Hong Kong

A Chinese and International Concern

Hong Kong

A Chinese and International Concern

EDITED BY

Jürgen Domes and Yu-ming Shaw

Westview Press
BOULDER & LONDON

Westview Special Studies on East Asia

This Westview softcover edition is printed on acid-free paper and bound in softcovers that carry the highest rating of the National Association of State Textbook Administrators, in consultation with the Association of American Publishers and the Book Manufacturers' Institute.

Published in 1988 in the United States of America by Westview Press, Inc.; Frederick A. Praeger, Publisher; 5500 Central Avenue, Boulder, Colorado 80301

Library of Congress Cataloging-in-Publication Data
Hong Kong, a Chinese and international concern.
  (Westview special studies on East Asia)
  1. Hong Kong—Politics and government. I. Domes,
Jürgen. II. Shaw, Yu-ming. III. Series.
DS796.H757H645   1988   320.951'25   87-29475
ISBN 0-8133-7449-9

Printed and bound in the United States of America

The paper used in this publication meets the requirements of the American National Standard for Permanence of Paper for Printed Library Materials Z39.48-1984.

6   5   4   3

Contents

Tables

Introduction

Jürgen Domes

On September 26, 1984, representatives of the government of Great Britain and the government of the People's Republic of China (PRC) initialed a Draft Agreement on the Future of Hong Kong, consisting of a Joint Declaration and three annexes (for the complete text, see the Appendix to this volume). After an assessment of the views of the Hong Kong populace (which, however, had no bearing upon the validity of the agreement) and the consent of the British Parliament, the prime ministers of Great Britain and the PRC—Margaret Thatcher and Chao Tzu-yang—signed the Anglo-Chinese agreement on December 19, 1984, in Peking.

In the Joint Declaration, the PRC declared that it will "resume the exercise of sovereignty over Hong Kong" on July 1, 1997, and Great Britain pledged to cede Hong Kong to the PRC on that date. After July 1, 1997, so the government of the PRC stated, Hong Kong will become a special administrative region of the PRC under the direct authority of the Peking central government. In this special administrative region, the government of which is supposed to "be composed of local inhabitants," the "current social and economic systems" and the "life-style," including civil rights and freedoms, "will remain unchanged" for fifty years, i.e., until July 1, 2047.

All these pledges notwithstanding, the Anglo-Chinese agreement of 1984 marks the first time since the Munich agreement of 1938 that the government of a country with a pluralistic representative system has formally promised to hand over a territory and its populace to the government of a country with a system of totalitarian, single-party rule. The almost 5.5 million people in Hong Kong—who, in 1985, produced a per-capita GNP seventeen times larger and earned a per-capita income nineteen times larger than those of the PRC, people who, while not really sharing political power, enjoyed almost unlimited economic and considerable political, personal, and religious freedom—are going to be converted into subjects of a Marxist-Leninist dictatorship, albeit with a number of privileges for fifty years. Their fate has been determined, not by themselves, but by their current government in negotiations with another government. The right of self-determination was denied to them in those negotiations; they have only an unbinding

1

right to air their views during a certain period of time. Hence, the Anglo-Chinese agreement of 1984, although received with approval by most representative governments the world over, is a significant departure from principles that such governments have long advocated and still hold to with respect to Zimbabwe, Namibia, and South Africa.

For the international academic community, the developments that led to the agreement, the agreement itself, and the future prospects for the people of Hong Kong are a great opportunity for research and debate. It is astonishing that, with the exception of two academic gatherings in Hong Kong itself, that opportunity has not yet resulted in intensive scholarly work. It is for this reason that the Institute of International Relations, National Chengchi University, Taipei, Taiwan, Republic of China (ROC), and the Research Unit on Chinese and East Asian Politics, the Saar University, Saarbrücken, Federal Republic of Germany, decided to cosponsor an international symposium, Hong Kong: A Chinese and International Concern. This symposium, which was attended by political scientists, economists, historians, sociologists, and scholars of international law from Great Britain, the Federal Republic of Germany, Canada, the United States of America, Australia, Japan, Hong Kong, and the ROC, convened in Taipei March 3–8, 1986. The contributions to this symposium, in versions revised after the discussions in Taipei, are presented in this book with the hope that academic debate will thus be stimulated. The editors and the authors are well aware that no chapter constitutes the final word on any particular subject. We hope we offer an intermediate balance-sheet, which consists of hypotheses that invite scholarly verification or falsification.

The papers and debates at the March 1986 symposium concentrated on ten main questions:

1. How did Hong Kong fare as a British crown colony?
2. For what reasons did Great Britain and the PRC open their negotiations, and under the influence of which determinants did the negotiations develop?
3. What was the impact of these negotiations on the economic and political scene in Hong Kong?
4. How, and to what extent, did the Hong Kong problem influence PRC domestic politics, and how did and will PRC domestic politics influence developments in and around Hong Kong?
5. What are the economic prospects for Hong Kong under the 1984 Anglo-Chinese agreement?
6. How does the government of the ROC on Taiwan view the developments in and around Hong Kong, and how do and will these developments influence the politics and the economic development of Taiwan?
7. What is the impact of the Anglo-Chinese agreement on Japanese and U.S. foreign policies?
8. What is the impact of the Anglo-Chinese agreement on the world economy?

9. How should the agreement be evaluated from the point of view of international law?
10. What are the overall prospects for the people of Hong Kong before 1997 and thereafter?

In this book, Chapters 1 and 2, both contributed by Dennis Duncanson, deal with the first two questions; the third is debated by Ambrose Y.C. King and Henry N. Geraedts. Jürgen Domes considers the answers to the fourth question, the interrelationship between PRC domestic politics and developments in and around Hong Kong, and the fifth question, dealing with Hong Kong's economic prospects, is addressed by Y. C. Yao. Yu-ming Shaw and Teh-pei Yu, both scholars from Taiwan, present the views held there concerning the political and economic impacts of the Anglo-Chinese agreement on the ROC, i.e., they venture to answer the sixth question.

Concerning the international aspects of the Hong Kong issue, the impact of the agreement on Japanese and U.S. foreign policies, the seventh question, is examined by the contributions of Mineo Nakajima and Hungdah Chiu. The chapter written by Jan S. Prybyla discusses the eighth question, the impact of the Anglo-Chinese agreement on the world economy, and Georg Ress—a recognized German authority on international law—raises the legal problems involved in the agreement, in particular the problem of self-determination. George L. Hicks attempts to answer the tenth question by discussing the situation in Hong Kong after the agreement, and to start a debate about the future prospects for the people of Hong King.

It is readily apparent that the contributors to this book do not entirely agree with each other, particularly with respect to the evaluation of the agreement itself and the future prospects for Hong Kong. Not only can areas of agreement and dissent be discerned among the different chapters in this book, they were also obvious in the rather intense academic debates during the symposium.

There is agreement that the development of Hong Kong between 1950 and the early 1980s represented a unique success story of a free market economy organized along the lines of traditional European liberalism. Yet this success was not duplicated by political development. Although the inhabitants of Hong Kong were free with respect to religion and the expression of political and social thought through comparatively free media, they had only a minimal share in the political decision making of the colony. In the same vein, the consultation of public opinion in Hong Kong concerning the Draft Agreement after the initialing of that document could not camouflage the hard fact that the right of self-determination had been denied to the Hong Kong populace.

The agreement itself contains numerous ambiguities and uncertainties. Even if the government of the PRC decides to abide by the contents of the Joint Declaration—a decision that is entirely up to that government after July 1, 1997, without any viable international guarantees or instruments of supervision—it can still interpret the text as it pleases. The government of the PRC has promised that the future Hong Kong Special Administrative Region "will enjoy a high degree of autonomy," but what does "high" mean to the Chinese Communist party's ruling elite? "The laws currently in force in Hong Kong will remain basically unchanged," but what does "basically" mean? And what is the meaning of the provision that "the chief executive will be appointed by the Central People's Government on the basis of the results of elections *or consultations* [italics added] to be held locally"? It is certain that this wording does not state that the chief executive is going to be chosen by the Hong Kong people in free elections. These and other similarly ambiguous phrases in the agreement leave considerable room for doubt about the future of Hong Kong between 1997 and 2047, not to mention the period after 2047, when all pledges given by the PRC in the Joint Declaration become formally invalid.

Such uncertainties were reflected in the disagreements among the participants of the symposium about the colony's future prospects. The views range from Y. C. Jao's comparatively optimistic evaluation of the economic prospects to Ambrose King's statement that "the future of Hong Kong in general and the fate of political democratization in particular are full of challenges, ambiguities, and uncertainties" to Henry Geraedts's projection that Hong Kong's fate will increasingly be tied in with that of the PRC: "Should the PRC actually manage to put its house in order, Hong Kong could retain some of its economic viability—to be sure, not in the way we have come to recognize it over the past twenty-five years or so, but an economic capacity nevertheless. However, if the PRC does not work, Hong Kong does not stand a chance at all." Jan Prybyla's conclusions are similarly critical of any euphoria:

> So what happens if Hong Kong is mucked up? From the standpoint of the world economy . . . , nothing much. Such a chance will be an inconvenience. . . . A couple of NICs may benefit, if they are quick enough to pick up the pieces by liberalizing their still rather restrictive financial and banking arrangements. The big loser will be mainland China, but the damage there will not be lethal: more of a shame than a loss. The biggest loser will be Hong Kong.

Yu-ming Shaw further argues that "Taiwan under the rule of the Republic of China is a completely different case than that of Hong Kong under British colonial rule." Hence, any attempt to also apply the "one country, two systems" formula to Taiwan would be "both unreasonable and impossible." In addition, he and other participants from Taiwan argued that the inclusion of Hong Kong in the PRC under a special status could provide the ROC with opportunities to influence the domestic political scene in the PRC: "The Chinese Communists will be unable to stop the flow into China from Hong Kong of the ideas of democracy and freedom, the capitalist system, and even the new Confucianism." European, U.S., and Japanese participants agreed that Taiwan's situation is not comparable to that of Hong Kong and therefore, the Anglo-Chinese agreement on the future of Hong Kong could hardly provide a blueprint for future developments in PRC-ROC relations.

Georg Ress goes further by suggesting that the people on Taiwan should claim the "(defensive) right of self-determination" to avoid being, at a certain point, forced to submit to PRC unification offers. His proposition, however, met with disagreement from a number of participants from Taiwan, who argued that the right of self-determination applies only to total political entities, not to a province, as Taiwan is still considered to be in the official view of the ROC government. The debate on this point became one of the most challenging during the symposium. It made the participants from Europe, Japan, and America realize the extent to which Taiwan still hopes for the eventual unification of all China. On the other hand, both sides again seemed to agree that Taiwan should continue to move toward political modernization and pluralization—and, indeed, Taiwan made considerable strides in that regard during 1986 and 1987.

As to the future of Hong Kong itself, George Hicks argues that an alliance of British colonial authorities, parts of the Hong Kong business establishment, and the Chinese Communist party is already shaping up. This alliance, he suggests, may result in the intermediate establishment of a system of "authoritarian capitalism," which, however, will most probably not work.

> In the end, of course, the people of Hong Kong will lose their freedom and probably their prosperity as well. Hundreds of thousands of the more prosperous and qualified, however, will escape to rebuild their lives in other parts of the world, taking with them the energy and dynamism that has made Hong Kong one of the great economic miracles in history. Other nations will benefit from the Hong Kong tragedy, although East Asia as a region will be the poorer for the loss of its most dynamic member. Britain and China will have to share the responsibility for what is a wholly predictable, but avoidable, disaster. Fortunately, neither is likely to escape unscathed.

Hicks's prediction differs greatly from the generally optimistic, if not euphoric, view with which the Anglo-Chinese agreement was acclaimed in most Western administrative and diplomatic establishments and by the majority of Western business circles, particularly those with vested interests in the Hong Kong economy and trade relations with the PRC.

Yet one can hardly deny that Hicks's analysis is broadly documented or that he knows Hong Kong rather well. Hence, his sobering conclusions give one considerable food for thought. I would not deny that there is a chance that the Anglo-Chinese agreement may work. But I consider this chance comparatively slight. To me, it appears more likely that the more active and economically viable parts of the Hong Kong populace will leave between 1990 and 1995, that after 1997, the communization of Hong Kong will proceed at a faster pace than is assumed today, and that a number of large Western enterprises may well lose a lot of property there. Hence, I would not now invest a single dime in what used to be one of the most dynamic economies in the world. If Hong Kong becomes what has been called a CRIC—a "collapsing recently industrialized country"[1]—its collapse will have occurred with the active cooperation and applause of large parts of the pluralistic and democratic world. But would Hong Kong's collapse prevent a repetition elsewhere?

Notes

1. Chalmers Johnson, "The Mousetrapping of Hong Kong: A Game in Which Nobody Wins," *Asian Survey* 24:9 (September 1984), p. 887.

PART ONE

Hong Kong: The Past and the Present

1

Hong Kong as a Crown Colony

Dennis Duncanson

The fact that Hong Kong's separation from China is the consequence of three Anglo-Chinese agreements of the nineteenth century, the second and third bringing about extensions of the territory conceded under the first, is by now such common knowledge that reiteration of the details is not called for here. The three agreements were concluded by plenipotentiaries and had the force, although two did not have the title, of treaties. The circumstances of limited force under which they were concluded were such that, since the very moment of their conclusion, they have afforded a plausible argument for an irredentist strand in Chinese attitudes toward Hong Kong, namely, that the circumstances were "unequal" and oppressive and ipso facto the agreements were never valid. Even if no more than a coincidence, it is a relative detail that the special commissioner of the Nanking government in Hong Kong, T. W. Kwok, who in 1948 stood up for China's reserved powers in Kowloon Walled City, had published a treatise on Jean Bodin, the sixteenth-century originator of the doctrine, which had long since been abandoned in the West but had been revived in China in the 1900s.[1]

The purpose and consequence of the first two Hong Kong treaties (1842 and 1860) were the removal of *restrictions* on one party without imposing any on the other, so that the logic of the plea that the *effect* was oppressive could be called in doubt. Moreover, the treaties were the outcome of very limited wars, and *peace* treaties are invariably unequal; the only practicable alternative to them is a fight to the finish (an outcome that is obviously much more "unequal") and the imposition by the victor on the vanquished of capitulations were onerous by far than befell China in the first two treaties. However, the inequality of the 1898 lease regarding the so-called New Territories is less clear-cut. Although it is true that, at a time when European arrogance was at its height, China was being bullied for concessions, territorial and other, by every foreign government that had gained diplomatic access to Peking on Britain's coattails, both Britain who demanded the grant and China who conceded it were actuated by motives of defense, similarly if not jointly, to ward off "oppression" from other predators. In this one respect, the case of the New Territories was a similar case to that of Wei-hai-wei at the same time. In Shantung, both Britain and China sought a strategic barrier against Russian expansion southward; at Hong Kong they sought a barrier (for Britain, at the moment of Fashoda) against a French advance north from the newly ceded Kwangchowan on the Lei-chou peninsula.[2]

Motives for the creation of Hong Kong on a sparsely inhabited tract of coastline were, of course, mixed on both sides and bear little resemblance to the reasons for safeguarding its continued existence a century and a half later. There are, however, features and trends that can be detected at every period in Hong Kong's history. One of the constant features still clearly visible today is the ambivalence of feelings about the territory's detachment from the mainland on the part of the Chinese people, from the lowly to the most exalted. On the one hand, the signing of the three treaties parting with land was a national affront—a humbling of Emperor Ch'ien Lung's haughty "tribute" pretensions and a turning by foreigners to their own advantage of the extraterritoriality by which he had tried to "oppress" them—so that the arrangement was likely to be annulled sooner or later. On the other hand, many utilities have accrued to both the state and the people in China from Hong Kong's detachment under the rule of successive regimes, so that the moment when repossession would appear on the Chinese side to be desirable was repeatedly put off.

There was little urgency—though admittedly some—for Hong Kong to be included with the treaty ports in the demand for the abolition of foreign privileges by which the Kuomintang courted popularity in the 1920s and early 1930s. When Britain and the United States were at last negotiating for the termination of treaty rights with the Republic of China in 1942 and 1943, during the Japanese occupation of Hong Kong, the Chinese side did ask that Kowloon (here meaning the New Territories) be included with Shanghai; but when rebuffed, Chungking did not persist.[3] British officials feared in 1945 that Chiang Kai-shek might insist on the return of Hong Kong after Japan's surrender. It is well known that Stalin taunted Churchill with that prospect at Yalta and that Roosevelt tried to put Chiang up to it, but in the event Chiang made no such demand. What was so peculiar about Hong Kong that it should be the only foreign enclave in China to survive, down to the present day, the peaceable moves for retrocession between the world wars and the upheavals of the Second World War, which removed all the other enclaves, as well as the seizure of power on the mainland by a Marxist-Leninist regime? The explanation must be an awareness in China that Hong Kong differed from other settlements and concessions—that the self-esteem lost because of its separateness was offset by the wealth gained—and for a great many people, undoubtedly, that Hong Kong provided the possibility of sanctuary from political persecution or economic disadvantage at home. The Hong Kong agreement ratified in May 1985 is concerned less with the terms of retrocession than with the terms under which separateness is to be prolonged—for another half century and for Peking's benefit rather than Hong Kong's.

On the British side, one can discern a trend, which gathered momentum after the First World War, toward the independence of Hong Kong from colony status. Regarded in 1842 merely as a safe haven in which merchants could careen their ships and store their wares, it took on, over the decades, an identity and vitality of its own, and the original merchants and their successors had progressively less of a say as the Cantonese inhabitants grew in both numbers and capability. The British officials began to preside over a Hong Kong community in which British commercial interests increased arithmetically but diminished geometrically in proportion to Chinese and international interests—more than servants of London, the officials became champions of Hong Kong for its own sake.

Writers on Hong Kong affairs in the West since the Second World War have been reluctant to admit that a colonial government, or its individual civil servants, could really be actuated by an unselfish sense of duty toward the governed; yet Hong Kong has never been an important possession for the United Kingdom, and hardly any expatriate residents who ever flourished there can be said to have played a significant part in the home country's affairs. Chinese commentators on the negotiations who have asserted that Hong Kong is not materially very valuable to Britain are right, but if they infer that the fate of the Hong Kong people is therefore immaterial to the officials who administer the colony or negotiate for its future, they are wrong. It is a fact that Hong Kong has advanced toward a unique form of home rule unconnected with the agitations or international pressures that dominated the precipitate process of colonial emancipation in other parts of the world—a form that includes recognition of Hong Kong as a quasi state by other countries when negotiating economic agreements, for example. When the Peking government protested to the United Nations in 1972 that the Committee on Decolonization had no business meddling in the future of Hong Kong because that was not a colonial matter, it had every justification to do so. However, whether that government was equally justified in adding that Hong Kong's future was a domestic concern of China alone (to the implied exclusion of the people of Hong Kong as well as of the United Nations) is hardly borne out by that country's willingness ten years later to enter into negotiations with Britain about the future of Hong Kong. The additional statement is instead to be regarded as a pretext for halting, not hastening, Hong Kong's progress in the direction of full independence under the circumstances outlined in the following pages.

Structure of Government

In British constitutional law, Hong Kong was and is a "crown colony."[4] It is ruled by a governor and commander in chief (the colloquial title is *ping t'ou* ["head soldier"]) under instructions signed by a sovereign in London—that is to say, under basic empowering Letters Patent (1843, 1888, and 1917, further amended half a dozen times in incidental clauses down to 1972) together with Royal Instructions on detail and procedure. Contrary to the assumption in many quarters more familiar with the status of American colonies or with that of French possessions like Algeria, a crown colony is not an extension of the United Kingdom. What is understood as "the British Government" does not rule Hong Kong, except for its strategic defense and an ever-diminishing range of external relations. Nor is Hong Kong "owned" by the United Kingdom in the informal sense, for barely 7 percent of the colony's capital investment is held through London. The Royal Prerogative (expressed in Arts. 8 and 9 of the Letters Patent) to approve or disallow Hong Kong legislation, and conversely to legislate for Hong Kong by order of the Privy Council sitting in London, is generally interpreted as implying that the British Parliament has the power to make laws for Hong Kong. Whether that interpretation is correct or not, the power has been but rarely exercised. Acts of Parliament do not automatically apply to Hong Kong, and money is not remitted from the Hong Kong treasury to the British exchequer save in settlement of mutual services— for instance, contributions toward maintenance of the garrison.

The only mention of London offices of state in the Letters Patent or Royal Instructions is a vague reference to the "principle secretaries of state" as the channel for communications between Crown and governor. The enormous growth in public business in London manifest frm the late 1860s onward led to the creation of a secretary of state expressly for the colonies, but the Colonial Office has no explicit function in Hong Kong's constitution, nor was it in existence in either 1843 or 1981. During its hundred-year lifetime, the Colonial Office wielded more influence than actual authority over the governors of Hong Kong, and although it provided advice on technical matters of every kind, the final decisions rested with Hong Kong itself. It is as much a British as a Chinese tradition to avoid friction between overlapping authorities, and the practice of prior informal discussion of contentious matters has extended to relations between London and Hong Kong as regularly as within the domestic government of the territory. Only once in recent memory has a governor been overruled by London: Sir David Trench, having, on the advice of his Chinese unofficial advisers, confirmed a sentence of death soon after Parliament had abolished capital punishment in the United Kingdom, was overridden by exercise of the Royal Prerogative of clemency in favor of the convict. That action is an example of influence at work instead of command, but also, it must be conceded, of British social values prevailing over those of Hong Kong.

The governor has at no period been invested with dictatorial powers: From the start, he has been required by the Letters Patent to consult the Executive Council (his cabinet), and new laws or regulations have been enacted by the Legislative Council. On the other hand, down to 1981 neither of these bodies had any elective element, nor was there universal suffrage. Both bodies have always had an "official" membership, which has included the senior secretaries of the government appointed by the Crown or with London's approval, and an "unofficial" membership of persons of local influence chosen by the governor, predominantly European at the beginning but predominantly Chinese by the 1970s. In 1981, the Executive Council had six official and nine unofficial members; the Legislative Council had twenty-four official and twenty-seven unofficial members, and this group's Finance Committee, which controls revenue and expenditure, comprised three official members and all the twenty-seven unofficial ones. The Finance Committee has proved a determined watchdog over the colony's fiscal independence; for instance, in 1972, when the pound sterling was under world pressure, the committee made the dramatic decision to diversify external balances out of sterling and to disengage the Hong Kong dollar from its customary (not statutory) fixed exchange rate to the pound. The London government was chagrined but had no power to gainsay the decision. For the next ten years the Hong Kong dollar had a floating but buoyant value, but the loss of confidence during the Anglo-Chinese negotiations lowered its value so sharply that a fixed standard had to be adopted again—this time the U.S. dollar instead of the pound sterling.

Many years ago, the thirty-six unofficial members of the two councils, though not elected, came together as an informal body, the Unofficial Members of the Legislative Council (UMELCO), which has its own offices and secretariat and discharges what in the United Kingdom is called "constituency work"—looking into grievances and keeping in touch with public opinion. As an extension of that function, UMELCO has increasingly acted as the mouthpiece for Hong Kong as a quasi state, in public and controversial representations both to the United Kingdom government and to other governments (including that of China), with regard to issues either too sensitive for the governor to take sides on or when his answerability to the Crown might be interpreted in Hong Kong or abroad as a prejudicial interest.

The main business of public administration, conducted through specialized departments, has been controlled in the town areas by the Urban Council (half elected on a limited property franchise, half appointed by the central authority) and in the rural areas by an entirely official district administration relying on an intricate network of unpaid committees able to voice commercial, industrial, and also traditional "lineage," interests. Under both arrangements, there has existed a myriad of local and technical committees, manned by residents of village standing and influence, which interact for mutual information and persuasion. This method of governance owes no less to Chinese than to British tradition—though hardly local tradition, for most of the people of even the New Territories are recent immigrants.

The objection has often been made—mostly by Western critics—that without the principle of open and universal election, the system falls short of the ideal for representative government. So far as district and urban administration is concerned, the Hong Kong government was by 1981 yielding to the criticism and making plans—which have matured since then—to substitute elected district councils for the entire territory. Until the conclusion of the Anglo-Chinese agreement, there were no other steps toward representative government or toward meeting the criticism that there

ought to have been a devolution of power at the constitutional level as
well to an elected central-government legislature long ago. As a matter of
fact, a move so to do was made by the socialist cabinet in London in the
1940s, and it might have been possible to persuade the oligarchy of UMELCO
to accept an electoral system in those days had the Nationalist government
in Nanking not been overthrown. But anxiety over the Communists'
intentions in the aftermath of the events of 1949, combined with doubts
and fears over the consequences of the deluge of refugee immigrants into
Hong Kong for two or three years thereafter, turned the Hong Kong
unofficials decisively against the idea in 1952, and London, true to custom,
refrained from pressing them—as British intellectual opinion at that time
would have liked—let alone advising the Crown to override them by an
Order in Council.[5]

So long as a substantial proportion of Hong Kong's population regarded
itself as transient, it was difficult to devise satisfactory measures for universal
suffrage anyway, and there was no popular agitation for it either. The
periodic demands came usually from expatriate unofficials or other professionals, themselves temporary residents, who had unsatisfactory arguments
for their position, such as that representative government was the way of
the world nowadays or that it was required by "British," or socialist, or
some other a priori precept. The permanent settlement of immigrants in
the most recent quarter century might have put a more favorable complexion
on the question but for the fact that the Hong Kong government has felt
constrained to comply more and more with the expressed, implied, or merely
inferred wishes of the People's government in Peking that the colony should
not enjoy liberal measures that might kindle an analogous demand across
the frontier or that might be interpreted as the impact of "a second China."[6]
By 1981, it was evident that Hong Kong had nevertheless taken on, by dint
of its development, numerous attributes of an independent state, and
conjectures about the uncertainties of its future made it imperative to devise
political machinery that was adapted somehow or other to letting the people
of the territory exercise self-determination. That is how the question of
constitutional advance stood at the beginning of the negotiations.

A comparable set of local problems long deprived Chinese personnel of
the fruits of high office in government, which the colonial power could
have used as another means of devolving authority into local hands. There
had never at any time been a shortage of Chinese workers for the lowlier
public positions, but it was harder to find educated Chinese recruits even
for the police let alone for higher grades. When tertiary education became
more easily accessible, especially at Hong Kong's two universities, the civil
service failed to attract the best graduates to the top administrative positions
now open to them; public service turned out to be only the second choice
of individuals whose prospects were poor in commerce or industry. With
the passage of time, the situation has improved: A locally based Public
Service Commission, set up in 1950 as an advisory body outside the
government, has been increasingly successful in finding recruits and in

inspiring confidence that promotion is fair and that the civil service is a genuine and honorable vocation. As a result, today all but 2 percent of the public employees are locally born Chinese. Yet there has still been a reason—rather delicate to air in public and peculiar to Hong Kong—why the Chinese civil servants may not necessarily want to qualify for highest preferment. From the 1890s onward, in order to avoid scandal, regulations were introduced in all crown colonies forbidding senior civil servants appointed from London from acquiring private financial interests in the country they administered. Such a regulation could be an embarrassment if a Chinese official moving into a post formerly held by an expatriate had close family interests in the ever-more-flourishing industrial and financial markets of Hong Kong.

Social and Economic Development

The philosophy of government in Hong Kong, shaped at first by British attitudes alone but after acquisition of the New Territories increasingly by Cantonese attitudes as well, has been centered on the idea of personal self-determination. The common name for this philosophy is laissez-faire—a well-justified description as long as it is not assumed to have derogatory import—but the Hong Kong government's own term is "positive nonintervention." A hundred years ago, it was British and a few other Western merchants who stood to gain from the free port and from a political regime that imposed few restrictions of other kinds, but as China modernized—financially as much as technically—the Europeans were joined by Cantonese competitors and partners. As the population has increased, the spheres of public service and regulation in the interest of a felt common good have widened, and a sense of community has emerged (even though the politically dominant Europeans have almost all retained an expatriate status and usually go home to retire, as did many Chinese people before 1949). The government has set about providing a physical infrastructure, starting with the reclamations of little coves and shallow beaches in the 1850s and culminating in the 1970s and 1980s with an extensive railway and motorway network tunneled through the peaks and under the harbor. A parallel moral infrastructure of law and regulation-by-convention endeavors to give free rein to enterprise in a society that defies Marxian analysis. The almost continuous expansion of Hong Kong has depended on its growing prosperity, which in turn has depended on confidence that the guerdon of enterprise is safe and on the money and labor invested in industries as a result of that confidence. The confinement of government initiative to public works, where neither overbearing ideology nor cocksure development science have found any place, has also been a major advantage. That the policy suits the Chinese economic and industrial culture is evidenced by the lack of takers some years ago for starting-up loans offered, on the suggestion of voices within UMELCO, through an Industrial Development Board.[7]

The unfavorable topographical conditions of Hong Kong mean that public works have been a big element in the economy, not only in the area of site formation (cutting down rocks and tipping the spoil into the sea, draining brackish inlets, engineering access roads and harbor works), but also in the design and construction of hydraulic works for catchment, storage, and pumping of water across country and under the harbor— sometimes in the teeth of strong opposition from villagers who do not benefit—in order to cope with the fast-growing demands of domestic users, hospitals, shipping, and industry. Notwithstanding use of salt water for a few purposes, and some water supplied from China since 1960, water rationing has been a fact of life in Hong Kong since time immemorial, so that reservoirs, whether for direct catchment or for storage of water bought from China, have been strong competitors for the scarce supply of land.

The fifty-two-square-kilometer port of Hong Kong is an example of private enterprise flourishing where the government has furnished the infrastructure of planning, regulation, moorings, and fire- and pollution-fighting craft while shipping interests have built wharves, gantries, docks, and repair and shipbuilding yards. The result has been a harbor that began as a watering place and typhoon shelter now being the third-biggest container port in the world, servicing 12,000 oceangoing vessels a year. The more recent airport has grown similarly, the government building runway and aprons and terminals in Kowloon Bay (reclaimed) while private enterprise has provided engineering and support services for more than thirty airlines and their 10 million passengers a year. No analysis of the general economy is possible in this chapter, but over the twenty years of the economy's decisive growth—namely, the 1960s and 1970s—no other country consistently out-performed Hong Kong,[8] and Hong Kong has become a major financial center that Tokyo fears, Taipei and Singapore envy—and Peking covets.

Noninterference in profitable enterprise has not debarred the government from accepting some responsibility for social services even when, during the years of overwhelming immigration, it curtailed them by comparison with standards in other British territories because of a reluctance either to impose direct taxation on working people to pay for them or to resort to borrowing. The economy has stayed solvent in years of trade deficit (more frequent now) thanks to the good luck of inflows of speculative capital, which could be regarded as an analogue of public borrowing but have the obvious advantage of not saddling the exchequer with public debt.

The revenues available for allocation have been raised from direct payment for certain urban services, from license fees and other forms of indirect taxation, and from land transactions—this last heading credited to nonre-current capital works. The predominance of land revenue in the budget is a reflection of the gradual expansion of the economy, especially the switch from trade and agriculture to industry that began in the early 1950s after the revolution on the mainland, but it had been a big item long before that. Even the British moves to acquire Kowloon and the New Territories in the nineteenth century, though justified at the time by arguments of defense needs, almost certainly owed something to Hong Kong's shortage of utilizable land and a desire to hold in check the exorbitance of economic rents that finally hit the colony in 1982. Direct taxes did not become a major revenue item until the late 1970s, and even in 1981 a maximum income-or-profits tax of 15 percent yielded only 26 percent of the total revenues of HK$30,626 million, compared with about 35 percent from land transactions. The "economic miracle" has led to many years of surplus, and large (though necessarily unpublished) reserves have been credited to what is now called the Exchange Fund, and that in turn is distributed among eighty-seven bank or security accounts in thirteen different countries.[9]

The first public social services ever provided in Hong Kong were rudimentary public health and medical services characteristic of the age. A medical school was opened in 1887 (and Sun Yat-sen was trained there), and it became the first faculty of the University of Hong Kong twenty years later. In modern times hospitals have afforded a major outlet for Chinese as well as British-missionary charity, and Hong Kong has long enjoyed—thanks to coordination between government and community—a health service that is comparable to similar services in Europe. Hong Kong has been particularly successful in controlling epidemics, with the ready collaboration of a common people who are educated and public-spirited in such matters. Less successful has been the control of drug addiction, in spite of an annual expenditure for that purpose of HK$260 million in 1981. Social welfare is another area of customary Chinese charitable endeavor, so that here too the government has been able to devote a large part of the public money available for it to training and procurement of expert skills and equipment while sharing with the private sector, and a prosperous community chest, the costs of maintaining services.

In contrast, conditions of labor and the welfare of workers are a purpose to which Cantonese idealism has not been much committed. Before Hong Kong's massive industrialization in the 1960s, the risk of detrimental or oppressive working conditions was of limited incidence; all the same, inspection of workplaces by government inspectors began in the 1920s, and legislation had been in force for many years for safety of machinery, standards of hygiene, and workmen's compensation, and the colony had a good record in implementation of the International Labour Office's conventions. Hong Kong remained backward in the promotion of model contracts of work and in measures to put a stop to exploitation of a labor force repeatedly swollen by immigrants, who were often destitute.

On the workers' side, there has been a conspicuous willingness to accept unsatisfactory conditions or wages because the alternative hardships are worse, and that fact lends a grain of truth to overseas competitors charges of "sweat labor." But workers have often made a stoical calculation of their alternatives, and when the world oil slump hit Hong Kong in 1974, a typically ready acceptance of lower wages quickly restored the volume of exports and, with it, workers' earnings while unemployment was kept down as low as 4 percent. Efforts were made in the 1950s to foster trade unionism, but, as had been the case when the first unions were formed in Hong Kong thirty years earlier (after repeal of an ordinance repressing their secret-society antecedents and banning strikes), the promoters were more concerned with political mobilization for the Nationalist or the Communist parties than with the personal welfare of their members. Happily, in part by way of reaction to the discreditable agitation from the mainland in 1967, Hong Kong's unions have caught up with their peers in Europe, and the colony has an ironic degree of international respectability as a result of strikes in both industrial and white-collar sectors.

The Hong Kong government has been criticized from time to time for leaving large parts of education to private, charitable initiative. Here again the customs of the Cantonese community, together with the eagerness to help of Western missionaries with high professional qualifications and substantial foreign donations to disburse—whose numbers were swollen by the exodus from the mainland after 1949—made joint social ventures particularly suitable in the territory. Although well-to-do families still pay to educate their children overseas, the facilities in Hong Kong lack for little in either professional scope or accessibility to rich and poor. Non-profit-making private schools have been encouraged by means of generous capital and caitation subsidies from the government, and the Chinese University benefits similarly, but the majority of rural schools, specialized schools, the Polytechnic, and the English University are supported by government funds—the last two through a grants committee funded by, but not subordinate to, the Education Department. Elementary schooling is universal and free, but there are fees for secondary and tertiary education (on admission by examination) although many means-tested grants and loans are available.

Great attention has been given to standards of performance, secured in the tertiary field by reference to external examiners, not necessarily from the United Kingdom. Nonetheless, the government has had to admit that standards have been declining in one very serious respect: As has also been found in Singapore, too many young people are unable to express themselves properly in either Chinese or English. In recent years, it has been official policy to urge development of Chinese at the expense of English (the opposite is true in Singapore), but the problem of choosing between Cantonese and Mandarin is harder to solve in single-dialect Hong Kong than in multidialect Singapore because in the former, Cantonese has taken on almost the character of a national symbol against the Communist party, which supports Mandarin. The major cause of poor literacy in Hong Kong has been shortcomings among teachers who, during the period of rapid expansion of the school system, easily found jobs without having to be properly qualified. In spite of the growing importance of China to Hong Kong, it may in the end prove even more important to raise the standard of English than that of Chinese, for English is the key to open the doors "Hong Kongers" want to go through in search of the modernism and technology, which the mainland hopes to get cheaper through Hong Kong after 1997 than in the past. One unexpected difficulty in the way of raising standards is related to a demographic factor: It was discovered in 1984 that the seventeen–twenty age group in the resident population will decline by nearly a third in the decade 1981–1990; with less competition for places, there may also be less incentive to excel.

The Hong Kong government sets aside money for innumerable cultural amenities and the environment, urban and rural, and has had to face huge expenditures to keep the water supply sufficient for the needs of industry and overcrowded tenements. But pride of achievement must go to the public housing program. There was none until after 1949. The first refugees squatted in shacks on the hillsides, where they could not be supplied with city water or sanitation, or even on street pavements and private roofs, which were marginally less insanitary. It was difficult for social services to reach these refugees, and above all they were exposed to the severities of the typhoon season. Kerosene stoves caused many fires until, at Christmas 1953, a single conflagration in a squatter area—not the last—made 55,000 refugees homeless in a night. The government embarked on a scheme for low-cost, bare-minimum housing that became a model—both for coping with emergencies and for upgrading the quality of accommodation subsequently to meet the wishes of a populace whose standard of living rose, thanks to industrial development, faster than anybody could have dared hope when the scheme began. The continuing influx of refugees from the mainland has made it difficult to eliminate all squatters, and there was actually a net gain in their numbers in 1979 and 1980 to around 200,000; since then, their numbers have reduced again. A great variety in quality and type of dwellings has resulted, and the revenues to pay for them were an invisible tax on the expanding economy—as well as an important form of public enterprise—and most of the early estates have been rebuilt. By 1981, 2 million people had been rehoused in public-owned estates (almost 40 percent of the population and as high a proportion as anywhere), apart from new home-ownership estates (strongly competed for) and many new private-sector developments.

This survey of the social and economic scene would not be complete without discussing another aspect of the infrastructure upon which Hong Kong has so thrived, namely, the system of law and justice, which occupied a prominent place in the Anglo-Chinese agreement. The financial and legislative independence of Hong Kong from the United Kingdom has been mentioned already; the courts and their procedures are more independent still. From the outset, Hong Kong courts have tried to respect Cantonese custom in civil matters, especially with regard to land titles in the New Territories after 1898.[10] Subject to a proviso to respect "different social conditions," the original Letters Patent decreed that the laws of Hong Kong should be the general common law and the principles of equity, together with the Statutes of England (that is, the special legislative enactments) as they existed in 1843.

The matter was stated more precisely by a Hong Kong ordinance of 1966, which defined the common law as that of England (not that of other nations who share it)—but did not, of course, define "equity" more narrowly. The ordinance also listed the UK Acts of Parliament that should apply, including both a medieval statute creating lay magistrates (justices of the peace) and the all-important Habeas Corpus Act of 1679, which had occasionally been relied on in Hong Kong courts in the past as if it had been part of the common law. The 1966 ordinance proved desirable because much of the received law of 1843 had since been repealed in England or superseded by more-recent Hong Kong ordinances, and an explicit list of English statutes in force in Hong Kong, as part of the local legislation, removed any shadow of doubt from what previously could have been reckoned a partly inferential reliance on the laws of England, above all in regard to protection of the individual from abuse of authority under habeas corpus.

It has to be admitted that the principle of common law and that of equity are not always easy to grasp for persons accustomed to comprehensive codes of law and, especially, to mandatory scales of punishment. In England, for one example, and therefore in Hong Kong by virtue of these reenactments, maximum penalties can be laid down by law but not minimum penalties, and it is one of the many points of equity to mitigate the severity of damages or compensation or restitution in cases in which circumstances may have changed since an injury was done the plaintiff or a contract breached so that a judgment applying the full rigor of the law would seem to a reasonable person to be unfair. The common law is not codified but jurisprudential; its essence is the validity of precedent. Precedents fall into two classes, mandatory ones and influential ones. In Hong Kong, only Hong Kong judgments fall into the first class, but precedents of the second class may be taken into account in fresh judgments, not exclusively from English courts but from courts anywhere in the world where the common law holds sway (Australia or the United States, for instance) if those seem more apt and more equitable to the Hong Kong judges. There may be argument between counsel in court about the aptness of a precedent, but as soon as the bench has given its verdict, that becomes a mandatory Hong Kong precedent if the same circumstances ever recur. Up to now, the supreme court of appeal for Hong Kong, as for certain other common-law countries, has been the Judicial Committee of the Privy Council in London—an arrangement that follows in logic from the sovereignty of the Crown over Hong Kong. These characteristics of law and justice were, as foreseen in London and Hong Kong, a source of difficulty during the negotiation of the Anglo-Chinese agreement.

Relations with China

There was no local resistance to the British seizure of Hong Kong Island in 1841 or of Kowloon in 1860, largely because neither place was garrisoned and the two Anglo-Chinese "wars" had been fought some way off; moreover, in 1860, the central government had cause to be preoccupied with foreign encroachments in the north and on the capital itself. But in 1898 the British occupation of Chinese territory did not precede the treaty authorizing it, and, although there were no Chinese troops to be withdrawn from the New Territories, there was enough of a local populace to put up a skirmish, even though ordered from Canton not to. The reaction of the British troops was not brutal but still high-handed, and although the neighborhood of the *yamên* ("office") of the magistrate appointed from Canton (Kowloon Walled City) was supposed to be excluded from the lease, the Hong Kong authorities seized that too in contravention (and reprisal) without further ado. In like mood—if also for want of an alternative—the governor proclaimed that the laws of Hong Kong henceforward applied to the New Territories equally and thereby ended any real distinction of tenure between one part of the colony and another. Resentment in the New Territories against the new regime did not last long, and immigration from across the new frontier was soon noticeable. London has never subsequently received any definite demand from China for retrocession earlier than 1997, although several diplomatic soundings were made from Nanking and Chungking in the 1920s (Washington Conference) and 1940s, and it is remarkable that the first step toward the recent talks on the post-1997 status came from the British, not the Chinese, side.[11]

Only once has there ever been threat of conflict over Hong Kong, and for a few years the garrisons' guns faced toward China, so to speak. That threat occurred in the aftermath of the overthrow of the Nationalist government when the Chinese Communist party adopted an attitude of acute animosity and virulent abuse toward the Hong Kong government, and, until called north for the Korean War, the People's Liberation Army stood to in belligerent posture. Relations with Canton were tense a few other times, as during the 1922 seamen's strike and the 1925 May 30 movement (both extended to Hong Kong by Communist-led agitation). In 1948 the Hong Kong government cleared the Walled City (its "walls" long since replaced by insanitary hovels) of the vice and disease that squatters who had flooded in after the Japanese surrender had brought there, and in retaliation for this hardly avoidable, and very humane, action, a mob in Canton burned down the British consulate-general on Shameen.

When the Nationalist government began to appoint its own consuls abroad, London opposed their appointment in dependent territories out of apprehension that they would be tempted to exert a political domination over Chinese residents, who, under Chinese law, were Chinese nationals by jus sanguinis wherever they might live. In 1946, however, a Chinese commissioner was accepted after all and got on excellent terms with the governor—until the former was implicated in the Walled City episode and asked to go, never to be replaced.[12] In 1956, and again in 1973, the People's government broached with the United Kingdom the question of representation in Hong Kong, by a special commissioner rather than a consul—in all probability because a consul would imply recognition of the fact that Hong Kong was other than an integral part of China. There was no agreement, because London insisted on a consul answerable to the Chinese ambassador in London.[13]

In the absence of official Chinese representation after 1949—especially when Hong Kong had so many other foreign consulates, consulates-general, and trade commissions accorded de facto diplomatic status—communication between Hong Kong and Canton was for a long time conducted through the Canton-Kowloon Railway administration and between Hong Kong and Peking (rather awkwardly) through the Foreign Office and the two chargé d'affaires' offices—the People's government withheld diplomatic relations with Britain at ambassadorial level for over twenty years. There is no knowing, of course, whether a Communist consul would or could have dissuaded his principals from interfering in the 1956 Triad riots, from the mobbing of Government House and other disturbances during the Cultural Revolution in 1967, or from the many malicious broadcast lies and furious campaigns of propaganda to stir up anti-British sentiment and destabilize Hong Kong. It appears unlikely that he could have done so—until Mao was dead and the light could dawn on the dinosaur of a Politburo that here was a goose whose golden eggs could be appropriated for the asking.

Although having a base from which to conduct trade up and down the China coast, unmolested by what international law quaintly calls "constraint of princes," was prominent in the original British desire to possess Hong Kong, the colony, unlike Macao, has never depended wholly on the China trade. For instance, the Hong Kong and Shanghai Banking Corporation made three huge loans to the viceroy of Canton to finance resistance to the French in Tonkin in 1884 but two or three years later was supplying banking services to the French authorities in Cochin China in anticipation of the opening of the Banque de l'Indochine. British demands that China "open its doors" to foreign intercourse were matched by a reciprocal open-door policy in Hong Kong. As a result, the colony was committed to participation in—and profited enormously from—a much wider, and continuously widening, area of Far Eastern trade relations than mere bilateral Anglo-Chinese exchanges. Indeed, by the 1860s, British interest in the Canton region was overshadowed by interest in Shanghai and upstream Yangtze ports, and that was the case until the Japanese invasion of China began to close the door again. Not only did Western firms other than British ones—especially shipping lines, of course—open offices and warehouses in Hong Kong, but they were soon joined by "modernizing" Chinese entrepreneurs.

In consequence, there was an early international interest in preserving the colony, the only exception being Japan, which appears never to have contemplated any positive use for Hong Kong until the present day and, having occupied it in 1941, treated it as a nuisance until evicted in 1945. Conversely, Chinese and other Hong Kong financial interests were able (with the help of a trade commissioner accredited to the Marunouchi military headquarters) to turn the recovery of Japan after 1945 to advantage as a more profitable area for investment than mainland China, which was torn by civil war. The Korean War and the UN embargo on trade with China, on a wide range of exports classed as potentially "strategic," hit Hong Kong severely after 1950, but the colony was far from being crippled, in part because of the simultaneous flight out of China of managers and laborers trying to escape Mao's Three-Anti and Five-Anti campaigns.

One might suppose that, on balance, Hong Kong's existence has been considered useful to China. On the official side, the Manchu rulers certainly manifested no more concern for it than for other distant provinces, on which they devolved an autonomy that extended to the point of making war across frontiers. By the time the Chinese Republic began to adopt policies with a more definite national horizon, from 1912 onward, the colony had become, ambiguously, an object of resentment as well as an object of admiration as a national achievement. But—like Shanghai or Wei-hai-wei or Kulangsoo—it was also a refuge or an El Dorado or a port for emigration for the dispossessed, the alienated, and the persecuted in all walks of life, and many waves of immigrants have entered Hong Kong from the mainland during the past seventy years—the influx reached 100,000 a year after the Communist victory. The causes of mass immigration have sometimes combined political and economic hardship at home, as when nearly 2,000 families of Pearl River fishermen escaped to Hong Kong after the setting up of fishermen's communes in China in 1958.[14] There was another upsurge of nearly 200,000 immigrants as recently as 1979-1980—presumably more for economic than for political reasons. Down to the Second World War, a high proportion of migrants moved on into Southeast Asia, but the Japanese conquests and subsequent colonial emancipations put a stop to that outlet; it is to the colony's credit—not least to its administration—that it has been able to absorb such a demographic accretion.

Governments in China have tended to welcome this safety valve for misfits, and whenever, for obvious practical reasons, the administration has tried to control entry, there have been protests that Hong Kong is part of China and that "the British" have no right to prevent Chinese people from settling in it, whatever the effects on the water supply or public health.[15] There were, in fact no controls until the invasion of 1950, and during a rush of immigrants to the frontier in 1962, some 2 million strong, the Canton authorities collaborated with Hong Kong in the forcible return of all of them. Spontaneous, large-scale moves back to China do not seem ever to have occurred. While upholding free speech, communication, and association, the Hong Kong government has obviously had to prevent a spread of China's various phases of civil strife to the colony, and before and after the First World War, the colony tried to deny its entrepôt facilities to arms dealers who were supplying the rebels in China, if not always with success. In the struggle between Nationalists and Communists, marches or other organized manifestations of partisanship have been banned because they might lead to street fighting, but advocacy through the press, education, or trade unions has been accorded total tolerance in accordance with the common law.

The eviction of foreign nations from the former treaty ports of China after 1950 brought Hong Kong a certain uniqueness as channel both for such exports as the Communist regime could produce and for importation of the few indispensable items of equipment the meager exports could pay for. Some of the claims that Hong Kong was the source of all China's foreign exchange earnings around 1958 were certainly exaggerated, but, given the colony's high consumption of food from China and the ruthless means by which the Canton authorities intercepted and taxed Hong Kong's traditional fisheries, it may have supplied as much as half for two decades. Even before 1949, the Hong Kong dollar was well established as the China coast's chief hard currency; in quite small towns, foreigners were expected to pay for their needs with it in preference to the Chinese dollar, and it was hoarded as an alternative to gold against inflation. Since the colony's industrialization and the post-Mao liberalization on the mainland, Hong Kong has, in a much more complicated manner than before, become both an important marketplace for China's advanced technology and a place for investment by the Chinese state in all kinds of industrial—and even speculative financial—undertakings, the profits of which are one kind of "state enterprise" that is better not talked about in the Party media. As a major financial center, Hong Kong has become, not only a gem the mainland Party desires to possess—and has, in a sense, been buying its way into through investment in property, the underground railway, and so on—but also a school in which to have mainland managers trained in the realities of what as Marxists they call the capitalist system, the better to manipulate the system later on. A two-stage land deal carried out by agents of Peking in 1981 and 1982 was largely instrumental in drawing both public and official attention in Hong Kong to the urgency of procuring a settlement of the future of the New Territories after 1997. Its implications are discussed in the next chapter.

Notes

1. According to *Who's Who in China* 1936: 132.

2. Young 1970: 69ff; also Atwell 1985: 6–11. The parallel between the British leased territories at the moment of acquisitions is explained fully by N. J. Miners in a foreword to Atwell.

3. Wesley-Smith 1983: 161.

4. For an admirable, professional appreciation of the legal position of Hong Kong, see Dicks 1983.

5. Grantham 1965: 158; also Hook 1983: 500–505.

6. Miners 1975: 28 (n.22). The prohibition is sometimes said to have been "hinted unmistakably" early in 1950 when the United Kingdom recognized the People's Republic.

7. See, for example, observation by Goodstadt in *China Quarterly* 63: 564.

8. Howe 1983: 512.

9. Pinkstone 1982: 46–47 and 53–54.

10. *Chinese Law and Custom* 1953; Wesley-Smith 1983: 92ff. A discussion of the Hong Kong practice with regard to customary family law (mixed with cases from other British dependent territories) can be found in Hooker 1975: 158ff.

11. The drift of the different official Chinese approaches to Britain under ever-changing circumstances of power in the Far East is dealt with objectively by Hungdah Chiu in Cohen, ed. 1972.

12. Grantham 1965: 130-133.

13. Miners 1975: 218-219.

14. Catron 1972: 417.

15. News item in *China Quarterly* 34: 189.

Bibliography

Atwell, Pamela. *British Mandarins and Chinese Reformers* (at Wei-hai-wei). London: Oxford University Press, 1985.

Catron, Gary. "Hong Kong and Chinese Foreign Policy." *China Quarterly*, no. 51 (1972).

Chinese Law and Custom in Hong Kong. Hong Kong: Government Printer, 1953.

Cohen, Jerome A. "The Chinese Communist Party and 'Judicial Independence' 1949-1959." *Harvard Law Review* 82:5 (1969):967-1006.

Cohen, Jerome A., ed. *China's Practice of International Law.* Cambridge, Mass.: Harvard University Press, 1972.

Dicks, Anthony. "Treaty, Grant, Usage, or Sufferance? Some Legal Aspects of the Status of Hong Kong." *China Quarterly*, no. 95 (1983):427-455.

Endacott, G. B. *A History of Hong Kong.* London: Oxford University Press, 1958.

England, Joe, and John Rear. *Chinese Labour Under British Rule.* London: Oxford University Press, 1975.

Friedmann, W., et al. *International Law.* Minneapolis, Minn.: University of Minnesota Press, 1969.

Grantham, Alexander. *Via Ports—from Hong Kong to Hong Kong.* Hong Kong: Hong Kong University Press, 1965.

Hook, Brian. "The Government of Hong Kong: Change Within Tradition." *China Quarterly*, no. 95 (1983):491-511.

Hooker, M. B. *Legal Pluralism.* London: Oxford University Press, 1975.

Howe, Christopher. "Growth, Public Policy, and Hong Kong's Economic Relationship with China." *China Quarterly*, no. 95 (1983):512-533.

Hsiung, James Chieh. *Law and Policy in China's Foreign Relations.* New York: Columbia University Press, 1972.

McNair, Lord. *The Law of Treaties.* London: Oxford University Press, 1961.

Miners, N. J. *Government and Politics of Hong Kong.* Hong Kong and London: Oxford University Press, 1975.

Parsons, M. J. *Hong Kong 1983* (official review for 1982). Hong Kong: Government Printer, 1983.

Pinkstone, M. *Hong Kong 1982* (official review for 1981). Hong Kong: Government Printer, 1982.

Wesley-Smith, Peter. *Unequal Treaty 1898-1997.* 2d ed. Hong Kong: Oxford University Press, 1983.

Who's Who in China. (China Weekly Review, Shanghai). 1936.

Young, L. K. *British Policy in China 1895-1902.* London: Oxford University Press, 1970.

2

The Anglo-Chinese Negotiations

Dennis Duncanson

Prelude to Negotiation

Attention was drawn in Chapter 1 to the areas in which, by 1981, the Hong Kong government had become increasingly complaisant to the Central People's government. The chief of them was the delay in introducing representative government or other measures of devolution of authority to the people. Another was disuse of the word "colony," even though the territory underwent no constitutional change. Among the explanations for Hong Kong's complaisance must be counted the hope of not giving Peking any positive cause to raise the question of rendition. The policy succeeded: On the rare occasions in recent years when Communist leaders were moved to make some pronouncement on Hong Kong's future, the purport was invariably to reassure the people that no revolutionary interference was planned, and therefore they on their side avoided, along with the word "colony," use of words like "rendition" or "retrocession" or "repossession."

When groups of Cantonese businessmen began to visit Peking in 1980 and 1981 and, with an eye to their investments, sought clarification of the People's government's intentions, they began to report that Teng Hsiao-p'ing replied they could set their minds at rest since China was not wanting to undermine the territory's flourishing economy—in 1979 he had told the governor of Hong Kong the same thing. This attitude gave rise to the widespread hope in Hong Kong that as one government in China after another had repudiated the principles on which the three basic treaties had been founded, to the point of saying in different ways, "We do not recognize them," the terminal date in the last of them, 1997, would be ignored by the People's government. In fact, the United Kingdom itself ignored the date when it underwrote a General Electric Company advance to the China Light and Power Company for equipment for the Castle Peak power station, the last repayment of which is not due till 2002.[1] Why then should London stir matters up by broaching discussion of the future in 1982, fifteen years in advance of the terminal date?

The reason is set out in the United Kingdom's introduction to the Joint Declaration of September 26, 1984: to safeguard confidence in the Hong Kong financial market, increasingly under threat from the shortening term of Crown leases in the New Territories (the area, including Castle Peak, of most valuable industrial and social development in recent times), which were all due to lapse on June 27, 1997, three days before expiration of the Anglo-Chinese convention of 1898. I pointed out in Chapter 1 that revenue from land—principally from the sale of leases on land bought from private owners more or less compulsorily ("resumption"), though at market rates, or else new land obtained by rock leveling or sea reclamation—had long been a major source of public funds and was applied in the main to capital works of infrastructure. The colony's treasury could not easily have made good a heavy fall in the land market engendered by uncertainty about the long-term future, and that problem, in turn, would have been concomitant with a general decline in the economy.

The question of Crown leases in British enclaves on the China coast or the Yangtze basin has a long history. Starting with Shanghai in the 1840s, the British practice in treaty ports was to recompense the Chinese government for the concession by paying an annual ground rent equivalent to the preexisting land tax—a sum of money kept low by the ill-advised promise of the K'ang Hsi emperor in 1712 that the Ch'ing dynasty would never raise this tax above its current level.[2] The British consul meanwhile bought out private Chinese rural owners at the market price, surveyed the land cadastrally, and then granted Crown leases on it—that is to say, leases under the Office of Works of the United Kingdom government—for 999 years at the same ground rent as was being passed on to the Chinese government. The Ch'ing authorities did not challenge the legality of this procedure. However, when the lease of Wei-hai-wei was granted Britain in 1898, for a term limited to the time that Russia might occupy Port Arthur, and the new British commissioner followed the treaty-port practice in one very small area of the territory needed for building Port Edward (Ma T'ou), Peking protested that 999-year Crown leases amounted to alienation of more than Britain "owned."[3] The protest was heeded, and after that developers had to buy land round Port Edward direct from the old owners[4]—as if they had been in a French, Russian, or other enclave. It seems likely that Peking's protest had some bearing on the decision in Hong Kong to restrict Crown leases in the New Territories to the term of Britain's tenure of the territory—down, that is, to 1997.

Peasant land in the New Territories also was declared to be Crown land, as it had been under the constitutional theory of the Chinese Empire, but existing rights were registered and subsequently overridden only by "resumption" for some public purpose, with more generous compensation. Some Crown leases were granted at one time on the permanently ceded lands of Hong Kong for 999 years, but eventually the term for all of them was standardized at 75 years, with right of renewal.[5] Whereas Crown leases in treaty-port concessions at one time yielded a modest income to the

United Kingdom treasury—a practice quite without moral justification—
Crown-lease income arising in Hong Kong has always remained in the
colony.

By 1979, tenure in the New Territories had fallen to twelve years—a
period shorter than the customary term for mortgages or even for the fast
amortization of capital that had become the rule in an economy long used
to boom conditions. The considerations that moved the London and Hong
Kong governments to make an approach to Peking have not been disclosed
other than in the general way referred to earlier, but it is safe to surmise
that there were two other, unspoken, factors. The first is that the unplanned
termination of British extraterritorial rights in some of the treaty ports in
the late 1920s, especially Hankow and Kiukang, had caused embarrassing
confusion over the fate of leaseholders' rights, even though, down to that
time, no Chinese government had ever declined to respect those rights
after taking over any foreign enclave. Second, the settlement pattern in the
New Territories was many times more complicated than it had ever been
in a treaty port, and it was essential to secure leaseholders' rights, well in
advance of 1997, for a span of time far after that date. The governor of
Hong Kong was invited by one of the Chinese ministers to pay an official
visit to Peking in 1979, and it was decided that he should sound his hosts
about the Central People's government's willingness to agree to terms under
which the Hong Kong government might extend leases—the whole lot due
to fall in on a single day, as we have seen—for a substantial period. The
Communist leaders he met were not willing to discuss Hong Kong's land
problem in isolation, probably on the grounds that it was incidental to the
main question of Hong Kong's future—not the other way round, as the
governor would see it. It is probable they judged that they did not know
enough about the territory's affairs to formulate a complete policy yet, for
when Foreign Minister Huang Hua went to London in October 1980 and
the topic was again sounded, he too rebuffed the approach.[6]

During the next two or three years, the People's government set about
buying its way into the Hong Kong economy and, at the same time,
cultivating more positively Cantonese tycoon leaders of industry (dubbed
on the local scene, unkindly, "the fat cats"). By mid-1981, there had developed
a lively debate in the Hong Kong Chinese press about the uncertainties of
the future, a debate that some thought responsible for an increase in
unemployment that year and for the beginning of what turned out to be
a grave slump in property values. *Ming Pao* called on Teng to "translate
his promise into internationally recognizable language," and *Ching-chi chou-
k'an* [Economic review] and others wanted Peking to extend the whole
New Territories lease there and then for another fifty years—even to throw
the recently designated special economic zone at Shenchen in with it. These
comments reflected the gossip of the marketplace at the time.

Peking concentrated that year on its "peace offer" for unification with
Taiwan, inevitably linked with Hong Kong, and the matter held fire for
another year. It was in the offer to Taiwan that the Chinese Communist

party first advanced the slogan "one country, two systems," which was destined to be its chief public bait for allaying popular fears that in the event of repossession of Hong Kong, standards of living were bound to be lowered. In January 1982, Peking spokesmen signaled to a visiting junior minister from London that they would soon be ready for discussions. There then occurred the land deals alluded to at the end of Chapter 1. In 1980, under the guise of China Resources, the Central People's government had bought 486 hectares of T'ienshuiwan in the New Territories for HK$600 million, with the hope of converting it into a housing estate. Finding the feasibility of such development too far in the future, two years later Peking called on the Hong Kong government to "resume" the site for a price thought by the press to be as high as HK$2,000 million. The government gave way, and immediately afterward the Bank of China bought from the government by private treaty a central public site for HK$1,000 million, a site that it was supposed could have fetched more than twice that price if the government had auctioned it in the usual way. China Resources was known to have been sold sites at cut prices before, and it was obvious that from now on Peking intended to abuse its whip hand by investing in Hong Kong in ways that milked profits from the capitalist system without incurring the attendant risks. As a result, the stock-exchange index suffered a major plunge, dragging property values and the currency down with it.[7]

The Course of the Negotiations

For the sake of the elusive intangible of confidence, therefore, the British prime minister's opening of the question of Hong Kong's future during her visit to Peking in September 1982, ostensibly for other reasons as well, was far from precipitate. But considerable controversy attended Margaret Thatcher's forthright manner during her talks with Teng Hsiao-p'ing and subsequent press conferences. The rights and wrongs of her statements as negotiating tactics and the significance of the offense taken by the Communists as determinants of the final outcome would be easier to gauge if we knew the opening positions adopted by the two sides, but they had agreed at the start that no account of the negotiations would be divulged until they were all over and an agreement had been reached. Although in the event, the Communists now and then deliberately leaked their version of what was going on in order to put pressure on the British side, the latter kept its promise, and it is to be feared that no actual record of what was said at the meetings at any stage will be accessible until about the year 2012 or later.

In anticipation of the encounter, Teng again invited certain Hong Kong tycoons to Peking to hear his intentions and promises: China was going to resume sovereignty over Hong Kong some time about 1997, but in such a way as to preserve its "stability and prosperity."[8] It seems that he bluntly said just that when the two prime ministers met on September 24, 1982, no doubt adding that the Central People's government did not propose to take any account of the three Hong Kong treaties because all of them were unequal and thus invalid. Thatcher's reaction to this understandably extreme opening bid was to adopt an extreme position on her side: Whether or not the treaties were unequal in either signature or effect had no bearing on their validity in international law. She pointed out that a state that broke a past treaty could hardly expect to be trusted in regard to future treaties. She refused to have "resumption of sovereignty" written in as part of the joint communiqué issued during her visit, but the New China News Agency added the term to its version.[9] It is a common practice in the diplomacy of Communist states to try to maneuver the other party into conceding the main point at issue before negotiations begin, and Thatcher will have been briefed to expect such an attempt.

Both sides made a show of being offended in their sincerity by the other: Safeguarding the future interests of the people of Hong Kong, said Thatcher, was a "moral responsibility and duty" for the United Kingdom; according to an infuriated Teng Hsiao-p'ing, since the Hong Kong treaties were invalid *ab origine* ("from the outset"), only the People's government had the right to talk about "moral responsibility"—an argument rather at variance with that government's insistence on other occasions on the principle *rebus sic stantibus* ("circumstances alter cases").[10] But the fact was that the Chinese and the British alike were looking over their shoulders at implications of a solution of what the Communists called "the Hong Kong problem" on other international issues.

For the Communists, Hong Kong was a precedent, useful not only for their plans for Taiwan but also for relations with the USSR, which still incorporated wide tracts of north and central Asia by virtue of even older unequal treaties with the Chinese Empire. Although the present regime in Peking had expressly forgone opportunities to press "the fraternal state" for restitution, that self-denial was offset by a caveat that the treaties were not on that account to be recognized as valid in law. The invalidity of unequal treaties is supported by Russian authorities themselves, for, when pronouncing on questions of international law, the Soviet Academy of Sciences has been quoted as asserting that "the sanctity of treaties (*pacta sunt servanda*) does not extend to treaties imposed by force and unequal in character, and their repudiation cannot be considered a violation of it."[11]

The British contention was that even though the wresting by one state of a treaty from another by coercion has been condemned since the conclusion of the Covenant of the League of Nations ("deplored" in the 1969 Vienna Convention on Treaties), earlier treaties are not thereby invalidated; that nearly all treaties follow hard bargaining and contain effects the parties would have liked to avoid; and that no case claiming invalidity of the most notorious unequal treaty of modern times, the Treaty of Versailles, on the eve of the covenant, was ever entertained by the Permanent Court of International Justice.[12] Indeed, China had been both a signatory and a beneficiary of the Treaty of Versailles, so that its insistence in 1982 on the Soviet doctrine smacked of special pleading—notwithstanding previous denunciations from Peking of new treaties among other states, to which the People's Republic was not even a party, as invalid because unequal.[13] But there was an ulterior motive, if not quite a specious element, in Thatcher's stand as well: In 1982, she had a special concern lest the disposal of Hong Kong should set a precedent in international opinion for the rendition of Gibraltar, British by virtue of the Peace of Utrecht (1713) and demanded back by Spain in the teeth of clearly expressed opposition on the part of its inhabitants.

Although the sanctity of treaties supported British retention of Hong Kong Island and Kowloon, it equally supported Chinese repossession of the New Territories, and since territorial division had to be ruled out (at one spot it would have meant westbound traffic driving through British territory, eastbound through Chinese) the legal principle alone could not be used to determine the ultimate agreement for the future governance of the territory. Nor could the Communist doctrine either, for, right or wrong, retrocession of Hong Kong in 1997 was going to be a much more complicated operation than its cession in 1842.

There remained, however, yet another question of principle important to London but dismissed by Peking, namely, the status and representation of Hong Kong as a political entity in its own right in any decision about its future. There was no precedent in modern British imperial history for the surrender of a colonial people to another power other than by an expression of self-determination as prescribed in the Yalta agreement and enshrined in the United Nations Charter—and London was at grips at the time not only with Spain's demands to do just that to the Gibraltarians but also with Argentine to do it to the Falkland Islanders.[14] The People's government, however, could have no sympathy for that particular problem: On the strategic level, the aim of negotiation was to detach Hong Kong from Britain and attach it to China, and it was hardly in doubt that the majority of people, if they could be given a chance to express a wish, would oppose that aim. As in nearly every case in which a Communist government is one party, therefore, the tactics of the People's government indicated "neutralization" of Hong Kong residents as political participants, and the best procedure to that end was to insist on bilateral negotiations between sovereign powers over the heads of the people.

In addition, standing on "sovereign rights" had hitherto served Communist states very well in international negotiations and—though a concept for which there was no term in Chinese political thought until the Japanese coined *shuken* ("sovereignty") in the 1860s—on this occasion, it gave the People's government a trump card against any British proposals that might prevent total control over Hong Kong in the future by the Politburo of the Chinese Communist party. "Sovereignty" does not occur in the Hong Kong treaties, and it leads to inflexibility, which English legal draftsmen rather shun, but there have been many occasions when the USSR especially has used the principle in international relations—not least the "limited sovereignty" of the 1968 Brezhnev Doctrine—to buttress prescriptive authority and totalitarian rule at home. It has not been made known how hard the Foreign Office pressed for representation of Hong Kong as such, but it was not so well placed to do so as it would have been had there been devolution to parliamentary government in the past. The failure (at Communist behest) to provide for consultation of the Hong Kong people as a factor in the negotiations was cited at one stage by Thatcher as enhancing her government's moral responsibility. In the event, Peking agreed (by way of "concession") to accept the credentials of the governor of Hong Kong as one member of the United Kingdom team—since he was not himself a Hong Konger but a direct servant of the Crown—but without any capacity as a representative of Hong Kong.

Requests in the colony in March 1984 for a debate in the Legislative Council on the colony's future *before* Britain and China reached a decision on the matter were ruled out by the People's government as a mere trick on Britain's part "to manipulate public opinion."[15] When, after a whole eighteen months of talks, a delegation from UMELCO went to Peking and asked to be received by Teng, its members were snubbed and told they did not represent the people of Hong Kong[16]—unlike the tycoons Teng was keeping in close touch with, as the alarmed local press repeatedly emphasized. Failure to win a place at the negotiating table for the voice of Hong Kong was the lesser of two disappointments destined to sadden the Foreign Office diplomats—I will discuss the second one later.

In spite of the wrangles, it was fortunate that, to judge from such evidence as we have been vouchsafed, when it came to opening the talks, both parties did concentrate on practical questions rather than on the sterile bids made during Thatcher's visit to Peking in September 1982. Soon after that date, the governor had let it be known in Hong Kong that preliminary points were being gone over by the British ambassador and Chinese foreign ministry officials, but slow progress seems to have been made, even with agreeing on an agenda, and the two sides were not ready for full formal negotiations until April 1983. From that time forward, sessions alternated between Peking and London.

The introduction to the London version of the Joint Declaration tells us that the British side was at pains in this second phase "to explain in detail the systems which prevail in Hong Kong and the importance for these systems of the British administrative role and link." The Chinese negotiators were probably tempted to attribute such reluctance to lay aside the "moral responsibility" to "exploitative" greed and special pleading against their own demand for straightforward rendition, which in turn would be based on the example of the Nationalist government's takeovers in the 1920s and 1930s of the infinitely smaller and less developed concessions in treaty ports. Down to this moment, there is reason to suspect that many of the Peking leaders understood little more about what they always called "cap-italism" (but the British rarely did) than what they had read about it in the works of Marx and Engels. They appreciated that the economic successes of both Hong Kong and Taiwan were the work of capitalists, but only since investing in Hong Kong themselves were they getting an understanding of the investor's point of view, and even that was like learning to drive without mastering the principle of internal combustion. Above all, since the objects of their two territorial ambitions were basically different in the detail of their administrative and legal systems, it would be hard to credit an assertion that Hong Kong's future prosperity was going to depend on a link with the United Kingdom when Taiwan's was not. All the same, their eventual agreement to tolerate most of the Hong Kong "detail" after 1997 is evidence that they became convinced, if not that Hong Kong's prosperity really was inseparable from it, at least that the Hong Kong people, the Chinese tycoons, and the foreign investors all believed that it was.

Although it was agreed that the progress of the negotiations should be confidential, and the British team kept to that agreement—except for informing and consulting UMELCO, on which the Foreign Office refused to be gainsaid—Peking proved skillful at feeding open indiscretions to a public anxious about its fate and, by rumormongering, pressed the other side of the table into giving way when it had been holding firm. As an example, it was rumored in June 1983 that Peking had set a deadline for reaching agreement or the Central People's government would impose a settlement, and shortly thereafter that the United Kingdom had said it was ready to cede its sovereignty over the island and Kowloon—both rumors were denied by the British.[17] Throughout this period, Peking spokesmen reiterated their formulas for the future as "one country, two systems" and "sovereignty with prosperity"; to the obvious question, if prosperity were to prove incompatible with sovereignty, which would come first, the answer was "sovereignty."[18]

By September, a testy atmosphere prevailed again: Margaret Thatcher, just reelected prime minister, told U.S. journalists that if it weren't for the New Territories lease, Hong Kong would have ceased to be a colony and become as independent as Singapore years ago, and non-Communist newspapers were proposing rendition of sovereignty but "lease-back" of administration; Peking responded that the People's Republic would "never agree to continuation of colonial rule."[19] For the perceptive, the dice had been cast in December 1982 by the enactment of the Fourth Constitution of the People's Republic by the National People's Congress: Its presenter had explained that Art. 31, taking powers to set up "special administrative zones," was drafted deliberately to enable "national reunification."[20] In the fall of 1983, the Chinese negotiators really did issue an ultimatum that agreement must be concluded by September 30, 1984, and this time London admitted the fact;[21] but whatever came out of the negotiations before then, stated a British junior minister on a visit, must be acceptable to all three parties (that is, including Hong Kong); no, Peking rejoined, there were only *two* parties to the decision.[22] Meanwhile, the stock exchange continued its mercurial ups and downs in response to Communist leaks to the press, property values continued to drift down, and the fall of the local dollar, long unpegged from sterling, was checked only because it was repegged to the U.S. dollar.

It seems to have been at this point that the U.K. government finally consented to surrender all three parts of Hong Kong to the People's Republic in 1997: Although the fact was not published explicitly, reassuring statements from the Communists that no fundamental points remained unsettled restored a little confidence to the financial market—less perhaps than if the rumors had been of Peking's yielding instead of Britain. Here was the Foreign Office's second disappointment: The British administrative "role and link" (Thatcher's way of putting it) had had to be abandoned in order to keep intact the British administrative "detail."

Because of the ultimatum, the rounds of talks speeded up, punctuated in spring and early summer 1984 by two visits to Peking from the foreign secretary himself, Sir Geoffrey Howe, who now acknowledged that preservation of the role and link he had been urging for eighteen months was not "realistic" after all.[23] With rendition no longer in doubt, Communist leaks ceased to be hostile to Britain but aimed instead at stilling anxiety in Hong Kong that too much of the territory's independence might have been surrendered, and individual members of UMELCO were at last invited to Peking to have their feelings mollified.[24] In particular, it was emphasized that, as in the Communists' offer to Taiwan, "capitalism" would be left alone for fifty years after 1997, that in the meantime the laws and the administrative structure need not be modified to any radical extent, and that the government after 1997 would be administered by Hong Kongers (*Kang-jen chih Kang*) answerable to elected representatives. The effect was reduced a shade, however, by a gloss from Teng himself in June that *Kang-jen* was to be understood as "patriotic compatriots" whom "China would not require all to favor China's socialist system but who must love the motherland as well as Hong Kong"—a qualification the Chinese Communist party would presumably deem itself to be sole judge of, not the people.[25]

In July, the Hong Kong government published a Green Paper (that is, a proposal for public consideration) on electoral reform, which, with a few changes, was put into effect in 1985. In 1984, however, it was received coolly by the Communist spokesmen, and there is reason to believe that they had envisaged the introduction of a representative government only after 1997, under their own auspices. The further negotiations, in the last months and weeks, apparently dealt with the precise procedures necessary to make the principles of the settlement a reality and with what the British side regarded as guarantees for the transition period up to 1997 more than with the years after 1997. At an earlier point in the talks, Chinese leaders had suggested that Hong Kong be administered until repossession by an Anglo-Chinese condominium, under which it was no more than prudent to foresee that the Chinese would have exercised the power while the British shouldered the responsibility, much as the Chinese had previously expected profits from "capitalism" while not accepting its risks.[26]

With a joint working group sitting full time in Peking in order to meet the deadline, the last phases of the negotiations were the fastest, and the final (twenty-second) session was held at the beginning of September 1984.

During the previous few weeks, People's Republic spokesmen had issued calming statements about the future safety of Taiwanese financial interests in Hong Kong and had held discussions in Peking on the same general subject with Japanese diplomats. As soon as it was known that a Joint Declaration was ready for initialing, the stock market surged again—for several weeks. The heads of the two delegations initialed the final Chinese and English texts in Peking on September 26. The stage was then set for giving the impending changes of Hong Kong's status, and the terms of it, constitutional effect—a step of enormous concern for Britain but of trivial concern for the People's Republic, which was not subject to constraints of public opinion. The first move was the consultation of public opinion in Hong Kong—a consultation after the event, like one of those plebiscites to confirm a fait accompli that were common in Europe in the nineteenth and early twentieth centuries. Ministerial consultation with UMELCO, in both Hong Kong and London, had been frequent during the talks; there had been debates about what *ideally* would be desirable in the Legislative Council and both houses of Parliament; and the press comments had been yet another element in the British negotiators' representations in Peking and London, but British consciences were still troubled because all of that fell short of a true procedure for self-determination by the people.

The day the Joint Declaration was initialed, an assessment office was opened in Hong Kong, with Peking's assent, and instructed, independent of Hong Kong government departments, to invite and collect submissions of views from representative bodies and private persons. It was open until November 15—seven weeks. The office's operations were overseen by two monitors appointed by the foreign secretary, a Hong Kong judge (Chinese), and the chancellor of Essex University—the last at one time a senior United Kingdom civil servant. Their duty was to report whether the "operations" were conscientious and impartial, and they duly did so. At the same time, a score of private organizations conducted their own opinion polls, with substantially similar results. The crux of the assessment office's report is contained in *Hong Kong 1985*.[27]

In summary, an overwhelming majority of acceptances of the Joint Declaration was recorded, and every one of the representative bodies in the colony met and passed a resolution to that effect, although in nearly all of them some votes were cast against. Fewer than 2,000 written submissions were received at the office, but the great majority accepted the agreement. Objections were raised to the lack of consultation before it was drawn up, the fact that Hong Kong's future was being determined by China and the United Kingdom on their own—above all with the People's Republic instead of the Republic of China—and the untrustworthiness alleged against Communists in general. Many people regretted the failure to settle the future constitution, which had been left to the Central People's government to decide on by itself, and a few questioned particular provisions. The general attitude, expressed with greater or more grudging fulsomeness, was that whereas keeping the status quo might have been best, the British side had

had no alternative but to give way on rendition and that if the future sovereign keeps his word, life will be tolerable under such an arrangement. There was great euphoria in Hong Kong; only the bar association and the law society (the two branches of the legal profession) were ominously unable or unwilling to give notice of general acceptance by their members of what had been negotiated.

Relieved and strengthened by what it cannot be denied was a massive yes vote, the two houses of Parliament debated at length a resolution to approve the draft Joint Declaration, and both passed it in the end without division. Prime Minister Thatcher then set out for Peking again and signed the declaration simultaneously with Chao Tzu-yang, prime minister of the Central People's government, on December 19, 1984. Members of UMELCO were invited by the Communists to attend, as private individuals, and several did, but others declined the invitation, evidently more as a mark of resentment of the shabby treatment meted out to their two councils during the previous two years than as a protest against the terms concluded. In preparation for ratification, a draft bill was presented to Parliament in January (No. 15 of 1985) that gave effect to the transfer of sovereignty in 1997 in two or three lines, and its various stages were completed early in April 1985. The opposition in both houses dwelt on only three points: criticism of Thatcher for alleged tactlessness in the talks—though without suggesting what better terms might have been obtained without it—the lack of proper consultation of the people concerned, and the Joint Declaration itself for leaving nationality questions in the air. There was, of course, no scope for amendment, and, on the whole, the favorable resolutions of the councils in Hong Kong were matched by hardly less satisfaction when passing the bill into law. The Joint Declaration was presented to the People's National Congress in April 1985 and adopted by a show of hands; ratification took place in May. The final step was to deposit the Declaration, "as a treaty in the most solemn form" (as Sir Geoffrey Howe described its status), with the United Nations, where the secretary-general, a Peruvian diplomat, perhaps with an eye on the United Kingdom's differences with Spain and Argentina, welcomed it as a model for diplomatic resolution of sovereignty disputes in the future.

The Agreement in Historical Setting

The Joint Declaration is printed in the Appendix of this book, and its effects—the consequences so far and the implications—are discussed in later chapters, but it may be worth concluding this account of the negotiations with a few comments on the declaration's place in history. Javier Perez de Cuellar's readiness to cite the agreement as a precedent in just the way Thatcher had hoped to avoid demonstrated the shallow hold the Yalta principle of self-determination has in the world today—the principle that peoples shall not be transferred from rule by one state to rule by another save of their own free will. Consultation there was, after decisions had been taken, but the acceptance of the agreement that so gratified the British spokesmen was acquiescence in an arbitrary act—there was no chance of decisive consultation beforehand. Without power of their own, the Hong Kong people's self-determination could not be vindicated under the United Nations Charter, and the power of the United Kingdom could not be invoked on their behalf because if Thatcher had stood out longer against the 1983 ultimatum from Peking and the People's Liberation Army had marched in, Britain would not have had a friend in the world and Hong Kong itself would have lain in financial if not physical ruins, with sections of its people (as it predicted) in tumult. Whether a less resolute British stand on the treaties and the importance of administrative details during the first year of negotiation would have found the People's government less resolute about sovereignty or more so cannot be answered with certainty. The circumstances of the rendition of Hong Kong are consequently not really paralleled by anything that has happened in the past or could happen in the future.

It is of more interest to consider the agreement as part of the history of China. Is it a departure from the traditional structure of China? Is it inconsistent with Marxism-Leninism? British negotiators and advocates of the merits of the Joint Declaration and its first annex, in which the People's government elaborates its intentions, have tended to assume that the idea of a special administrative zone, under the local-autonomy section of the 1982 constitution of the People's Republic, is ingenious, novel, and unique, but it has its precursors in Chinese history. The empire, in its pretensions to universal suzerainty, had a long-standing policy of both yielding to the expediency of allowing distant provinces a large measure of autonomy and of working on their political culture ideologically but then watching for opportune moments to incorporate them in the central administrative structure—the policies of *t'u-ssu* and of *kai-t'u kuei liu*. To this extent, the Chinese Communist party's establishment of autonomous districts and regions soon after it seized power—"autonomy" having different meanings in different parts of the country—could be said to have imperial antecedents, and having a chief executive appointed by the Politburo to preside over Hong Kong is reminiscent of a Ch'ing *ting-pien* (governor or chief resident) in the northwest.

Equally, the agreement has antecedents in the Leninism of Russia: On the one hand, Lenin advocated self-determination as a tactic to detach dependent territories from empires not yet ruled by the Communists—as did Marx before him—and on the other, he argued from the premise that any group of people who did not wish to be under Communist party rule must ipso facto be bourgeois and wicked, and he urged a seizure of opportunities to bring them into the Soviet system. As the late Leonid Brezhnev once pointed out, the USSR is a union of "autonomous republics," united in the dominion over all of them of a single Communist party. The term "special administrative region" has its origins in the practice of the Republic of China of not reincorporating treaty-port concessions wholly into the National administration when they had lapsed, either as a result of the Treaty of Versailles or by negotiated agreement with Western powers: For an unspecified period (though presumably not forever), they were to continue with their municipal organization, regulation, taxation, and judiciary under the designation "special administrative district." With the partial exception of Wei-hai-wei, for which the evidence has been collected by Atwell, one cannot say how the system would have worked over a span of years because it was overtaken by the Japanese occupation and the civil war, but the 1930s precedent must have been in the minds of the Chinese negotiators of the Joint Declaration, and perhaps of the British too. The answer to the first question above, therefore, is no.

The second question is more one of judgment than of fact, but it is one that has had some importance for Peking leaders, whom Nikita Khrushchev once taunted in the United Nations for their toleration of the colonial status quo in Hong Kong and Macao. Even before Thatcher's first visit to Peking, Secretary-General Hu Yao-pang saw fit, at the moment of the controversial land deals, to explain that adoption of the "one country, two systems" formula to solve the problem of sovereignty over Hong Kong and Macao was to be regarded as following the example of Lenin's 1920 attitude over concessions to capitalists;[28] in other words, using capitalists to undo capitalism. What Hu was referring to was the clear-cut distinction Lenin drew between indispensable "tactical compromises" with capitalism, in order to draw on its own resources in the struggle against it, and "strategic compromises," by which Communists might commit themselves so far to a "minimum program" of cooperation that they put in jeopardy the "maximum program" of the Party's absolute power. The question for answer here is whether the undoubted compromises in the Hong Kong agreement fall within the bounds of the purely tactical or are so fundamental as to shape strategically the course of future developments in the ex-colony or in China itself. Hu appeared to be saying that they were tactical, and, as the eventual Joint Declaration turned out, by committing the Party to the policy in it for only fifty years after British withdrawal—a provision no more than realistic anyway, some might feel—the effect is not to incur the permanent sort of strategic compromise Lenin condemned, in his personal jargon, as "opportunism."

Nevertheless, there is a little more to the matter. All Peking's utterances, before and during the negotiations, stayed within Marxian limits, in that what was proposed and then promised was preservation of "capitalism": that is to say, the whole issue was envisaged as simply one of economics. It looked as if all the Party meant to promise was continuation of the characteristics of Hong Kong from which there was expectation of deriving profits and other material advantages for the Party on the mainland. It seems likely that for all their condemnation of the Great Proletarian Cultural Revolution, Teng and Hu and their followers were conscious that the extreme severity of the revolution's intimidation of "individualism" did succeed in cowing the masses into acceptance of the Party's monopoly of power once and for all, so that it would take much more than capitalism under the red flag in Hong Kong to upset it.

But it is noneconomic characteristics that articulate opinion in Hong Kong has made plain are prized there—the social, political, and above all legal infrastructure—and it is perpetuation of those, not of the tycoons' fortunes, that constituted the moral responsibility the British negotiators harped on. There was indeed the precedent of Lenin's own new economic policy (tolerating "freedom of trade, something we consider criminal")[29] to justify "one country, two systems of economic management," as Hu argued, and that compromise in the agreement was therefore tactical—for as long as the Hong Kong goose continued to lay golden eggs. But the promise to tolerate common-law precedents—equity, English rules of evidence, and the Habeas Corpus Act—in a judiciary not susceptible to "guidelines" from the Politburo must raise Leninist eyebrows. At present, the people of Hong Kong do not enjoy their liberties in pursuance of a bill of rights granted by a benevolent monarch, because there is no bill of rights in the United Kingdom: Liberty is understood to be immanent in the individual man or woman until limited by statute. That concept has no place in either Confucian or Marxist-Leninist tradition, in neither of which do rights exist until conferred "benevolently." Insofar as existing Hong Kong liberties are protected in what amounts to a summary bill of rights in the Joint Declaration, instead of by continuation of the present administration and ultimate recourse to the Crown, they could equally be rescinded, even earlier than 2047, by exercise of the "sovereignty" Peking negotiators so demanded: What a sovereign has granted can be taken away again. To this extent, even in regard to the noneconomic aspect, it might just be conceded that the agreement is not a strategic compromise with Marxism-Leninism, whereas to have left the link with Britain alone would have been one.

It must, of course, have occurred to the Communists, facing British diplomats across the table, that rescission of the liberties on the list could not be perpetrated at the stroke of a pen without at least some risk of international scandal and the opprobrium of the broken word. Furthermore, so long as those liberties continued to be respected in Hong Kong, there must be the old danger that mainlanders would hanker after them too—even demand them. The previous excuse that Hong Kong was a separate political entity was no longer going to apply after repossession, so that critics might point to the danger that the tactical compromise in Hong Kong might grow into a strategic one in China as a whole. Presumably, that likelihood was taken into account, and the obviating of it may have been a contributory factor in Peking's refusal to have a constitution giving effect to the executive's "accountability"—something less than *answerability?*—to elected representatives spelled out in detail,[30] for if the British had had their way over this point, the people's will in Hong Kong might have blocked rescission, even in 2047. By leaving the Basic Law out of the Joint Declaration, the Communist party made sure of a firm fallback position behind which to entrench its absolute power over Hong Kong against spontaneous demands for self-determination from below, which might undermine the Politburo's standing as the sole authority for "correct" decision making.

The oligarchic democracy-by-corporate-consultation set up by the colonial government, even allowing for the enlarged franchise of the 1985 structure, must have looked ideal for penetration and subversion: It ought to be possible for experienced Leninists to preserve its manipulability in the Basic Law while paying the same lip service to representative government as on the mainland and in the end, work their will, by contrivance, over the political and legal infrastructures of Hong Kong. For instance, during the lifetime of the 1954 constitution of the People's Republic, independence of the judiciary from the *state* was proclaimed but in practice subverted by the *Party* through various overt and clandestine devices.[31] The Peking negotiators agreed that the Hong Kong courts should exercise final adjudication themselves, and thereby forwent the right of overt interference, but they also procured by it abolition of appeal to the Privy Council, which hitherto had been the ultimate guarantor of judicial independence. Isolation from external protection of the "bourgeois system" within the framework of a "socialist state" ought, after a few years, to render the bourgeois system amendable to subversion and, if desired, gradual assimilation to the "proletarian system"—outwardly by the free choice of its own practitioners. If that interpretation is accurate, Hu and the Chinese diplomats are justified in feeling that they have not been guilty of a strategic compromise in underwriting the common law in the Joint Declaration to the limited degree that they have.[32]

Notes

1. *Far Eastern Economic Review*, October 23, 1981.
2. The fact is well known among historians of China; one reference is by A. Feuerwerker in Fairbank and Liu 1980: 60.
3. Details are taken from a 1927 minute by Sir John Pratt in Foreign Office file 371/31659 (Confidential Print) at the Public Record Office, London.
4. Inferred from Atwell 1985: 54 and 107, although that author has not clarified the position explicitly.
5. Needless to say, this statement about Hong Kong land administration is incomplete. For fuller treatments of the law and policy, see past government annual reports.
6. *Far Eastern Economic Review*, March 13, 1981.
7. Ibid., June 11, June 18, and August 13, 1982.
8. Ibid., July 16, 1982.
9. *Keesing's Archives* 32623 (1984).
10. Hsiung 1972: 248.
11. Quoted by Friedmann, et al. 1969: 334. For Chinese Communist references to the doctrine as essentially Marxist-Leninist, see quotations in Chiu 1972: 258–259.
12. McNair 1961: 209.
13. Examples in Hsiung 1972: 252–253.
14. At first sight, Britain had breached its policy when surrendering the people of Eritrea to Ethiopia in 1952. But that instance was not a precedent for Hong Kong, because Eritrea was temporarily occupied, not a British colonial territory, and the handover was in obedience to a resolution of the UN General Assembly.

15. *Beijing Review* 27:11 (March 12, 1984).
16. *Times,* June 25 and June 26, 1984.
17. Ibid., June 21, June 30, and July 1, 1983.
18. *Beijing Review* 26:16 (April 19, 1983).
19. E.g., *Hsin Pao,* September 22, 1983; New China News Agency, October 4, 1983.
20. New China News Agency, December 4, 1982.
21. *Times,* September 21, September 29, and October 1, 1983.
22. *Jen-min jih-pao,* September 30, 1983.
23. *Draft Agreement* 1984: Introduction, 3.
24. *Times,* June 18, 1984.
25. *Keesing's Archives* 33093 (1984).
26. Hints to this effect that this was the official Peking view were denied by Prime Minister Chao Tzu-yang (*Times,* October 29 and December 17, 1982), perhaps in order to get the benefit of a leak without the blame.
27. Knight 1985: 31–38.
28. As reported by the Hong Kong monthly, *Cheng Ming* [The Contender, from Mao's phrase "let the Hundred Schools contend"] no. 58 (August 1982): 10.
29. *Collected Works,* vol. 31, p. 458.
30. Sect. 1 of Annex 1, *Draft Agreement* 1984: 14.
31. Cohen 1969: 981 ff.
32. It has to be taken for granted that key personalities like Teng and Hu understood what was involved in the common law from the translation, *p'u-t'ung fa.* It is possible they did not.

Bibliography

Atwell, Pamela. *British Mandarins and Chinese Reformers* (at Wei-hai-wei). London: Oxford University Press, 1985.

Chiu, Hungdah. "Comparison of the Nationalist and Communist Chinese Views of Unequal Treaties." In Jerome A. Cohen, ed., *China's Practice of International Law.* Cambridge, Mass.: Harvard University Press, 1972.

Cohen, Jerome A. "The Chinese Communist Party and 'Judicial Independence' 1949–1959." *Harvard Law Review* 82:5 (1969):967–1006.

A Draft Agreement Between the Government of the United Kingdom of Great Britain and Northern Ireland and the Government of the People's Republic of China on the Future of Hong Kong. Parliamentary White Paper Cmnd. 9543, June 1984, Treaty Series no. 26. London: Her Majesty's Stationery Office, 1984.

Evans, D. E. "Chinatown in Hong Kong: The Beginnings of Taiping-shan." *Journal of the Hong Kong Branch of the Royal Asiatic Society* 10 (1970):69–78.

Fairbank, J. K., and K.-C. Liu. *The Cambridge History of China.* Vol. 11, pt. 2. Cambridge: Cambridge University Press, 1980.

Friedmann, W., et al. *International Law.* Minneapolis, Minn.: University of Minnesota Press, 1969.

Hsiung, James Chieh. *Law and Policy in China's Foreign Relations.* New York: Columbia University Press, 1972.

Knight, Bill. *Hong Kong 1985.* Hong Kong: Government Printer, 1985.

McNair, Lord. *The Law of Treaties.* London: Oxford University Press, 1961.

3

The Hong Kong Talks and Hong Kong Politics

Ambrose Y.C. King

The negotiations between the government of the United Kingdom and the People's Republic of China (referred to hereafter as the PRC government) over the future of Hong Kong started in September 1982 in Peking. During the two years of prolonged and strenuous talks, they were not devoid of dark moments and despair for the people of Hong Kong, who were totally denied any role in the negotiations. It should be mentioned that before the talks started, the British did make a point that the people of Hong Kong should have their representatives in the talks. However, the PRC government sternly rejected this proposal, attacking it as a "three-legged-stools" concept, which was considered to infringe on the sacred right of the PRC government, which alone represents the whole Chinese people, including the people of Hong Kong. As a result, the Joint Declaration was exclusively the work of the British and PRC governments. At last, a spirit of so-called mutual understanding and mutual accommodation prevailed, and a Joint Declaration on the question of 1997 was signed between the two governments on September 26, 1984.[1] The main thrust of the Declaration is as follows: On the day of July 1, 1997, the sovereignty of Hong Kong will be restored to China. Hong Kong shall become a special administrative region (referred to hereafter as SAR) enjoying a high degree of autonomy. Hong Kong will continue to preserve its present form of capitalist system with executive, legislative, and independent judicial power, including that of final adjudication for fifty years from 1997 onward. In a nutshell, this is the widely publicized concept of "one country, two systems." The British and PRC governments jointly engineered a spectacular show, the ceremony for the initialing of the Declaration, which, of course, was intended to

This chapter is reprinted from *Issues and Studies*, Vol. 22, No. 6, June 1986, with permission from the Institute of International Relations, Taipei, Taiwan, Republic of China.

attract world attention. Undoubtedly, the initialing of the Joint Declaration signified that Hong Kong has entered a new historical stage.

Judging from the reactions, the Joint Declaration was indeed well received and even enthusiastically welcomed. The United States and Japan, the two major trading partners of Hong Kong, rendered their endorsement to the agreement immediately after the Declaration was announced. Supportive also were the European Economic Community (EEC) and other countries in Asia. The affirmative reaction of the international community to the Declaration created positive effects on confidence in the future of Hong Kong since it did give the Joint Declaration status like that of bilateral treaties. As for the 5 million people in Hong Kong, they had, in fact, only the Hobson's choice, that was no choice. Having been subjected to tremendous frustration and anxiety during the prolonged period of secretive negotiations, the people of Hong Kong showed a sign of relief when the content of Declaration was made known. True enough, as late as 1982, people in Hong Kong were still mesmerized in an optimistic mood thinking that the status quo under the British administration, or at least with some form of British responsibility, could be maintained after 1997.[2] However, on April 20, 1984, the optimists were totally shattered by the statements of Sir Geoffrey Howe, the foreign minister of the British government, that Britain had conceded sovereignty to China. Since then, Hong Kong people have become realistic and practical enough not to have illusions. By the time the agreement was released, the people of Hong Kong were presented with the fait accompli of either having an agreement as it is or having no agreement at all. Under the circumstances, they felt that having this agreement was better than having none. From what we can gauge from editorials, comments, and reports in the press, as well as survey findings of independent research institutes, the overwhelming majority of the population were in favor of the Declaration, though most of them were not without reservations of one kind or another.[3]

The Transitional Phase

From a political viewpoint, the future of Hong Kong has been settled. To be sure, what will actually happen after 1997 in Hong Kong is something which cannot be assuredly prescribed by the Declaration, simply there are too many uncertain factors involved. Nevertheless, one thing is now certain. The Joint Declaration made it crystal clear that from the day the Joint Declaration is ratified up until June 30, 1997, the government of the United Kingdom "will be responsible for the administration of Hong Kong with the object of maintaining and preserving its economic prosperity and social stability, and that the Government of the People's Republic of China will give its cooperation in this connection." This stipulation rules out the possibility that the British might withdraw from Hong Kong before 1997, thus creating inadvertently a political vacuum leading to political chaos. This indeed was perceived as highly probable when the negotiations were more than once turned into a war of words between the two governments. With the Declaration internationally proclaimed, it could therefore be expected with reasonable certainty that Hong Kong would have for another thirteen years a political environment the people of Hong Kong have been accustomed to for so long. The irony of the matter was that the Declaration had given the continuing administration of British rule of the colony a new legitimate basis.

Since the negotiations started in the fall of 1982, the British–Hong Kong government (referred to hereafter as the Hong Kong government) has been repeatedly under attack for its colonial nature and unrepresentativeness of Hong Kong people, directly or indirectly, by the PRC government and its agents in Hong Kong. Not only did it create a situation that embarrassing for the Hong Kong government, but also the very basis of government's legitimacy was unequivocably shaken. The "lame duck" image of the Hong Kong government inevitably emerged as a result. Thanks to the Declaration, which has met the maximum mutual interests of the two governments, a new basis of mutual cooperation between the two was thus provided. The aim the two governments could happily share is to see Hong Kong have a prosperous and stable transition. It is no exaggeration to say that China is even more eager than the Hong Kong government to assure a prosperous and stable transition for the colony. The reason is simple: China has more at stake. Without a successful transition, there will certainly not be another fifty years of capitalist Hong Kong, thus not only turning Hong Kong an asset into a liability to China but also making the "one country, two systems" concept totally an unrealizable dream. It will make China's unification idea a remoter proposition than ever. Therefore, it is quite true that the thirteen-year transition is the most crucial period for the long-run development of Hong Kong.[4]

It is no gainsaying that the people of Hong Kong would wish a prosperous and stable transition. Indeed, it was the common interest of the three parties, namely, China, Britain, and the people of Hong Kong, and their combined efforts which constituted the fundamental motivational forces behind the speedy recovery of the Hong Kong economy today. Understandably, the Republic of China (ROC) on Taiwan would not recognize the validity of the Declaration between Britain and the People's Republic of China. However, the ROC was also realistic and pragmatic enough to decide to have its representative agencies continue to remain in Hong Kong at least up to the date of June 30, 1997. Taiwan's realist stance serves its best possible interests under the given circumstances. It serves Hong Kong's interests too. Not surprisingly, mainland China also overtly welcomed Taiwan's continuing presence in the postagreement Hong Kong. The continuing presence of Taiwan's representative agencies can indeed be seen as an indicator that Hong Kong still remains as a politically free society, immune from the interference of Communist China.

Intensification of Politics

It has been a little more than a year since the ratification of the Declaration. The general social and economic situation in Hong Kong during the initial period of transition was more than good. Hong Kong's economic indicators in real growth rates, volume of trade, stocks and real property were all very encouraging. Despite the fact that the long-term prospect of Hong Kong remains uncertain, the will to emigrate by professionals shows no sign of lessening. However, short-term confidence is restored. Although Hong Kong people have not returned to their previous level of optimism, the once rampant pessimism and defeatist attitudes are now something from yesterday. Hong Kong seems steadily returning to the normality of the pre-1997 issue era. Though this could hardly be dismissed as the postsettlement euphoria, nevertheless, looking at the deeper level, Hong Kong has changed; it is no longer possible to return to its prenegotiation situation. Hong Kong has been already, willy-nilly, undergoing deep change. The change took place primarily in the realm of politics. It was brought about by the negotiations, the Joint Declaration and the transition.

The basic change taking place in the realm of politics in Hong Kong is the deepening and intensification of politics in society. For long Hong Kong had been a politically inactive and economically dynamic city which was ruled and administered by a vast and efficient Weberian type of bureaucracy. The colonial government has never taken initiative in instilling political consciousness into the citizens. The low and middle strata had been basically politically indifferent and apathetic, in spite of the fact that the political culture of these strata had undergone significant changes since the 1960s.[5] The Hong Kong government never seriously thought to transplant the British or other Western types of democracies into the colony. However, the Hong Kong government was never too insensitive and too arrogant to be concerned with the feeling and the mood of the public. For decades, the Hong Kong government had consciously and deliberately created hundreds of consultative committees at various levels of the bureaucracy, through which the views and feelings of the industrial-business elites, professionals, and even ordinary citizens were fed back into the administrative decision-making processes. The Legislative and Executive councils are the two organs which serve as important mechanisms to co-opt the socioeconomic elites into administration. Through the extensive institutionalized process of consultation and absorption, Hong Kong has developed a unique brand of political system which can be characterized as one variant of elitist politics. The essence of the political system is the bureaucratization of politics. It should be mentioned that the system's performance in efficiency and effectiveness is easily one of the very best in Asia, if not in the world. The continuing and timely absorption of potential political elites into the administration has made politics almost unnecessary outside of the government. To a significant extent, it has contributed to the political stability of the colony in the past decades. I have called this phenomenon "administrative absorption of politics" some years ago.[6] Naturally, the great absorber of politics was the Hong Kong government. However, the administrative absorption of politics, a kind of system of "elite integration," could only work well in a society where the level of politicization was relatively low. Hong Kong is such a case in point. When the political consciousness of the citizens is heightened and the level of politicization increased, the legitimacy of the government can no longer afford not to take the views and support of the masses into account. In other words, a system of "elite integration" has to be displaced by a system of "elite-mass integration."

It was a small wonder that in 1982 the Hong Kong government put forward an Administrative Development Plan which divided Hong Kong into two regions, and eighteen district boards as a response to a new political milieu. The composition of the district boards has members, apart from government-appointed ones, directly elected, through a broad franchise by the people in districts. The explicit purpose of the Administrative Development Plan was to bring a group of grassroots leaders into the government administration in order to bridge the gap between the government and the people. Though this plan was mainly aimed at increasing the political effectiveness of the administration, it did provide a vehicle to channel the rising demand for political participation into local, and hence, manageable areas.[7] Indeed, the district board election in 1982 which was unprecedented event in the colony's political history should be conceived as a step, though a small one, toward political democratization.

The Emergence of a Political Market

Since the 1997 issue was on the political agenda, the politicization at the societal level has begun to accelerate and intensify, especially at the middle stratum. Pressure groups and political activists emerged one after another. The conspicuous rise of politically oriented groups and individuals were mainly precipitated by three factors: Firstly, professionals, petty capitalists, and intellectuals found themselves suddenly facing a new political situation in which their fate was at stake. Secondly, the political participation at the local level was intentionally encouraged by the Hong Kong government since 1982, at the time the 1997 issue began to emerge. The high turnout rate of candidates for district board seats (404 candidates for 132 openings) was very much due to the effort of "candidate mobilization" by the government.[8] The "candidate mobilization" later become "elite participation" when the Legislative Council was partially opened for election. Thirdly, China's slogan of "Hong Kong people rule Hong Kong" was indeed most inviting to a no small number of people who were politically motivated. To be sure, very importantly, the new British decolonization policy has created a catalytic effect on elite political participation. The Hong Kong government, in fact, provided structural venues for political activities. The increasing interests shown by industrial-business elites and professionals in politics resulted from the "supply" side of political system just as much as from the system's "demand" side. For decades, Hong Kong could be characterized as an economic market in which the dynamism of economics was devoid of politics. But now a "political market" is opening up. This is, to a large extent, intentionally or unintentionally created by both the Hong Kong and PRC governments. Admittedly, the rules of game of the two markets are different; to be successful in one market is no guarantee to be so in another. However, the mutual interaction and mutual influence of these two markets are inevitable and the assets in the economic market can be, to a certain extent, transferred into the political market for political gains. The reverse process can also happen but not too much so at this stage simply because the Hong Kong political market is still in an incipient form.

Hong Kong has abundant big capitalists but no politicians of grand stature. What is interesting is that both the Hong Kong and PRC governments would like to see more capitalists and professionals play a guardian's role in the increasingly expanded political market. Both are of the belief that capitalists and professionals are the pillars of the economic market of Hong Kong and with their participation and involvement in the political market, the spirit and inner logic of capitalist economy can be guarded against the possible distortion by democratic sentiments and welfarist ideologies of the latter, thus assuring a prosperous and stable transition. It is indeed a great paradox that both governments have consciously and unconsciously opened up and expanded the political market for very different motives, yet they have both tried hard, for the same goal (prosperity and stability) to fight against the tendency of mass-oriented democratization which they believe will damage Hong Kong's economic market. In this respect, the Hong Kong government's attitude toward the political market is very different from its attitude toward the economic market which has been proudly coined by Haddon-Cave, the former financial secretary, as positive noninterventionism. In the political market, the Hong Kong government has from the very beginning played an active role in initiating and deciding the pace and form of political reform.

With the clear understanding that the sovereignty of Hong Kong is going to be restored to China, the British seem to have a sense of urgency in carrying out political reform. Within a limited space of thirteen years, Britain must implement decolonization policy and prepare an "exit-in-glory" for 1997. To the British, power needs to be delivered into the hands of the Hong Kong people through a process of political democratization. This is not only the logical and necessary way to legitimize and strengthen the British rule during the transition, it was also the traditional practice of British decolonizers elsewhere. Moreover, in the Joint Declaration, it is clearly spelled out that the government and legislature of the special administrative region will be composed of local inhabitants. The chief executive will be selected by election or through consultations held locally and be appointed by the Central People's government. The executive authorities will be required to act in accordance with the law and will be accountable to the legislature, and the legislature will be elected. Therefore, it is clear that the future legislature as the source of the highest authority in Hong Kong's Special Administrative Region government must be an elective organ. Thinking retrospectively, it was no coincidence that the Hong Kong government issued a Green Paper on *The Further Development of Representative Government in Hong Kong* on July 18, 1984, just about two months before the Joint Declaration was signed, and a White Paper on the same topic was finally published in November 1984, just about two months after the Joint Declaration.[9] It was an important political document for Hong Kong. For one thing, it expanded the local district boards by adding members through direct election; the elective members were increased from 132 in 1982 to 237 in 1985. This indicates that Hong Kong's local politics is heading toward a democratic mode of direct election. For another, more importantly, the White Paper gives a new structure to the Legislative Council at the central level by introducing an elected element. The composition of the Legislative Council in 1985 added two new categories of elected members. Apart from the existing categories, i.e., official members (high-ranking officials) and appointed members (appointed by the governor) which had ten and twenty-two seats, respectively, in addition, ten new seats were elected by the new category of functional constituencies which referred to finance, banking, industry, law associations, medical community, unions, and other professional organizations. This novel device enabled, with assurance, the industrial-business elites and professionals to have a disproportionate, weighted voice in the new Legislative Council. The other new category enabling the local political-administrative bodies including the Urban Council, the Regional Council, and district boards to send their representative to the Legislative Council was expected to be able to bridge the gap between the local people and the central level, though it is through a mode of indirect election. Another important change of the Legislative Council is that, apart from the organizational restructuring, the nature and function of the council shall be changed from the consultative or advisory to decision making. With regards to the election of the Legislative Council in 1985, the electoral turnout for the functional constituencies was 57.6 percent which could not be viewed as having too much political enthusiasm given the fact that the Hong Kong government had made great effort in selling the idea to the special stratum of the population who have rather high educational standards. The election of the electoral college constituencies was something of a different nature. These contests were quite fierce and marked by intense factional rivalries. Of these two kinds of elections, individual attributes of the candidates stood out as an outstanding factor in the vote-getting game.[10] The general impression was that the two new modes of elections of the Legislative Council, particularly the electoral college, did not really add too much democratic respectability to the Legislative Council. Nevertheless, the Legislative Council has had a new face and its modus operandi cannot remain to be the same.

The political structural reform conceived in the White Paper is, rightly or wrongly, perceived by the pro-China groups as a British model of "Hong Kong people rule Hong Kong." One thing is clear, the Hong Kong government has obviously turned away from the practice of what I call "administrative absorption of politics." It has consciously stepped down as an absorber of politics; it has realized that politics can no longer be circumvented in Hong Kong as in the past. It has now pushed for a more representative form of government. However, the new model of representative system gives disproportionate weight to the interests of the established elites of the capitalist system, and the indirect election of the electoral colleges provides no room for a role by ordinary citizens. Not surprisingly, it has met strong criticism from democratic activists.

On the issue of political democratization, the Hong Kong government was in an awkward predicament. As mentioned above, on the one hand, it wanted to create an open political market paving the way for the development of local political leadership for the post-1997 Hong Kong. On the other hand, it has to shape and manipulate the newly created political market so as to prevent the operation of the economic market from being distorted and jeopardized. The dilemma facing the Hong Kong government is gigantic: After 1997, it has to deliver the power to the people of Hong Kong in order to have a genuine form of "Hong Kong people rule Hong Kong" in 1997; yet it can ill-afford to see Hong Kong turn into an independent political entity as a result of democratization, because this is simply intolerable to the PRC government. The Hong Kong government has been reminded again and again that decolonization of Hong Kong could in no way be allowed to restore the sovereignty to the people of Hong Kong. Thus, as argued by two social scientists, "The goal of decolonization without independence necessarily holds the tasks of democratization in play."[11] Indeed, this is a kind of decolonization the British have never experienced before. By the time the British depart, the best possible situation to be hoped for is that Hong Kong has had a stable political system enjoying a high degree of autonomy as an SAR, acceptable to China, yet independent enough to make the undue interference on Hong Kong affairs from the north difficult, if not impossible. Surely, this would need a kind of political engineering of the first order. Can this be accomplished within a short span of time?

The Challenge of Political Restructuring

Although clearly stated in the Declaration, the Hong Kong SAR shall enjoy a high degree of autonomy, the nagging question remains, What is a high degree of autonomy? And, the real important question is rather under what kind of political structure can Hong Kong be assured to have a high degree of autonomy? Most students of Hong Kong politics of different political stances and ideological affiliations would probably agree on principle that it needs some sort of representative or democratic government. However, as to the questions on the form of democracy and how fast it should be established, then views diverge. The Hong Kong government seems to be inclined to adopt a gradual process and has made it known that Hong Kong will not follow the Western type of adversary politics or mass democracy. Generally speaking, this stance is basically in line with most of the newly emerging political groups which, with few exceptions, do not favor blindly copying the Western models of democracy.

Today, Hong Kong is very much preoccupied with the issue of democratization. Of the local elites or semi-elites, established or newly emerging, they feel that in order to have a legitimate base of governing, they must go directly to the people. And there are a few persons who began both in words and action to form political parties, or quasi parties in substance if not in name.[12] It is no secret that there is a strong feeling among a number of people that a form of democratic government should be established before 1997 in order to make it possible for the post-1997 Hong Kong SAR government to resist the interference from China after 1997.[13]

Judging from the direction the political reform has moved in recent years, it is reasonable to assume that the Hong Kong government has been seriously restructuring the colonial system into a more democratic form of government. Furthermore, given the increasing pressure and mounting demands coming from local activists for further democratization, and in light of the fact that several local elections held in the last two or three years have proved to be smooth and "successful," there has developed some expectations that a limited direct election method would be adopted as a mechanism of political recruitment for the future Legislative Council. The Hong Kong government has repeatedly pledged to review and assess the political reform in 1987. Indeed, the politically minded people in Hong Kong have shown a great concern in government's review exercise one year from now. Naturally, the PRC government is no exception.

At this juncture, it should be emphatically pointed out that though the political democratization now in force is a deep concern to the PRC government, it has kept silence on the whole development only until very recently. For a fairly long time, the PRC government has publicly adopted a rather indifferent, or a noncommittal attitude toward Hong Kong's political reform. The PRC government, however, did make its position known that "this [political reform] is solely the British–Hong Kong governments' doing," making it unequivocally clear that it has absolutely nothing to do with it. True, since mid-1984, there were signs that the PRC government was extremely uneasy and suspicious about the motive behind the White Paper. In fact, warnings, subtle or otherwise, were conveyed to the Hong Kong government as early as July 1984. Chi P'eng-fei, director of China's Hong Kong and Macao Affairs Office, expressed that the PRC government was in favor of "stability and prosperity," not "prosperity plus reform."[14] In August 1985, Hsü Chia-t'un, director of the Hong Kong New China News Agency (NCNA), publicly warned against any hasty change in the Hong Kong government structure before 1997.[15] On October 19, Chi P'eng-fei told Mr. P. H. Liao, secretary for district administration, that Hong Kong's political reform must consider its linkage problems with the Basic Law, and he commented in no ambiguous terms that Hong Kong's future political system could only be stipulated by the Basic Law.[16] Notwithstanding, the Hong Kong government's determination for further development of representative government seemed undisturbed, believing that it had and has the sole responsibility and right for Hong Kong affairs, including political reform, up until 1997. High-ranking officials of the Hong Kong government no other than Peter William, secretary for general duties, and Michael Thomas, attorney general, have made their views known that the Hong Kong government has no need to consult the PRC government on the issue of political reform and that the purpose of the political restructuring is to develop a system with its power rooted in the people of Hong Kong.[17]

At this point, it is not too difficult to detect that there was a lack of consensus between the two parties, namely, China and Britain, with regard to the issue of political reform during the transitional phase. Then on November 21, 1985, Hsü Chia-t'un dumbfounded the people in Hong Kong by charging that "some people are not observing the Joint Declaration."[18] This strong statement reflected no small degree of seriousness of lack of consensus between the two governments. The next day the Hang Seng index of stock prices dropped nearly fifty points, reflecting as much the nervousness of Hong Kong's economic market as that of its political market. This is the first sign of a Sino-British rift since the agreement. The rift is clearly caused by their different perceptions and attitude toward political reform introduced by the Hong Kong government. It should be pointed out that the PRC government had indeed exercised considerable self-restraint in refraining from publicly commenting on Hong Kong's development of a representative system, fearing that doing so would be interpreted as an act of interference on Hong Kong's administration. However, rightly or wrongly, the PRC government was more and more convinced that the Hong Kong government and its alleged "Chinese agents" have engaged in a conspiracy by developing Hong Kong into a British model of "Hong Kong people rule Hong Kong" as a fait accompli, before 1997, leaving China no choice. According to the sources close to China, the PRC government was indeed of the belief that the development of representative government was a conspiracy of *min-chu k'ang-kung* ("using democracy to resist communism"); it was not intended to preserve the characteristics of capitalism, instead, it was to transform Hong Kong into a "separate political entity," a city-state of its own, subject to no constraints from the Central People's government.[19] Thus perceived, Hsü Chia-t'un's bombshell in August is not beyond comprehension. Chi P'eng-fei is quoted as saying that "during the transition the British will be responsible for Hong Kong's administration, but things involving the transfer of Hong Kong's sovereignty, the Chinese Government shall be consulted."[20] Understandably, the British can ill-afford to see the Sino-British rift unhealed. In fact, before Chi P'eng-fei's goodwill visit to Hong Kong in December 1985, it was believed that Britain had yielded to Chinese pressure, agreeing to discuss Hong Kong's political reforms and its linkage problem with the Basic Law at the forthcoming meeting in March

1986 by the Joint Liaison Group, which was established under the terms of the agreement. And moreover, Sir David Akers-Jones, chief secretary, who had before his assumption of duty spoken of the need of compatibility between the Chinese political system and the evolving one of Hong Kong, had expressed that in the 1987 review exercise on the representative system, the PRC government will be consulted before the publication of the Green Paper.[21] Obviously, the British–Hong Kong government and the PRC government have now reached an understanding that they will jointly search for a consensus for the synchronization of ongoing political reforms and the forthcoming drafting of the Basic Law.

Penetrated Political System and Dual Authority

The authority structure of Hong Kong has undergone fundamental change since it entered the phase of transition. The most conspicuous phenomenon is that Chinese influence has deeply permeated into the body politic of Hong Kong. More and more, a new authority structure is emerging from the political scene, paralleling that of the Hong Kong government. Admittedly, according to the agreement the Hong Kong government has the sole authority for administration before 1997, and the representative agencies of the PRC government in Hong Kong have consciously adopted a policy of what may be characterized, to borrow Haddon-Cave's terminology, "positive nonin-terventionism," toward Hong Kong politics. Nevertheless, it is a common perception that China's representative agencies, together with the Hong Kong government, have formed a dual authority structure in Hong Kong.[22] To begin with, a Joint Liaison Office is being established under the terms of the agreement. The Joint Liaison Office is specifically meant not to be a power organ—it will neither participate in Hong Kong's administration nor will it exercise supervisory function—but it does have the right to discuss with the British government "matters relating to the smooth transfer of government in 1997." Therefore, it is not illegitimate to say that China has an important say on Hong Kong affairs during the transition phase. And in Hong Kong, China's authority is embodied in the New China News Agency (NCNA). NCNA is not just a news organization, it is China's de facto diplomatic mission in Hong Kong and has a large organizational structure, with a strength of hundreds. The NCNA has existed in Hong Kong for a long time, but its presence has always been low-postured, nonconspicuous, and amorphous. Then, in 1983 it underwent a dramatic transformation. It quickly emerged as the authoritative voice of China in Hong Kong. The appointment of the new director of NCNA, Hsü Chia-t'un, who is an important political figure in the Communist party, enjoying a ministerial status, was unmistakenly a sign that NCNA had been substantially upgraded. During the Sino-British talks, NCNA acted unabashedly as the Chinese authority in the colony, tolerated, if not recognized by the Hong Kong government. There was no shortage of tensions between the NCNA and the Hong Kong government through the whole period of Sino-British talks. The relationship between the two, however, has become much more cooperative, cordial, and friendly, at least at the level of public relations in the aftermath of the agreement. The NCNA's representing of the Chinese authority is now duly recognized by the Hong Kong government. The governor, Sir Edward Youde, has found no uneasiness in appearing together with Mr. Hsü, the director of NCNA, in public. Through his personal charm and flexible attitude on ideological issues, Mr. Hsü has made himself the most sought-after politician by the Hong Kong media. It cannot be overexaggerated to say that de facto, if not de jure, the NCNA and the Hong Kong government are the two authority systems in Hong Kong. Hong Kong is now governed by a peculiar form of condominium "synarchy," or co-ruling. Theoretically speaking, the NCNA can be conceptualized as a "penetrated political system."[23]

The NCNA as a penetrated political system derived its authority from the fact that it is the official representative of China, and naturally, its continuing ascendency and growing influence have everything to do with the approaching date of 1997. Without doubt the penetrated political system is bound to divide and penetrate the existing authority, namely, the Hong Kong government. However, during the transition period the weakening authority of the Hong Kong government is paradoxically strengthened and reinforced by the Chinese penetrated political system. Because of the common aim of maintaining stability and prosperity, the PRC government has a built-in interest in rendering support to the Hong Kong government, since any decisive sign of weakening of the latter will scare away the capital and the professionals. The coexistence of two authority systems is indeed a very intricate phenomenon. A precarious balance has somehow been maintained through a delicate modus operandi of the two authorities. It is a commonplace knowledge that when the two cooperate, both benefit; when in conflict, no one can be the winner. This symbiotic relationship has made each party extremely cautious toward the power situation in Hong Kong. The NCNA is certainly reluctant to publicly interfere in the administration of the Hong Kong government, and the latter has also good reason not to push for something at the risk of offending the NCNA. As a matter of fact, both authorities have indirectly and implicitly joined hand in hand to salvage Hong Kong's confidence crisis.

Looking from a developmental perspective, the authority of the Hong Kong government is bound to become increasingly weakened and eventually disappear by June 1997. On the other hand, the authority of the penetrated political system of the PRC government will grow and continue to grow until it totally replaces the authority of the Hong Kong government. Nevertheless, authority cannot be devoid of responsibility. The role of the NCNA, in fact, has been transformed from a "critic" of the system as an "outsider" to a "protector" of the system as an "insider" after the agreement. Although NCNA is not legally responsible for the "smooth transition," it is politically obliged in the eyes of the people to ensure the prosperity and stability of Hong Kong before and after 1997. The NCNA is having more and more problems as its authority increasingly expands and inflates. At present, NCNA is facing a severe test of a challenging nature: how to help draft a Basic Law which will be the constitution of the Hong Kong SAR government acceptable to the people of Hong Kong.

The Political Absorption of Economics

The Joint Declaration states that the Basic Law will stipulate that the socialist system and socialist policies practiced in the People's Republic of China will not be extended to the Hong Kong SAR and the Hong Kong's capitalist system and life-style will remain unchanged for fifty years after the establishment of the SAR. It is indeed quite striking that socialist China would agree to let the Hong Kong SAR continue to have its capitalist system after 1997 for another fifty years. This is of course embodied in what is called the "one country, two systems" concept. However, the Joint Declaration is a political document. The spirit of it has to be translated into a legal code, the Basic Law, under which the future Hong Kong SAR government will be governed. Therefore, the drafting of the Basic Law becomes the most important thing, next probably only to the Declaration with respect to the fate of the people of Hong Kong.

As was mentioned above, Hong Kong people were denied by the PRC government to have any formal role in the Sino-British talks. The PRC government was of the view that the talks were the business of two sovereign states. It is an external matter, therefore, there is no room for the Hong Kong people who are but a part of the Chinese population. However, the drafting of the Basic Law is something of a different nature. It is purely an internal matter, and this is no business of the British government. But then the question is, Will the people of Hong Kong have a say in drafting the Basic Law? The people of Hong Kong are fully aware that to take a part in the process of drafting the Basic Law is the only and last chance to protect their own future. And they did show no reluctance in expressing fiercely their demand for participation, thanks to the freedom of the press which is well established in Hong Kong. The Chinese leaders in Peking were cognizant of the fact that Hong Kong people's confidence is essential to the success of Hong Kong as a special administrative region as well as the "one country, two systems" strategy. Therefore, it is understandable that the PRC government made enormous efforts in staging a grand political show to demonstrate its willingness and eagerness to have the people of Hong Kong participating in the holy mission of drafting the Basic Law.

In July 1985 China announced the establishment of a Basic Law Drafting Committee under the auspices of the National People's Congress. The composition of the committee was quite impressive. Of the fifty-nine members, thirty-six were appointed from the mainland and twenty-three from Hong Kong. Of the twenty-three appointees from Hong Kong, with only a few exceptions, they are prominent figures belonging to the high and high-middle strata. Economic elites constitute the core: Not a few of them are either the leaders of the economic market or the reputable personalities of various professions. This carefully-thought-out membership list by the PRC government was clearly intended to please the strategic elites of the Hong Kong economy, and it is indeed with a purpose to augment the capitalist system in Hong Kong. What is more significant about the membership is that two appointees are the serving members of the Legislative Council of the Hong Kong government. This unusual arrangement can only be interpreted as China's intention to connect directly the authority system of the "penetrated political system" to the authority system of the Hong Kong government. Naturally, these two appointments (the two legislative councillors) would have the blessing of the Hong Kong government. With the overlapping memberships of the two authority systems, not only at a technical level, the communication between the two authority systems can be more easily facilitated, though it is not totally inconceivable that a situation of "role conflict" might occur to those who work for two systems. At the symbolical level, it creates an image for the "penetrated political system" as one which is not incompatible with the Hong Kong government. From the arrangement engineered by the NCNA, we can tell that China is interested in maintaining the status quo; it shows no sign of discontinuing the elitist politics which has been the dominant mode of politics in the colony for years. The model used by the Hong Kong government in the past, as was argued above, was the "administrative absorption of politics," what China seemed to adopt is a model which could be called the "political absorption of economics." From the time when the 1997 issue became crystallized, the Hong Kong government has step by step abdicated its role as an "absorber," while the NCNA as a "penetrated political system" consciously and unconsciously took up the role of "absorber" in no time.

Following the establishment of the Basic Law Drafting Committee, the NCNA took a great deal of effort in setting up the Basic Law Consultative Committee which has a membership of 180. The Basic Law Consultative Committee (referred to hereafter as BLCC) was supposed to be a Hong Kong–wide civic, nonofficial organization which will have full representation of the Hong Kong people from all walks of life. The basic functions of the BLCC are twofold: firstly, to serve as the bridge between the Hong Kong people and the Basic Law Drafting Committee; secondly, to serve as a channel to reflect the views of Hong Kong people on the Basic Law and to make recommendations thereupon.[24] The establishment of the BLCC was no easy task, and the process of formulation of the membership of the committee was not without frictions and unhappy moments. Although the establishment of the BLCC was a job for the members of the Basic Law Drafting Committee who reside in Hong Kong, yet it was public knowledge that the BLCC was engineered by the NCNA.[25]

The composition of the BLCC is comprised of representatives from the following eight constituencies: namely, industrial and business, financial and real property, legal, professional, media and press, civic, religion and non-Chinese. By a rough estimate, of the 180 members, 60–70 percent represent the established interests (industrial-business elites and professionals), 30–40 percent the nonestablishment and grassroots. It is no denying the fact that among the members there are individuals who either have political integrity or have critical attitudes toward Communist ideology and the status quo of Hong Kong. Nevertheless, the great majority of them are pragmatic realists who found no difficulty in sharing the basic outlook for the future of Hong Kong of the NCNA. To an important extent, the NCNA has absorbed, through the BLCC, a significant number of respectable citizens, who enjoy various degrees of representatives of their respective constituencies into the "penetrated political system." It can be well expected that the BLCC will share, if not monopoly, the voice and influence in the political market in the days to come, with those representatives, particularly the elected members of the Legislative Council, of Hong Kong's authority system.

The Future of Political Democratization

China's overwhelming concern with the political stability and economic prosperity of Hong Kong is fully understandable. Questions still remain as to how to achieve prosperity and stability after 1997. Can it be achieved without change or reform in the existing political system of Hong Kong? Furthermore, what form should the future SAR government take? Regarding these questions, views and stances are diverse not only between the PRC government and the Hong Kong government but also among elites and political groups. Broadly speaking, there are two camps of views and convictions, each trying to captivate Hong Kong's political market.

One camp is charge-oriented, of the view that reform of Hong Kong's present system is necessary and the only logical way is to develop Hong Kong into a representative form of government, with its legitimacy and power rooted in Hong Kong. This is basically the Hong Kong government's position, and most of the politically motivated pressure groups and democratic activists are in general support of this line of thinking. However, they are by no means in consensus concerning the pace and form of democratic change; not a small number of them are advocates of more radical change, arguing for society-wide direct elections for the Legislative Council and party politics along the line of Western democracies. In this connection, the Hong Kong government can only be seen on the conservative end of the spectrum of the camp, judging from the pace and scope of the political reform initiated to date.

The other camp of which the PRC government seems to be the leading force is status quo–oriented. (Chi P'eng-fei's explicit rejection of the "prosperity plus reform" concept illustrates this orientation well.) Most of the capitalists and economic elites are the staunch exponents and supporters of this general view. China's preference for the status quo is not difficult to understand. The present system is perceived to be a time-honored system responsible for social stability and economic prosperity, and the current governmental structure is not unattractive to China, as Lau and Kuan pointed out:

Like every other colonial constitution, the political system in Hong Kong is dependent on an external force for its legitimacy, relatively immune from political pressures originated from the society, executive-centered rather than legislative-dominant, and operative in a top-down policy-making mode. Isn't it convenient for China to remain in ultimate control of Hong Kong if these essential features are preserved while those "colonial" components such as appointment of the governor by the Queen are removed? In essence, it involves nothing more than the replacement of the master.[26]

Furthermore, this camp does see the value of the current political system which in fact is positively identified by the great majority of the Hong Kong people.[27] It fears that political reform toward a democratic system will inadvertently result in group activism, mass behavior, and ideological conflict, thus jeopardizing stability and prosperity. And, moreover, as was mentioned above, the PRC government is even worrying that democratic reform will lead the Hong Kong SAR to become a politically independent entity. It felt that Hong Kong's political democratization has already gone too fast and too far.

Against this background, it is not surprising that the PRC government called a halt in no subtle terms to the development of political reform to the Hong Kong government in late 1985. On December 22, 1985, it was reported that during his visit in Peking, Mr. Timothy Renton threw a strong hint that Hong Kong's further development of democratic reform is being put on hold. He stated that the British government agreed with the view (of China) that there was a need for building a linkage between the ongoing political reform in Hong Kong and the forthcoming Basic Law.

In search of a political system for the future Hong Kong SAR government, the Hong Kong government knows well enough that it is a thankless, if not totally futile, job without having consensus with the PRC government. In the 1987 review exercise on the representative system, it can be expected that the Hong Kong government will try hard to avoid a collision, instead, to seek a point of convergence, with the PRC government, even at the expense of alienating political groups and individuals who aspire to a highly democratic SAR government in 1997.

Despite the fact that the PRC government has grave reservations about political democratization, the Hong Kong government is prepared to search, together with the PRC government, for a converging point between the ongoing political reform and the forthcoming Basic Law. However, this does not mean the issue of political reform can have an easy solution. Ever since 1982, when the future of Hong Kong became an issue, the structure of political consciousness of Hong Kong people has changed. The political market has grown and is expanding. Indeed, the demand for political democratization is no longer confined to a small group of democratic activists. It should not be forgotten that it is the very Sino-British agreement which made it so clear that Hong Kong will be ruled by the Hong Kong people after 1997. Then, the question is how this could be realized under what kind of political structure. It is a commonplace conception that change or reform is inevitable. What should be studied is how much change or reform is needed. And furthermore, it is also widely perceived that democratization of the existing government structure is necessary. Again, what should be studied is what form of democracy should be adopted. It is no secret that what worries Hong Kong people most is that the future Hong Kong SAR government will turn out to be "Peking people rule Hong Kong," instead of "Hong Kong people rule Hong Kong."

At this juncture, it is worth mentioning that a recent survey's findings showed that the Hong Kong people have a very low degree of trust with regard to the PRC government. When asked whether they believed that China would let Hong Kong people rule Hong Kong after 1997, 66.3 percent (N=337) of those who gave answers (N=508) responded in the negative.[28] Given the distrust the Hong Kong people have toward China's pledge for "Hong Kong people rule Hong Kong," the future Hong Kong SAR government, if not augmented with some degree of democratic respectability, will have tremendous difficulty in commanding the confidence of the Hong Kong population. Therefore, the ongoing development of the representative system engineered by the Hong Kong government can ill afford to be treated with contempt, let alone hostility.

Unquestionably the political structure of Hong Kong will be changed and is being changed. But what next? The next step of the political reform will be, to a large extent, shaped and determined by two events, namely, the Hong Kong government's review of the representative system in 1987 and the drafting of the Basic Law around 1990. The latter one is definitely more crucial and decisive insofar as the future of democratization is concerned. However, there is no indication what form of government the future Hong Kong SAR will eventually take. There is no shortage of speculation, of course. Indeed, there is again a wait-and-see attitude prevalent among the anxiety-stricken population of Hong Kong. What we can say is that the political system of Hong Kong, during the transition period, is still in the formulation process, subject to internal and external forces. The future of Hong Kong in general and the fate of political democratization in particular are full of challenges, ambiguities, and uncertainties.

Notes

1. Text in *A Draft Agreement Between the Government of the United Kingdom of Great Britain and Northern Ireland and the Government of the People's Republic of China on the Future of Hong Kong* (Hong Kong: Government Printer, September 26, 1984).

2. Joseph Y.S. Cheng, ed., *Hong Kong in Search of a Future* (Hong Kong: Oxford University Press, 1984), p. 79.

3. A fair description of the reaction to the agreement by the Hong Kong people can be found in the extract from "Report of the Assessment Office on Arrangements for Testing the Acceptability of the Draft Agreement on the Future of the Territory," in *Hong Kong 1985* (Hong Kong: Government Publication, 1985), pp. 31–39.

4. Ambrose Y.C. King, "Without Thirteen Years, There Will Be No Fifty Years," (in Chinese) *Ming-pao yueh-k'an* [Ming Pao monthly], no. 222 (June 1984): 3–5.

5. Regarding the political culture of Hong Kong of the sixties and early seventies, see Stephen Hoadley, "Hong Kong Is the Lifeboat: Notes on Political Culture and Socialization," *Journal of Oriental Studies* 8 (January 1970): 206–218; and Ambrose Y.C. King, "The Political Culture of Kwun Tong: A Chinese Community in Hong Kong," in Ambrose Y.C. King and Rance P.L. Lee, eds., *Social Life and Development in Hong Kong* (Hong Kong: Chinese University Press, 1981), pp. 147–168. The change of political culture of Hong Kong since the sixties is discussed in Lau Siu-Kai and Kuan Hsin-Chi, "The Changing Political Culture of the Hong Kong Chinese," Occasional paper, Centre for Hong Kong Studies, The Chinese University of Hong Kong, November 1985. Lau and Kuan write, "The overall direction is clearly the institutionalization of a set of participatory norms. Actual participative behavior, nevertheless, lags behind normative orientation." Their study shows that the Hong Kong Chinese today exhibit "an early-modern, and hence unmature, form of participatory political culture."

6. Ambrose Y.C. King, "Administrative Absorption of Politics in Hong Kong: Emphasis on the Grass Roots Level," *Asian Survey* 15:5 (May 1975): 422–439.

7. Lau Siu-Kai and Kuan Hsin-Chi, "District Board Elections in Hong Kong," *Journal of Commonwealth and Comparative Politics* 22:3 (November 1984): 303–317.

8. Ibid.

9. White Paper, *The Further Development of Representative Government in Hong Kong* (Hong Kong: Government Printer, November 1984).

10. See note 7 above.

11. Lau Siu-Kai and Kuan Hsin-Chi, "Hong Kong After the Sino-British Agreement: Limits to Institutional Change in a Dependent Polity," Occasional paper no. 9, Centre for Hong Kong Studies, The Chinese University of Hong Kong (1985), p. 9.

12. See Fong Shu, "First Steps in the Political Transformation: Elections of the Legislative Council," *Chiu-shih nien-tai* [The Nineties], no. 188 (September 1985): 22–24.

13. Martin C.M. Lee, a newly elected member of the Legislative Council, explicitly argued for this position in a meeting of the Legislative Council in November 1985.

14. See *Ming Pao* [Daily], July 25, 1984.

15. Ibid., August 6, 1985.

16. See Ku Hsing-hui, "Signs of Hope for the Political Reform Controversy," *Ching-pao* [The Mirror], no. 103 (February 1986): 6–10.

17. See Ho Li, "Political Reform Controversy Swept Hong Kong," *Chiu-shih nien-tai*, no. 190 (November 1985): 14–18. It should be pointed out that Michael Thomas's view is not different from what was said in the White Paper of 1984, which stated, "The main aim of the proposals are a. to develop progressively a system of government that authority for which is firmly rooted in Hong Kong, which is able to represent, authoritatively, the views of the people of Hong Kong, and which is more directly accountable to the people of Hong Kong."

18. "Xu's [Hsü's] Speech Jolts Hong Kong Optimism," *Asian Wall Street Journal*, November 25, 1985.

19. Ku Hsing-hui, "What Are the Main Issues in the Political Reform Controversy?" *Ching-pao*, no. 102 (January 1986): 6–11.

20. Ho Li, "Entering the Year of Showdown," *Chiu-shih nien-tai*, no. 192 (January 1986): 42–45.

21. Ho Li, "East Wind Prevailed over the West Wind," ibid., no. 193 (February 1986): 35–38.

22. Ambrose Y.C. King, "The Political Change During Hong Kong's Transition," *Chung-kuo shih-pao* [The China times], October 17–18, 1985.

23. The concept of penetrated political system is borrowed from James N. Rosenau, see J. N. Rosenau, "Pre-theories and Theories of Foreign Policy," in R. B. Farrell, ed., *Approaches to Comparative and International Politics* (Evanston: Northwestern University Press, 1966), pp. 27–92.

24. Yu Chi-wen, "Basic Law Consultative Committee: Created for the Manipulation of Public Opinion?" *Chiu-shih nien-tai*, no. 192 (January 1986): 46–49.

25. Ibid.

26. Kuan Hsin-Chi and Lau Siu-Kai, "Hong Kong in Search of a Consensus," Occasional paper, Centre for Hong Kong Studies, The Chinese University of Hong Kong (November 1985), p. 23.

27. In a survey conducted in the summer of 1985 when people in Hong Kong were asked whether the current system albeit imperfect was still was best under the existing circumstances, 74 percent of the total sample (767) agreed (ibid., p. 28).

28. Ibid., p. 7.

4

Hong Kong: The Economics of Political Dictates

Henry N. Geraedts

Miracles are propitious accidents, the natural causes of which are too complicated to be readily understood.

George Santayana, 1863–1952

Many people in the international media, in government at various levels, and in the business community appear to be decidedly more bullish with regard to the prospects for economic growth and a stable sociopolitical environment in both Hong Kong and the People's Republic of China than a careful examination of the facts perhaps warrants. In my view, a healthy degree of skepticism is called for. Our understanding of the linkages between the central elements of the Hong Kong equation, on the one hand, and the dominant mechanisms of PRC domestic politics and policy formulation, on the other, is best served by a collected and cautious review of the facts and not by indulgence in the pleasures of wishful thinking. Also, any reflection on the available facts about the Hong Kong issue that takes into account our knowledge of the central elements of PRC politics leaves little place for optimism. Finally, skepticism is also called for where the merits of what is best viewed as "prescriptive writing" are concerned. As much as this style appears to be in favor, no useful purpose, other than the gratification of the author, is served by such an approach.

The September 1984 Draft Agreement

People familiar with Hong Kong know of the remarkable ability of this city/territory to adapt to change and overcome adversity; together with the industriousness of its people and the promise of future opportunities to be successfully exploited, this characteristic is the essence of what makes Hong Kong "tick." Although the changes the colony has experienced since the end of World War II have been many and at times dramatic, it is more than probable that the run-up to 1997 holds the seeds of even more profound changes; including in particular, considerable alterations in the territory's economic and political modus operandi.

On September 26, 1984, the United Kingdom and the People's Republic of China (PRC) initialed a joint agreement regarding the future of Hong Kong.[1] In a number of ways, the document represented an out-of-the-ordinary achievement; in particular, it proved to be far more detailed than was thought possible at the outset of the negotiations. Central among the issues addressed was the expiration of the ninety-nine-year lease on the New Territories in 1997, when all of Hong Kong is to revert from British rule to that of the PRC. As of that date, Hong Kong is to become a special administrative region (SAR) under the direct authority of the central government in Peking. One of the document's stated roles is to serve as a framework for the transition from British colonial rule to administration as a special economic region. With that objective in mind, the document contains provisions for policies for the new entity covering constitutional arrangements and government structure, legal and judicial systems, public service, financial and economic systems, external economic relations, monetary system, shipping, civil aviation, culture and education, external noneconomic relations, defense, security and public order, rights and freedoms, rights of abode, travel documents, and immigration.

The joint agreement specifies that the SAR's government and legislature are to be composed locally, with its chief executive appointed by Peking in conjunction with some form of—as yet unspecified—local elections. The legislature is to be vested with legislative powers and constituted by elections. The present judicial system is to be maintained, with the final court of appeal in the SAR. Judges and lawyers may be recruited from other common-law jurisdictions. Both Chinese (not specified whether this is to be Mandarin or Cantonese) and the English language will be acceptable in court.[2]

It is intended that the Hong Kong SAR will handle its finance, budget, and revenue exclusively; it is also the intention that current systems of taxation, accountability, and public expenditure will be maintained. Likewise, it is the intention that the PRC central government will not levy taxes on the special administrative region but will receive reports "for the record." The SAR is to have the latitude to decide its own economic and trade policies and to participate in relevant international organizations and trade agreements such as the General Agreement on Tariffs and Trade (GATT).[3] Representatives of the Hong Kong SAR may participate as members of the PRC delegation on negotiations affecting the SAR. To maintain Hong Kong's position as an international financial center, there will be no exchange controls, and the Hong Kong dollar will continue to circulate and remain freely convertible. In addition, the special administrative region will be authorized to issue local currency.

Under the agreement, land leases are to be protected during the pre-1997 period. However, more stringent measures governing new land policies may take effect after the official transfer of power. Land leases extending beyond 1997 and all rights in relation to such leases will also be recognized and protected. All leases without a right of renewal that expire before June 30, 1997, may be extended for fifty years without payment of an additional premium. New land leases, on the other hand, may be granted for a fifty-year term at a premium and a nominal rent until 1997.[4]

Although the United Kingdom will retain the right to establish a consulate-general in the SAR without special approval, other foreign consular and semiofficial missions will need such approval from the PRC government. Finally, military forces sent by the Peking central government for the purposes of defense are not to ("shall not") interfere in the internal affairs of the Hong Kong SAR. In the same vein, the internal policing of Hong Kong is to remain the exclusive purview of the SAR.

With the stated intent of providing a forum for discussion and coordination between the United Kingdom and the PRC, a Joint Liaison Group was set up in conjunction with the joint agreement. It is presently active in Peking and London and will be permanently based in Hong Kong between 1988 and 1997.

On the whole, the joint agreement to a certain extent reflects the effort made to address a number of issues in some detail.[5] Available information with respect to the negotiations suggests that this degree of specificity was not the wish of the PRC negotiators but the result of persistent pressure on the part of the British. The final document, however, is flawed by a number of crucial omissions. These omissions are due (1) to the manner in which the negotiations were initiated and subsequently conducted and (2) to the PRC's stated views with respect to sovereignty. Quite simply, a number of important points were never specified. For instance, the document remains vague as to the process by which the local legislature is to be elected or the mechanism by which the top executive is to be appointed after 1997. Of equal importance, although the agreement states that a Basic Law will be enacted for the Hong Kong SAR, it does not specify the provisions for future amendments to this law. Also in the legal domain, the agreement stipulates that any existing local law found to be in conflict with the Basic Law will be considered invalid, omitting, however, to indicate who is to determine this. Clearly the most important omission, however, is the absence of a reliable mechanism for verifying the actual implementation of the provisions of the joint agreement after 1997.

Peking's stance in this regard has been explicit: It argues that since Hong Kong will be under its jurisdiction after 1997, the matter is of concern to no other party.

The Economy, 1983–1985

Prior to the 1984 agreement, four factors, in particular, had affected the Hong Kong economy: the generally depressed world economy since 1981–1982, the severe domestic crisis of confidence during the autumn of 1982, the substantial devaluation (US$1/HK$9.5) of the Hong Kong dollar as a result of a second crisis of confidence in September 1983, and the renewed strengthening, in late 1983, of Hong Kong's main export markets. Although the first two factors obviously had a negative impact, the latter two subsequently allowed for a short-term revitalization of the territory's economy.

The scope of this new growth—led by such traditional industries as textiles and low-technology electronics—fell far short of that experienced in 1980 (11.0 percent) and 1981 (9.4 percent); however, the 6.5 percent (in real terms) registered in 1983 was a significant improvement over the dismal results of 1982 (2.9 percent). In spite of this overall improvement, the Hong Kong economy in 1983 experienced a marked lack of growth in plant, machinery, and equipment investment; having registered −14.3 percent in 1982, growth in 1983 was negative again, −4.2 percent. It should be noted that there typically is a lag of some three to six months between the occurrence of a substantial pickup in exports and the subsequent increase in capital investments; 1983 was noteworthy in that no such commitments were made.[6]

The Hong Kong government, faced with the problem of a most severe lack of confidence in the future of the territory and—it must be clearly understood—the virtual collapse of the existing financial and monetary system, made an attempt to promote a climate of stability and support the economic upswing. The exchange rate was effectively pegged at US$1/HK$7.8 as of November 1983, and although this action initially had the effect of driving up interest rates from 8.5 percent in March of 1984 to a high of 17 percent in July, the prime rate dropped to a more manageable level of 10 percent later during the year.

In 1984, Hong Kong's gross domestic product (GDP) grew by 9.4 percent. The foreign sector of the economy accounted for the bulk of this increase, representing approximately 40 percent of the overall growth. On the domestic side, private consumption growth figures fell to 6.1 percent from the 8.1 percent registered in 1983, and other components of demand remained weak. The latter is largely explained by the Hong Kong government's not yet having recovered from the loss of revenue normally derived from land sales/leases following the breakdown of the property market. The inflation rate, which had averaged some 10 percent during 1982 and 1983, declined to approximately 8 percent in 1984 as a result, among other things, of the moderating effects of lower import prices, the new-gained stability of the Hong Kong dollar, the decline in property prices, and the slowdown in money supply growth. The initialing of the joint agreement in September 1984 did much to remove the cloud of political uncertainty under which Hong Kong lived, and it contributed to a relative stabilization of the economy. As a result, at the beginning of 1985, GDP growth of some 7 percent was expected to be the figure of reference.[7] As well, growth in domestic demand was expected to offset some of the effects of a projected decline in exports on overall growth.[8]

At the time of writing, however, it has become evident that the Hong Kong economy did not perform nearly as well in 1985 as was expected. The growth rate for domestic exports, estimated at 11 percent in the 1985 budget, was actually negative. The budget-projected GDP growth for the year was revised at midyear to 4.5–5 percent; in reality, the GDP grew by, at the most, 1 percent. Although the growth rate for total exports of goods declined during the year, reexports registered 28 percent growth versus 30.5 percent in 1984. This trend was visible fairly early on; compared to the same period in 1984, domestic exports, with the exception of those to the PRC, declined by some 6 percent in real terms during the first six months of 1985.[9] In a parallel development, the Hong Kong dollar experienced an appreciation against the currencies of its major markets as well as against those of its major competitors after mid-1984, which reduced the competitiveness of Hong Kong products.[10]

It is of interest to note that as of 1984, the PRC became the second-largest market for Hong Kong domestic exports. Hong Kong's domestic exports to this market increased markedly after mid-1984, growing by approximately 69 percent in real terms.[11]

Reexports proved to be a buffer in 1985. Exports in this category consisted mainly of consumer goods, raw materials, and semimanufactures, which accounted for 36 percent and 40 percent of the total value in this category.[12] Although Hong Kong, of course, also reexported to other countries, such as the United States (13 percent), Japan (5 percent), Taiwan (4 percent), and Singapore (4 percent), the PRC continued to be its largest reexport market. During the first two quarters of 1985, the value of reexports to the PRC grew by 140 percent and accounted for 47 percent of the total value of goods reexported through the colony. These reexports consisted chiefly of textiles, telecommunications equipment, electrical machinery, office machines, data processing equipment, and road vehicles. In addition to being the principal market, the PRC remained the most important source of the goods subsequently reexported through Hong Kong. However, mainly because of the more rapid increases in reexports from Japan and Taiwan, the PRC's percentage share declined from 36 percent during the first two quarters of 1984 to 30 percent during the same period in 1985. In terms of composition, products from the PRC for reexport via Hong Kong were dominantly textile yarn and fabrics, clothing, and light industrial/low value products.[13]

On the domestic side, the unemployment situation for the labor force as a whole remained largely stable during 1985, with a seasonally adjusted rate of approximately 3 percent.[14] The continued expansion of the entrepôt trade sector and of the finance and other related services sectors appears to have helped ease some of the negative effects of the weak domestic export performance.

1986 and Beyond

Will the joint agreement indeed turn out to be the framework for transition, as is its intended purpose? Or will it be used to wallpaper over, if that is at all feasible, the virtually irreconcilable differences that are part and parcel of the entire Hong Kong question? The very existence of the document has, so far, brought both a measure of stability to the territory by alleviating some of the more immediate pressures brought about by the pre-1984 climate of general uncertainty, but it has also had the effect of immediately allowing for the development of a new set of uncertainties.

The document has, for instance, had the effect of giving rise to the articulation of a number of expectations and demands with regard to the territory's political makeup that were essentially unknown prior to the U.K.-PRC negotiations and the final agreement. However much viewed as undesirable by both signatories of the agreement and basically unacceptable to Peking, these expectations and demands are now, nevertheless, part of the Hong Kong issue. The conclusion of the negotiations and the signing of the agreement have also given rise to a generally carefully articulated, if not always genuinely felt, confidence in the future of the territory. These professions of confidence are themselves not unusual. They tie in with the objectives of most of the people involved since the economy must be kept alive; regardless of one's views on the issue as a whole, much money remains to be made (and lost) in this territory where doing business has traditionally been the ultima ratio.

As far as Hong Kong's status—economic or otherwise—is concerned, it has been suggested that the territory is not really a British colony, but rather an essentially Chinese city-state that has found it profitable and expedient to sail under a flag of convenience.[15] For the people who find this suggestion debatable, the same proposition suggests that both the major political parties in the United Kingdom, on the one hand, and the PRC government, on the other, albeit for different reasons, appear to have been in tacit agreement as to this de facto state of affairs long before the Hong Kong issue became the subject of negotiations.[16]

There is much to be said for this observation. Confining ourselves to the years since World War II, Hong Kong, quite apart from its de jure status, has de facto played a number of varying but specific economic roles. Some of these roles have persisted over time. Although not always immediately apparent, Hong Kong's role as an entrepôt, for instance, has in fact survived both recurring political turmoil in the PRC and external factors, largely because its port and communication links are far superior to anything available within the PRC itself. Other roles, such as the city's importance as a considerable financial center, albeit of a somewhat more recent date, are still developing. On the whole, it must be viewed as highly unlikely that much of this importance would have been possible had the results not been of tangible benefit to Peking.[17] Having opted in favor of doing so tacitly during the 1950s and 1960s, the PRC leadership has since the early 1980s increasingly demonstrated, if not always a commanding understanding of the quintessential economic and social factors at work in Hong Kong, at least the importance it attaches to the territory's overall economic capabilities and potential.

A review of Hong Kong's importance in economic terms must include some observations with respect to two crucial elements of the equation, namely, Hong Kong's population and the present socioeconomic characteristics of the territory. For all practical purposes, the fruits of Hong Kong's economic success have given rise to what is essentially a middle- to upper-middle-class city. The 1985 per capita GDP was likely to reach US$6,000— fourth in Asia after Brunei, Japan, and Singapore. As a matter of fact, for the first time the territory is, so to speak, within "GDP striking distance" of the United Kingdom itself. Apart from a large variety of boutiques, the extent of the territory's general affluence is amply demonstrated by the near-catastrophic proliferation of cars. It is a place of vast differences in wealth, its population ranging from the extremely rich to the destitute; it might be added that there is little evidence to suggest the existence of a widespread urge to alter this state of affairs. Aside from being affluent, Hong Kong is essentially urban, thoroughly capitalist, very cosmopolitan, and above all young; less than 7.5 percent of the population is over sixty-five years of age. Today, the majority of the population is Hong Kong born, as opposed to being refugees from the PRC.

By Asian and even by Western standards, Hong Kong is relatively liberal and certainly well-educated.[18] Entrepreneurial initiative, hard work, and a fast pace are its hallmarks. Hong Kong is a place where there is virtually unrestricted economic freedom, a fair legal system, relatively little corruption (certainly by Asian standards), good communications, and low taxes. The government prides itself on applying a philosophy of "positive nonintervention," leaving business either to prosper or to go broke. The same government also believes it should do no more than provide the framework for a stable social order. As a consequence, Hong Kong relies on a relatively thin, closely knit, elite stratum to ensure this stability. In addition to some 2,000 key senior civil service and approximately 6,000 police officers, Hong Kong has approximately 4,000 entrepreneurs (who, it is worth noting en passant, provide close to 1 million jobs), 1,200 solicitors, 200 barristers, 1,400 engineers, and 900 architects.[19]

Finally, Hong Kong is a place where the overwhelming majority of the population has no particular wish to be governed by anybody. In fact, the majority does not appear to care much whether a British or a Chinese flag flies over the Government Secretariat building, providing the officials inside have (1) little power and (2) and more important, little or no inclination to tell the business community what to do.[20] Most residents would agree that the government should not meddle in the activities of business. The extent of this conviction was illustrated a year or so ago when even such a relatively benign proposal, by the Hong Kong government, that entrepreneurs might pool funds to be earmarked for research and development purposes in the territory was firmly rejected by the business community. The tenor of the reaction clearly was, if the rejection of the proposal meant that some business ventures surely must go broke, so be it.

At the risk of stating the obvious, Hong Kong's people, together with the views they espouse, represent the linchpin of Hong Kong's economic achievements. This fact appears, however, to have been overlooked during recent times; in particular by the people who, by virtue of the joint agreement, will rule Hong Kong after 1997 and who are already in the process of influencing decisions likely to have far-reaching consequences. Remove from the Hong Kong equation the industriousness, the determination, the willingness to gamble and to take financial and other economic risks—and the *primus motor* of it all, the pervasive and near-obsessive predilection for money—of the people in Hong Kong, and one can rest assured that the entire mechanism as we know it will rapidly grind to a halt. To entertain any other conclusion is tantamount to delusion.

The people who are ultimately most likely to affect the Hong Kong equation are the elite. As far as is known, of Hong Kong's total population of some 5.5 million people, at least 250,000 have already secured the means—fund transfers, travel papers, permits of residence or documents attesting to a new nationality—of leaving the territory should they decide it wise to opt out. It is also more than likely that another 300,000 to 350,000 are in position to secure similar avenues of departure. Apart from the purely mathematical aspects, it should be fairly evident for other reasons that members of the elite are contained in this group. It is no secret that the first of the people to prepare for their exit from the colony were Hong Kong's successful entrepreneurs. The reason for their decision is largely historical, and their assessment of the situation as it has developed since 1982 is relatively straightforward. Virtually all of the territory's major entrepreneurs have their roots in either Canton or, more likely, Shanghai. Following the rise to power of the Communists in 1949-1950, the Chinese Communist party (CCP) assured these people that they were indispensable to the modernization of their country, that they would be free to continue to run their businesses, and that they would be asked to assist in the management of the economy under the guidance of the CCP. Many of those who listened lost everything, and that lesson has not been forgotten.[21]

What, then, are Hong Kong's prospects? Most of the foregoing, especially when put into perspective against some other factors, does not bode well. In tune with its traditional time horizon, Hong Kong's most immediate concern over the short term will remain its economy.[22] On the whole, the performance of the Hong Kong economy was expected to remain flat during 1986 and 1987. Economic performance of the OECD market was not expected to change much from that of 1985, and in particular it was not quite clear whether the U.S. economy could be counted upon to provide the needed demand. As a result, Hong Kong's GDP growth was unlikely to exceed 4-5 percent at best. After their decline in 1985, domestic exports were also likely to remain flat. Viewed market by market, the prospects for Hong Kong domestic exports were not very encouraging. Export growth to the PRC was expected to decline, conditions in the European markets were likely to remain poor, and the Japanese market had to be regarded as a major question mark—Hong Kong's domestic exports to this market actually declined by approximately 13 percent in 1985. Prospects for a significant recovery of domestic exports to the U.S. market were also regarded as poor. This assessment did not apply to 1986 alone but extended to the short-term period (i.e., until 1987) as a whole.

Although some people still view reexports as the bright spot in Hong Kong's export picture, both the extent and some of the effects of the territory's dependence on its reexport links with the PRC were likely to be highlighted in 1986. Almost half of Hong Kong's reexports are destined for this largely unstable market, but over the short term, the PRC's very substantial 1985 trade deficit[23] can be expected to force a slowdown in the country's economy as a whole and in its foreign economic activity in particular. Although it is true that demand for Hong Kong goods in the mainland market is likely to remain relatively strong, it is far from clear whether an increased dependence on this fickle market is desirable in the longer term. Since the outlook for reexports to other major markets remains largely similar to that of 1985, the rate of overall reexport growth in 1986 probably slowed to approximately 15 percent.

Over the short term, Hong Kong's merchandise trade balance can be expected to deteriorate. However, the territory's current account balance of payments will remain well in surplus—expected at HK$22 billion for 1985—as a result of substantial earnings from services. Due to developments in the export sector, the merchandise trade surplus perhaps declined by as much as 50 percent in 1986, and the surplus in services was also likely to be less substantial, leading to a decline in the current account surplus, which was expected to remain substantial at HK$14 billion.

On the domestic side, economic conditions are weak but generally steady. A sectorial review indicates that the industries most affected by this state of affairs are electronics and fabricated metal products. Also weak, but somewhat less so, are the watch and clock and the textile and wearing apparel sectors. Orders in hand continue to decline in most areas, and there is relatively little likelihood that conditions will improve over the medium term. Sagging exports can be expected to continue to affect plant and machinery investment and are likely to result in further declines in retained capital goods imports. With prospects for merchandise sales uncertain due to economic conditions in the principal markets, manufacturing investment can be expected to remain weak over the medium term. It must be viewed as unlikely that the relatively rapid rate of upturn in the construction sector experienced in 1984 and early 1985 would be maintained in 1986. Although investment in residential real estate was substantial in 1985, the decline in investments in the public sector, as evidenced, in particular, by the relatively low levels of public works projects, is likely to result in generally depressed conditions in this category over the short term.[24] Domestic consumption, which had been relatively subdued, was likely to gain some momentum during 1986. With buying power strong, private consumption perhaps grew somewhat, possibly by as much as 7 percent.

A discussion of likely economic conditions in Hong Kong over the medium to long term would be incomplete without the inclusion of a number of political factors with which the territory and the people who operate there will have to contend. Some of these factors will affect Hong Kong from within and some externally; all will be directly linked to the PRC.

It must be viewed as increasingly evident that both Hong Kong's economic performance and its prospects will be affected by political decisions and the ensuing social reactions much sooner than many had anticipated, hoped, or professed. We have been in a position to gauge the impact of the introduction, in 1982 and 1983, of a negative political element into the Hong Kong equation once before. Many people have taken the view that the signing of the joint agreement effectively eliminated most of those negative effects. I do not agree. Private consumption/consumer spending is a case in point, and the trend in this category could prove to be highly illustrative. Although this component of the GDP recovered somewhat during 1985, it did not do so nearly as strongly as was expected. In terms of disposable income, 1984 and 1985 were relatively good years; pay increases averaged more than double the rate of inflation. Consumer spending, however, remained unaffected; savings were up, and borrowing was down.

It was not unlikely that this tendency would become more pronounced during 1986 as it became increasingly clear that the PRC, for all intents and purposes, was already in the process of erecting its own political infrastructure in Hong Kong. Peking has, much earlier than expected by most, shown how it intends play its hand with regard to the political system it wishes to introduce in the territory. This situation has led to the parallel, unpleasant realization in the colony that the British administrators do not have nearly the degree of independence they used to enjoy in the past or, more important, that they are supposed to have by virtue of the joint agreement. In terms of consumer spending, there exists more than just the mere possibility that the people in Hong Kong with the most purchasing power—i.e., those most likely to emigrate—will prefer to save for their future rather than to consume now. The depressing effects of this realization are unlikely to remain confined to the realm of economics.

As recently as 1985, the dominant perception with regard to the Hong Kong issue was that Peking's wishes would eventually, of course, have to be taken into account. The notion that the PRC's designs with respect to the sociopolitical system it had in mind for Hong Kong or that its handling of the transition period could actually negatively affect the territory's prospects was generally viewed as pessimistic. Didn't the joint agreement contain sufficient safeguards? Hadn't Peking's negotiators shown reason and restraint? The notion of the "China factor" as a threat to Hong Kong's prospects until 1997 tended to be dismissed out of hand.

In terms of Hong Kong's prospects, all the discussion is likely to be beyond the point. For all intents and purposes, Peking, as of the autumn and winter of 1985, has established its de facto control over the territory. For those who find this conclusion debatable, I would like to go one step further and suggest that Peking's objective of controlling developments in

Hong Kong's political infrastructure is likely to increasingly cast doubts as to whether the United Kingdom will retain full responsibility for Hong Kong up to 1997 and must be viewed as having a direct bearing on the stability of the territory's administration and its institutions.

Fundamental differences have emerged between the PRC leadership and the Hong Kong administration; also involved are a number of local political groupings with views as to how they wish the territory to be run in future. Ostensibly, the differences center around the issue of how Hong Kong's political infrastructure should evolve between now and 1997. At the risk of appearing somewhat cynical, the notion of any sort of evolution is naive. The differences are better viewed as signals from Peking that (1) it does not wish any fundamental change in the way the colony has been governed until now and most certainly no changes that would tend to introduce a "Western style" democratic system and (2) that if there has to be change, it must conform to Peking's blueprints.

The fact that Peking has no intention of tolerating more than a token input from other sources was established beyond a doubt by its representatives to the territory. Hsü Chia-t'un[25] established the fact in no uncertain terms in a public statement in November 1985 in which he declared that the Hong Kong government should put a halt to all political reforms until 1990, when Peking's political framework for the territory, the so-called Basic Law, is supposed to come into being.[26] Hsü explicitly stated that the political system of the Hong Kong SAR should be viewed as the PRC's concern alone. London has since, for all intents and purposes, thrown in the towel and declared that it will consult with Peking on any change it might have in mind for the territory.

This development must be viewed as one of the potentially most harmful to the territory because the degree of popular respect for the British administration will be pivotal to Hong Kong's prospects over the medium term. Given that Peking has effectively established the rules of the political/administrative game, popular confidence in the British administration, which will increasingly be viewed as having no genuine authority, and its ability to administer Hong Kong independently is likely to decrease substantially over this time period. Conversely, it is highly unlikely that a proportional increase will take place in the already low popular confidence in Peking's ability to promote a stable economic and political system in the territory.

I do not mean to suggest that this change with regard to London's authority will necessarily lead to tangible forms of social unrest. What will occur, however, is that morale, in the business community and the various branches of the civil service, will be negatively affected. The much-publicized outflow of managerial talent continues, and although an inflow of the same type of talent admittedly does occur, it is essentially confined to people who have already secured their foreign residency and who have returned to Hong Kong only for as long as they judge that it presents more favorable business opportunities.

In terms of the civil service, the effects are likely to have far-reaching consequences for the territory's governability. Indications are that expatriate police officers will be confined to administrative duties as of 1990; all operational activities will be the responsibility of local personnel. This possibility has some quite worrying implications because although there is no lack of Hong Kong Chinese who are both interested and competent to handle other branches of the civil services, the same is not true where the police force is concerned. The Hong Kong government is likely to face increased difficulties in attracting qualified local personnel to replace the expatriate officers—this may in fact prove to be a major problem. As an extension, a deterioration in the quality and efficiency of the police force can be expected to have substantial negative effects on social stability. For instance, groups such as the triads are reportedly already exercising a more pervasive influence. Although unlikely to pose a serious problem in the short term, increased levels of crime and social instability are most likely to trigger a more detailed, direct intervention in Hong Kong's affairs by Peking over the medium term. It is highly unlikely that Peking will allow anything beyond minor changes in Hong Kong's stable social fabric. A rise in the incidence of crime, in particular of the economic variety, is the most likely change to provoke intervention by Peking.

Concluding Remarks

Peking, it has been argued, understands the importance of Hong Kong and can be expected to act in such a manner as to ensure that the transition from British to its own rule results in a stable and functioning SAR. The PRC, it has further been argued, has changed its principles of economic management and is committed to an economic development similar to some of the mixed economies found elsewhere in the world. Hong Kong, it is said, is of great importance to the PRC in this pursuit of economic modernization—probably more so than Peking appears to understand.

The people—whether in the business community, government, or academe—who entertain some of the above propositions and who, in addition, adhere to the comforting notion that the PRC has passed the "teething" stage of the economic and political reform policies introduced since the early 1980s could well be in for a few surprises. Unfortunately for Hong Kong, it is likely to be at the receiving end of most of those surprises. "Socialism with Chinese characteristics" is what Teng Hsiao-p'ing has called the objective of the changes he has attempted to introduce in the PRC. It has been pointed out that, so far, this slogan has looked more like a set of ad hoc reactions to Maoism than a coherent ideology and much less like a policy description,[27] which in part explains the stop-and-go nature of the economic reforms introduced since the late 1970s.

As far as Hong Kong is concerned—quite apart from the effects of the fluctuations in its other main markets—the very fact that the attempts at economic modernization in the PRC have failed to gain a more permanent foothold, particularly politically, is likely to have significant implications for the territory. Hong Kong's usefulness to the PRC government and the regimes that preceded it has resided in the fact that the territory was both a part of China and apart from it.[28] Unfortunately, Hong Kong's ultimate reintegration with the PRC will put an end much of the colony's raison d'être. Someone with a genuine understanding of what Hong Kong really represented once said that it was a "borrowed place," living on "borrowed time."[29] Politics have dictated that this "loan" be called. Although, theoretically, Hong Kong's best hope for the future would be being allowed to maintain through some distance the substance of its usefulness, in practice, the dictates of integration will make this hope as good as impossible.

Those same dictates will tend to increasingly intertwine the fates of Hong Kong and the PRC; not only in purely economic terms, but particularly in terms of the socioeconomic spin-off of occurrences on the PRC's domestic political scene. Should the PRC actually manage to put its house in order, Hong Kong could retain some of its economic viability—to be sure, not in the way we have come to recognize it over the past twenty-five years or so, but an economic capacity nevertheless. However, if the PRC does not work, Hong Kong does not stand a chance at all. Many people in Hong Kong, it would seem, have already concluded that given the track record to date, the balance of probability is that the PRC will not work.

Notes

Normal academic standards of reference have, wherever possible, been used in this paper. However, some of the source material is of a nature that renders its further discussion impossible.

1. *A Draft Agreement Between the Government of the United Kingdom of Great Britain and Northern Ireland and the Government of the People's Republic of China on the Future of Hong Kong* (London and Hong Kong, September 26, 1984).

2. I must admit I discuss this particular subject with quite some doubt. If there exists one single area in which differences in perception are near-total, it must surely be the legal area.

3. At first view, this arrangement makes sense. If the PRC, as is expected, seeks to renew its membership in GATT (which would take some time), the arrangement would, theoretically, give Peking two voices in international trade negotiations.

4. There are indications that the very issue of the land leases led the United Kingdom to first consider discussing the Hong Kong issue with Peking. Some people would suggest that the matter was considered to be of such importance that Prime Minister Thatcher's "faux pas" in Peking in 1982 was essentially one of form.

5. For further details and the exact wording of the provisions of the joint agreement, see *A Draft Agreement*, pp. 11–29.

6. See William H. Overholt, "Hong Kong After the Chinese-British Agreement," *Asian Perspective* 9:2 (Fall-Winter 1985), p. 263.

7. "Business, Business, Business. . . ." *Economist* (London), May 11, 1985, p. 11 (survey). Growth of approximately 7.5 percent in private consumption and 4.0 percent in public consumption and an inflation rate of 6.5 percent were also expected. The upswing in the rates of investment apparent as of late 1984, was expected to result in growth in private investment in machinery in excess of 10 percent in 1985. The last is best viewed as a reflection of the physical wear and tear on

equipment since the beginning of the economic upswing, compounded by the necessity to maintain competitiveness by means of the acquisition of more sophisticated equipment.

8. Ibid. The construction sector has shown some signs of renewed vitality subsequent to the bottoming out of the real estate/property market; private investment in this sector was expected to rise by 2 percent, compared to a 9.5 percent decline in 1984.

9. Hong Kong Government, *Half-Yearly Economic Report 1985* (Hong Kong 1985), para. 1.1 and 1.2. The slowdown in economic growth in the territory's major markets, in particular the United States, accounts for much of this decline.

10. Ibid.

11. Ibid., para. 2.3. To a large extent, Hong Kong exports to the PRC consisted of semimanufactures, reflecting the importance of compensation trade and processing arrangements. During the first two quarters of 1985, fabrics and textile yarn alone accounted for some 11 percent of these exports. At the same time, domestic exports of consumer durables to this market registered very substantial, but likely only temporary, increases in value terms.

12. Ibid., para. 2.15. As a share of total exports, reexports rose substantially, from 37 percent in the first two quarters of 1984 to 47 percent in the same period 1985.

13. As a comparison, the figure for reexports/total value of exports for the same period in 1984 was 28 percent (ibid., para. 2.16 and 2.17).

14. Ibid., para. 4.2.

15. See Chalmers Johnson, "The Mousetrapping of Hong Kong: A Game in Which Nobody Wins," *Asian Survey* 24:9 (September 1984), p. 888.

16. Ibid., pp. 888–889.

17. "Partners Again," *Economist* (London), May 11, 1985, p. 17 (survey). From 1949, when the Communist regime came to power in Peking, until the beginning of the 1980s, the PRC's external trade balance recorded deficits for twelve years. However, the incidence of such deficits would be twice as high if the PRC's trade with Hong Kong were excluded. Although it is undeniable that the PRC in turn represented a sizable advantage to Hong Kong in that it provided cheap food, raw materials, and the like, Peking has consistently viewed its two-way trade with Hong Kong as a source of foreign exchange earnings. The balance of trade between the two has been in the PRC's favor continuously since 1952, and its cumulative trade surplus since that year has been valued at some US$25 billion. From approximately one-fifth during the mid-1970s, earnings through Hong Kong represented some 37 percent of total PRC foreign exchange earnings at the beginning of the 1980s, and this proportion has since remained in the same order of magnitude. The role played by Hong Kong as a point of legal or illegal access to foreign technology has grown over the years, enhanced in the late 1970s and early 1980s by the renewed importance accorded by Peking to the use of advanced technology as an engine of economic modernization and the establishment of the special economic zones in Guangdong Province.

18. "Perhaps, Perhaps, Perhaps," ibid., p. 1 (survey).

19. Overholt, "Hong Kong After the Chinese-British Agreement," p. 261.

20. See "Perhaps, Perhaps, Perhaps," p. 2.

21. The ingenuity displayed by those determined to secure shelter elsewhere is probably best illustrated by the increasing incidence of Hong Kong mothers giving birth to their children in countries such as the United States, Canada, and Australia (which is technically illegal). The rationale that underlies the decision to do so is

that since the family thus now has at least one member legally a citizen of that country, immigration authorities will look more favorably at a family-wide application for permanent residence.

22. As much as possible distinctions are made among the outlooks for the short term (1986–1988), the medium term (until the early 1990s), and the long term (1995–1997). The various factors likely to affect Hong Kong can be expected not to come into play all at the same time.

23. The PRC's trade deficit for 1985 can reasonably be estimated at US$12 billion and could well have reached US$14 billion. As regards the figures supplied by the various PRC authorities, confusion appears to be near-total. The Ministry of Foreign Trade claims a deficit of US$7.61 billion (six times the 1984 figure), and the Customs Bureau estimated the deficit at US$9.2 billion for the first nine months alone. As has been the case over the years, the discrepancies have been attributed to different methods of calculation.

24. Over the medium term, some growth can be expected in public expenditures as the government is likely to go ahead with several major projects in the construction sector. The second crossharbor tunnel and the extension of the Kwai Chung container port should have stimulatory impact.

25. Hsü Chia-t'un is the director of Xinhua news agency in Hong Kong and is generally regarded as Peking's principal representative in the territory. The composition of the Xinhua representation was recently extensively altered and must now be regarded as constituting Peking's "shadow administration" in Hong Kong.

26. The Basic Law, being drafted by Peking with the participation of twenty-three Hong Kong representatives, is intended to serve as a miniconstitution for the Hong Kong Special Administrative Region. It is supposed to contain the letter and the spirit of the joint agreement; however, the mere process of appointing the Basic Law drafting-body members became a demonstration of Peking's heavy-handedness (see *Far Eastern Economic Review*, November–December 1985, for numerous articles on the various aspects of this issue).

27. Anthony Rowley, "A Certain Skepticism Should Inform Assessment of China's Capitalism," *Financier* (November 1985), p. 20.

28. "Perhaps, Perhaps, Perhaps," p. 2.

29. The expression was coined by the late doyen of Hong Kong's foreign correspondents, Richard Hughes. There is much to his observation. Per extension, it also suggests that there never was a realistic possibility, however much desired by some in the colony, of Hong Kong's becoming a separate sovereign entity.

PART TWO

Hong Kong: A Chinese Concern

5

The Impact of
the Hong Kong Problem and
Agreement on PRC Domestic Politics

Jürgen Domes

During the course of the Sino-Japanese War from 1937 to 1945, and again during the twenty-three years of conflict with the USSR from 1959 to 1982, the Chinese Communist party's (CCP) elite created, among legions of foreign observers, the impression that it was highly dedicated to the sovereignty, independence, and national self-determination of China; in other words, that it was—and is—as nationalistic as it is Marxist-Leninist. Given this impression, one would assume that the fact that Hong King has remained a Chinese irredenta for at least thirty-five years of the history of the People's Republic of China (PRC) has played a rather important part in the manifold developments of domestic politics on the Chinese mainland. In considering the present and future of Hong Kong not only as an international but also as a Chinese concern, it seems appropriate to look at the possible impact on the political scene of the PRC of the fact that Hong Kong did survive as a British colony. Furthermore, it is time to discuss the possible interdependence between the development of PRC domestic politics and the Sino-British talks from 1982 to 1984 as well as the impact of the Sino-British agreement on Hong Kong on the political events in Peking since the fall of 1984. Finally, we should ask how different projections of the perspectives for the political system in the PRC could affect the future of Hong Kong.

In order to advance some very initial hypotheses on these problems, this chapter addresses six questions. First, what were the positions of the CCP elite on the future of Hong Kong before the Cultural Revolution and which role did the Hong Kong problem play in PRC domestic politics between 1949 and 1965–1966? Second, what was the impact of the Cultural Revolution on Hong Kong and which role did the disturbances in the British colony between May and September 1967 play for the development of intra-elite politics in the PRC during that period? Third, was there any recognizable impact of the Hong Kong problem on domestic PRC politics between the end of the Cultural Revolution and the eve of the Sino-British talks, i.e., between 1969 and 1982?

Fourth, what were the configurations of intra-elite group formation within the CCP in 1982 and which role did the Sino-British talks play in the context of these configurations? Fifth, to what extent did the Sino-British agreement on Hong Kong influence domestic political developments and intra-elite group formation in the PRC between the fall of 1984 and early 1986? Sixth, what are the alternative projections for the future of domestic politics and the political system in the PRC and how could they affect the future prospects of Hong Kong?

1949–1966

From the establishment of the PRC on October 1, 1949, until the unfolding of the great systemic crisis, which is referred to by the misleading name Cultural Revolution, in late 1965 or early 1966, the Chinese mainland experienced the politics of reconstruction and the implementation of a developmental concept modeled after the USSR in the Stalinist period. Then followed Mao Tse-tung's gigantic effort at development through mass movements for enthusiastic austerity and the utter failure of that effort, which resulted in the greatest famine in China of this century. Next came the revisions of the Maoist concept and the ensuing differentiation within the elite, which set the stage for the crisis of 1966–1969. Since the Hundred Flowers Campaign in the spring of 1957, cycles of intra-elite conflict have dominated the political scene in the PRC. Latent opinion groups condensed into program-based factions vying for control of the power positions as well as recommending irreconcilable political platforms. Also during this period relations of the PRC with the USSR deteriorated into an open confrontation, which shook the very foundations of the international Marxist-Leninist camp.

Yet throughout all these twists and turns, trials and tribulations, Hong Kong, to the best of my knowledge, was not even once mentioned in any official CCP document of any single important Party conference, not even in the proceedings of the first and second plenary meetings of the Eighth Party Congress in September 1956 and May 1958. Nor do I find any mention of the British colony in any internal Party document of the sixteen-year period between 1949 and 1965 that is available outside the PRC. In his succinct general review of PRC foreign policy from 1949 to 1965, Harold C. Hinton mentions only that the CCP elite "did not molest" Hong Kong in the early period of its rule over the Chinese mainland but that, later, "whenever the CPR [PRC] has found a Taiwan Strait crisis on its hands it has generally stirred up trouble of some sort in Hong Kong." He also points to the mass exodus of Chinese refugees to the colony in May 1962, and he indicates that Hong Kong was a major channel of overseas Chinese remittances to the PRC.[1] But that is all.

Even when Nikita Khrushchev, at a session of the Supreme Soviet on December 12, 1962, scolded Mao Tse-tung as a "wise monk" who tended to give "anti-imperialist advice" to the USSR, but "kept mum on the fact of imperialist occupation of Hongkong and Macao,"[2] the CCP reacted rather late and not very explicitly. Only almost three months after Khrushchev's speech did a *People's Daily* editorial give passing mention to the "convention on the extension of Hongkong in 1898" as an "unequal treaty."[3] In October, in the fourth of the nine commentaries on the open letter of the Central Committee of the Communist party of the Soviet Union (CPSU) of July 14, 1963, the CCP leadership finally responded to Khrushchev's attack with the very general allegation that the Soviet elite was "betraying the fight against imperialism and colonialism" all over the world.[4] There was no special reference to a rebuttal of the Soviet leader's remarks about Hong Kong and Macao. It was only on the eve of the Cultural Revolution, at a time when the open rift within the CCP elite had become unavoidable, that a major Party leader addressed himself to the question of Hong Kong in a more threatening manner.

In September 1965, at an enlarged meeting of the Standing Committee of the CCP Politburo in Peking, a request by Mao to start a new purge of critical intellectuals was turned down by the majority of the assembled leaders, a decision Mao was not willing to accept.[5] It was at this moment that the consensus on procedures among the CCP elite broke down. With this event, the period of differentiation within the Peking leadership ended, and the period of confrontation began.

On September 29, 1965, the then-minister of foreign affairs, Marshal Ch'en Yi, obviously highly tense because of the impact of the bitter intra-elite debates, met with international press correspondents and indulged in a diatribe during which he invited the United States, the USSR, Japan, and India to "invade China." In the context of his remarks, Ch'en warned the government of the United Kingdom:

> The fact that Britain and the Hongkong authorities allow the U.S. to use Hongkong as a base for aggression against Vietnam has caused the anxiety of local inhabitants. The Chinese government considers the question not only one of using Hongkong as a base for aggression against Vietnam but also of preparing to use it in the future as a base for aggression against China. The Chinese government is firmly opposed to this. This action of the British government is most stupid. We hope that it will choose a wiser course in its own interests. Otherwise, China will take measures when necessary. . . . China sees not just the question of Taiwan, the question of Hongkong, and the question of Macao, each on its own. What we see is the global strategy of U.S. imperialism.[6]

Ch'en Yi's statement should be considered as a precursor to the aggressive CCP language during the Cultural Revolution. The PRC moved toward its major systemic crisis, and against this background, the status of Hong Kong became one of the instruments of conflict, albeit even now one of rather limited importance.

Although we may assume that there was a general, even if vague, consensus among the CCP elite that Hong Kong should be returned to PRC sovereignty sometime in the future, this brief review of developments between 1949 and 1965 allows only one conclusion: During that period, the Hong Kong problem was of extremely marginal, if any, importance for domestic politics in the PRC. The CCP elite did not develop any specific policies to solve the problem; it was basically a nonissue for the Peking leadership.

1967

The situation changed drastically, although only for a period of not more than five months, in 1967, the year that marked the high tide of the Cultural Revolution."[7] On January 4 and 5, Red Guards and "revolutionary rebels" seized power in Shanghai. Soon, popular resistance to the assault by the forces of Maoism led to strikes, the closure of factories, attacks on transport facilities, the storming of rural grain storage facilities and banks, and even to the return to individual farming in some places in twenty-six out of the twenty-nine provinces. By late January, the CCP center had to call for military intervention, and the regional military leaders seized control, taking over from the defunct Party and state administrative machines. Yet the People's Liberation Army (PLA) not only toppled the adversaries of Mao in the provinces, but also turned against the supporters of the Cultural Revolutionary Left around Mao, Lin Piao, and Mme. Chiang Ch'ing, the Maoist mass organizations that had started violent factional struggles among themselves.

In February and March, it seemed for a few weeks as if the PLA had managed to stabilize the situation. But then, during the first half of April, the organizations of the Left, mobilized by the central Cultural Revolution group under Chiang Ch'ing, Ch'en Po-ta, and K'ang Sheng and with the consent of Mao and Lin Piao, started a second offensive. From early May through late July, many provinces of China—in particular Kuangsi, Kueichou, Such'uan, Kuangtung, Hunan, Hupei, Chekiang, Fukien, Honan, Shensi, Shansi, Shantung, and Liaoning—became the scene of armed struggle between leftist and moderate factions as well as of attacks by the leftists on PLA installations and personnel. A number of regional commanders were dismissed from office, and from July 20 to July 26, an open rebellion by the commander in chief of the Wuhan Military Area, General Ch'en Tsai-tao, was suppressed with great difficulty by airborne and naval units under direct central command. The Wuhan events and the occupation of a number of ministries, including the Ministry of Foreign Affairs, in Peking by Red Guards and revolutionary rebels between August 12 and August 20, however, marked the turning point in the Cultural Revolution. By mid-August, Lin Piao had reached an agreement with the regional commanders, securing their support for the purge of the opponents of Mao in the center by entrusting them definitely with regional control and allowing them to start disciplinary actions against the Maoist mass organizations.

The PLA finally succeeded in suppressing the extreme Left in often rather bloody fighting between the beginning of September 1967 and late August 1968. During the spring and summer of 1967, Prime Minister Chou En-lai and the majority of the regional PLA commanders tried desperately to prevent a large-scale civil war and to put an end to armed clashes while the central Cultural Revolution group poured fuel on the fire, calling for attacks against "persons taking the capitalist road within the army," until, finally, even Chiang Ch'ing was forced to endorse the disciplinary actions of the PLA in a speech to Red Guard representatives from Anhui on September 5, 1967.[8]

These developments were exactly reflected in the province of Kuangtung, north of Hong Kong. Here, the commander in chief of the Canton Military Area, General Huang Yung-sheng, who had seized power in the city of Canton in early February, found himself confronted with an onslaught by the Left from early May through late August 1967.[9] After the beginning of June, Huang became the object of a systematic propaganda campaign by the leftist organizations in Canton,[10] and in July and August, that southern Chinese city and almost the whole of Kuangtung Province became the scene of heavy armed clashes between the Red Flag mass organizations, which were in contact with the Cultural Revolutionary Left in Peking, and the East Wind mass organizations, which supported Huang and the regional PLA. These clashes claimed hundreds, if not thousands, of lives,[11] and they subsided only after comparatively moderate PLA forces, led by followers of Huang, had taken over control of Canton by late August and of most of Kuangtung by the second half of September.

In early May 1967, these developments on the Chinese mainland in general and in Kuangtung in particular spilled over into Hong Kong. On the afternoon of May 6, the workers of an artificial flower factory in Sanpokong, led by leftist—i.e., PRC-influenced—trade unions, went on strike and occupied the premises of the plant. Hong Kong police moved in, drove the workers from the plant, and made twenty-one arrests.[12] This was the beginning of the Hong Kong "riots" of 1967, the only major crisis to hit the British colony between the early 1950s and 1982. Beginning on May 10, the riots spread over many parts of Kowloon,[13] and on May 22, they reached Hong Kong Island.[14] During the following weeks, the PRC-influenced unions and other leftist organizations continued with demonstrations, a rather successful bus strike—which the non-Communist population countered with the introduction of the so-called public light buses—and increasing violence. Soon, the government of the PRC declared open support for the rioters, first by sending a very strongly worded statement by the Peking Ministry of Foreign Affairs to the British government, which ended as follows:

The Chinese government hereby solemnly declares: The Chinese government and the 700 million Chinese people firmly support their compatriots in Hong Kong in their heroic and just struggle and resolutely stand behind them as their powerful backing. The Chinese government demands in all seriousness that the British government instruct the authorities in Hong Kong as follows:

- Immediately accept all the just demands put forward by Chinese workers and residents in Hong Kong;
- Immediately stop all fascist measures;
- Immediately set free all the arrested persons (including workers, journalists, and cameramen);
- Punish the culprits responsible for these sanguinary [sic] atrocities, offer apologies to the victims, and compensate for all losses; and
- Guarantee against the occurrence of similar incidents.[15]

The British government and the British authorities in Hong Kong must immediately and unconditionally accept the above-mentioned and just demands of the Chinese government. The Chinese government and people are determined to carry the struggle through to the end. Should the British government and the British authorities in Hong Kong cling to their perverse course, they must be held responsible for all the grave consequences arising therefrom.[16]

The Hong Kong colonial government, however, increasingly supported by the overwhelming majority of the Chinese inhabitants of the colony, did not bend, even when the authorities of Kuangtung Province remitted HK$10 million to aid the leftists,[17] when the PRC cut off the supply of water to Hong Kong in late June,[18] or when, on July 9, Chinese Communist militia forces clashed with Hong Kong border police near Lowu, killing five policemen and wounding twelve others.[19] During the month of July, the leftists attacked Hong Kong police and British soldiers and committed acts of arson and bombing assaults in many parts of the colony. The non-Communist organizations reacted with a boycott of PRC-owned shops and Communist schools, which was obeyed by more than three-fourths of the Hong Kong populace, and on July 29, the colonial government issued emergency regulations, which allowed the police to arrest rioters and terrorists for a period of up to one year.[20] In response, the Maoist organizations, which then controlled the headquarters of the All-Chinese Federation of Labour Unions in Peking, sent another HK$10 million to support the leftists in Hong Kong,[21] some of whom, during mid-August, started to attack the harbor ferries.

By late August, however, the disturbances had started to subside. The last bombs were thrown at British soldiers, wounding three of them, on September 4,[22] and on September 10, the last major demonstration, a protest by several thousand pupils of PRC-run schools, occurred.[23] Altogether more than 3,000 rioters and cadres of leftist organizations were arrested by the Hong Kong police between early May and late September, and during the disturbances, more than fifty policemen and soldiers lost their lives while several hundreds were wounded. By the end of September, however, the PRC resumed the water supply to Hong Kong, and life in the British colony returned to normal.

The course of these events in Hong Kong developed almost parallel to events within the PRC. The riots started at the time of the beginning of the second leftist offensive in early May; reached their peak in July and the first part of August, when forces loyal to the Cultural Revolutionary Left were in control of many parts of Kuangtung; and began to subside after the CCP central elite had turned against the extreme Left. During the second half of September, a circular by the Canton Military Area Command labeled the riots in Hong Kong "leftist adventurism" and warned the mass organizations of Kuangtung not to support any further activities in the British colony.[24]

By October, a period during which events in Hong Kong were influenced by the domestic political crisis within the PRC had ended. There can be no doubt that the disturbances in Hong Kong were directly instigated, as they were openly supported, by the Cultural Revolutionary Left within the CCP leadership. The faction around Chiang Ch'ing—and probably for some time between May and August 1967, Mao and Lin Piao as well—seems to have believed that Hong Kong could be forced into submission and taken over by means of riots. Premier Chou, on the other hand, supported by the diplomatic subsystem—or rather, by what was still left of it—and a number of leading regional commanders, doubted the effectiveness of such a strategy. Thus, the Hong Kong "struggle" became increasingly the concern of one faction rather than that of the whole CCP leadership. As soon as the position of the Cultural Revolutionary Left had weakened, after mid-August, and particularly after the defeat of the leftist Red Flag organizations in Kuangtung in late August and September, the Hong Kong leftists were abandoned by the PRC authorities, and the former had to learn that, at least for the time being, there was no choice for them but to accept British rule. For five months, Hong Kong had, finally, played a role in PRC domestic politics, but as an instrument used in the conflict over power and policies on the Chinese mainland rather than as a true political issue in China.

1969–1982

When the CCP convened its Ninth Party Congress in April 1969, Hong Kong had again almost entirely disappeared from the agenda of the PRC elite. Even in his report to the congress, Lin Piao made no single substantial statement concerning the present or future of the colony but only mentioned its name when, toward the end of his speech, he claimed that the "great unity" which supposedly had been achieved "under the great Red Banner of Mao Tse-tung thought" embraces—among others—"the vast numbers of patriotic Overseas Chinese and our patriotic compatriots in Hong Kong and Macao."[25] This was to be the last mention of Hong Kong in an official CCP document for thirteen years—until 1982.

During that thirteen-year period, the PRC first experienced Lin Piao's attempt to restore the Maoist concept of development by mass mobilization and class struggle, the overthrow of Lin in a palace coup in Peking, a return to the policies of economic readjustment—which had initially been implemented between 1961 and 1965—under the dominating influence of

Chou En-lai in 1972 and 1973, new attempts of the Cultural Revolutionary Left in 1974 to return to the policies of the Cultural Revolution, and again a turn toward the policies of readjustment under the influence of Teng Hsiao-p'ing in 1975.[26] Then there followed another leftist counterattack after the death of Chou, which led to the second purge of Teng in April 1976, and an anti-Maoist mass movement developed that began to threaten the very foundations of CCP rule during the spring and summer of 1976. Mao Tse-tung died on September 9 of that year, and Chiang Ch'ing and the other members of the leadership core of the Cultural Revolutionary Left were purged and arrested in a military coup d'état on October 6. Hua Kuo-feng, a lackluster civilian Party cadre with close security connections who had risen to the central level as a result of the Cultural Revolution, assumed the leadership of the CCP, but he was, in fact, manipulated by two powerful Party veterans with orthodox Bolshevik viewpoints, Marshal Yeh Chien-ying and Li Hsien-nien.

In July 1977, Teng Hsiao-p'ing was once again rehabilitated. After having built up his base, particularly within the ranks of the provincial Party leadership and the PLA, he set out in May 1978 to eliminate Hua and other remaining Maoists from the central decision-making organs and to change the political course of the PRC toward economic liberalization and a limited and controlled opening to the world. Finally, on December 5, 1980, Hua was removed from Party leadership by a decision of the Politburo,[27] and this action was confirmed by a decision of the sixth plenum of the Eleventh CCP Central Committee in June 1981, which also passed a resolution that devastatingly criticized the Cultural Revolution and introduced a mild form of de-Maoization.[28]

During the conflicts and crises of these thirteen years, the problem of Hong Kong did not even play a marginal role in CCP intra-elite politics. Yet the colony had indirect importance for the people in the Chinese mainland in two respects. First, it served as a haven for those people living in southern China, particularly in Kuangtung, who wanted to escape the miseries of life under socialism. From 1967 to 1972, at least 78,795 people, most of them in their twenties, made this escape.[29] Between 1977 and 1980, the figure rose to more than 400,000.[30] Second, the colony served as a constant reminder of what a Chinese populace can achieve economically if it does not have to operate under Marxist-Leninist rule. In 1981, Hong Kong had only 0.61 percent of the population of the PRC and the British colony together, yet is produced 8.06 percent of the combined GNP and 49.32 percent of the combined exports. In terms of per capita GNP, the PRC ranked 139th among 175 countries and territories in the world, and Hong Kong ranked 38th. With the increasing influx of foreign and overseas Chinese visitors to the Chinese mainland since 1978, information on the economic success story of Hong Kong, which had hitherto mainly been confined to Kuangtung and some other parts of southern China, spread all over the PRC.

Yet despite these indirect influences, there is not the slightest indication that the existence of Hong Kong or the problem of its future had any impact on the intra-elite conflicts and policymaking during the thirteen years from early 1969 to early 1982. Until the spring of 1982, Hong Kong was definitely not a major PRC policy concern.

1983

The situation changed, however, when the problem of the future of Hong Kong became one of the many policy issues debated by the CCP elite in the spring of 1982. Before I attempt to present some very initial considerations about the impact of the problem of Hong Kong's future in general and the Sino-British talks in particular on intra-elite politics in the PRC, it seems necessary to look at the configuration of intra-elite group formation within the CCP leadership during the period of the talks and since the Sino-British agreement of September 1984. During that period, the patterns of intra-elite group formation never became dominated by *factions*, i.e., by coherent circles, based on alternative platforms and exclusive claims to political power and overall control—in other words, by tight platform-based coalitions.[31] Instead, they were characterized by the existence of *opinion groups*, i.e., by latent alignments, based on common views concerning particular policy issues—in other words, by loose issue-based coalitions.[32]

The results of almost thirty years of observation of the political scene in the PRC has taught us that as long as opinion groups characterize the patterns of intra-elite group formation, the elite consensus on procedures prevails and all groups that participate in the decision-making process are willing to form fluctuating alliances and to arrive at compromises. Such was the case after the demolition of Chairman Hua Kuo-feng in late 1980, and it continues to be the case today.

By early 1982, at least three such opinion groups had emerged.[33] First, there was a reformist (or revisionist) group around Teng Hsiao-p'ing and Prime Minister Chao Tzu-yang, and it pressed for a thoroughgoing liberalization of economic policies and for a widening of the parameters of competition in all nonpolitical matters, particularly in the area of culture. This group also seems to have had the support of Hu Yao-pang, chairman of the CCP Central Committee until September 1982 and since then secretary-general of the CCP Central Committee's Secretariat. Second, there was an enlightened Bolshevik group around Ch'en Yün and P'eng Chen, which promoted a limited and controlled economic liberalization but argued for tight political control, even in the cultural area, and for strict Leninist discipline within the Party. Third, there was an orthodox Bolshevik group around Marshal Yeh Chien-ying and Li Hsien-nien, including the remnants of the disappearing Maoist faction (for example, Ni Chih-fu and, until September 1982, Hua Kuo-feng), which stood for centralized planning and the strict enforcement of Party control in all sectors of the society.

Between the spring of 1982 and the Twelfth Party Congress in September of that year, the reformists were able to muster eight votes among the full members of the Politburo; the enlightened Bolsheviks, six to seven; and the orthodox Bolsheviks, who, during that period, were mostly confronted by an alliance of the first two groups, eight to nine. After the personnel decisions of the first plenary session of the Twelfth CCP Central Committee on September 11, 1982,[34] the new lineup of forces was nine to eleven reformists (including Liao Ch'eng-chih who died on June 9, 1983), seven to eight enlightened Bolsheviks, and seven orthodox Bolsheviks. Yet between 1983 and today, the number of areas of agreement between the reformists and the enlightened Bolsheviks has been reduced, and the disagreements between these two groups have been on the increase.

The results of the Politburo reshuffle that immediately followed the CCP National Delegates' Conference in September 1985 at first glance appeared to have sealed a clear majority for the reformists in the new Politburo[35] as the reformists now seem to rally twelve of the twenty full members of the Politburo. But this superficial impression has to be modified. Hu Yao-pang and three new members who originated from the Communist Youth Corps machine (which Hu led from 1952 to 1965) tend to follow Teng Hsiao-p'ing's policy concepts, yet for reasons of personal loyalty rather than political conviction, so that this group of four should not indiscriminately be considered reformist. If we follow this differentiation, then the current Politburo consists of eight dedicated reformists, four moderately and insecurely reformist members of the group around Hu, five enlightened Bolsheviks, and three orthodox Bolsheviks, with the group around Hu holding the balance between the revisionist and the traditionalist forces in the CCP leadership core. It is in these varying configurations that the major decisions on the future of Hong Kong were—and are to be!—taken.

Until the spring of 1982, the future status of Hong Kong was obviously not at the center of attention for the CCP elite. In the fall of 1977, Li Hsien-nien had quoted Mao who once said that "as far as Hong Kong is concerned, we will worry about it after we have liberated Taiwan."[36] But in January 1982, the deputy foreign secretary of the United Kingdom, Sir Humphrey Atkins, visited Peking in order to prepare for a visit of his prime minister, Margaret Thatcher, later in the year. In the context of his visit, he informed the PRC leadership that his government planned to cease British rule over Hong Kong as soon as the lease of the New Territories expired on July 1, 1997. This information seems to have brought the problem of the future of the colony to the attention of the CCP elite, which now started to work out a PRC position on the solution of this problem. By late June, the conclusions seem to have been reached that Hong Kong, as well as Macao, should be returned to Chinese—i.e., PRC—sovereignty, and "not in the distant future," and that in order to facilitate a solution, the principle of "one country, two systems" (*I kuo liang chih*) should be applied, which would mean a continuation of the market economy and a "capitalist" society in Hong Kong with the British colony remaining a free port.[37]

There were, however, alternatives to that policy. The PRC could have agreed to make Hong Kong a territory under PRC sovereignty but administered, for a considerable period after 1997, by the British, or it could have agreed to accept Hong Kong as a nearly independent entity under PRC suzerainty. That the PRC line on Hong Kong was shaped along the lines of a definite end to British rule *and* administration, Chinese sovereignty, and a comparatively large amount of autonomy under the control of the central government and within the limits set by the constitution of the PRC must be attributed to policy compromises within the CCP leadership. This leadership, at the time the policy was shaped, was preparing for the Twelfth Party Congress, the results of which, in terms of structural reforms as well as personnel decisions, signaled a middle-of-the-road position between the reformist and the orthodox Bolshevik groups, mostly reflecting the views of the enlightened Bolsheviks.[38] I suggest that the Hong Kong compromise was one of many issues that formed the overall compromise package of 1982.

From September 22 through September 26, Prime Minister Thatcher visited Peking, discussing Hong Kong—among other less important issues— with Chao Tzu-yang and Teng Hsiao-p'ing.[39] During these talks, she seems to have tried to establish a British negotiating position by acknowledging that the New Territory lease would definitely expire in 1997 but pointing out that the treaties which gave Britain the sovereignty over Hong Kong Island and Kowloon would remain valid, thus making it necessary to work out a compromise agreement for all of Hong Kong, most likely with the aim of achieving a status with PRC sovereignty but British administration. Only a few days after she had left China, the CCP elite, however, made it crystal clear that this was not the road to be taken: "It must be pointed out that these treaties which involve the Hong Kong area were products of British Imperialism's 'gunboat policy' and invasion of China in the 19th century. . . . The Chinese people have always held that these treaties are illegal and therefore null and void."[40]

During the ensuing Sino-British talks (altogether twenty-two sessions between October 1982 and the end of September 1984), the British side at first attempted to bargain for the abolition of the treaties that secured British sovereignty over Hong Kong Island and Kowloon, together with the expiration of the 1898 lease, in exchange for a continued British administrative presence in the territory of Hong Kong after 1997. This proposal, however, was adamantly refused by the PRC negotiators, and the United Kingdom finally gave in. During a visit to Hong Kong in April 1984, the British foreign secretary, Sir Geoffrey Howe, publicly announced that "it would not be realistic to think of an agreement that provides for continued British administration of Hongkong after 1997."[41]

With this concession, the deadlock in the talks was broken. The position of the PRC, in my view a compromise between the reformist and enlightened Bolshevik groups to which the orthodox Bolsheviks only grudgingly agreed— accepting the fact that they were in the minority concerning this problem— had been accepted by the British, without taking into account the views of the people whose fate was decided in this manner, the Hong Kong populace.

1984–1986

On September 26, 1984, the Sino-British Joint Declaration on Hong Kong was initialed, to be signed on December 19 and ratified by June 30, 1985. Shortly after the initialing of the agreement, the third plenary meeting of the Twelfth CCP Central Committee convened in Peking. On October 20, the plenum passed a "Draft Resolution on the Reform of the Economic System," which introduced sweeping changes in the management and planning structures of the Chinese mainland economy.[42] This resolution was, without doubt, a victory for the reformists around Teng Hsiao-p'ing and Chao Tzu-yang, and they continued their victories with the introduction of sweeping personnel changes in the provincial Party leadership between November 1984 and July 1985. Finally, in the immediate aftermath of the National Delegates' Conference of the CCP, which convened September 18–22, 1985, the strength of the orthodox Bolshevik group on the Politburo was cut from seven to three, or from 29.1 to 15 percent. Since then, the orthodox forces could influence the making of CCP policy only if they joined the enlightened Bolsheviks, and this coalition drew at least some support from the newly emerging group around Hu Yao-pang, the former Communist Youth Corps cadres.

These developments seem to me to suggest that although the political position of Teng never depended on the outcome of the Sino-British talks, the Hong Kong agreement may very well have been viewed by a considerable part of the CCP elite as a personal victory of the two persons who were most directly involved in the negotiations and the forcing of the PRC line on the British, Teng and Chao Tzu-yang. Therefore, the Sino-British agreement on Hong Kong seems to have made a definite impact on PRC domestic politics in 1984 and 1985: It helped to strengthen the positions of Teng and Chao in the intra-elite group configuration. But the agreement was certainly not the only, and hardly the most important, element in the temporary victory of the reformists. At least as important, if not much more so, were the obvious successes of the decollectivization of agricultural production in the framework of continued collective land ownership (i.e., the introduction of a new system of tenancy in China's villages) and the revitalization of the rural as well as the urban economy through the introduction of limited market factors.

Moreover, during the second half of 1985, the impact of the Hong Kong agreement on PRC domestic politics, however important it may have been for some time, began to wear off. Instead, inflation, an upsurge of corruption and black-marketeering to proportions unknown on the Chinese mainland since the final years of the civil war, and a marked decrease in foreign exchange reserves created new problems, which have definitely strengthened the hand of the traditionalist against that of the revisionist forces. By the beginning of 1986, there were increasing indications that a readjustment of the policies of reform was under way, which may well result in a strengthening of the structures of bureaucratic control, though not in very dramatic, or short-term changes.

The ripples of these new waves in the PRC made themselves immediately felt in Hong Kong, too. On November 21, 1985, Hsü Chia-t'un—since 1983 director of the Hong Kong New China News Agency, the highest representative of the CCP elite in the colony—warned, in a short speech, against the formation of political parties and the broadening of voting rights in Hong Kong before 1997.[43] Soon after this speech, political activities in the colony decreased remarkably. Whether or not Hong Kong ever had an impact on PRC domestic politics worth mentioning, there can be no doubt that since the ratification of the Sino-British agreement, the impact of PRC domestic politics on Hong Kong has become rather strong.

The Future

Before I turn to the future prospects of Hong Kong in the light of alternative projections for the future of the political system in the PRC, it seems appropriate to summarize, in five points, the answers found to the question concerning the impact of the Hong Kong problem and the Hong Kong agreement on PRC domestic politics.

1. Between 1949 and 1966, the future of Hong Kong played only an extremely marginal role in PRC politics. The CCP elite had not developed a definite policy concerning the colony, nor was such a policy needed because Hong Kong was not a major concern for the CCP elite.

2. For five months in 1967 the status and the future of Hong Kong became an issue in Chinese factional confrontations, with the Cultural Revolutionary Left instigating and supporting the Hong Kong riots while the more moderate segments of the state administrative machine and a number of regional commanders criticized the leftist policy, abolishing it as soon as they were able to do so. If Hong Kong was a CCP concern during the Cultural Revolution, it was the concern of only a faction.

3. From 1969 to 1982, the problem of the future of Hong Kong did not play even a marginal role in CCP intra-elite politics. Until the British raised the question of how to arrange for Hong Kong's future status, the colony was definitely no major policy concern for the PRC elite.

4. From 1982 to 1984, the Sino-British talks seem to have played a considerable, though not decisive, role in PRC domestic politics, being used as part of larger-scale, intra-elite policy compromises.

5. Although the political position of Teng Hsiao-p'ing definitely did not depend upon the outcome of the Sino-British talks, the agreement between the PRC and the United Kingdom seems to have been viewed by parts of the CCP elite as his and Chao Tzu-yang's personal victory. Thus, the outcome appears to have strengthened their political position. This impact, however, has already started to wear off, and today, the impact of PRC domestic politics on Hong Kong is becoming ever stronger. With the ratification of the Sino-British agreement, the major decisions for the future of Hong Kong have been moved from the international arena to the arena of CCP intra-elite politics.

The last being the case, the future prospects for Hongkong can only be presented by connecting them with the future projections for the political system of the PRC. Since the early 1980s, many Western observers of the Chinese political scene have tended to consider these future projections in terms of only two alternatives: a continuation of the current reformist policies (often called "pragmatic," although hardly anybody has ever made an attempt at a precise definition of that term) or a return to the policies of development by mass mobilization and to the doctrines of Maoism. I suggest that these possibilities are not perceptive enough, although I readily admit that they are very reassuring for any wishful thinkers who dream about a continuation of the policies of reform and the opening toward the West. Instead, it seems to me necessary to present at least four alternative projections for the future of the political system in the PRC:

1. The continuation and further broadening of the policies of reform, resulting in a slow but continuous economic and social progress, which could achieve a thoroughgoing modernization of the Chinese mainland during the first three decades of the twenty-first century.
2. A return to the policy concepts and organization structures, as well as to the doctrines, of late Maoism, which dominated the Chinese scene between 1958 and 1960 and again between 1966 and 1972. This alternative would most probably mean new economic and social crises of immense proportions, and it would postpone the modernization of the Chinese mainland indefinitely.
3. A "freezing" of the reforms in the economy and the society at the present status for a long period. This possibility would call for enhanced bureaucratic control, which, in turn, would clash with the dynamics unleashed by the reforms between 1979 and 1985 and thus provoke a series of domestic political crises with an uncertain outcome.
4. A gradual and slow, but effective, strengthening of the elements of planned economy and bureaucratic control, with the abolition of the most daring reforms, while the policies of a limited opening toward the West and some of the changes introduced on the domestic scene would be sustained, at least for a period of five to ten years. This alternative would result in the development of a partially modernized bureaucratic socialist system, or, in other words, the political, economic, and social present of the USSR would show us the features of the future for the PRC. In this case, a thoroughgoing modernization of the Chinese mainland would have to wait until the second half of the twenty-first century.

Within the framework of these future projections for the political system of the PRC, three alternative future projections for PRC policies toward Hong Kong until the takeover in 1997 and during the first years after that takeover can be proposed. First, if the first projection should materialize, there would be a scrupulous adherence to the Sino-British agreement combined with considerable efforts to ensure the preservation of economic and social stability in Hong Kong. Second, if the second projection should materialize, there would be a sudden turn against the contents of the agreement after about 1990, or at least immediately after 1997, which would trigger a major economic and social crisis in Hong Kong. Third, if the third or the fourth projection should materialize, there would be a general adherence to the agreement until 1997 combined with a rather restrictive, "socialist" interpretation of its contents, which would most probably result in a gradual destabilization of the economy and society of Hong Kong between 1990 and 1997. After the takeover, there would be a definite assertion of the priority of the general provisions in the constitution of the PRC over those of the Basic Law for Hong Kong, which would end the current social status of Hong Kong within a very few years.

Given the current configurations within the CCP leadership, and the general outlook of the younger groups among the ruling elite in the PRC, the fourth projection for the future of the political system of the PRC—the "Sovietization" of China—could have a higher probability than the first. The first projection, currently, could be ranked second in any probability rating; the third could be ranked third; and the second, fourth. Therefore, the third alternative projection for the future development of PRC policies toward Hong Kong would have a higher degree of probability than the other two. For the West, there is very little that can be done to change this outlook. Hence, there is only rather limited room for optimism regarding Hong Kong's future.

Notes

1. Harold C. Hinton, *Communist China in World Politics* (Boston: Houghton Mifflin, 1966), pp. 24, 147, 271, and 407.

2. *Pravda* [Truth] (Moscow), December 13, 1962.

3. *Jen-min jih-pao* [People's daily], Peking (hereafter, *JMJP*), March 8, 1963.

4. "The Proponents of Neo-colonialism," *JMJP*, October 22, 1963.

5. See Franz Michael, "Moscow and the Current Chinese Crisis," *Current History* 53:313 (September 1967), p. 147, and Philip Bridgham, "Mao's Cultural Revolution: Origin and Development," *China Quarterly*, no. 29 (January-March 1967), p. 16.

6. New China News Agency, Peking (hereafter, NCNA), September 29, 1965.

7. For my account of domestic political developments in the PRC, see Jürgen Domes, *The Internal Politics of China, 1949–1972* (London: C. Hurst and Company, 1973), pp. 171-202.

8. *JMJP*, September 17, 1967.

9. For a detailed account of the Cultural Revolutionary developments in Kuangtung, see Jürgen Domes, "General and Red Guards: The Role of Huang Yungsheng and the Canton Military Area Command in the Kuangtung Cultural Revolution," *Asia Quarterly* (Brussels), nos. 1 and 2 (1971).

10. Ibid., no. 2, pp. 125 ff.

11. Ibid., pp. 126 ff.

12. *Hsing-tao jih-pao* [Star Island daily], Hong Kong (hereafter, *HTJP*), May 7, 1967.

13. Ibid., May 11–14, 1967.

14. Ibid., May 23, 1967.

15. These points were soon to become known as the Five Demands.

16. NCNA, May 15, 1967.

17. HTJP, June 15, 1967.

18. Ibid., June 28 and June 29, 1967.

19. Ibid., July 10, 1967.

20. Ibid., July 30, 1967.

21. Ibid., August 1, 1967.

22. Ibid., September 5, 1967.

23. Ibid., September 11, 1967.

24. This document is not yet available to researchers, but the contents of it were quoted by former Red Guard refugees to me during interviews in Hong Kong in September 1972.

25. The English version of Lin Piao's report can be found in *Peking Review*, April 28, 1969, special supplement.

26. For my account of developments from 1969 to 1973, see Jürgen Domes, *China After the Cultural Revolution: Politics Between Two Party Congresses* (London: C. Hurst and Company, 1975), passim; for developments from 1975 to early 1982, see Jürgen Domes, *The Government and Politics of the PRC: A Time of Transition* (Boulder, Colo., and London: Westview Press, 1985), pp. 123–183.

27. "Notice of the Meeting of the Politburo of the CCP Central Committee," December 5, 1980, *Chung-kung yen-chiu/Studies on Chinese Communism* (Taipei), 17:4 (April 1983), pp. 82 f.

28. See "Resolution on Several Problems of Party History Since the Establishment of the PRC, Unanimously Approved by the 6th Plenum of the Eleventh CCP Central Committee," June 27, 1981, *Hung-ch'i* [Red flag] (Peking), no. 13 (1981), pp. 3–27.

29. Figures estimated by Hong Kong police in 1973 (see *Chung-yang jih-pao* [Central daily news], T'aipei, September 12, 1973).

30. Chalmers Johnson, "The Mouse-Trapping of Hong Kong: A Game in Which Nobody Wins," *Issues and Studies* (T'aipei) 20:8 (August 1984), p. 28.

31. See Domes, *Government and Politics of the PRC*, p. 82.

32. Ibid., p. 81.

33. Ibid., pp. 182 f.

34. NCNA, September 12, 1982.

35. JMJP, September 24, 1985.

36. Information by Mr. George L. Hicks on a conversation Li Hsien-nien held with leading Hong Kong property developers in late September or early October 1977.

37. *Cheng-ming* [Debate] (Hongkong), no. 7, (July 1982).

38. See Domes, *Government and Politics of the PRC*, pp. 184–188.

39. JMJP, September 23–25, 1982.

40. NCNA, September 30, 1982.

41. *Times* (London), April 22, 1984.

42. JMJP, October 21, 1984.

43. HTJP, November 22, 1985.

6

An ROC View of
the Hong Kong Issue

Yu-ming Shaw

Hong Kong's Historical Role

Starting in the year 1842, Hong Kong began to play a role in modern Chinese history that was to become an unusually complicated one, and one full of contradictions. To the great majority of Chinese, Hong Kong was the beginning of a series of unequal treaties and the symbol of Western imperialism's incursion into China. To the British, Hong Kong, a British-run crown colony, has long been a bridgehead of trade between the British Empire and China.

However, to the majority Hong Kong's residents, Hong Kong's most important function is that it has offered temporary shelter from the Taiping Rebellion, battles between the Chinese warlords, Japanese aggressions in China, and from tyrannical Communist rule. The refugees of these strifes and their descendants may themselves not necessarily be fully aware of the fact that Hong Kong, during the past one hundred years or so, has played the very significant role of bringing about several major overall changes in the areas of politics, economics, and culture on the Chinese mainland. In other words, Hong Kong has long been a major catalyst of change on the mainland, not simply a passive place of refuge.

Hong Kong as a Political Catalyst

The recent transfers of political power on the Chinese mainland have all been somehow linked to Hong Kong. Over seventy years ago, Hong Kong exercised a great influence in bringing about the collapse of the Manchu Ch'ing dynasty (1644–1911), the first phase of the process beginning in the final years of the dynasty. Both K'ang Yu-wei, leader of the reform faction, and Sun Yat-sen, leader of the revolutionary faction, derived their inspirations for transforming traditional Chinese society from their stays in Hong Kong. K'ang Yu-wei's firsthand observation of Hong Kong in 1879 unambiguously affirmed his dedication to Western studies and his conviction to work for reform.[1] Sun Yat-sen's stay as a student in Hong Kong (1883–1892) confirmed his revolutionary resolution to overthrow the autocratic Manchu rulers.[2] Both leaders independently came to have the same desire, namely, to make all of China as clean, orderly, and efficiently run as Hong Kong was.

Because the Ch'ing government was rapidly becoming more and more impotent in extricating itself from the West's firm grip on China, coupled with the refusal of the Manchu royalty to release political power to Han Chinese, the revolutionary faction under Sun Yat-sen's leadership after 1905 soon became the mainstream of the Chinese political movement, which was strongly supported by the people of Hong Kong. Of the donations by overseas Chinese to finance the eleven revolutionary uprisings, a significant portion came from the Hong Kong area.[3] Hong Kong was also a major source of revolutionary thought and activity, as well as a key base for promoting the revolution and launching uprisings.

After the outbreak of the Hsin-hai Revolution on October 10, 1911, the Revolutionary party finally succeeded in establishing the first republic in Asia, the Republic of China. This action broke the dynastic cycle of Chinese history, in which, it has been said, "there are only revolts, no revolution," and succeeded in implanting a new tradition in China—democracy. Its establishment was also Hong Kong's first major wave of influence on China in the area of politics.

The founding of the republic in 1912 was originally a cause for celebration for the Chinese people; later, however, because of Yuan Shih-k'ai's usurping of power and his ambitions to be emperor, Hong Kong became one of the bases of the Nationalist party (KMT) and supported its revolutionary work in mainland China, for example, the movement to topple Yuan Shih-k'ai and another to protect the constitution. In 1920, over 1,000 machinery workers in Hong Kong staged a major strike lasting nineteen days, virtually paralyzing Hong Kong's transportation and public services. The foreign companies and the British authorities in Hong Kong had no choice but to give in to the workers' demands for a raise (25–30 percent) in order to have these services resumed. This was the first victory of Chinese workers in a major strike called for economic reasons, and it did much to encourage workers in inland China to establish unions for themselves, to organize and unite to strive together for improvements in their life and the protection of their rights. That same winter, the China Seamen's Benevolence Association (Chung-hua Hai-yuan Tz'u-shan Hui) reorganized itself to become the General Industrial Federation of Chinese Seamen (Chung-hua Hai-yuan Kung-yeh Lien-ho Hui), a name chosen by Sun Yat-sen. The federation is commonly referred to in Chinese as the Hai-yuan Kung-hui, and Ch'en Ping-shen was its first chairman. Two years later, seamen in Hong Kong held a second major strike,[4] and the worker organizations later joined the KMT in staging many of its revolutionary activities.

After the outbreak of the incident of May 30, 1925, which sprang forth from a tide of general anti-imperialistic sentiment across the country, Hong

Kong workers, together with Chinese workers in the concessions in Shameen lease, Canton, launched the Great Kwangtung–Hong Kong Strike. Over 100,000 people participated, and the strike lasted sixteen months before it was finally settled in October 1926. The British were never again to belittle the force of the Chinese workers' movement,[5] and its success served to inspire inland workers to action, to the consternation of the warlords. Thus, Hong Kong also played a key role in the Northern Expedition, which was Hong Kong's second wave of influence on the Chinese mainland in the area of politics. The CCP in 1927 also used Hong Kong as the base for its Communist revolution.[6]

In 1946, as the political situation in China deteriorated, the flight of people from the China mainland to escape Communist rule caused Hong Kong's population to leap from 1.55 million in 1950 to 2.237 million within four short years.[7] Thus began the third phase of Hong Kong's reactive relationship with mainland China.

In this phase, millions of originally penniless Hong Kong residents, under the Hong Kong government's "active nonintervention" policy and system of "administrative absorption of politics"[8] and in an environment of free thought and a free economy, succeeded in achieving an economic "miracle out of a bare rock."[9] This success sent a clear message to the people living under Chinese Communist rule on the mainland that Hong Kong was not only a free port but also a "heaven on earth," with no class struggle. At the same time, Hong Kong has acted as a medium in spreading knowledge of the achievements of the Republic of China on Taiwan under the Three Principles of the People, which has made the people in mainland China realize that the socialist road of Marx, Lenin, Stalin, and Mao is not the only possible one for China. At present, Hong Kong still continues to carry out this role. The continuation and intensification of this role of prodding the China mainland into becoming a more democratic and free state[10] will be the task of Hong Kong's fourth phase of influencing mainland Chinese politics.

Hong Kong as an Economic Catalyst

Britain's seizure of Hong Kong was, according to the pretext that Britain gave, a manifestation of the commercial Pax Britannica that put economics before politics.[11] However, with the huge amounts of opium flowing in and the huge amounts of silver flowing out,[12] China's national treasury was in serious straits by the end of the Ch'ing dynasty. Even more serious was the fact that traditional Chinese society was gradually being torn apart at the seams because of an influx of various kinds of inexpensive machine-made foreign goods, which entered the inland market through Hong Kong. In practice, these inexpensive goods made it impossible for locally made goods to compete, a severe blow to the small-farm economy, which was based primarily on agriculture and secondarily on handcrafted goods.[13] Even after Shanghai was opened to international trade in 1856, and this geographically advantaged city downstream of the Yangtze River tended somewhat to gradually replace Hong Kong in its special role, Hong Kong was still the largest entrepôt trade center in southern China.

After 1950, Hong Kong again gradually regained its function in entrepôt trade from Shanghai. At the same time, through a visible trade of goods and an invisible in- and outflow of capital, the connections between Hong Kong and mainland China were drawn even closer. According to one study, of the US$26.5 billion of foreign investments in China from 1979 to the end of 1984, US$6.6 billion, or 25 percent, originated in the Hong Kong–Macao area. Of the US$10.3 billion invested directly by foreign companies, US$6.5 billion, a full 63 percent of the total, stemmed from the same area. Of the US$15.6 billion in foreign investments actually expended by Communist China, overseas capital accounted for approximately two-thirds of the total, but most of this capital originated in Hong Kong. On the other hand, mainland Chinese investment in Hong Kong has in recent years reached HK$30 billion (approximately US$3.84 billion) in enterprises ranging from finance and real estate to department stores and publishing.[14]

At the same time, since the implementation of the so-called open-door policy by the Chinese Communists after 1978, Hong Kong has again begun, in differing degrees, to reassume its role as an entrepôt trade center by exporting various types of consumer items (such as television sets, motorcycles, refrigerators, and tape recorders) to the China mainland. Because the Chinese Communists are now making efforts to reform their system of management, they have in recent years been sending a steady stream of cadres to Hong Kong to "learn from abroad," i.e., to learn capitalist methods of management. From January to December of 1985, the number of people holding a mainland China passport who entered Hong Kong exceeded 100,000.[15] It is still too early to say exactly what kind of and how much influence they will have on their country after returning from their learning experience in Hong Kong, but Hong Kong's aggressive spirit of high efficiency will inevitably exert a considerable amount of psychological pressure on these people. If, after a certain period of time, presently unimaginable changes occur on the mainland, they should not be viewed with too much surprise.

Hong Kong as a Catalyst of Culture and Ideology

Since Robert Morrison introduced the news media into China as a method of imparting new knowledge, all forms of reform thought in China— be it "good words to admonish the age" (Ch'üan-shih liang-yen), which so deeply influenced Hung Hsiu-ch'üan;[16] Wing Yung's sending young people to study in America;[17] Kuo Sung-t'ao's appeal to learn from abroad, or even the north-south news publications Hsün-huan jih-pao [Circulation daily news] founded by Wang T'ao[18] and Young J. Allen's Chinese Globe Magazine (Wan-kuo kung-pao);[19] Ho Kai and Hu Li-huan's new government reforms; K'ang Yu-wei and Liang Ch'i-ch'ao's reform and restoration; or Sun Yat-sen's revolutionary thought—can be traced back to Hong Kong. K'ang Yu-wei and Sun Yat-sen both clearly attested to the fact that the turning point in their thought occurred because of the new knowledge and insights they acquired while in Hong Kong. Hong Kong has thus long served the function of transmitting Western thought to China.

After the establishment of the Chinese republic, this transmission function of Hong Kong was upstaged to a considerable extent by Shanghai and Peking at different points in time. However, since the Communist takeover of the entire Chinese mainland in 1950, followed by suppression of free intellectual thought on the mainland, Hong Kong and the Republic of China on Taiwan have taken over the important role of rebuilding Chinese culture and education. The founding of the *Tsu-kuo chou-k'an* [Motherland weekly], the *Min-chu p'ing-lun* [Democratic review], and the New Asia College were all enlightened actions of intellectuals who were unwilling to live under Chinese Communist rule and subsequently drifted to Hong Kong to sigh about the destruction of Chinese culture. In 1957, Mou Tsung-san, Hsü Fu-kuan, Chang Chün-mai, and T'ang Chün-yi published an article, "Chinese Culture and the World,"[20] in which they reaffirmed the importance of Chinese culture. They formally established a new Confucian school of thought out of their concern for the future development of Chinese culture, and to open up a new area for exploration. Mainland Chinese intellectuals of today have lost their confidence in communism, and even the Chinese culture.[21] Looking to the future, Hong Kong's and Taiwan's new Confucian culture will continue to be a challenging influence on intellectual thought in mainland China, and will undoubtedly serve to hasten the disintegration of the Communist culture in mainland China.

The ROC's Stand on the Hong Kong Issue and Actions It Is Taking

Hong Kong was a product of unequal treaties, and the "abrogation of unequal treaties" was the first and foremost goal of the national revolution.[22] On June 15, 1928, the Nationalist government declared to the world that it was willing, through normal administrative procedures, to revise treaties with each country on a base of equality and mutual respect of sovereignty. On July 7, the Nationalist government declared invalid all unequal treaties that had by that time expired and said that new treaties were to be negotiated; those that had not yet expired were to be revised; and for old treaties that had expired and had yet no new one to replace them, a "temporary regulation" was to be followed.[23] The Nationalist government at this time reopened negotiations with the British regarding recovery of the various leased territories; thus, it has always been one of the fundamental stands of the ROC to reclaim Chinese territories.

In 1930, the Nationalist government officially recovered Wei-hai-wei, which had previously been leased to Britain. The recovery of Hong Kong and Kowloon through peaceful talks was to have been the next task. But because of the occurrence of the Mukden incident on September 18, 1931, this matter was temporarily set aside, under the pressure of the war with the Japanese and their expanded invasion of China.

In 1943 and 1944, when China and Britain negotiated and signed the Abrogation of British Extraterritoriality in China and Other Related Special Privilege Treaties, the ROC requested that the leased territory of Kowloon be included in the conference agenda, but this request was temporarily set aside when Britain refused to agree to it.[24] When the treaty was finally signed on January 11, Foreign Minister Sung Tzu-wen sent an official memorandum to notify the British ambassador to China, Sir Horace James Seymour, of a proposal that "the Chinese Government reserves the right to resubmit at a later date this question [of the Kowloon leased territory rights]" in hopes that the issue of ownership of Hong Kong Island, the southern Kowloon Peninsula, and the New Territories could all be resolved at the same time.[25]

Japan declared its unconditional surrender on August 14, 1945, and Hong Kong, as part of the Chinese war zone, should have been surrendered to China. The troops under Chang Fa-k'uei had already entered the northern portion of the New Territories and should have been able to use the opportunity to retake Hong Kong. However, in the interest of maintaining friendly Sino-British relations, the Nationalist government did not wish to take advantage of the opportunity that the surrender provided by taking unilateral action and reclaiming Hong Kong.[26] Thus, all that transpired at the September 9 ceremony celebrating the Japanese surrender of Hong Kong was the attendance at the ceremony by representatives of both the Chinese and the British governments.[27]

This restraint demonstrates that the ROC has from the outset never abandoned its resolution and efforts to recover Hong Kong but if and when it is to do so, it will be part of an overall action. The Republic of China would in no case rashly attempt to take any action before the time is ripe.

On January 7, 1950, Great Britain was the first democratic country to accord recognition to the Chinese Communist government and break off official diplomatic relations with the Republic of China. This action rendered the ROC unable to continue its efforts to recover Hong Kong. Nevertheless, that fact did not change the ROC's stand on recovering all Chinese territory. However, because the ROC realizes that the political system in force on the China mainland is an unreasonable one, and that the majority of Hong Kong's residents are unwilling to accede to Chinese Communist rule, the ROC is opposed to the return of Hong Kong to the Chinese Communist government.

For this reason, the stand taken by the ROC over the past thirty-plus years has been, there is in fact no "Taiwan problem"; there is only a "China problem."[28] Not until the China problem is completely and satisfactorily resolved can the Hong Kong problem be resolved. In other words, if all the Chinese people were to gain freedom and democracy, the people of Hong Kong would of course be included.

On September 26, 1984, ROC Premier Yü Kuo-hua made a declaration on the Hong Kong question. In addition to declaring nonrecognition of the agreement draft announced by the Chinese Communist and British governments, he announced the following (summarized) steps being taken by the ROC government to assist the people of Hong Kong in their current situation:

1. Continue to expose the Chinese Communists' conspiratorial activities in the Hong Kong–Kowloon area.
2. Continue to promote world support for the protection of freedom and prosperity in Hong Kong; help compatriots in Hong Kong fully express their love for freedom and democracy and their opposition to Communist rule.
3. Utilize various methods and ways to assist and support those people who wish to remain in Hong Kong and actively struggle for freedom.
4. Support the uniting of strength, participation in elections, and striving for the protection of freedom and democracy of those people who wish to remain in Hong Kong.
5. Establishment by the Overseas Chinese Affairs Commission of a Hong Kong Compatriots Relocation Service Center, which is presently providing advice, services, and general assistance for Hong Kong compatriots wishing to settle in Taiwan.
6. Permit Hong Kong compatriots to apply for a multiple entry and exit permit valid for one year.
7. Do its utmost to help those people who plan to move to Taiwan before the Communist takeover scheduled for 1997.
8. Give priority processing and assistance in applying for housing loans to Hong Kong compatriots wishing to settle in Taiwan.
9. Give priority processing and assistance to Hong Kong compatriots wishing to go to Taiwan to invest or trade.
10. Assistance by offshore banking centers to Hong Kong compatriots wishing to deposit funds in Taiwan, which may be taken in or out of the country without restriction.
11. Make priority arrangements for and give assistance to children of Hong Kong compatriots wishing to study in Taiwan.[29]

On January 15, 1986, Premier Yü again explained the position of the ROC government and people that China must be united, but this unification must be under the condition that all Chinese people will be able to live in a free and democratic system and prosperous society. The Chinese Communist policy on Hong Kong is to use Hong Kong's position over the short term to obtain large quantities of foreign exchange, with the goal of gradually incorporating this free area into the Communist totalitarian system, and the ROC cannot accept this policy.[30] At the same time, regarding concrete measures, Premier Yu announced that when necessary, the ROC government could adopt flexible, expedient measures to help professional people from Hong Kong and Kowloon go to the ROC.

The Hong Kong Study Group of the Executive Yuan, made up of various pertinent government officials, has long been looking into various ways to give necessary assistance to the people of Hong Kong to go to Taiwan to live, work, and study.[31] This work and the above measures and declarations all clearly demonstrate that the ROC is putting its full efforts into helping maintain the freedom and well-being of the people of Hong Kong.

A Critique of "One Country, Two Systems" and "Hong Kong Ruled by Hong Kong People"

The slogan "one country, two systems" and the Hong Kong formula have been the focus of Communist China's propaganda in recent years. Teng Hsiao-p'ing first mentioned the idea of "one country, two systems" to a professor from the United States, Winston Yang of Seton Hall University, in June 1983.[32] The Chinese Communists further played it up during the negotiations with Britain over Hong Kong, repeatedly touting it as a reasonable and practical formula. However, judging from its contents, it is in fact unreasonable and impractical.

The idea of "one country, two systems" is established on two basic premises: (1) Mainland China will continue to regard socialism as its principal component and will never evolve into a capitalist society, and (2) "one country, two systems" is a "transitional formula" for the settlement of the Hong Kong and the Taiwan issues. For people who do not believe in Marxism-Leninism-Stalinism and Mao Tse-tung thought, mainland China's adherence to socialism is unreasonable. In the past thirty-some years, the difference in economic development on the two sides of the Taiwan Strait and the bankruptcy of socialism in mainland China have already proved that the socialist system is inefficient, and the Chinese Communist attempt to force people to support that system is irrational.[33] On the other hand, the Republic of China's stand is that a future China must be built on the basis of an open society that is politically democratic and economically free.

The second premise is based on the erroneous analogical deduction that Taiwan, under the rule of the Republic of China, and Hong Kong, under British rule, can be placed on a par. Taiwan and Hong Kong are absolutely different in status. The Republic of China, which was established long before the founding of the Chinese Communist party, has been active in the international arena as a political entity with national sovereignty as well as having an independent defensive capability. The confrontation between the Republic of China and the Peking regime across the Taiwan Strait not only points up the contrast between two different ways of life but also brings into focus the continuous competition between the practice of two different ideologies. Hong Kong is Chinese territory that was seized by imperialist and colonialist Britain under the gunboat policy. Hong Kong is a colony without sovereignty and has no military forces of its own. Hong Kong and the Republic of China thus cannot be put on a par with each other.

According to Professor Byron Weng of the Chinese University of Hong Kong, the very idea of "one country, two systems" is full of problems, because its contents are self-contradictory, because it is based on the predominance of the Peking regime, and because it is supposed to be transitional. It is contradictory because such a highly centralized socialist society as the Peking regime would not, over time, tolerate the practice of the capitalist system in areas under its jurisdiction. Second, the Peking regime insists on its predominance in the implementation of the "one country, two systems" model. If Hong Kong and Taiwan were one day to hold the upper hand politically and assume mainland China's present international leadership role, it is doubtful whether Peking would continue to uphold the "one country, two systems" formula. Finally, if one of the two sides did not "swallow up" the other in the practice of "one country, two systems," the formula should not be "transitional." The Peking regime thus expects that Hong Kong and Taiwan would eventually effect a transition to socialism.[34]

A few years ago, the Chinese Communists proposed to let "Hong Kong be ruled by the Hong Kong people" as a way to put the idea of "one country, two systems" into practice. This proposal, however, is incapable of inspiring much confidence among the people in Hong Kong and elsewhere. Furthermore, since the end of June 1985, on Peking's order, Chinese Communist units in Hong Kong have refrained from mentioning such a measure.[35] In addition, the Peking regime began to change its attitude when quantities of politically awakened bourgeoisie in Hong Kong enthusiastically took part in an indirect election (a political reform) of members to the Legislative Council of Hong Kong. In October 1985, Chi P'eng-fei, director of the Chinese Communist Hong Kong and Macao Affairs Office, asserted that future reforms of Hong Kong's administration should be linked to the Basic Law, which will determine the political system in Hong Kong after 1997.[36] Hsü Chia-t'un, director of the Hong Kong branch of the New China News Agency, made the criticism that the efforts to promote representative government in Hong Kong were not in accordance with the Joint Declaration signed between the Peking regime and . Britain.[37] These comments have helped to dispel the illusion that the Peking regime will not intervene in Hong Kong affairs.

During a visit to Hong Kong in January 1986, Lu P'ing, secretary-general of the Hong Kong and Macao Affairs Office under the Chinese Communist State Council, even described the concept of "Hong Kong ruled by the Hong Kong people" as unscientific[38] and asserted that the idea was not first proposed by Chinese Communist leaders.[39] Liao Ch'eng-chih, the late vice-chairman of the Standing Committee of the National People's Congress and director of the Hong Kong and Macao Affairs Office, had mentioned this disclaimer on November 20, 1982, to a delegation of Hong Kong manufacturers,[40] but Huan Hsiang, Chi P'eng-fei, Teng Hsiao-p'ing, and P'eng Chen had all at one time or another used the same phrase to describe this policy of the PRC toward Hong Kong.[41]

Since the establishment of the Basic Law Drafting Committee in June 1985 and the Basic Law Consultative Committee in December of the same year, many events have led the Hong Kong people to have misgivings about Peking's promise to grant "a high degree of autonomy" to Hong Kong after 1997. For instance, when the Basic Law Consultative Committee elected its Standing Committee members in December 1985, there was an "illegal nomination of candidates by Hsü Chia-t'un," "unanimous approval by acclamation," and the "illegal participation in a meeting by Mao Chun-lien who was not even on the Consultative Committee."[42] These actions violated Hong Kong's tradition of abiding by the rule of law.[43] Current developments in Hong Kong point to the probability that the slogan "Hong Kong ruled by the Hong Kong people" will have to be changed to "Hong Kong ruled by Communist party members in Hong Kong" or even "Hong Kong ruled by Communist party members."

There is further evidence to support that conclusion. First, because of the training in the past thirty-some years of various Chinese Communist units in Hong Kong (including Communist-run schools such as the Heong Dao Middle School), there is in Hong Kong a "fifth column"—even if the Peking regime does not send any cadres to Hong Kong—consisting of several tens of thousands of Communist party members, pro-Communist elements, and employees of Communist-run organizations. In recent years, through the Hong Kong branch of the New China News Agency, the Chinese Communists have even publicized their intention to recruit new Party members in Hong Kong (in the past such work was done only surreptitiously). Second, some high-ranking Chinese Communist cadres have been traveling back and forth between mainland China and Hong Kong to lead existing Communist cadres in Hong Kong and to unite the pro-Communist Hong Kong people so as to realize the "rule of Hong Kong by Communist party members," or the "rule of Hong Kong by cadres from Peking." Quite a number of such Chinese Communist cadres have recently been sent to Hong Kong.[44]

The Republic of China thus believes that the Peking regime has no intention of fulfilling its promises in the Joint Declaration, and that the concepts of "one country, two systems" and "Hong Kong ruled by the Hong Kong people" are just a ruse on the part of the Chinese Communists to annex Hong Kong and to advance the united front work against the Republic of China.

Conclusion

Judging from the current situation in Hong Kong as well as the colony's role in the modern history of China, I subscribe to the following views on the Hong Kong issue.

1. The Chinese Communist government's main purpose in retaking Hong Kong is to gradually transform it from being a free area into one under Communist control, thus removing any threat to the long-term existence of Chinese communism.

2. At present, Hong Kong is the most important point of contact between mainland China and Taiwan. Out of a concern for compatriots in Hong Kong as well as for the purpose of making Hong Kong a springboard in the attempt to spread freedom and democracy to mainland China, the Republic of China will in no case abandon Hong Kong. The ROC is, in addition, continuing to devise various methods to provide its Hong Kong compatriots with effective assistance in their resistance of Chinese Communist oppression.

3. There is no possibility of success for the "one country, two systems" formula advocated by the Chinese Communists because of its many irreconcilable contradictions and difficulties. Thus, Peking's dream to transplant this formula to Taiwan is both unreasonable and impossible. Taiwan under the rule of the Republic of China is a completely different case than that of Hong Kong under British colonial rule. The Republic of China is an international judicial entity. It has an independent government with sovereign rights and a sufficient defensive capability.

4. In the past century or so, Hong Kong has played a catalyzing role in many changes in mainland China and has exercised considerable influence on mainland China in the areas of politics, economics, culture, and ideology. The Chinese Communists, therefore, will discover that Hong Kong, after its reluctant merger with mainland China, is a time bomb, ready to go off at any minute. The Chinese Communists will be unable to stop the flow into China from Hong Kong of the ideas of democracy and freedom, the capitalist system, and even the new Confucianism, which will have the effect of negating Marxist-Leninist-Stalinist and Mao Tse-tung thought. Moreover, the success story of the Republic of China will be gradually spread among the people on the mainland and will become a significant threat to the ideology, political and economic systems, and the life-style of mainland China. The Chinese Communists will find it very difficult to cope with these changes, which will inevitably accelerate the decline of the Communist government. I therefore conclude that the Hong Kong issue of today provides the Republic of China with a turning point in its struggle to bring freedom and democracy to the entire Chinese mainland and to move another step toward the eventual unification of China.

Acknowledgments

The author wishes to express his thanks to his colleagues, Mr. Camoes C.K. Tam, who helped in the writing of the original Chinese version of this paper, and to Ms. Karen S. Chung, Ms. Oi-va Kwan, and Ms. P'ing Ho, who translated it into English.

Notes

1. Hsiao Kung-ch'üan, "Ideal and Reality: Kang Yu-wei's Social Thought," in *Chin-tai ssu-hsiang jen-wu-lun—she-hui chui-i* [Comments on modern intellectuals—

socialism], ed. Hsiao Kung-ch'üan, et al., 4th printing (Taipei: Shih-pao wen-hua Publishing Company, 1985), pp. 45–46.

2. Regarding evidence that Dr. Sun Yat-sen gained inspiration from Hong Kong, see Sun Yat-sen, "Sun Wen Hsüeh-shuo" [Dr. Sun's doctrine], in *Kuo-fu ch'üan-chi* [Complete works of Dr. Sun Yat-sen], comp. Party History Committee of the Kuomintang (Taipei: Party History Committee of the Kuomintang, 1965), vol. 1, pt. 3, pp. 161–163; "We Cannot Construct Our Nation Without Scholarship: A Speech Delivered at Ling-nan College, Canton, on May 7, 1912," in ibid., vol. 2, pt. 8, pp. 18–19; and "The Emergence of Revolutionary Thought: A Speech Delivered at Hong Kong University in February 1923," in ibid., pp. 156–157.

3. Ch'en Shu-ch'iang, "Research on Contributions of Southeast Asian Overseas Chinese During the Revolution of 1911" (Paper delivered to the Symposium on the 1911 Revolution and Overseas Chinese of Southeast Asia, Taipei, Republic of China, February 17–19, 1986), p. 16. Of the approximately HK\$3.94 million contributed to the revolution by overseas Chinese, HK\$1.11 million (28.15 percent) came from the Hong Kong area, the largest amount of contributions from any single area. Also, according to a paper presented at the same conference by Chiang Yung-ching, "Pre-Hsin-hai Revolution Support for Sun Yat-sen's Revolutionary Movement from Southeast Asian Overseas Chinese," p. 15, the largeset amount of contributions from overseas Chinese to sponsor the ten uprisings from the Chung-hsing Hui to the T'ung-meng Hui period came from Thailand and Vietnam; Hong Kong, however, was among the six largest contributors.

4. Ch'en Ming-ch'iu, "The May Fourth Movement and the Labor Movement," in *Wu-szu yen-chiu lun-wen-chi* [A collection of essays on the May Fourth movement], ed. Wang Jung-tsu (Taipei: Linking Publishing Company, 1978), pp. 80–85, and Jean Chesneaux, *The Chinese Labor Movement 1919–1927*, trans. H. M. Wright (Stanford, Calif.: Stanford University Press, 1968), pp. 180–187.

5. Kuo T'ing-i, *Chin-tai Chung-kuo shih-kang* [An outline of modern Chinese history] (Hong Kong: Chinese University Press, 1980), 2:549–551; G. B. Endacott, *A History of Hong Kong*, 2d ed. (Hong Kong: Oxford University Press, 1964), pp. 289–290; and Chesneaux, *Chinese Labor Movement*, pp. 290–318.

6. For example, Liao Ch'eng-chih had been active in Hong Kong for a long time before Japan occupied Hong Kong in December 1941. Liao later fled in disguise to Kwangtung Province and resumed his secret activities there. In May 1942, the Nationalist government captured Liao in Lech'ang in northern Kwangtung Province. At the same time, the government also destroyed the Communist Southern Bureau (Nan-fang-chü), which rendered Kwangtung's Communist party organization empty. Thus, in October 1949, after occupying Canton, the Communists were reluctant to transfer all the personnel of the Hua-shang Pao, the Communist media agency in Hong Kong, to Canton. By this time, the problem of the shortage of Party cadres in Canton had been temporarily resolved (see Warren Kuo, *Analytical History of the Chinese Communist Party*, 4 vols. [Taipei: Institute of International Relations, 1969–1971], 4:453).

7. Cheng Tong Yung, *The Economy of Hong Kong*, rev. ed. (Hong Kong: Far East Publications, 1982), p. 52.

8. Ambrose Y.C. King, "Administrative Absorption of Politics in Hong Kong: Emphasis on the Grass Roots Level," *Asian Survey* 15:5 (May 1975): 422–439.

9. Hsing Mu-huan, "The Miracle of a Rock: The Story of Hong Kong's Economic Growth," *Chung-kuo shih-pao* [The China times] (Taipei), June 18–21, 1982, p. 2.

10. Many of Hong Kong's professionals and intellectuals also maintain similar opinions. For example, references concerning the pressure group Point of Convergence

(hui-tien) are collected in Min-chu kai-ke yü kang-jen-chih-kang—'hui-tien' wen-chien-an [Democratic reforms and Hong Kong ruled by Hong Kong people: The case of Point of Convergence] (Hong Kong: Shu-kuang Press, 1984), p. 1, and Ai Fan (Liu Nai-ch'iang), Kang-jen-chih-kang, hsing! [Hong Kong ruled by Hong Kong people, fine!] (Hong Kong: Kuang-chiao-ching Press, 1984), p. 6.

11. G. B. Endacott, Government and People in Hong Kong, 1841–1962: A Constitutional History (Hong Kong: Hong Kong University Press, 1964), pp. v–vi.

12. The main contributor to Britain's export surplus in its trade with China was the opium trade, however this surplus was not attained through direct trade with China but through other indirect measures. First, Britain exported a large quantity of opium into China through colonial India. Britain then demanded that India pay colonial tribute and loans as well as compensate British investment there, mainly in railway construction. As a consequence of these measures, Britain was able to maintain its superiority in the Anglo-Chinese trade. See Ch'en Tz'u-yü, "A Research on China's Foreign Trade in the Nineteenth Century from the Point of View of Sino-India-British Trade," in Chung-kuo hai-yang fa-chan-shih lun-wen chi [A collection of essays on Chinese maritime development] (Taipei: Institute of the Three Principles of the People, Academia Sinica, 1984), pp. 131–173.

13. Fei Hsiao-t'ung, a noted Chinese sociologist, maintains a similar viewpoint; see his Hsiang-t'u ch-'ung-chien [The reconstruction of rural society] (Shanghai: Observer, 1948), pp. 33–41, 65–78.

14. Wu Chung-lih and Tung Jui-ch'i, A Study on the Relations Between Hong Kong and the Chinese Communists: From an Economic Viewpoint (forthcoming).

15. Sing Tao Jih Pao [Star Island daily] (Hong Kong), January 12, 1986, p. 10.

16. Chien Yu-wen, T'ai-p'ing-t'ien-kuo Ch'üan-shih [A complete history of the Taiping Rebellion] (Hong Kong: Chien-shih Men-chin Book Company, 1963), 1:20–22.

17. Lo Hsiang-lin, Hsiang-kang yü chung-hsi wen-hua chih chiao-liu [Hong Kong and the Sino-Western cultural reciprocity] (Hong Kong: China Society, 1961), pp. 77–122.

18. Ibid., pp. 43–76, and Lin Yu-lan, Hsiang-kang pao-yeh fa-chan-shih [A history of the development of the Hong Kong press] (Taipei: World Book Company, 1977), pp. 10–15.

19. Thomas Lee and Shih Li-tung, Lin Le-chih yü wan-kuo-kung-pao: chung-kuo hsien-tai-hua yün-tung chih ken-yüan [Young J. Allen and the Chinese Globe Magazine: The origin of the Chinese modernization movement] (Taipei: Association of Taipei Journalists, 1977), pp. 16–18, 23–24.

20. T'ang Chün-yi, Shuo Chung-hua-min-tsu chih hua-kuo p'iao-ling [Discussions on the disintegration of the Chinese culture], 2d ed. (Taipei: San-min Bookstore, 1976), pp. 125–192, and Tu Wei-ming, et al., Chung-kuo wen-hua ti wei-chi yü chan-wang—tang-tai yen-chiu yü ch'ü-hsiang [The crisis and future of the Chinese culture—contemporary research and tendencies] (Taipei: Shih-pao wen-hua Publishing Company, 1981), pp. 103–161.

21. Recently, philosophers on the Chinese mainland have again begun to appeal to nationalism. Some discussions concerning this tendency and its characteristics and limits are presented in Fu Wei-hsün, "Comments on the Philosophical Research on the Chinese Mainland," Chung-kuo lun-t'an [The China Forum] (Taipei), no. 241 (1985): 29–33.

22. "Dr. Sun Yat-sen's Will," in Kuo-fu ch'üan-chi, vol. 2, pt. 5, p. 17.

23. Kuo, Chin-tai Chung-kuo shih-kang, p. 623.

24. Wellington Koo, "Wellington Koo on the Negotiations Concerning Hong Kong During World War II," *Ming Pao Monthly* [Light daily monthly] (Hong Kong), no. 225 (1984): 10. This article is a translation from one part of Koo's memoirs.

25. Quoted in Kuan Kuo-hsüan, "From the New Sino-British Equal Treaty to the Sino (Communist China)–British Agreement on Hong Kong," *Chuan-chi wen-hsüeh* [Biographical literature] (Taipei) 46:3 (March 1985): 10.

26. Hungdah Chiu, "A Study on Hong Kong's Legal Status," in *Kuan-yü chung-kuo ling-t'u te kuo-chi-fa wen-t'i lun-chi* [Collection of essays regarding the issue of the Republic of China's territory in international law] (Taipei: Taiwan Commercial Press, 1976), pp. 138–139.

27. Endacott, *History of Hong Kong*, pp. 304–305; G. B. Endacott (edited and with additional materials by Alan Birch), *Hong Kong Eclipse* (Hong Kong: Hong Kong University Press, 1978), pp. 236–240.

28. Chiang Ching-kuo, "The Three Principles of the People Will Eventually Triumph over Communism and Reunify China: President Chiang's Message on the Eve of the National Day," *Chung-yang jih-pao* [Central daily news] (Taipei), October 9, 1984, p. 1, and Sun Yün-hsüan, *China Issue and China's Reunification: Remarks at the Reception Honoring Participants in the 11th Sino-American Conference on Mainland China, June 10, 1982, Taipei* (Taipei: Government Information Office, Republic of China, 1982).

29. *Chung-yang jih-pao*, September 27, 1984, p. 1.

30. Ibid., January 16, 1986, pp. 1, 2.

31. *Lien-he pao* [United daily news] (Taipei), February 4, 1986, p. 1.

32. Teng Hsiao-p'ing, *Chien-she yu Chung-kuo t'e-se te she-hui chu-i* [To construct socialism with Chinese characteristics] (Peking: People's Publishing House, 1984), pp. 17–20.

33. Teng said to Professor Yang: "Of course, it will take time to accomplish the peaceful reunification of China. However, it would be a lie to say that we are not anxious. We are all advanced in years, and of course desire an earlier reunification" (ibid., p. 18).

34. Byron Weng, "My Thoughts on 'One Country, Two Systems': Its Conception, Nature, Contents, Difficulties, and Perspective," *Chiu-shih nien-tai* [The nineties] (Hong Kong), no. 191 (1985): 34–36.

35. Editorial, "The Short Life of the Doctrine 'Hong Kong Ruled by Hong Kong People,'" *Cheng-ming Monthly* (Hong Kong), no. 94 (1985): 3.

36. *Ta Kung Pao* [General daily] (Hong Kong), October 20, 1985, p. 1.

37. Ibid., November 22, 1985, p. 4.

38. *Ming Pao* (Hong Kong), January 10, 1986, p. 1.

39. Ibid., January 12, 1986, p. 2.

40. Ibid.

41. Regarding Huan Hsiang's and Chi P'eng-fei's opinions, see *Ta Kung Pao*, November 22, 1983, p. 1; for Teng Hsiao-p'ing's opinion, ibid., June 28, 1984, p. 1; and for P'eng Chen's opinion, ibid., March 30, 1985, p. 4.

42. *Ming Pao* [Light daily], December 8 and 9, 1985, p. 1. On December 11, 1985, under the pressure of public opinion, the Communists had to reselect their members to the Standing Committee. However, the list of nominees, except for those who renounced their candidacy in order to avoid suspicion, was the same as that advanced by Hsü Chia-t'un and Pao Yü-kang—this was the so-called illegal nomination.

43. Norman Minors, *The Government and Politics of Hong Kong*, 3d ed. (Hong Kong: Oxford University Press, 1982), pp. 70–72, and Endacott, *Government and People in Hong Kong*, pp. 229–247.

44. For a more detailed account, see two special collections compiled by *Chiu-shih nien-tai:* "Chinese Trade Under Uncle's Pressure," no. 181 (1985): 29–44, and "New Image Under Uncle's Pressure," no. 189 (1985): 51–67.

7

Economic Links Among Hong Kong, PRC, and ROC— with Special Reference to Trade

Teh-pei Yu

Over a hundred years ago, Taiwan, Hong Kong, and the Chinese mainland were all part of a united China. In 1842, Hong Kong became a British colony under the Treaty of Nanking, and in 1949, the National Chinese government moved to Taipei when the mainland was taken over by the Communists. The different political and economic systems developed on either side of the Taiwan Strait over the past thirty-seven years are designated the Republic of China (ROC) and the People's Republic of China (PRC).

These three entities—Hong Kong, the ROC, and the PRC—have experienced different processes of economic development in the past four decades. Since World War II, Hong Kong has become one of the world's major centers of trade, finance, and transshipment, and Taiwan has been described as an "economic miracle" because of its high rate of economic growth in the past twenty-five years. The average annual real growth rates for Hong Kong and Taiwan between 1961 and 1985 are as high as 9 percent each, making them two of the "Asian dragons."[1] However, the Soviet-style, centrally planned economic model adopted by the PRC has constrained the economic growth of mainland China. The average growth in its national income was around 6 percent during the same period.[2]

Although the three territories have different political ideologies, they are linked economically with one another. Hong Kong has maintained a very close economic and trading relationship with both the ROC and the PRC, while at the same time it has become the major transshipment center for indirect trade between Taiwan and the Chinese mainland—people in Taiwan are not allowed to trade with the mainland directly for political reasons.

At the third plenary session of the Chinese Communist party's Eleventh Central Committee in December 1978, the PRC decided to adopt an open-door policy in order to attract foreign capital and technology to assist in the country's domestic economic development. The new economic policies on the mainland have further advanced the economic and trading links among the three areas both directly and indirectly.

Politically, the PRC authorities have nullified the unequal treaties forced on the Chinese by foreign powers in the past. For example, they have regained sovereignty over Hong Kong beginning July 1, 1997. According to the Joint Declaration initialed by the PRC and Britain on September 26, 1984, Hong Kong will be treated as a special administrative region under the PRC and its capitalist system and way of life will be allowed to continue for fifty years.

What are the economic prospects for Hong Kong after 1997? What changes might take place in the Hong Kong-Taiwan-mainland China economic and trade relationships? These are the questions that all Chinese and people all over the world are asking. This chapter will incorporate two themes: first, a review of the three areas' trading relations over the past four decades; second, a projection of their trade ties in the near future.

Economic and Trade Links
Between Hong Kong and the PRC

Historically, Hong Kong and the Chinese mainland were separated, both economically and politically, over a hundred years ago. And yet, in the past forty years they have depended heavily on each other, especially economically. First, the PRC has been an important source of human capital and a supplier of natural resources for Hong Kong during the latter's postwar economic development process. Since the late 1940s, there has been a large influx of mainlanders into Hong Kong, and they have supplied that labor market with an abundance of skilled and unskilled labor. As a result, wages have increased very slowly in the territory in comparison with other developing countries.

Second, poor land structure has limited Hong Kong's agricultural development. Therefore, 80 percent of all agricultural raw materials and food products have to be imported, and 50 percent of these imports come from the mainland. An additional consideration is that raw materials and consumer goods from the PRC are 25–50 percent cheaper than those from other sources.[3] Both the slow increase in local wages and the low price of imported raw materials and food products have contributed to the high competitiveness of Hong Kong's exports in the world market.

The PRC has played an important role in Hong Kong's import and export business over the past forty years. At the end of the 1940s, Communist China's internal chaos caused it to isolate itself from the rest of the world, and Hong Kong, because of its geographic position, became the PRC's only link with the rest of the world.

From Table 7.1, one can see that the volume of trade between Hong Kong and the Chinese mainland grew at an average annual rate of 53 percent between 1949 and 1951. Reexports from Hong Kong to the Chinese

TABLE 7.1. Trade between Hong Kong and mainland China, 1947–1984 (Unit: 100 million HK$)

Year	Total Trade Between HK and MC	Growth Rate of Trade Between HK and MC (%)	Trade Between HK and MC/Total Trade of HK (%)	Rank of HK's Trade with MC	IM from MC	Growth Rate of IM from MC (%)	IM from MC/HK's Total IM (%)	Rank of HK's IM from MC	EX to MC	Growth Rate of EX to MC (%)	EX to MC/HK's Total EX (%)	Rank of HK's EX to MC out of Total EX	HK's REX to MC	Growth Rate of HK's REX to MC (%)	HK's REX to MC/HK's Total REX (%)	Rank of HK's REX to MC out of Total HK's REX
1947	6.49		23.5	1	3.82		24.6	1	2.67		21.9	1				
1948	7.11	9.55	19.4	1	4.31	12.83	20.7	1	2.80	4.87	17.7	1				
1949	11.78	65.68	23.2	1	5.93	37.59	21.6	1	5.85	108.93	25.2	1				
1950	20.43	73.43	27.2	1	7.83	32.04	20.7	1	12.60	115.38	33.9	1				
1951	24.67	20.75	26.5	1	8.63	10.22	17.7	1	16.04	27.3	36.2	1				
1952	13.50	-45.28	20.2	1	8.30	-3.82	22.0	1	5.20	-67.58	17.9	2				
1953	13.97	3.48	21.1	1	8.57	3.25	22.1	1	5.40	3.85	19.8	1				
1954	10.83	-22.48	18.5	1	6.92	-19.25	20.1	1	3.91	-27.59	16.2	1				
1955	10.80	-0.28	17.3	1	8.98	29.77	24.1	1	1.82	-53.45	7.2	5				
1956	11.74	8.70	15.1	1	10.38	15.60	22.7	1	1.36	-25.27	4.2	7				
1957	12.54	6.81	15.4	1	11.31	8.96	22.0	1	1.23	-9.56	4.1	7				
1958	15.53	23.84	20.5	1	13.97	23.52	30.4	1	1.56	26.83	5.2	6				
1959	11.48	-26.08	14.0	1	10.34	-25.98	20.9	1	0.09	-94.23	0.4	37	1.05		10.6	3
1960	13.06	13.76	13.3	2	11.86	14.70	20.2	1	0.13	44.44	0.5	30	1.07	1.9	10.0	3
1961	11.27	-13.71	11.4	3	10.28	-13.32	17.2	1	0.08	-38.46	0.3	41	0.91	-14.95	9.2	3
1962	12.98	15.17	11.7	4	12.13	18.00	18.2	1	0.08	0	0.2	45	0.77	-15.38	7.2	3
1963	15.57	19.95	12.6	3	14.87	22.59	20.1	1	0.08	0	0.2	47	0.62	-19.48	5.3	4
1964	20.30	30.38	14.2	2	19.70	32.48	23.0	1	0.13	62.50	0.3	36	0.47	-24.19	3.5	8
1965	23.94	17.93	15.5	2	23.22	17.87	25.9	1	0.18	38.46	0.4	34	0.54	14.89	3.6	8
1966	28.38	18.55	16.1	2	27.69	19.25	27.4	1	0.15	-16.67	0.3	36	0.54		2.9	9
1967	23.30	-17.90	12.1	3	22.82	-17.59	21.8	1	0.06	-0.60	0.1	65	0.42	-22.22	2.0	13
1968	24.74	6.18	10.7	4	24.29	6.44	19.5	2	0.09	50.00	0.1	60	0.36	-14.29	1.7	16
1969	27.37	10.63	9.7	4	27.00	11.16	18.1	2	0.07	-22.22	0.1	73	0.30	-16.67	1.1	20
1970	28.94	5.74	8.8	4	28.30	4.81	16.1	2	0.30	328.57	0.2	38	0.34	13.33	1.2	20

Year															
1971	33.92	17.21	9.1	4	33.30	17.67	16.4	2	0.19	-36.67	0.1	51	0.43	26.47	1.3	19
1972	39.50	16.45	9.6	3	38.47	15.53	17.7	2	0.21	10.53	0.1	47	0.82	90.70	2.0	13
1973	59.05	49.49	10.7	3	56.34	46.45	19.4	2	0.49	133.33	0.3	35	2.22	170.73	3.4	7
1974	62.87	6.47	9.8	3	59.91	6.34	17.6	2	0.99	102.04	0.4	33	1.97	-11.26	2.8	8
1975	69.70	10.86	11.0	3	68.05	13.59	20.3	2	0.28	-71.72	0.1	27	1.37	30.46	2.0	13
1976	79.08	13.46	9.3	3	77.61	14.05	17.9	2	0.24	-14.29	0.1	30	1.23	-10.22	1.4	17
1977	82.88	4.81	8.9	3	80.82	4.14	16.6	2	0.31	29.17	0.1	32	1.75	42.28	1.8	14
1978	108.45	30.85	9.3	3	105.50	30.54	16.7	2	0.81	161.29	0.2	24	2.14	22.29	1.6	15
1979	170.48	57.20	10.5	3	151.30	43.41	17.6	2	6.03	644.44	1.1	15	13.15	514.49	6.6	6
1980	281.95	65.39	13.43	3	219.48	45.06	19.66	1	16.05	166.17	2.35	8	46.42	253.00	15.44	1
1981	404.78	43.56	15.54	2	295.10	34.45	21.33	1	29.24	82.22	3.64	5	80.44	73.29	19.27	1
1982	447.33	10.51	16.55	2	329.35	11.61	23.05	1	38.06	30.16	4.58	4	79.92	-0.65	18.02	1
1983	612.37	36.89	18.22	2	428.31	30.05	24.41	1	62.23	63.50	5.96	4	121.83	52.44	21.64	1
1984	951.00	55.30	21.38	2	557.53	30.17	24.96	1	112.83	81.31	8.18	3	280.64	130.35	33.61	1

Source: *Hong Kong Economic Yearbook* (Hong Kong: Sing Jao Jih Pao Press, 1981–1984).

mainland grew even more, however, and this reexport experience was the foundation of Hong Kong's role as an important entrepôt in the world market later on.

In 1951, the United Nations imposed a trade embargo on mainland China, which caused the trade flow between Hong Kong and the mainland to drop drastically, plummeting by as much as 45.3 percent in 1952. The trade flow started to pick up again in 1956 and reached an annual growth rate of 23.8 percent in 1958 despite the 1957–1958 world economic recession. Briefly speaking, in the 1950s, trade (imports and exports plus reexports) between Hong Kong and mainland China fluctuated, and reexports to the Chinese mainland withered.

This phenomenon slowed Hong Kong's economic growth in the 1950s, but it also forced the colony to beef up the development of labor-intensive processing industries, especially in the areas of textiles, plastics, etc., and products from these industries were Hong Kong's main exports in the 1960s. The territory's economic development strategies eventually changed the structure of its export commodities, which, in turn, led to a rapid growth in the economy in the following years.

In 1949, mainland China's economy was reconstructed according to a policy of self-reliance plus economic aid from the Soviet Union. At the end of the 1950s, the Soviets cut off their aid. The lack of financial support and the failure of the Great Leap Forward forced mainland China to revise its economic and trade relationships with the rest of the world by shifting its close economic links with the Soviet Union to Western countries and Japan. However, during the Cultural Revolution in the 1960s, the PRC's economic ties with the Soviet Union and its East European allies were reestablished. Even during the period of 1960–1977, trade between Hong Kong and mainland China still grew at an annual rate of 12.5 percent; the figure for Hong Kong's exports to the mainland was 33 percent, and that for reexports, 13 percent.

Generally speaking, mainland China was Hong Kong's biggest trade partner between 1947 and 1959. However, the trade growth slowed down after this and in 1977, the PRC ranked as Hong Kong's third-biggest trade partner. A breakdown of the trade between the two territories suggests that mainland China was Hong Kong's most important export market in the late 1940s. However, the mainland's ranking gradually fell to forty-seventh in 1963, dropped to seventy-third in 1969, and rose again to thirty-second in 1977. The PRC was the third-largest market for Hong Kong's reexported goods in 1959, but later the growth rate of those reexports began to decrease, and the PRC was the fourteenth-largest buyer in 1977.

However, after 1977 trade between the PRC and Hong Kong started to grow rapidly. During the period 1978–1984, the average annual growth rate was 42.8 percent, of which imports from mainland China grew by an average of 32.2 percent and exports to the PRC, by an average of 175.6 percent. Entrepôt trade also expanded by an annual average of 149.3 percent during the same period. This trade growth was due to mainland China's modernization programs, which began with the economic reform of 1978. Changes in economic policies and strategies have forced the PRC to depend heavily on foreign capital and technology. Given Hong Kong's geographic location and its role as an important financial and trade center in the world market, the territory may be expected to play an even more significant role as a major supplier of capital and as an entrepôt trade center for the PRC.

From 1979 to 1983, the PRC attracted US$2.6 billion in foreign investment, 60 percent of which was from Hong Kong.[4] About 37.6 percent of the foreign investment went to the special economic zones, especially Shenzhen, and more than 90 percent of the foreign investment in Shenzhen was from Hong Kong. The rest, 62.4 percent, was distributed among major inland cities and along the coast. In Shanghai, 40 percent of the foreign investment came directly from Hong Kong.[5]

On the other hand, capital has also flowed from the PRC to Hong Kong. The PRC's investment in Hong Kong has taken two main forms: banking and real estate. By increasing the number of its banks in Hong Kong, mainland China has introduced a substantial amount of capital into the British colony, and by using large amounts of capital to speculate in the Hong Kong property market, the PRC has made huge profits. For example, between 1977 and 1980, the mainland authorities bought HK$10 billion worth of property to boost real estate prices.[6]

According to the PRC's official figures, the mainland has invested US$5 billion in more than 300 different businesses in Hong Kong while Hong Kong's investment on the mainland is only US$4.5 billion.[7] Moreover, the oil drilling in the South China Sea might also be favorable to Hong Kong's economy. Given the colony's natural deep harbor, good communications facilities, experience in shipbuilding and ship maintenance, and other advantages, Hong Kong could become one of mainland China's logistic bases for oil. It has been reported that the PRC will invest US$2 billion in its oil bases, and it has been estimated that about 25 percent of this money will go to Hong Kong.[8] This investment will not only assist Hong Kong's economic growth but will also strengthen economic relations between the two parties. In 1984, mainland China and Hong Kong signed an agreement to establish joint businesses in ship maintenance, oil exploitation, and other areas.[9]

The above analysis seems to suggest that the PRC has been gradually getting involved in Hong Kong's economic activities according to a well-planned strategy since the late 1970s. The expansion of trade and business cooperation between the two territories will continue if the PRC continues its open-door policies, and the faster the expansion, the easier the integration of these two economies will be. A high degree of economic integration will help to ease political tension that might arise at the time of the takeover of Hong Kong in 1997.

Economic Relations Between Hong Kong and Taiwan

Hong Kong is Taiwan's third-largest trade partner, although the trade between them has accounted for only 5 percent of Taiwan's overall trade in recent years (Table 7.2). Hong Kong is also Taiwan's third-largest market, and the trade surplus is in Taiwan's favor. Hong Kong's importance lies in the fact that Taiwan has been using its trade surpluses with the colony and the United States to balance its large deficit with Japan.

In addition to being a surplus producer, Hong Kong is also a major entrepôt for Taiwan's exports to the rest of the world. As shown in Table 7.3, 90 percent of Taiwan's exports to Hong Kong were for local consumption prior to 1979, but since 1980, this percentage has declined to between 70 and 80 percent.

Imports from Hong Kong account for between 1 and 2 percent of Taiwan's total imports, and statistics show that approximately 70 percent of Taiwan's imports from Hong Kong actually originate in a third country (see Table 7.4). It is clear that in the period 1974–1983 Hong Kong played a more significant role as a market for Taiwan than as a supplier.

There is also a movement of capital between Hong Kong and Taiwan. Investment from Hong Kong fluctuated during the 1974–1983 period with a 3 percent average decrease annually, but it dropped substantially in 1982 and 1983, by 37.7 percent and 28.1 percent, respectively. This phenomenon can probably be explained by the talks on the future of Hong Kong that were going during that period. The outflow of capital from Hong Kong has mainly gone to the United States, Canada, Singapore, and Australia; Taiwan is not considered a desirable place for investment. Most Hong Kong people feel that a PRC takeover of Taiwan along the lines of the so-called Hong Kong formula is probable, so to minimize risk to their capital, they prefer countries other than Taiwan.[10] Prior to 1978, most of Hong Kong's investment in Taiwan was concentrated in plastics, textiles, and other labor-intensive industries; since then, investment has gradually switched to chemicals, electronics, transportation, and services. In addition, most of Hong Kong's investment goes to small- and medium-sized enterprises.

Capital also flows from Taiwan to Hong Kong. During the period 1974–1983, the average annual growth rate of Taiwan's investment in Hong Kong was 54.2 percent, but the high growth dropped rapidly to 1.1 percent in 1982 and 0 percent in 1983. Again, the slowdown in Taiwan's investment in Hong Kong was mainly caused by uncertainty about Hong Kong's future during the talks between the PRC and Britain.

The prospects for economic relations between Taiwan and Hong Kong are not very promising if the political situation on either side of the Taiwan Strait does not change much before 1997. If Taiwan were united with mainland China, its trade with Hong Kong would be considered a domestic economic activity. However, if the ROC government continues to refuse to do business with the Chinese Communists, Taiwan will lose a major export market in Hong Kong. However, Taiwan's imports from Hong Kong would not be seriously affected, since 80 percent of these are indirectly supplied by third countries and Taiwan could always buy them directly, or look for another entrepôt, although the costs would be higher.

Indirect Trade Between the ROC and the PRC

Officially, Taiwan has banned trade with mainland China since 1949, although certain government agencies are allowed to buy mainland commodities via Hong Kong. However, the products purchased from mainland China are limited to those that are either unavailable locally or whose local supply is inelastic. However, the Taiwan authorities have no way of controlling the products once they are shipped to Hong Kong, and they are well aware that they are dealing with mainland China. Taiwan's trade with the mainland via Hong Kong continued for quite a long time without its volume growing significantly. However, the open-door policy that affects the PRC's foreign trade in general inevitably affects its trade with Taiwan.

The growth of Taiwan-mainland trade through Hong Kong has been phenomenal: Between 1980 and 1984, the annual growth in indirect trade between these two areas was 139 percent (see Tables 7.5 and 7.6). Taiwan has become the leading source of Hong Kong's reexports to the mainland since 1980, and Taiwan's dominant role in the reexport trade is primarily attributed to the competitiveness of its products compared to those from Japan and South Korea. The comparatively closer and stronger ties between traders in Taiwan and Hong Kong have also helped promote the trade.

The extent of the price advantage or disadvantage of Taiwan products over products from other countries is indicated by the ratios of the unit values of selected commodities. Commodities from Taiwan and three other places of origin—South Korea, Hong Kong, and Japan—were reshipped to mainland China (see Table 7.7). If the ratio exceeds 1, the implication is that the Taiwan commodity enjoyed a price advantage; if the ratio is under 1, Taiwan suffered from a price disadvantage. It is evident that Taiwan has enjoyed large price advantages over Japan and Hong Kong and a slight advantage over South Korea.

In addition, the political policies and tactics adopted by the PRC have also influenced indirect trade. In order to create an impression, both domestically and internationally, that the political unification of the mainland and Taiwan has been going on through an expansion of indirect trade, the PRC started encouraging indirect trade through Hong Kong and Macao in 1978. This policy became obvious in 1980 when the PRC government removed the export tax on mainland products sold to Taiwan and the import duties on Taiwan goods. Consequently, indirect trade grew by as much as 1,032 percent that year.

However, this duty-free policy left customs officials confused and gave rise to speculation and uncertainty among Hong Kong reexporters. The policy cost the PRC government tremendous losses in tax revenues, and the difficulty faced by customs officials in carrying out the rules forced the mainland government to change the policy in May 1981.

TABLE 7.2. Trade between Hong Kong and Taiwan, 1950–1983 (Unit: 100 million HK$)

| | Total Trade | | | | Imports | | | | Exports | | | | | | | |
| | | | | | | | | | of HK Products | | | | Reexports | | | |
	Total Trade Between T and HK	Growth Rate of HK's Trade to T (%)	Percentage of HK-T Trade out of HK Total Trade (%)	Rank of Trade to T out of HK's Total Trade	IM from T	Growth Rate of IM of IM From T (%)	IM From T/HK's Total IM (%)	Rank of IM from T out of HK's Total IM	EX to T	Growth Rate of EX to T (%)	EX to T/HK's Total EX (%)	Rank of HK's EX to T out of HK's Total EX	HK's REX to T	Growth Rate of HK's REX to T (%)	HK's REX to T/ HK's Total REX (%)	Rank of HK's REX to T out of Total HK's REX
1950	2.76		3.7	8	0.75		2.0	12	2.01		5.4	5				
1951	2.02	-26.81	2.2	10	0.62	-17.33	1.3	19	1.39	-30.85	3.1	9				
1952	2.52	24.75	3.8	8	0.45	-27.42	1.2	19	2.07	48.92	7.1	5				
1953	1.80	-28.57	2.7	9	0.74	64.44	1.9	12	1.06	-48.79	3.9	7				
1954	1.27	-29.44	2.2	10	0.47	-36.49	1.4	17	0.80	-24.53	3.3	8				
1955	0.77	-39.37	1.2	12	0.40	-14.89	1.1	18	0.37	-53.75	1.5	15				
1956	0.98	27.27	1.3	12	0.51	27.50	1.1	19	0.47	27.03	1.5	15				
1957	1.33	35.71	1.6	11	0.72	41.18	1.4	15	0.61	29.79	2.0	14				
1958	1.12	-15.79	1.5	10	0.50	-30.56	1.1	18	0.62	1.64	2.1	11				
1959	1.61	43.75	2.0	10	1.02	104.00	2.1	13	0.10	-83.87	0.4	35	0.49		4.9	6
1960	2.00	24.22	2.0	10	1.24	21.57	2.1	11	0.14	40.00	0.5	28	0.62	26.53	5.8	5
1961	2.17	8.50	2.2	10	1.54	24.19	2.6	8	0.10	-28.57	0.3	32	0.53	14.52	5.3	5
1962	1.99	-8.29	1.8	10	1.36	-11.69	2.0	10	0.09	-10.00	0.3	44	0.55	3.77	5.1	6
1963	2.31	16.08	1.9	9	1.72	26.47	2.3	10	0.09	0	0.2	43	0.50	9.10	4.3	5
1964	2.48	7.36	1.7	10	1.78	3.49	2.1	9	0.15	66.67	0.3	34	0.55	10.00	4.1	7
1965	2.40	-3.23	1.5	10	1.54	-13.48	1.7	10	0.17	13.33	0.3	33	0.69	25.45	4.6	5
1966	2.66	10.83	1.5	11	1.69	9.74	1.7	11	0.25	47.06	0.4	29	0.72	4.35	3.9	6
1967	3.91	46.99	2.0	10	2.60	53.85	2.5	8	0.47	88.00	0.7	19	0.84	16.67	4.0	5
1968	5.78	47.83	2.5	8	4.13	58.85	3.3	5	0.65	38.30	0.8	15	1.00	19.05	4.7	5
1969	7.14	23.53	2.5	7	5.02	21.55	3.4	6	0.87	33.85	.8	17	1.25	25.00	4.7	5
1970	11.21	57.00	3.4	6	8.20	63.35	4.7	5	1.47	68.97	1.2	10	1.54	23.20	5.3	5

Year															
1971	14.05	25.33	3.8	6	9.92	20.98	4.9	5	2.13	44.90	1.5	9	2.00	29.87	5.9	5
1972	18.93	34.73	4.6	6	13.09	31.96	6.0	5	2.33	9.39	1.5	10	3.51	75.50	8.4	4
1973	27.49	45.22	5.0	6	16.86	28.80	5.8	5	3.90	67.38	2.0	9	6.73	91.74	10.3	3
1974	28.19	2.55	4.4	6	17.65	4.69	5.2	6	3.62	-7.18	1.6	9	6.92	2.83	9.7	3
1975	27.79	-1.42	4.4	6	19.43	10.08	5.8	4	2.36	-34.81	1.0	10	6.00	13.29	8.6	3
1976	41.92	50.85	4.9	6	30.57	57.33	7.1	4	3.20	35.59	1.0	11	8.15	35.83	9.1	4
1977	45.01	7.37	4.8	7	32.54	6.44	6.7	4	3.75	17.19	1.1	12	8.72	6.99	8.9	5
1978	59.89	33.06	5.1	7	42.57	30.82	6.8	4	5.11	36.27	1.3	12	12.21	40.02	9.3	4
1979	84.70	41.43	5.2	5	60.35	41.77	7.0	4	7.06	38.16	1.3	14	17.30	41.80	8.6	4
1980	110.21	30.12	5.3	6	79.61	31.91	7.1	4	8.36	18.41	1.2	16	22.29	28.84	7.4	5
1981	141.41	28.31	5.4	6	107.62	35.18	7.8	4	9.61	14.92	1.2	16	24.20	8.57	5.8	6
1982	138.87	-1.80	5.1	5	101.98	-5.24	7.1	5	10.27	6.87	1.2	14	26.62	10.00	6.0	5
1983	172.04	23.89	5.1	5	124.48	22.06	7.1	4	13.02	26.79	1.2	13	34.54	29.75	6.1	5

Source: *Hong Kong Economic Yearbook* (Hong Kong: Sing Jao Jih Pao Press, 1981–1984).

TABLE 7.3. Taiwan's exports to Hong Kong and reexports via Hong Kong, 1971–1984
(Unit: million HK$)

	(1) Total Exports to HK	(2) Growth Rate of (1)	(3) Reexports via Hong Kong	(4) Growth Rate of (3)	(5) Direct Exports to HK[a]	(6) Growth Rate of (5)	(7) [(3)/(1)]x 100%
1971	991		76		915		7.7
1972	1,309	32.09	118	55.26	1,191	30.16	9.0
1973	1,686	28.80	177	50.	1,509	26.70	10.5
1974	1,765	4.69	243	37.29	1,522	0.86	13.8
1975	1,943	10.08	196	–19.34	1,747	14.78	10.1
1976	3,057	57.33	258	31.63	2,799	60.22	8.4
1977	3,254	6.44	362	40.31	2,892	3.32	11.1
1978	4,257	30.82	402	11.05	3,855	33.30	9.4
1979	6,035	41.77	898	123.38	5,137	33.26	14.9
1980	7,961	31.91	2,134	137.64	5,827	13.43	26.8
1981	10,762	35.18	3,379	58.34	7,383	76.70	31.4
1982	10,198	–5.24	2,500	–26.01	7,698	4.27	24.5
1983	12,448	22.06	2,573	2.92	9,875	28.28	20.7
1984	17,347	39.36	3,327	29.30	14,020	41.97	19.2

[a](5) = (1) – (3)

Sources: *Hong Kong Review of Overseas Trade* (1973–1984), *Hong Kong External Trade Year Book* (1981), Hong Kong government, Census and Statistics Department.

TABLE 7.4. Taiwan's imports from Hong Kong and reimports via Hong Kong, 1971–1984
(Unit: million HK$)

	(1) Total Import from HK	(2) Growth Rate of (1)	(3) Imports of HK's Products	(4) Growth Rate of (3)	(5) Reimports via Hong Kong	(6) Growth Rate of (5)	(7) [(5)/(1)]x 100%
1971	413		213		200		48.4
1972	584	13.08	233	9.39	351	75.5	60.1
1973	1,063	82.02	390	67.38	673	91.74	63.3
1974	1,054	–0.85	362	–7.18	692	2.82	65.7
1975	836	–20.68	236	–34.81	600	–13.3	71.8
1976	1,135	35.77	320	35.59	815	35.83	71.8
1977	1,247	9.87	375	17.19	872	6.99	69.9
1978	1,732	38.89	511	36.27	1,221	40.02	70.5
1979	2,436	40.65	706	38.16	1,730	41.69	71.0
1980	3,065	25.82	836	18.41	2,229	28.84	72.7
1981	3,381	10.31	961	14.95	2,420	8.57	71.6
1982	3,689	9.11	1,027	6.87	2,662	1.10	72.2
1983	4,756	28.92	1,302	26.78	3,454	29.75	72.6
1984	6,479	36.23	1,611	56.86	4,868	40.94	75.1

Source: *Hong Kong Review of Overseas Trade* (1973–1984).

TABLE 7.5. Hong Kong's reexports of Taiwan origin to mainland China (Unit: million HK$)

	(1) HK's REX Value of Taiwan Origin to Mainland China (at current prices)	(2) Rate of Growth	(3) HK's REX Value of Taiwan Origin (at current prices)	(4) [(1)/(3)]/100%
1974	0.048		243.34	0.20
1975	0.068	41.0	191.20	0.40
1976	0.013	−81.0	257.58	0.005
1977	0.154	1,085.0	362.08	0.40
1978	0.240	56.0	402.23	0.60
1979	106.517	44,282.0	898.10	11.86
1980	1,205.407	1,032.0	2,134.0	56.47
1981	2,182.308	81.0	3,379.0	64.58
1982	1,263.944	−42.0	2,500.0	50.56
1983	1,226.541	−3.0	2,573.0	47.67
1984	3,327.000	171.0		

Sources: Hong Kong government, Census and Statistics Department; Ronald Hsia, *The Entrepot Trade of Hong Kong with Special Reference to Taiwan and the Chinese Mainland* (Seattle: University of Washington Press, 1984).

TABLE 7.6 Hong Kong's reexports of mainland China origin to Taiwan (Unit: million HK$)

	(1) HK's REX Value of China Origin to Taiwan (at current prices)	(2) Rate of Growth	(3) HK's REX Value of China Origin (at current prices)	(4) [(1)/(3)]x100%
1974	105.97		1,582.22	6.70
1975	129.17	22.0	1,743.02	7.41
1976	191.93	49.0	2,402.35	7.99
1977	142.77	−26.0	2,491.54	5.73
1978	218.44	53.0	3,658.99	5.97
1979	279.17	28.0	5,663.50	4.93
1980	390.54	40.0	8,393.90	4.65
1981	426.60	9.0	12,834.0	3.32
1982	546.05	28.0	14,694.0	3.72
1983	698.33	28.0	19,681.0	3.55
1984	990.00	43.0		

Sources: Hong Kong government, Census and Statistics Department; Ronald Hsia, *The Entrepot Trade of Hong Kong with Special Reference to Taiwan and the Chinese Mainland* (Seattle: University of Washington Press, 1984).

TABLE 7.7. Price ratio of selected commodities exported/reexported from Hong Kong to mainland China, 1981 (Price ratio for Taiwan products = 1.00)

	Place of Origin		
	S. Korea	Hong Kong	Japan
Plywood	1.40	2.17	
Woolen yarn	0.99	0.90	1.12
Nylon grey yarn	1.03	1.45	1.04
Terylene grey yarn	1.40	1.03	
Orlon grey yarn	0.76	1.09	1.15
Orlon yarn, other than grey	0.90	1.12	1.16
Nylon woven fabric	0.62	0.79	1.29
Terylene woven fabric	0.76	0.82	1.06
Polyester knitted fabric	1.10	1.26	0.95
Sewing machines (household)			1.18
Television receivers (monochrome)	1.23	1.41	1.67
Television picture tube (cathode ray)	0.98		1.01
Bicycles		1.48	3.35
Umbrellas		0.93	

Source: Ronald Hsia, *The Entrepôt Trade of Hong Kong with Special Reference to Taiwan and the Chinese Mainland* (Seattle: University of Washington Press, 1984), p. 60.

In addition, at the end of 1981, there was an apparent rise in trade protectionism on the part of the PRC. All of these factors led to a decline in the growth of indirect trade in 1982 and 1983 (42 percent and 3 percent, respectively). The mainland's temporary easing of import controls in 1984, done in order to moderate a high level of domestic inflation, brought about another great leap in its trade with Taiwan, which grew by a striking 171 percent in that year (see Table 7.5). Obviously, the frequent and sudden changes in the PRC's trade policies have contributed to the instability of Taiwan's reexports to the mainland.

Table 7.6 shows the volume of mainland Chinese products shipped to Taiwan via Hong Kong from 1974 to 1984. This trade has grown rapidly since the beginning of 1978 with an average annual growth of 32.7 percent. However, the proportion of mainland Chinese products reexported to Taiwan in Hong Kong's overall reexports of mainland China's products has remained quite stable since 1978—growing from between 3.3 and 6.0 percent. In other words, from the mainland's point of view, the possibility of depending on Taiwan as a major market is very low.

The structure of major commodities in the most recent trade between the mainland and Taiwan via Hong Kong is given in Tables 7.8 and 7.9, and a comparison of the two tables reveals a striking contrast. The flow from mainland China to Taiwan is characterized by an overwhelming proportion for crude animal and vegetable materials, while exports from Taiwan to the mainland are almost completely dominated by manufactured goods. This contrast reflects the essential differences in the economic development of the two areas. While Taiwan long ago became one of the

TABLE 7.8. Structure of major commodities of mainland China exports to Taiwan via Hong Kong by broad category, 1978–1983 (Unit: 1,000 HK$)

	1978	1979	1980	1981	1982	1983
Fish, crustaceans and molluscs, and preparations thereof (SITC 03)	281.6 (0.13%)	163.3 (0.06%)	7,234.9 (1.85%)	12,552.3 (2.94%)	14,645.6 (2.68%)	40,698.9 (5.83%)
Oil seeds and oleaginous fruit (SITC 22)					198.2 (0.03%)	17,322.1 (2.48%)
Textile fibres (other than wool tops) and their wastes (not manufactured into yarn or fabric) (SITC 26)	2,850.4 (1.30%)	4,146.9 (1.48%)	12,621.3 (3.23%)	28,653.4 (6.67%)	3,733.01 (0.68%)	28,393.5 (4.07%)
Crude fertilizers and crude minerals (excluding coal, petroleum, and precious stones (SITC 27)	1,220.2 (0.56%)	6,555.3 (2.35%)	13,583.6 (3.48%)	17,262.8 (4.05%)	18,670.5 (3.42%)	23,680.6 (3.39%)
Crude animal and vegetable materials (SITC 29)	198,834.4 (90.83%)	230,376.9 (82.52%)	285,763.6 (73.18%)	286,138.8 (67.08%)	383,770.2 (70.28%)	394,268.3 (56.46%)
Medicinal and pharmaceutical products (SITC 54)	1,982.02 (0.88%)	687.3 (0.25%)	5,727.1 (1.4%)	9,016.7 (2.11%)	13,953.5 (2.56%)	22,971.1 (3.29%)
Textile yarn, fabrics, made-up articles, and related products (SITC 65)	83.3 (0.04%)		93.4 (0.02%)	977.5 (0.23%)	14,670.4 (2.72%)	26,111.6 (3.76%)

Note: Percentage figures don't add up to 100 because only major commodities are considered.

Sources: Hong Kong government, Census and Statistics Department; Chung-Hua Institution for Economic Research, T'aiwan yü chung-kuo ta-lu chin Hsiang-kang chün-kung mao-yi chih-yen-chiu (Taipei: Chung-Hua Institution Press, 1985), p. 36.

newly industrialized economies, mainland China has stayed more or less in a state of underdevelopment.

Crude animal and vegetable materials were the most important commodities reexported to Taiwan throughout the period of 1978-1983. This commodity group is composed almost exclusively of Chinese medicinal herbs, and its relative weight for the period averaged 73.4 percent. However, the relative weight of this commodity group is tending to decrease, while those of textile yarns and textile fibers are increasing.

In contrast to the mainland-Taiwan trade flow, the distribution of the Taiwan-mainland trade by commodity groups is less unbalanced. The largest commodity group during the period 1978-1983 was that of textile yarns, fabrics, made-up articles and related products, and it had an average weight of 58.9 percent. The second-largest commodity group was that of telecom-

TABLE 7.9. Structure of major commodities of Taiwan exports to mainland China via Hong Kong, 1978–1983 (Unit: 1,000 HK$)

	1978	1979	1980	1981	1982	1983
Textile fibres (other than wool tops) and their wastes (not manufactured into yarn or fabric) (SITC 26)			66,214.5 (5.5%)	38,630.5 (1.77%)	3,309.4 (1.06%)	10,880.3 (0.89%)
Cork and wood manufactures (excluding furniture) (SITC 63)	21.9 (50.7%)	2,329.6 (2.2%)	37,257.3 (3.1%)	65,318.8 (3.0%)	14,364.2 (1.1%)	27,862.8 (2.3%)
Textile yarn, fabrics, made-up articles, n.e.s. and related products (SITC 65)	69.4 (28.9%)	82,512.0 (77.3%)	696,158.7 (57.8%)	1,443,991.3 (64.2%)	885,995.0 (70.1%)	678,257.7 (55.3%)
Non-metallic mineral manufactures, n.e.s. (SITC 66)		13.6 (0.0%)	115.9 (0.0%)	47.7 (0.0%)	3,219.8 (0.2%)	40,396.1 (3.3%)
Iron and steel (SITC 67)			8.5 (10.0%)	471.8 (0.0%)	10,207.9 (0.8%)	10,565.7 (0.9%)
Metalworking machinery (SITC 73)		54.3 (0.1%)	5,874.9 (0.5%)	87,012.5 (4.0%)	32,992.9 (2.6%)	206.2 (0.0%)
Telecommunications and sound recording and reproducing apparatus and equipment (SITC 76)		2,642.2 (2.0%)	92,979.7 (7.3%)	90,882.7 (3.0%)	25,669.4 (0.7%)	12,591.7 (2.0%)
Electrical machinery, apparatus and appliances, n.e.s, and electrical parts thereof (including non-electrical counterparts, n.e.s. of electrical household type equipment) (SITC 77)		10.8 (0.0%)	42,881.9 (3.6%)	10,080.5 (0.5%)	46.0 (0.0%)	156.9 (0.0%)
Road vehicles (including air cushion vehicles) (SITC 78)		5.4 (0.0%)	7,796.1 (0.6%)	42,306.8 (2.0%)	10,741.0 (0.8%)	27,864.8 (2.3%)
Photographic apparatus, equipment and supplies and optical goods, n.e.s.; watches and clocks (SITC 88)			4,120.7 (0.3%)	13,502.7 (0.7%)	544.6 (0.0%)	132.7 (0.0%)
Miscellaneous manufactured articles, n.e.s. (SITC 89)		108.8 (0.1%)	16,442.8 (1.4%)	21,007.9 (1.0%)	8,364.6 (0.7%)	120,406.7 (10.0%)

Note: Percentage figures don't add up to 100 because only major commodities are considered.

Sources: Hong Kong government, Census and Statistics Department; Chung-Hua Institution for Economic Research, *T'aiwan yü chung-kuo ta-lu chin Hsiang-kang chün-kung mao-yi chih-yen-chiu* (Taipei: Chung-Hua Institution Press, 1985), pp. 38–40.

munications and sound recording and reproducing apparatus and equipment, because of the mainland's modernization programs.

The expansion of indirect trade depends on political and economic policies on both sides of the Taiwan Strait. The Peking authorities started to discourage imports from Taiwan in 1985 while the Taipei government, on the contrary, made it clear in the same year that it would not interfere with the country's indirect exports to mainland China. As a result, the trend of trade development between the two sides in the near future will be determined mainly by economic factors. However, a continued expansion of Taiwan's indirect exports to the mainland would cost individual traders the opportunity to develop new products and seek new markets, and in the country's economy as a whole, the pace of upgrading technology through investment in research and development would slow down.[11]

In summary, the indirect trade costs Taiwan more than it gains. And Taiwan would have more to lose should the mainland change its policy overnight, by, for example, suspending imports from Taiwan.

Conclusion

Historically, Hong Kong, Taiwan, and mainland China have had very close economic, cultural, and political relations. The expansion of their economic links depends on many factors. First, if mainland China could arrange a smooth takeover of Hong Kong before 1990, then the territory's economic prosperity could continue and Hong Kong could remain an international trade, finance, and transshipment center. After 1997, trade activities between Hong Kong and the mainland would be considered part of the PRC's domestic economy, and Hong Kong would become the country's chief foreign trade center and surplus producer.

Given this assumption, trade links between Taiwan and Hong Kong will change tremendously in the next few years. Taiwan has to seek a new entrepôt for the products it imports from mainland China; it also has to look for another harbor to replace Hong Kong as a transshipment center for products indirectly sold to the PRC (Singapore might act as the replacement). To minimize the loss in trade when Hong Kong's status is changed, Taiwan's exporters will have to search for new markets.

However, if the Peking authorities cannot guarantee Hong Kong's stability, indicators of instability—such as a huge outflow of capital and people—will appear approximately around 1990. If this happens, Hong Kong will not be able to maintain its economic prosperity. Under these circumstances, Tokyo and Singapore are the two candidates for Hong Kong's status as one of the world financial centers.[12]

If Hong Kong loses its importance in the international economy, its functions as the mainland's chief foreign trade port and trade surplus maker would be weakened. As a result, Hong Kong would gradually play a less significant role in Taiwan's exports.

Last but not least, the issue of Hong Kong's future after 1997 is worrying both the government and the people of Taiwan. However, these worries have their positive effects as they will force Taiwan to speed up the upgrading of its technology and consequently improve its overall economic structure. Taiwan business people have also been prompted to look for new buyers in other countries, which will help in the expansion of Taiwan's overseas market and economic growth.

Notes

1. The real growth rate is calculated in terms of GNP for Taiwan and GDP for Hong Kong.

2. The national income of the PRC is in nominal terms due to limited statistics. Also, the national income is not adjusted to include the production of service industries, which has been included in the GNPs of Taiwan and Hong Kong.

3. See *Kuang-chiao ching* [Wide angle] (Hong Kong), no. 130 (July 16, 1983): 42.

4. See *Kuo-chi mao-i* [International trade] (Peking), no. 5 (1984): 13.

5. See *Economic Reporter* (Hong Kong), no. 1865 (April 16, 1984): 9.

6. See *Kuang-chiao ching*, no. 130 (July 16, 1983): 45.

7. Quoted from Wang Tung-yin, *Ta Kung Pao* [General daily] (Hong Kong), November 10, 1984.

8. See *Ta Kung Pao*, May 27, 1982. Also, see note 5 above.

9. See *Economic Reporter*, No. 1863 (April 2, 1984): 12.

10. Chung-Hua Institution for Economic Research, *Hsiang-kang ch'ien-t'u chi ch'i ch'i-yeh tung-hsiang* [Hong Kong's future and the direction in which its enterprises are moving] (Taipei, April 1984).

11. See Teh-pei Yu, "Reexport Trade: A Study," *Ching-chi jih-pao* [Economic daily news] (Taipei), August 23, 1985. See also Teh-pei Yu, "Countermeasures Against Reexport Trade and Smuggling at Sea," *Lien-ho pao* [United daily news] (Taipei), June 23, 1985.

12. For detailed discussion, please see Chung-Hua Institution for Economic Research, *Hsiang-kang i-chiu-chiu-ch'i wen-t'i chi ching-chi yuan-ching* [The Hong Kong 1997 issue and its economic prospects] (Taipei, June 1985), pp. 23–27.

PART THREE

Hong Kong:
An International Concern

8

The Hong Kong Agreement and Its Impact on International Law

Georg Ress

Despite the legal regulations in the Joint Declaration of December 19, 1984,[1] and the British Hong Kong Act of 1985,[2] the future of Hong Kong still raises some rather complicated legal problems. The Joint Declaration and the related statute of Great Britain and the forthcoming Basic Law on Hong Kong of the PRC are but means to secure a peaceful transition from the status of a crown colony to that of a special administrative region of the PRC designed to secure stabilization and the continuation of the economic and political interests of both sides.[3] International public law provides some specific techniques for such a peaceful change, and there exists the example of other delicate areas whose status is defined in international treaties for the sake of international peace and security—e.g., Berlin, which though not similar in the legal framework has also a special legal status.[4] In the light of international public law some intriguing questions may arise, such as whether the right of self-determination should be exercised by the population of Hong Kong as a crown colony or whether the right to opt for an effective British nationality should not be granted to those inhabitants of Hong Kong who now have the status of British Dependent Territories citizens.[5]

This chapter will mainly deal with the problem of the new status of Hong Kong after 1997 until the year 2047, a period during which Hong Kong will be a special administrative region under the sovereignty of the PRC but its internal political, social, and economic regime will be regulated by an international treaty, the Joint Declaration, with Great Britain. During this period, Hong Kong will not be an internationalized territory but a Chinese territory under the sovereignty of the PRC. Nevertheless, the period between 1997 and 2047 may be called a period of an *internationally protected* regime. Even after the expiry of this regime in 2047, Hong Kong could continue to enjoy a special legal status under the sovereignty of the PRC, i.e., as a special administrative region with the same legal particularities that are the source of its present economic prosperity.

The continuation of such a regime beyond 2047 will depend on the sovereign decision of the PRC. It therefore may be doubtful whether such a unilateral continuation of a special legal status is safe and attractive enough for international investors. It is evident that this consideration will depend on the question whether the PRC is able to maintain in Hong Kong a Western-type security of law and court system. It is this security of law and the existence of an independent court system that—despite the necessity of arrangements and negotiations in economic relations and even considering the special Chinese and Asian approach to law in general—in the past accounted for a large part of the economic prosperity. It is perhaps expedient in this context to note that the ROC (Taiwan) and Japan adopted and incorporated many elements of the German civil law and civil procedure in their legal orders and despite the fact that their practices are somewhat different from that in Germany, this kind of legal regulation has provided for a fairly evident economic success.

Notwithstanding its solely Chinese-regulated special status after 2047, Hong Kong could be a party to international agreements, e.g., to the GATT and other multinational conventions and treaties, and in this way could obtain an internationally accepted position, though it would be considerably weaker than under the Joint Declaratioin with the United Kingdom. The reason for this weaker position is, inter alia, that the recognition in international agreements of the special status of Hong Kong after 2047 will be carried out only by international organizations, not on a bilateral basis with states.

Some new developments that have occurred since the material in this chapter was first presented in a paper to a conference in Taipei in 1986 require some consideration. First of all, the Order in Council regulating the question of nationality (British Nationals Overseas) of persons residing in Hong Kong and having now the status of British Dependent Territories citizens was promulgated.[6] However, despite this regulation, the situation of the holders of a BNO passport remains rather delicate, and there is no satisfactory solution for those persons who do not have Chinese nationality. It has rightly been pointed out that with respect to the meaning of nationality for travel purposes, a passport represents the issuing state's willingness to receive the holder. Thus, if a person's presence in a foreign country becomes undesirable, he or she can be repatriated or compelled to leave.[7] The former BDTC passport equivalent is actually of little meaning as a document per se. In fact, its utility for traveling depends solely on the Chinese assurance in the Joint Declaration and on the forthcoming Basic Law regarding the rights of holders to exit, entry, or residence in the Hong Kong SAR.

Another change was the adherence of Hong Kong to the GATT.[8] This adherence and its continuation beyond 1997 raise important problems of application of the GATT rules, which will be treated accordingly. Other problems relate to civil aviation and the inclusion of Hong Kong in air service agreements after 1997 and to the continuation of land leases after 2047.[9]

Nevertheless, it is clear that the Joint Declaration largely helped to recover economic stability in Hong Kong, and the Hang Seng index illustrates the extent of confidence on the part of international investors in the stability of the situation in Hong Kong after 1997.[10]

The Joint Declaration and Its Context

The Joint Declaration of the government of the United Kingdom and of the government of the PRC on the question of Hong Kong, providing for the "transfer of governance"[11] of Hong Kong, is an *international treaty*[12] with interesting and even unique elements that might also serve as a model treaty for other non-self-governing territories such as Gibraltar or the Falkland Islands. According to the preamble, it was concluded as a "settlement of the question of Hong Kong," which was considered to be "conducive to the maintenance of the prosperity and stability of Hong Kong and to the further strengthening and development of the relations between the two countries on a new basis." According to the British view the agreement "met the needs of the people of Hong Kong"[13] in providing for the establishment of a Hong Kong Special Administrative Region (SAR) under Chinese sovereignty as of July 1, 1997, the date on which the lease of the New Territories[14] will end, and for fifty years following the transfer. At least during the period[15] until 2047 the social and economic systems and even the "life-style" of Hong Kong, which has become the world's third-largest financial and gold-trading center,[16] shall be preserved. The agreement consists of the text itself (a preamble and eight paragraphs) and three annexes: one an elaboration by the government of the PRC of its basic policy regarding Hong Kong until the year 2047, a second on a Sino-British Joint Liaison Group, and a third on land leases. According to para. 8 of the Joint Declaration, the declaration and its annexes are equally binding.

For an evaluation of the consequences, it is necessary also to consider the provisions of the British Hong Kong Act of 1985[17] together with the Orders in Council mentioned in the schedule of Sec. 2(2) of that act. Furthermore, on the very day of the signature of the Joint Declaration, two memoranda[18] related to the status after 1997 of persons who are now British Dependent Territory citizens (BDTCs) were exchanged explaining the respective positions of the two governments.

The Joint Declaration fails to mention or to define the legal status of these memoranda. In the light of Art. 31, sec. 2, lit. b, of the Vienna Convention on the Law of Treaties (VCLT), they can be looked upon as instruments that form part of the context of the treaty besides the text, the preamble, and the annexes and that have to be taken into account for the interpretation of the treaty.[19] As a consequence, the memoranda may clarify on which points no agreement was reached so that the Joint Declaration and the annexes themselves cannot be interpreted in such a way as to suggest that an agreement was reached.

Self-Determination

What is the impact on international law of this Joint Declaration? One of the first questions, since the agreement relates to Hong Kong as a crown colony,[20] would be, How does this agreement fit into the framework of international resolutions on decolonization and to what extent is it in accordance with the international public law rules on self-determination? It is somewhat amazing that the United Kingdom, which fought for the self-determination of the Falkland inhabitants[21] and regards the Gibraltar question to be largely dependent on the will and opinion of the inhabitants of Gibraltar,[22] has concluded an agreement, according to its own interpretation on the transfer of sovereignty and a cession of territory, without a referendum. Can the Joint Declaration therefore be regarded as a model for specific cases of decolonization? The British government considered the situation of Hong Kong "of course sui generis," incomparable with any other cases in which the United Kingdom has divested itself of sovereignty over territory. "In this case we are entering into an agreement with another power to terminate sovereignty as from a certain specific date."[23]

Does there exist a "people of Hong Kong" as a subject of a (defensive) right of self-determination,[24] or is the Hong Kong people's right of self-determination only a part of the right of self-determination of the entire Chinese people?[25] For those who consider also the (defensive) right to self-determination as a rule of *jus cogens*, the question might arise whether the Joint Declaration is not null and void in the light of Art. 53 of the Vienna Convention on the Law of Treaties. But in my view it is rather doubtful in the case of Hong Kong that such a (defensive) right of self-determination exists because Hong Kong has never been a "state" and the United Kingdom is under the obligation to restore at least the New Territories to China in 1997. The British government has also acknowledged that the remaining portion of Hong Kong will "not be viable alone." The government of the PRC insisted that the settlement of the question of Hong Kong was a matter of Chinese sovereign right and that, as a consequence, Hong Kong should not be included in the list of colonial territories referred to in the UN General Assembly Declaration on the Granting of Independence to Colonial Countries and Peoples.

However, even if the situation of Hong Kong was considered in the light of the UN decolonization resolution 1514 (XV) the conflict between the two principles of *self-determination* and *territorial integrity* remains obvious. According to § 5 of that resolution, "immediate steps shall be taken, in trust and non-self-governing territories or all other territories which have not yet attained independence to transfer all powers to the people of those territories, without any conditions or reservations in accordance with their freely expressed will and desire." But § 6 states that "any attempt aimed at the partial or total disruption of the national unity and the territorial integrity of a country is incompatible with the purposes and principles of the Charter of the United Nations." The latter section was applied to Gibraltar (Res. 2353 [XXII]),[26] and it is obvious that the argument would also apply to Hong Kong. The point is that the United Kingdom insisted on holding a referendum in Gibraltar and that the General Assembly of the United Nations declared this referendum to be in contravention of its resolution 2231 (XXI). But the fact remained "that the Gibraltarians had been given an opportunity to exhibit their aspirations and desires to the view of the entire world and that they had done so in an unmistakable fashion."[27]

Some Open Questions

There arise some questions in relation to problems of public international law for which there exist no ready-made answers. First, Is this Joint Declaration a kind of model treaty with respect to so-called unequal treaties? It is obvious that the technique of the agreement—declarations on both sides— is but a means to rule out different views on fundamental legal questions such as the validity of the unequal treaties. At least since 1949,[28] China has asserted that the three treaties with Britain[29] are not binding and can be invalidated because they are unequal treaties. In 1982, the PRC stated:

> Hong Kong is part of Chinese territory. The treaties concerning the Hong Kong area signed between the British Government and the Government of the Qing Dynasty of China in the past are unequal treaties which have never been accepted by the Chinese people. The consistent position of the Government of the PRC has been that China is not bound by these unequal treaties and that the whole Hong Kong area will be recovered when conditions are ripe.[30]

The doctrine of the legal invalidity of unequal treaties has not been *generally* accepted as a rule of public international law.[31] It is impossible to classify treaty conditions, in particular those in peace treaties, according to the equality or inequality in the bargaining power of the parties and the benefits and burdens created by the treaty itself. Despite the opposite view of some Chinese and Soviet jurists,[32] there is no rule in public international law demanding that there must be a "balance" or "equality" of the treaty obligations for both sides. Therefore, unequal treaties do not become invalid on account of the "unequality" of rights and duties of the contracting parties but on account of the *conditions* that actually lead to such material inequalities, e.g., coercion of a state by the threat or use of force, this being admitted in Art. 52 of the VCLT,[33] which does not use the term "unequal treaties." Any discussion of the problem along the lines of the VCLT should include the fact that the VCLT does not have a retroactive effect and that in the nineteenth century, threat—even war— was considered a legally admissible instrument of national policy. This legal situation was changed only by the Covenant of the League of Nations and, in particular, by the Briand-Kellogg Pact.[34]

As no agreement could be reached on the question of the invalidity of the treaties, the legal technique resorted to (diverging declarations by each party in a joint document) did not settle the dissent, which also includes the question whether there is a "transfer" of sovereignty at all.[35] In Germany, the controversy about the validity of the Munich agreement of 1938[36] led to the Treaty of Prague of December 11, 1973,[37] which settled the question of the invalidity only "under the present treaty" between the Federal Republic of Germany and Czechoslovakia leaving, e.g., nationality unaffected.[38] No agreement was reached as to the retroactive nullity of the Munich agreement, and the same is true for the Joint Declaration. It becomes clear from the text that for the PRC, the measures taken by the authorities of the crown colony are valid and so are the legal rights and attained positions, despite the argument about the "nullity" of the three treaties.

Two other questions are, Is the Joint Declaration a model for the unification of Taiwan with China?[39] and, Is this treaty a kind of model of a "one country, two systems" approach, a kind of "special joint venture" of capitalism and communism with an international commitment in relation to the internal structure of this region? The ROC has rejected the first prospect and the underlying ideal of "one country, two systems" from the beginning as a "political plot" of the Chinese Communists.[40] Since both Chinese governments, the government of the Republic of China (Taiwan) and the government of the PRC, claim to be the government of the one and only country, the question may arise whether the United Kingdom—from a legal point of view and viewed through the eyes of the government of the ROC— concluded the agreement with the legitimate government of China.

What is—from a political point of view—the actual significance of sovereignty if essential parts of the internal order are, in connection with the "transfer of sovereignty," withheld from the disposal of the sovereign? The practice of international agreements can substantiate by more than one example the fact that despite the solemn declaration of sovereignty by one of the parties, full sovereignty was not granted or was not achieved.[41] Nevertheless, from a legal point of view it is fairly likely that the PRC will have full sovereignty over the entire Hong Kong area as of July 1, 1997, as after that date "Her Majesty shall no longer have sovereignty or jurisdiction over any part of Hong Kong."[42] For this reason, the legal situation cannot be compared to one in which "certain rights and responsibilities" are retained or preserved in relation to the restoration of "full" sovereignty to the other party.[43]

If the PRC failed to fulfill the obligations concerning the future internal order of Hong Kong, that failure would simply be a breach of an international treaty, such as the Joint Declaration, but not interference with the United Kingdom's internal sphere, implying that some sovereignty of the United Kingdom is preserved. What will be the consequences then if the PRC does not comply with para. 3 of the Joint Declaration concerning the elements of the basic policies regarding Hong Kong, especially the maintenance of the current social and economic systems and the guarantee of rights and freedoms laid down in sec. 5 of para. 3? It is evident that this kind of treaty—as, e.g., the Treaty on the Basis of Relations between the two German States also[44]—leaves hardly any possibility for suspension or termination of the treaty in case of breach,[45] nor for the automatic recovery of sovereignty (status quo ante) through the United Kingdom.[46] Executed treaties (*traités exécutés*) may be terminated if a material breach of their provisions becomes evident, but this termination does not change the territorial status or sovereignty of the ceded territory.[47] On the other hand, neither the PRC nor the United Kingdom could refer to a fundamental change of circumstances after the date of the conclusion of the treaty in support of a termination or suspension of the Hong Kong agreement. As this is a territorial treaty that establishes a boundary (Art. 62, sec. 2, lit. a, of the VCLT) and a territorial status[48] until the year 2047, it is not possible for the PRC to argue in the future that by reason of a fundamental change of circumstances (whatever these may be) the clauses of the Joint Declaration, in particular para. 3, which is related to the internal structure of the Hong Kong SAR, must be renegotiated or changed in the light of Art. 62 of the VCLT.[49]

Another question of some importance in this context is whether in the Hong Kong agreement there are any elements of a *guarantee* treaty under public international law. There are many examples of international guarantees concerning domestic legal circumstances.[50] The legal history of Germany reveals, e.g., that parts of its internal constitutional structure have often been regulated and in some way been guaranteed by external powers.[51] The quadripartite agreement on Berlin of September 3, 1971, may also be regarded as a kind of collective guarantee of a complicated legal situation in that city.[52] Can the Joint Declaration be compared with these agreements?

The Legal Nature of the Joint Declaration

Although the document is called a "declaration," there is no doubt that it is an international agreement as any other international treaty between states. The international juridical effect of a treaty does not depend on the name given to the document.[53] Nevertheless, the agreement, which is composed of different unilateral declarations of the parties and which, in substance, is but a promise of each respective party in relation to the other, represents a fairly special technique. Irrespective of the fact that it is a joint declaration and that all declarations in this agreement are connected in a reciprocally binding form, this special technique, which was also resorted to by the Soviet Union and the three Western powers in the Berlin agreement of 1971, gives each party the opportunity to reserve its particular legal opinion in drafting its respective declaration.[54] The reason for this technique may also be seen in the fact that the unilateral declarations are to be found in the first three paragraphs, but the substance of the Declaration is only at the disposal of one party (as e.g., the restoration of Hong Kong to the PRC through the government of the United Kingdom to take effect on July 1, 1997).

In this respect, the wording of the first two paragraphs of the Joint Declaration is of some interest. The different legal status of the three parts of Hong Kong—i.e., Hong Kong Island, Kowloon, and the New Territories—is in no way mentioned. The island of Hong Kong and Kowloon were ceded by China to Great Britain for all time in the Treaty of Nanking and the first Peking convention, whereas the New Territories were leased in the second Peking Convention of 1898 for ninety-nine years. In para. 1 of the Joint Declaration, the government of the PRC declares that it has decided "to resume the exercise of sovereignty"[55] over Hong Kong, i.e., over all three parts, "with effect from 1 July 1997." This declaration is an expression of the Chinese view of the validity—or better, invalidity—of the unequal treaties of Nanking and Peking.[56] Although the United Kingdom does not recognize this legal view by its declaration in para. 2, it is surprising that in the text of the declaration, the United Kingdom refers to the "restoration" of Hong Kong to the PRC rather than to a transfer of sovereignty. The United Kingdom has to restore on that date only the New Territories, and the use of one single term in relation to Hong Kong as a whole could be considered as in some way slightly recognizing the well-foundedness of the PRC's claims in relation to the so-called unequal treaties. However, in my view it appears more consistent to interpret this point in such a way that both declarations reflect the underlying and continued dissent on the legal question whether a real "transfer"[57] of sovereignty or only a resumption of a still existing sovereignty is stipulated.[58] There can be no doubt that on July 1, 1997, the sovereignty of China over the entire Hong Kong area will be restored, and, as the British Hong Kong Act of 1985 puts it, British sovereignty and jurisdiction over Hong Kong will end. In this respect, the Hong Kong Act is more precise than the Hong Kong agreement. The former provides for the termination of British sovereignty over ceded parts of Hong Kong and the termination of British jurisdiction over the whole territory.[59]

Is this sovereignty perhaps limited insofar as the government of the PRC promises in para. 3 of the Joint Declaration to follow and implement specific elements of basic policies in relation to Hong Kong, policies that concern the internal legal structure of this area? There is no evidence in the Joint Declaration that the United Kingdom has retained parts of the sovereignty over the area of Hong Kong. The United Kingdom has an obligatory right with regard to the PRC, but it has waived any further exercise of sovereignty. Therefore, it is doubtful whether the United Kingdom could ever demand the re-restoration of sovereignty, even if the PRC does not comply with the obligations it accepts in the Joint Declaration. The PRC would argue that even a termination of the agreement would not imply a restoration of sovereignty to the United Kingdom as the United Kingdom was under all circumstances bound to restore sovereignty over all parts of Hong Kong to the PRC. The United Kingdom on the other hand would of course argue that this obligation holds only for the New Territories and not for the other parts of the Hong Kong area and that there is no valid argument in international public law in favor of revising the results of so-called unequal treaties.

Therefore, the ending of the United Kingdom's sovereignty and the resuming of the exercise of sovereignty over Hong Kong by the PRC are definite and not limited. Treaty commitments do not limit sovereignty itself (the legal *capacity* to act) but are simply the expression of the sovereign's right to limit itself (the freedom to act within a state's capacity).

The technique used in the Joint Declaration is not new to an international lawyer because it has been resorted to often in the process of decolonization. The characteristic feature in this special case under consideration is that Hong Kong does not become a new independent state with some obligations toward the mother country enshrined in a treaty of independence; instead, a kind of treaty of cession (or in the eyes of the Chinese government, a treaty of resumption of sovereignty) with another state was concluded. The value of such entrenched clauses as are in para. 3 of the Joint Declaration is a rather disputed one.

The Hong Kong Special Administrative Region (SAR)

National Unity and the Question of Consular Protection

The establishment of the Hong Kong SAR (in accordance with the provisions of Art. 31 of the constitution of the PRC)[60] has to be interpreted in the light of the maintenance of national unity and territorial integrity (para. 3 of the Joint Declaration). "National unity" means that there will be no special population or special nation of Hong Kong. For the PRC, the people of Hong Kong are part of the "entire Chinese people" (para. 1). If the Hong Kong population enjoys a special legal status, that fact raises the particular question of nationality that is dealt with in the two memoranda and in the British Hong Kong Act of 1985.

The government of the PRC has declared in its memorandum that under the nationality law of the PRC, "all Hong Kong Chinese compatriots, whether they are holders of the 'British Dependent Territories citizens' Passport' or not, are Chinese nationals." Nevertheless, they may "use travel documents issued by the Government of the United Kingdom for the purpose of travelling to other states and regions." The Chinese Memorandum makes it quite clear that these Chinese nationals "will not be entitled to British consular protection in the Hong Kong Special Administrative Region and other parts of the People's Republic of China on account of their holding of the above-mentioned travel documents." On the other hand, the United Kingdom Memorandum (item d) makes it clear that "those who have obtained or been included in passports issued by the Government of the United Kingdom . . . will be entitled to receive, upon request, British consular services and protection when in third countries."[61] Since it becomes clear from the Chinese Memorandum that the PRC is not a third country in this respect,[62] it must be concluded that the British government has admitted that in relation to the PRC the effective nationality of these people is the Chinese one. Since the Chinese Memorandum precludes only British consular protection in the Hong Kong SAR and other parts of the PRC, it is evident that the PRC has conceded that the United Kingdom will protect these Chinese nationals upon request in third countries. The respective third country may decide at its own discretion whether to admit the consular protection of the United Kingdom or that of the PRC in regard to these persons.[63] Since there is no mention of "diplomatic protection," it is not quite clear whether the same rules apply also to that kind of protection. It appears that there is no reason in this respect to differentiate between diplomatic and consular protection.

Territorial Unity and the Special Legal Status

The Hong Kong SAR is to be incorporated as a part of *upholding territorial integrity*. The Hong Kong SAR, therefore, will be a part of the territory of the PRC despite the fact that the history of Hong Kong and the special exercise of executive, legislative, and judicial powers in the Hong Kong SAR will make it a kind of territory with a special status. The Hong Kong SAR will not be "an internationalized territory,"[64] nor are sovereignty and territorial jurisdiction to be in the hands of different states. The Hong Kong SAR is to be part of the national territory of the PRC, with effect from July 1, 1997, though with a *special legal status* according to the binding effect of the Joint Declaration. Although the Hong Kong SAR will not be an independent entity under international public law, it will enjoy limited powers to conduct foreign relations.[65] These limited powers have to be looked upon in the light of the clause according to which foreign affairs of the SAR in general are under the responsibility of the Central People's government.

Nevertheless, under the name of "Hong Kong China," it will have a status similar to or even beyond that of states within a federal state[66]— e.g., the right to conduct its own relations and agreements with states, regions, and international organizations in "appropriate" fields including the economic, trade, financial, and monetary areas[67] and participation in international organizations and conferences not limited to states.[68] Whether international organizations will recognize these special capacities of Hong Kong China is doubtful, or at least cannot be automatically derived from the Joint Declaration. The exceptions to the "moving treaty frontiers rule" require acceptance by the other parties, and that will depend on a careful analysis of every international treaty and by each international organization as to whether Hong Kong, after having changed its legal status from a British crown colony to a Chinese SAR in 1997, is able to continue participation or to maintain its former legal status.[69] It makes a great difference for all parties of a treaty—as e.g., of GATT—whether the treaty applies under British responsibility to Hong Kong as a British crown colony or under Chinese responsibility to Hong Kong as a Chinese SAR.

Meanwhile, in accordance with GATT regulations, Hong Kong became on April 23, 1986, a contracting party under Art. XXVI, 5(c), by declaration of the United Kingdom. The same day, the People's Republic of China notified the GATT Secretariat that Hong Kong shall remain a member of GATT after July 1, 1997, since "the Hong Kong Special Administrative Region will meet the requirements for a customs territory to be deemed to be a CONTRACTING PARTY as prescribed in GATT Article XXVI, 5(c), to be deemed to be a contracting party to the General Agreement on Tariffs and Trade."[70] The GATT regulations have been applied to Hong Kong by the United Kingdom since 1948, and representatives of Hong Kong have participated for a long time as part of the British delegation in GATT meetings. The procedure under Art. XXVI, 5(c), is the more attractive one as it does not involve any new negotiations and does not presuppose a "sovereignty" of Hong Kong. Since the PRC is negotiating now to "resume" its status as a contracting party (the membership of China came to an end in 1950 by a declaration of the Chinese government in Taiwan), and since Portugal could issue a similar declaration with respect to Macao, it cannot be precluded that in the near future the PRC will be represented three times in the GATT, for the procedure according to Art. XXVI, 5(c), provides: "If any of the customs territories, in respect of which a contracting party has accepted this agreement, possesses or acquires full autonomy in the conduct of its external commercial relations and of the other matters provided for in this agreement, such territory shall, upon sponsorship to a declaration by the responsible contracting party establishing the above-mentioned fact, be deemed to be a contracting party."

The Continuation of Hong Kong's "Life-Style" from 1997 to 2047—and Beyond?

The establishment of the Hong Kong SAR as a part of the basic policies will "remain unchanged for 50 years" (para. 3, sect. 12). Therefore, in 2047 China will be free from internationally binding commitments in relation to the internal legal structure of the region. This situation may also have a bearing on the decision of third states to grant Hong Kong China the continuation of treaty relationships. The Joint Declaration and Annex III do not provide for any special regulations on the question of what will happen to land leases after 2047, although Annex III states that the SAR agrees to extend the rights of existing leases beyond June 30, 1997, without indicating a date of expiry. The provisions dealing with lease renewals and the granting of leases before 1997 have been interpreted to mean "that China and Britain intended the land lease policy to be renegotiated before 2047."[71]

During the fifty years, the Hong Kong SAR will "enjoy a high degree of autonomy, except in foreign and defence affairs which are the responsibilities of the Central People's Government" (para. 3, sec. 2). The Hong Kong SAR will have its own executive, legislative, and independent judicial powers, including that of final adjudication, and the laws currently in force in Hong Kong will remain basically unchanged. Moreover, the current social and economic systems in Hong Kong will remain unchanged and so will, according to sec. 5 of para. 3, "the life-style." The rights and freedoms and even private property, ownership of enterprises, legitimate right of inheritance, and foreign investments will be protected by law. It is obvious that parts of the Western "capitalist" approach to individual fundamental rights and freedoms have been accepted for this part of the Chinese territory by the PRC.

For the period of transition until June 30, 1997, the government of the United Kingdom is "responsible for the administration of Hong Kong with the object of maintaining and preserving its economic prosperity and social stability," and the government of the PRC has promised to give its cooperation in this connection (para. 4). To ensure "a smooth transfer of government in 1997" (para. 5), a Sino-British Liaison Group will be set up according to Annex II of the Joint Declaration.

Some Specific Problems

It is not possible to enter into all the details of the interpretation of each of the clauses of the agreement, especially all the subsections of paragraph 3 of the Declaration and Annex I, but I will discuss some basic problems of the whole arrangement.

Continuation of West-European Liberalism?

First of all, it is rather unusual for a socialist or a communist country to declare that "the socialist system and socialist policies shall not be practised" in a part of its national territory, i.e., "in the Hong Kong Special Administrative Region," or "that Hong Kong's previous capitalist system and life-style shall remain unchanged for 50 years." According to Art. 1 of its constitution, the PRC is a socialist state "under the people's democratic dictatorship." The socialist system is the basis of the PRC, and any sabotage of that system by an organization or individual is forbidden. What guarantee is there that the legal system of the Hong Kong SAR can preserve its specific West-European liberal elements?

No Specific Provision for the Settlement of Disputes

Other international agreements, e.g., the quadripartite agreement on Berlin of 1971, contain clauses on the establishment of special committees or special procedures in the event of disputes relating to the implementation of the agreement. It is one of the striking facts of the Joint Declaration that it does not contain any such particular rules for the settlement of disputes or for the establishment of some sort of observatory commission until the year 2047. The Joint Liaison Group, whose main task is "to ensure a smooth transfer of government in 1997" and only at a second stage "the effective implementation of this Joint Declaration" (para. 5), shall continue its work only until January 1, 2000 (para. 8 of Annex II). The PRC may have a particular interest in demonstrating that it is not only law abiding and a trustworthy party to international agreements but also that the Hong Kong agreement can serve as a model treaty for a solution to the "question of Taiwan." Still, it is nevertheless obvious that "in case of negotiating a settlement on a dispute relating to the application or interpretation of the Joint Declaration, the U.K. is in an unfavourable position" because, despite the lengthy content of the documents, the Declaration contains certain subtle gray areas, weak in nature, that would allow the PRC to maneuver its application without literally violating its provisions.[72]

The PRC seems to reject third-party adjudication in the settlement of international disputes, at least in relation to inherited commitments from previous Chinese governments. It does not accept the jurisdiction of the International Court in the Hague and refuses to recognize the validity of the Republic of China's acceptance of that court's jurisdiction in 1946.[73] Therefore, it appears highly expedient for the United Kingdom and the PRC to agree to the continued existence of the Sino-British Liaison Group beyond January 1, 2000. The question may be raised as to what specific interest the PRC might have in seeing such a mixed commission continue its work, as it does not have any obligation to do so. The main reason is presumably that the PRC has an interest in demonstrating its readiness to fulfill promptly and strictly all the terms of the Joint Declaration until the year 2047. It is also conceivable that third countries or international organizations in which Hong Kong China's membership is considered expedient might require the establishment of such procedures to ensure the fulfillment of the obligations through Hong Kong China.[74] Another reason may be that the establishment of such a commission, especially with respect to boundary treaties, is a common way to solve disputes[75] and may be regarded as an expression of the obligation under the Charter of the United Nations.

The existing arrangement is characterized by a step-by-step diminishing influence of the United Kingdom with respect to the Joint Declaration and its annexes. There will be the Sino-British Joint Liaison Group "to ensure a smooth transfer of government in 1997" (with the regulation in para. 5 of Annex II that provides for a closer cooperation and therefore an intensification of the Chinese influence after the first half of the period between the establishment of the Joint Liaison Group and July 1, 1997.[76] After that date and during the post-transitory phase, the Joint Liaison Group will continue to work until January 1, 2000. From that date until the end of the fifty-year period, there will be no instrumentalized British influence on the implementation of the Joint Declaration.

It is obvious (not only from sec. 12 of para. 3 of the Joint Declaration, but also from the wording of Annex III) that June 30, 2047, is the date when all obligations relating to the internal structure of Hong Kong come to an end. After that date, the PRC is free to change all the basic policies set forth in para. 3 of the Joint Declaration, even to abolish Hong Kong as a SAR. Nevertheless, the establishment of such a unit with a specific, though limited, foreign relations power may—and probably will—create international obligations toward third countries that may call for a further transitory period provided there is no *explicit* limitation to the year 2047 of all specific rights and obligations in agreements concluded by Hong Kong China.

The "High Degree of Autonomy"

Although granting a "high degree of autonomy" is an international obligation of the PRC,[77] it has also to be interpreted with a view to the regulations of the Joint Declaration itself. It has been argued[78] that the Joint Declaration itself contains many regulations that may raise serious doubt concerning the durability and credibility of such autonomy. The Basic Law of the Hong Kong SAR will be stipulated by the National People's Congress of the PRC,[79] and Hong Kong will have only some 40 delegates in the NPC out of a total of 3,400 delegates. The Standing Committee of the NPC has the power "to interpret statutes," so the high degree of autonomy does not embrace the competence either to legislate or to interpret the elements of basic policy contained in the Basic Law of the Hong Kong SAR. Chiu has concluded that under such circumstances, the so-called high degree of autonomy is at the mercy of the NPC and thus without any credible guarantee.[80] The term "autonomy" does not mean that the Hong Kong SAR, being vested with executive, legislative, and independent judicial powers, including that of final adjudication, will have the competence of final decisions in all legislative matters. This statement also applies to the laws previously in force in Hong Kong, which will be preserved except those that eventually are contrary to the Basic Law.[81] If they are in contrast to the Basic Law, the Standing Committee of the NPC can annul them.[82] A quite interesting question in this context is, What are the relationships between the power of the Standing Committee to interpret the statutes and the competence of the Hong Kong courts for final decision? Since there is a commitment of the PRC to regard final adjudication as final, I believe that there is no supervisory power of the judiciary. Therefore, the Standing Committee cannot annul judicial decisions.

It has been argued that the Standing Committee of the NPC, which has the power to annul local regulations or decisions of autonomous regions that contravene the constitution, the statutes, or the administrative rules and regulations, has therefore also the power to annul laws and regulations of the Hong Kong legislature. It does have that power, but on the other hand, the Standing Committee of the NPC has to interpret the provisions of the Basic Law (which is not yet promulgated) in the light of the Joint Declaration, which has incorporated fundamental rights and freedoms according to the Western liberal approach (separation of state and society instead of a socialist identity).[83] The interpretation of the Basic Law by the Standing Committee has to be guided by this conception if the PRC is prepared to implement paragraph 3 of the Joint Declaration.

In my view, it cannot be argued that the Standing Committee can annul all local Hong Kong regulations or decisions of the organs of state power just because they contravene, assessed formally and in an isolalated manner, the Basic Law, any Chinese law, or administrative rules or regulations. The point is that the Standing Committee itself has to take into account the provisions of the Joint Declaration. The same is true with respect to the power of the PRC's State Council (cabinet) under Art. 98, sec. 14. The State Council can interfere with the Hong Kong government's administrative functions because it has the power "to alter or annul inappropriate orders and decisions issued by local organs of state administration at different levels."[84] However, it cannot interfere on a merely discretionary basis, only with regard to the Joint Declaration. In my view, the expediency and appropriateness of the decisions and orders are part of the autonomy of the Hong Kong government. The Standing Committee of the NPC has the power to exert a legal supervision but has no control of expediency.

The status of the Hong Kong SAR differs in one respect considerably from the status of a state in a federal country. Art. 1, para. 3 of Annex I provides that "the chief executive of the Hong Kong Special Administrative Region shall be selected by election or through consultations held locally and be appointed by the Central People's Government." This method of selection indeed gives the Central People's government the final decision.[85] The high degree of autonomy therefore is rather limited, which becomes clear from the text of the Joint Declaration and Annex I. However, the change of status of this special administrative region is not only "an internal affair of China";[86] since this status is fixed in the Joint Declaration and in Annex I, it is an *international* affair for China and, as such, part of the bilateral legal relations between the United Kingdom and the PRC.

The Military Presence of the PRC

The defense of the Hong Kong SAR is to be the responsibility of the Central People's government. Article 12 of Annex I provides that "military forces sent by the Central People's Government to be stationed in the Hong Kong Special Administrative Region for the purpose of defence shall not interfere in the internal affairs of the Hong Kong Special Administrative Region." The garrison of British armed forces will be withdrawn upon the transfer of governance. Chiu has compared the development of Tibet under the PRC between 1950 and 1959 with the eventual development of Hong Kong.[87] This historical background may raise serious doubts whether the military forces sent by the Central People's government will really abstain from interfering in the internal affairs of the Hong Kong SAR. Also, for some German commentators, the entrance of military forces and of Chinese police forces represents the decisive item. Those observers are rather pessimistic, arguing that there is no freedom of expression in the PRC and that those people whose opinions are oppressed are not only students and Christians but in particular persons in the so-called autonomous region of Tibet.[88]

The Position of the Judges and Common Law

Another remarkable regulation is that although the executive and the administration should be composed of local inhabitants, the same does not apply to the judiciary. According to Art. 3 of Annex I, "the power of final judgment of the Hong Kong Special Administrative Region shall be vested in the court of final appeal in the Hong Kong Special Administrative Region, which may as required invite judges from other common law jurisdictions to sit on the court of final appeal."

This is the replacement of the jurisdiction of the Privy Council, which so far has dealt with Hong Kong's judicial affairs in the final instance. Up to now, British common law has been one of the main sources of law in Hong Kong. It was accepted by the Chinese government that "the courts shall decide cases in accordance with the laws of the Hong Kong Special Administrative Region and may refer to precedents in other common law jurisdictions." The precedents in other common-law jurisdictions are—according to the legal history of the Hong Kong area—precedents especially of British courts. The common-law system, with its acceptance of the main features of a liberal, capitalistic legal system, the freedom of contract, the freedom to sell and buy, the freedom to choose labor relations, etc., could not be abolished without abolishing the main features of "the current social and economic system in Hong Kong" (sec. 5 of para. 3 of the Joint Declaration). For the survival of the system for the fifty years after 1997, it is therefore vital not to exclude the participation of judges trained in the application of the common-law system.[89]

International Treaties:
The "Moving Treaty Frontiers Rule"

It is commonly accepted as a rule of customary international law that apart from some exceptions, territorial changes alter treaty frontiers but the regime of already existing treaties is itself not affected. If a territory undergoes a change of sovereignty for whatever reason, it passes from the treaty regime of the preceding state to that of the acquiring one.[90] As H. Waldock stated, the rule on moving treaty frontiers has two aspects: "The positive aspect is that the treaties of the successor state begin automatically to apply in respect of the territory as from the date of the succession. The negative aspect is that the treaties of the predecessor state, in turn, cease automatically to apply in respect of the territory."[91] Therefore, it could normally be expected that treaties concluded by the United Kingdom and applicable in the Hong Kong area would automatically cease to be in force in that area as of July 1, 1997, and that all treaties concluded by the PRC would be extended to Hong Kong.

The moving treaty frontiers rule provides for an exception only in the case of those treaties that are *specifically localized* (e.g., granted fishery or navigation rights on a river or lake in the region). However, the parties to the Joint Declaration excluded (at least until 2047) some of the consequences from the succession of states. The rule on moving treaty frontiers does not form part of *jus cogens*, which means that states may agree otherwise. Furthermore, according to state practice and the prevailing doctrine, the moving treaty frontiers rule does not automatically apply to the acquisition of territorial sovereignty over dependent territories. The normal procedure is to settle this problem in the treaties themselves, a procedure that has been followed in the Joint Declaration (Annex I, Art. 11, para. 2). Nevertheless, third state parties to the treaties are not automatically obliged to accept new parties within their treaty relations. The Joint Declaration uses rather vague formulations (*appropriate arrangements* for the application to the Hong Kong SAR of international agreements to which the PRC is not a party) and refers to the participation in "an appropriate capacity" of Hong Kong in international organizations. Since the provisions of Annex I, Art. 11, do not have an *erga omnes* ("binding all others") effect but require acceptance by third states, there is a rather large field for complications and influence of third states in the future development of Hong Kong.

The question of the participation of Hong Kong China as a contracting party in the GATT after 1997 deserves some attention. The rule in Art. XXVI, 5(c), clearly differentiates between the "responsible contracting party" and "customs territories," which acquire full autonomy in the conduct of their external commercial relations. Upon declaration the latter are deemed "to be a contracting party." By this declaration, the customs territory acquires the right de iure and/or de facto to act on its behalf and to fulfill its obligations.[92] The formulation "to be deemed" was chosen in order to clarify that these customs territories may also be represented by the "responsible contracting party" apart from a representation on their own rights. The whole procedure is based on a relation between a responsible contracting party and a separate customs territory that possesses full autonomy in the conduct of its external commercial relations. The question remains whether Hong Kong China after 1997 may continue "to be deemed a contracting party" when the People's Republic of China itself is not a member of GATT.[93] There can be no doubt that when a government becomes a contracting party under Art. XXVI, 5(c), does so on the terms and conditions previously accepted by the metropolitan government on behalf of the territory in question. The conditions under which Hong Kong is now to be deemed a contracting party of GATT are those that previously have been negotiated by the United Kingdom. The question remains whether Hong Kong China may continue to be deemed a contracting party after 1997 when it becomes part of the People's Republic of China. It is clear that Art. XXVI, 5(c), applies also when the customs territories become an independent state.[94] But in the case of Hong Kong China, the customs territory does not gain independence but becomes a dependent part of the People's Republic of China as a special administrative region.

The reason for questioning whether Hong Kong China may continue to be deemed a contracting party after 1997 is based on the fact that after that date, the responsible government for the territory will change and the new one is not (for the time being) a contracting party of GATT. For the other contracting parties of GATT it makes quite a difference whether a British crown colony, i.e., a territory for which the United Kingdom is and has been responsible and for which the relevant conditions have been negotiated, or a territory for which the People's Republic of China is responsible becomes automatically a contracting party or is "deemed to be a contracting party" without a new negotiation of the conditions. The Joint Declaration itself does not have any effect *erga omnes* and does not oblige third states, and therefore no contracting party of GATT, to agree to such a continuation after 1997. It is therefore the question whether in this case GATT Art. XXXIII, in connection with the protocol of annecy of October 10, 1949, on the conditions of accession, becomes applicable or not. Art. XXXIII reads:

> A government not party to this agreement, or a government acting on behalf of a separate customs territory possessing full autonomy in the conduct of its external commercial relations and of the other matters provided for in this agreement, may accede to this agreement, on its own behalf or on behalf of that territory, on terms to be agreed between such government and the contracting parties. Decisions of a contracting party under this paragraph shall be taken by a two-thirds majority.

The article is based on the presumption that a government acting on behalf of a separate customs territory, like the People's Republic of China for Hong Kong China after 1997, may become a contracting party only for such a separate customs territory, but there is no regulation saying that a separate customs territory which does not gain independence may continue to be deemed a contracting party when it changes its dependence from the former "responsible contracting party" to a state that is not a contracting party of GATT. Therefore, the declaration of the People's Republic of China that Hong Kong China will continue to be deemed a contracting party after 1997 refers without any justification to Art. XXVI, 5(c). If the GATT Secretariat accepted this statement and if all the other contracting parties accepted it in the same way, it might be considered as fulfilling the conditions of Art. XXXIII, but it is by way of the procedure under Art. XXXIII that Hong Kong China could continue to be deemed a contracting party after 1997.

Questions of Nationality

The Right of Abode

The Joint Declaration regulates the right of abode in the Hong Kong SAR[95] but fails to regulate citizenship. The right of abode is vested in all Chinese nationals born in Hong Kong or who have ordinarily resided there continuously for seven years, their children if of Chinese nationality, all other persons having resided in Hong Kong for seven years *and* having taken it as their place of permanent residence, their children under twenty-one years of age born in Hong Kong, and, finally, any other persons who had the right of abode in Hong Kong before the establishment of the SAR.[96]

A Right to Opt to Retain the Former Nationality?

International law contains some rules on the effects of moving frontiers on the nationality of the population. Generally speaking, the population loses the nationality of the state that cedes a ceretain territory and acquires the nationality of the state that assumes the exercise of sovereignty over the territory.[97] The acquisition of the new nationality is a legal obligation of the successor state because, otherwise, the population living in the territory that changes sovereignty becomes stateless.

It is questionable whether under international public law the population is entitled to opt to retain the former nationality. This kind of option has often been combined with the compulsion for those people wishing to retain their former nationality to leave the territory.[98] The regulation in the Joint Declaration and especially in the two memoranda and the British Hong Kong Act of 1985 in relation to nationality is particularly interesting. The British Hong Kong Act of 1985, stating that as from July 1, 1997, "Her Majesty shall no longer have sovereignty or jurisdiction over any party of Hong Kong" (Art. 1, sec. 1), contains a schedule that shall affect specific matters, such as nationality, which are considered as "consequential on or connected with" the ending of sovereignty or jurisdiction. The regulation of nationality is therefore, completely in accordance with the general rules of public international law, regarded as a matter that is consequential on the transfer of territory. According to Art. 2 of the schedule, the nationality of the Hong Kong population may be regulated by Order in Council, whereby (a) British Dependent Territories citizenship canont be retained or acquired on or after the relevant date by virtue of a connection with Hong Kong, and (b) persons who are British Dependent Territories citizens (BDTCs) by virtue of any such connection may before that date (or before the end of 1997 if born in that before the relevant date) acquire a new form of British nationality, the holders of which shall be known as British Nationals (Overseas) (BNOs).

The New Form of British Nationality

The Hong Kong Act of 1985 thus creates a new form of British nationality. For those Hong Kong residents who now have British Dependent Territories citizenship, that kind of citizenship will automatically end in 1997, but they "may," before July 1, 1997,[99] acquire the new form of British nationality. The Order in Council will not only regulate the procedure (and discretion) of how to acquire the new British nationality but also may "require application in respect to the new status . . . to be made before such time or times as are specified in the Order" (Art. 2, para. 2, of the schedule).

In the Hong Kong (British Nationality) Order of 1986, which has been approved by Parliament and shall come into operation on July 1, 1987, the government defined in Art. 2 the cases in which a connection with Hong Kong is established. According to Art. 4, para. 2, of the order, any person who is a British Dependent Territories citizen by virtue (wholly or partly) of his or her having a connection with Hong Kong and who would not be such a citizen without having a such connection (cf. Art. 3) shall be entitled before July 1, 1997 (or before the end of 1997 if born in that year before that date) to be registered as a British National (Overseas) and to hold or be included in a passport appropriate to that status.[100]

The rule that no person can retain the former British Dependent Territories citizenship by virtue of a connection with Hong Kong may be regarded as deriving from the fact that the transfer of sovereignty is definite; there is no intermediate status of mixed sovereignty between 1997 and 2047. The fact that no person born in the Hong Kong area after 1997 can acquire the new form of British nationality is a clear departure from the rule of jus sanguinis. As the White Paper of October 17, 1985, states, the status "that Hong Kong BDTCs will be eligible to retain"—i.e., the status of a British National (Overseas)—"will not be transmissible to any subsequent generation and that only those people who are already BDTCs by virtue of a connection with Hong Kong on June 30, 1997, may retain it." It can be anticipated that after 2047 there will be only a small number of persons having the status of British Nationals (Overseas) in Hong Kong. This is a clear result of the U.K. Memorandum's provision that "no person born on or after 1 July 1997 will acquire the status referred to," that of a British National (Overseas).

Is this new type of British nationality (BNO)—i.e., nationality without continued connection to Hong Kong and without the right to reside and live in the United Kingdom—a nationality at all?[101] The procedure is a transfer of jurisdiction over a population of more than 6 million people as the descendants of BNOs born after 1997 who are Chinese nationals will be *exclusively* Chinese nationals and will not have dual nationality.[102]

Will the regulation lead to an exodus of many "Chinese nationals in Hong Kong who were previously called 'British Dependent Territories citizens' "[103] and who can afford to use their travel documents issued by the U.K. government to travel abroad, in particular to the United Kingdom? The British Hong Kong Act of 1985 does not indicate whether by the new form of citizenship British Nationals (Overseas) are entitled to entry and residence in the United Kingdom. The title suggests that they will *not* be so entitled, and the British White Paper of September 26, 1984, states that the new status "will not give them the right of abode in the United Kingdom, which they do not possess at present, but it will carry benefits similar to those enjoyed by British Dependent Territories citizens at present, including the entitlement to use British passports and to receive British consular services and protection in third countries."[104]

The Legal Status of the British Nationals (Overseas)

These arguments reveal that the Hong Kong BDTCs do not enjoy the right to opt when acquiring the new status. They lose their right to live under British protection in Hong Kong without obtaining the right to opt for a real British nationality. The new form of nationality is a form of "transitional" nationality, valid for the present and the next generation, fixed to their holders and not transferable. Furthermore, it is a "nationality" with rather weak relationships to the United Kingdom,[105] and it may well be argued that for diplomatic (and even consular) protection, a *genuine* link, in the sense of the Nottebohm case,[106] does not exist and therefore a third state could refuse to accept the United Kingdom's protection. The White Paper does not expressly mention this questionable position but indirectly refers to it. According to the White Paper, the U.K. government "will do all they can to secure for holders of these British passports the same access to other countries as that enjoyed at present by holders of British Dependent Territories citizens passports."[107] This careful wording indicates that third countries might refuse access to these people who are Chinese nationals and will be only more or less *virtually* British nationals.

A BDTC was entitled, if not to abide in the United Kingdom, at least to reside and to stay in a specific British Dependent Territory. The British National (Overseas) will have no right of abode on British territory at all.[108] The procedure chosen in the Hong Kong Act and in the memorandum is, not that of a right to opt, but a kind of *transformation of nationality*, and for "all Hong Kong Chinese compatriots" (formulation of the Chinese Memorandum) who are Chinese nationals pursuant to the Nationality Law of the PRC, this is just a procedure to deprive them of their former British nationality.[109] The rather problematic position of the former BDTCs is reflected in the negotiations on the new passports (BNO passports for the population of Hong Kong, in particular for those persons who are not ethnically Chinese but are of other Asian origin). These persons are neither Chinese nor "real" British nationals; they are—or will be—mere holders of a BNO passport, which will enable them eventually to obtain access to other countries. But it remains doubtful whether they have a right to reenter Hong Kong. The government of the PRC refuses to recognize that there is any indication in the present Hong Kong passport of the right of abode in Hong Kong.[110] If these persons are not granted the right of abode in Hong Kong, and if there is no legal basis for extradition to Hong Kong after all, third countries will be even more reluctant to give them access to their own territory, be it only on a temporary, limited basis.[111] The position of non-Chinese Hong Kongers who live abroad—somewhere in Southeast Asia—could be even worse. They could be, as a member of the British Parliament put it, in "a ghastly limbo of lostness."[112]

With a view to the facts that China itself is a multinational country and that free access of skilled labor—even though workers are of another ethnic origin—is a basic principle of developed "capitalist" systems (e.g., the free movement of workers in the EEC),[113] there is no reason why the

PRC should not handle this matter generously by giving these persons at least the right of abode. International public law could be quoted in support of the fact that a transfer of territory automatically implies a change of nationality. If this—controversial—rule of general customary international law is applied, not only the persons who under the PRC's Nationality Law are considered Chinese nationals, but *all* former holders of a Hong Kong BDTC passport would have to be considered Chinese citizens. This implication might be in contrast with these persons' interests. Therefore, the question remains whether the inhabitants of Hong Kong who are not Chinese nationals should not be granted at least a right to opt for an *effective* British nationality. Even if in the past the option of nationality was not regarded as a generally accepted rule of public international law,[114] it appears at least as a substitute to the right of self-determination, or better, as an expression of its human rights elements. Given that sovereignty over the population of a territory is being transferred together with the territory without the population's consent and that the population cannot obstruct the transfer, the population should be granted the right to opt for the nationality of the country that is transferring the territory. It is not Hong Kong but the United Kingdom that is transferring Hong Kong to the PRC, and therefore it is the United Kingdom's responsibility to grant such a right. The right of self-determination is rooted in the concept of human rights[115] and so is the right of option of nationality in the case of a transfer of territory. It is true that today's idea of the human being may suggest or even demand such rights.[116]

Conclusion

The Joint Declaration is another example of a treaty that provides for an objective territorial regime.[117] The Hong Kong treaty regime contains a large number of provisions that require the consent and recognition of third parties, but the Joint Declaration does not have an *erga omnes* effect as such. Only if this arrangement was made in the general interest of the international community and if it was intended to be valid for parties other than the parties concluding the treaty may it receive specific recognition as an objective status treaty. There are many provisions to be found in the Hong Kong agreement that point to the fact that the new regime should be respected by third countries. Third countries may subject themselves independently to the order asserted by the parties of the treaty and may do so even tacitly in the form of acquiescence or implied recognition. It will largely depend on the conduct of third countries whether they accept such a temporary, limited regime or whether they insist on certain commitments on the part of the PRC concerning continuation after 2047.

The status of Hong Kong between 1997 and 2047 as a SAR of the PRC under *special* international law obligations is another example of a region whose status is internationally fixed in the interest of peaceful relations between East and West.[118] Whether the Joint Declaration will succeed in achieving a feasible solution for the future of Hong Kong "will ultimately depend in considerable measure on the will and good faith of its signatories."[119] Recent declarations of the PRC concerning elections in Hong Kong raise doubts as to the PRC's position and have given rise to some criticism.[120]

When the British government received from Chinese leaders at the highest level "solemn assurances of China's commitment to full implementation of the agreement"[121] and their "intention to consult Hong Kong's opinion on the drafting of the Basic Law on a wide basis,"[122] could it have foreseen these difficulties? Why did the United Kingdom not strengthen the representative government in Hong Kong earlier, or hold a referendum of the people of Hong Kong? Isn't it too late to give support to the representative government in Hong Kong until 1997[123] when it is obvious that the PRC is not really interested in such a government in Hong Kong in the fifty years after 1997? Hong Kong has been "straightjacketed" was one of the comments when the PRC warned that the democratic development in Hong Kong (election of twenty-four representatives from the population of Hong Kong to the council) deviates from the Joint Declaration.[124] What is the legal background of the dispute? In 1990, the NPC will enact the Basic Law, which will be in force in the Hong Kong SAR after July 1, 1997. If Hong Kong had a democratically elected representative organ by that time, the PRC would have to choose between either accepting this Western type of representative government or curtailing that freedom and introducing a more authoritative system and thereby running the risk of discrediting itself in the eyes of Western states. But since Hong Kong did not have really democratic institutions until September 1985[125] even though the capitalist economic and commercial systems flourished, it may have been the PRC's idea that the "two systems, one country" concept applied only to the economic, not the political, field.[126] The Joint Declaration does not provide for an autonomous, representative type of government. Only the legislature of the Hong Kong SAR "shall be constituted by elections"; the chief executive and all principal officials will be appointed by the Central People's government (Annex I, Art. 1). This arrangement clearly indicates the rather limited role of democratic institutions in the Hong Kong SAR.[127]

Finally, let me raise a fairly hypothetical question. Could the Joint Declaration serve as a model for the unification with Taiwan? This question raises more problems than solutions.[128] Is the "two systems, one country" model acceptable for Taiwan and its population? Who would be the representatives of the *one* country? The government of the ROC will claim to be the legitimate and only representative of the *one* China, and so will the government of the PRC.[129] The "two countries, one China" model, similar to the German example, has so far not met with general approval either in the PRC or in the ROC. Moreover, the Joint Declaration might not be a particularly attractive solution because

1. The population of Hong Kong did not participate in its final determination; no referendum was held.
2. The "two systems" model is limited to fifty years.

3. The influence of the central government and of the NPC on the elaboration and interpretation of the internal legal structure in Hong Kong is fairly strong.
4. The military presence is of paramount importance for the influence of the PRC government.

Probably any answer to the question will depend on the democratic development of the PRC itself and on the continuation of the liberal legal system, the granting of individual freedoms, and the functioning of security of law and of an independent court system in the Hong Kong "experiment." Furthermore, a decisive factor will be the will of the people of Taiwan and an answer to the question of how trustworthy they consider the PRC government to be. For example, any solution of the division of Germany will depend on the free exercise of the right of self-determination of the entire German people. The Federal Republic of Germany has admitted that it would accept a free decision of the population of the German Democratic Republic against reunification, provided that the decision is really free.[130] This position should also be applied to the relations between the PRC and the ROC, i.e., any form of unification should be made dependent on the expression of the free will of the Chinese population on Taiwan. There are, of course, forms of eventual cooperation, but the Joint Declaration, if at all, can only to a limited extent serve as a model for unification. In one very essential element the status of Hong Kong cannot be compared to that of Taiwan. The ROC succeeded—or from an objective point of view is at least on the way—in being established as a subject of international law, a state of separate legal identity, from which it follows that the people of the ROC may exert the (defensive) right of self-determination.[131]

Acknowledgments

This chapter is a revised and an enlarged version of a paper presented at the international symposium on Hong Kong: A Chinese and International Concern, March 3–8, 1986, Taipei. For his support in compiling the material on the Joint Declaration I would like to thank Mr. Martin Scheuer, research assistant of the Institute of European Studies. An abridged version of this chapter appeared in *Zeitschrift für ausländisches öffentliches Recht und Völkerrecht* 46 (1986), pp. 647–682.

For valuable critical comments I would like to thank Prof. David Edward, University of Edinburgh, and Prof. Maurice D. Copithorne, University of British Columbia.

In the chapter I have used the following abbreviations:

AJIL	*American Journal of International Law*
BayVGH	Bayerischer Verwaltungsgerichtshof
BDTC	British Dependent Territories Citizen

BNO	British National (Overseas)
BYIL	*The British Yearbook of International Law*
CMLR	*Common Market Law Review*
EEC	European Economic Community
EPIL	*Encyclopedia of Public International Law*, ed. R. Bernhardt (New York: Oxford University Press, 1981)
FBIS	Foreign Broadcast Information Service
GA	General Assembly
GATT	General Agreement on Tariffs and Trade
H.C.	House of Commons
H.C. Debs.	House of Commons, Standing Committee, Parliamentary Debates
ICJ Reports	*International Court of Justice, Reports of Judgements, Advisory Opinions, and Orders*
ILM	*International Legal Materials*
ILR	*International Law Reports*
NJW	*Neue juristische Wochenschrift*
NPC	National People's Congress
PRC	People's Republic of China
ROC	Republic of China
SAR	special administrative region
SI	Statutory Instruments
VCLT	Vienna Convention on the Law of Treaties
YILC	Yearbook of the International Law Commission

Notes

1. Joint Declaration of the Government of the United Kingdom (UK) of Great Britain and Northern Ireland and of the Government of the People's Republic of China (PRC) on the Question of Hong Kong of December 1984, Treaty Series No. 26 (1985), Cmnd. 9543. The Joint Declaration and annexes (hereafter cited as the Hong Kong agreement) were initialed on September 26, 1984, and entered into force on May 27, 1985. An evaluation of this treaty from a legal point of view is given, inter alia, by L. W. Pye, "The International Position of Hong Kong," *China Quarterly*, no. 95 (1983), p. 456 ff.; A. G. Kühn, "Hong Kong—Gegenwart und Zukunft in Fernost," *Aussenpolitik* 36 (1985), p. 438 ff.; M. D. Landry, "Commentary," *Harvard International Law Journal* 26 (1985), pp. 249-263; T. L. Tsim, "Blick auf 1977: Pekings Strategie in der Hongkong-Frage," *Europa-Archiv* (1984), ser. 1, pp. 23-30; A. Dicks, "Treaty, Grant, Usage, or Sufferance? Some Legal Aspects of the Status of Hong Kong," *China Quarterly*, no. 95 (1983), p. 427 ff.; Susan L. Karamanian, "Legal Aspects of the Sino-British Draft Agreement on the Future of Hong Kong," *Texas International Law Journal* 20 (1985), p. 167 ff.; Guiliano Bertuccioli, "L'accordo sino-britannico su Hongkong-Valutazioni storico-politiche," *La Comunità Internazionale* 40 (1985), p. 257 ff.; Lawrence A. Castle, "The Reversion of Hong Kong to China: Legal and Practical Questions," *Williamette Law Review* 21 (1985), p. 327 ff. On the military consequences, cf. R. N. Kaul, "The Hong Kong Sino-British Accord: An Analysis," *Foreign Affairs Reports* 34 (1985), p. 1 ff. There was, even before 1984, a quite intensive debate on the guarantees that had to be included in

an agreement between the United Kingdom and China on the question of Hong Kong; cf. G. Newsham, "Rethinking Hong Kong: A Blueprint for the Future," UCLA Pacific Basic Law Journal 1 (1982), p. 247 ff. (especially p. 263 f.).

2. Of April 4, 1985 (1985 c. 15).

3. S. E. Finer, "Hong Kong 1997: When the Kissing Has to Stop," Political Quarterly 56 (1985), p. 262, qualifies the joint agreement from the British standpoint as "an exercise in damage-limitation."

4. Cf. the remarks of U. Scheuner on Berlin and Hong Kong in K. Doehring, Das Selbstbestimmungsrecht der Völker als Grundsatz des Völkerrechts, Berichte der Deutschen Gesellschaft für Volkerrecht, vol. 14 (Karlsruhe: C. F. Müller, 1974), p. 61. On the legal status and political problems of Berlin, cf. the documents compiled in G. Doeker and J. A. Brueckner, The Federal Republic of Germany and the German Democratic Republic in International Relations, vol. 1 (Dobbs Ferry, N.Y.: Oceana Publications, 1979), p. 205 ff.; cf. also H. Schiedermair, Der Völkerrechtliche Status Berlins nach dem Viermächte-Abkommen vom 3. September 1971 (Berlin: Springer Verlag, 1975), and K. Doehring and G. Ress, Staats- und Völkerrechtliche Aspekte der Berlin-Regelung (Frankfurt am Main: Athenäum Verlag, 1972).

5. The report by the commissioner, Assessment Office, on the views expressed in Hong Kong on the Draft Agreement (presented to the governor of Hong Kong, November 1984) reveals the anger of the Hong Kongers who now hold a BDTC passport and in 1997 will receive a BNO passport instead: "host of those who commented [on the regulation on nationality] did so in adverse or critical terms." According to Finer, "a feeling that the U.K. had failed in its moral obligation towards the two million Hong Kong BDTCs led to expressions of frustration and sometimes anger, particularly from those who recalled their pledges of loyalty on naturalization" ([note 3], p. 268). Finer discloses that the obstacles came in fact, not from the British, but from the Chinese side, since China on September 10, 1982, decreed a Nationality Act that expressly rejected dual nationality. Finer asserts that "like its predecessors of three thousand years the present [Chinese] regime is exceedingly xenophobic and rabidly nationalistic" (p. 269).

6. The Hong Kong (British Nationality) Order 1986, SI 1986/948 (in force on July 1, 1987); Halsbury's Laws of England, 4th ed., Cumulative Supplement 1987, pt. 1, vol. 4, para. 947C 1.

7. Tung-Pi Chen, "The Nationality Law of the People's Republic of China and the Overseas Chinese in Hong Kong, Macao, and Southeast Asia," Journal of International and Comparative Law (New York Law School) 5 (1984), pp. 281, 319.

8. On April 23, 1986, Hong Kong became (as ninety-first member) a contracting party to the GATT. In 1985, Hong Kong was the world's fourteenth biggest exporter and fifteenth biggest importer in terms of the value of international trade (cf. GATT Newsletter [Focus], no. 39 [1986], p. 2).

9. Cf. Karamanian (note 1), p. 174 ff.

10. Cf. Neue Zürcher Zeitung, January 1, 1987, p. 13.

11. Landry (note 1), p. 249. Whether a "transfer of sovereignty" occurred is a disputed question.

12. Karamanian (note 1), p. 181 ff.

13. Sir Geoffrey Howe, secretary of state for foreign and Commonwealth affairs, H.C., January 21, 1985 (Hansard, vol. 71, p. 733).

14. In the second Peking Convention (between Great Britain and China regarding an extension of the Hong Kong Territory) of June 9, 1898 (cf. P. Wesley-Smith, British Dependent Territories: Hong Kong, Vol. 4 of A. Blaustein and E. Blaustein, eds., Constitutions of Dependencies and Special Sovereignties, 6 vols. (Dobbs Ferry,

N.Y.: Oceana Publications, 1975–), p. 10), the New Territories (376 square miles of land on the mainland opposite Hong Kong Island—that is, 92 percent of the whole land area of Hong Kong) were leased for ninety-nine years, a term that will end on June 30, 1997.

15. Landry (note 1), p. 250.

16. Cf. "Peking Is Ready to Negotiate but Hong Kong Is Still Jittery," *New York Times*, September 26, 1982, p. E3, col. 1 (quoted from Landry [note 1], p. 252).

17. Hong Kong Act 1985 (1985 c. 15) of April 4, 1985.

18. Cf. the White Paper of the British government of September 26, 1984, p. 31 (United Kingdom Memorandum) and p. 33 (Chinese Memorandum)—with explanatory notes on p. 45 ff.; on the background of this "ambivalent exchange of memoranda" see Finer (note 3), p. 269.

19. As to the relevance of such instruments, cf. T. O. Elias, *The Modern Law of Treaties* (Dobbs Ferry, N.Y.: Oceana Publications, 1974), p. 75 f., and G. Ress, *Die Rechtslage Deutschlands nach dem Grundlagenvertrag vom 21. Dezember 1972*, Beiträge zum ausländischen öffentlichen Recht und Völkerrecht, vol. 71 (Berlin: Springer Verlag, 1978), p. 121 ff.

20. Hong Kong is ruled by a governor appointed by the Crown. The power of the governor is subject to the Letters Patent and to any Royal Instructions (cf. Hong Kong Letters Patent 1917 to 1976, Arts. I and II. He must consult an appointed Executive Council (five ex officio members and regularly nine other members). For the enactment of laws by the governor, the advice and consent of an appointed Legislative Council, the size of which has steadily increased since World War II (1980, official members twenty-two, unofficial ones twenty-seven), are necessary. Cf. N. Miners, *The Government and Politics of Hong Kong*, 3d ed. (Hong Kong: Oxford University Press, 1981), pp. 81, 126; Landry (note 1), p. 252; B. Hook, "The Government of Hong Kong: Change Within Tradition," *China Quarterly*, no. 95 (1983), p. 491 f.

21. The United Kingdom voted against the resolution of the GA on negotiations on sovereignty "because it made no reference to the right of self-determination" (H.C. Debs., vol. 997; Written Answers, vol. 424: January 28, 1981; and BYIL, vol. 52 [1981], p. 386). Cf. also Denis Healy in H.C., January 21, 1985, p. 742: "in the Falklands . . . experience with Hong Kong would prove of vital importance and set interesting precedents." Whether the Falklands case is a case of the self-determination of this population is doubtful (cf. M. A. Sanchez, "Self-determination and the Falkland Islands Dispute," *Columbia Journal of Transnational Law* 21 [1983], p. 577 ff.). On the differences between Hong Kong, the Falklands, and Gibraltar in this respect, cf. S. C. Roy, "The Hong Kong Agreement: An Assessment," *China Report* 21 (1985), p. 169 ff. A right of self-determination for the inhabitants of the Falklands is rejected by R. Dolzer, *Der völkerrechtliche Status der Falkland-Inseln (Malvinas) im Wandel der Zeit* (Heidelberg: R. v. Decker and C. F. Müller, 1986), p. 133 ff.

22. Lisbon statement of April 10, 1980 (Parliamentary Papers, H.C., 1980-1981, Paper 166 i, p. 4): "The British Government will fully maintain its commitment to honor the freely and democratically expressed wishes of the people of Gibraltar as set out in the preamble to the Gibraltar Constitution." Cf. also Lord Carrington, secretary of state for foreign and Commonwealth affairs, H.C. Debs., vol. 416, col. 766: January 28, 1981 (BYIL, vol. 52 [1981], p. 386).

23. Howe (note 13), p. 753. Although the Hong Kong Act is "different from an independence Act," similar provisions are necessary.

24. Cf. on these questions the systematic study by D. Murswiek, "Offensives und defensives Selbstbestimmungsrecht: Zum Subjekt des Selbstbestimmungsrechts der Völker," Der Staat 23 (1984), p. 523 ff.

One may argue that the United Kingdom was obliged to restore the New Territories, but only within the limits of public international law. If public international law grants to the people of colonies a right of self-determination on the question whether their colony should become independent, part of the sovereignty that leased the territory, or even remain under the jurisdiction of the leaseholder, then one might well query the legality of the whole agreement. The right of self-determination is considered to be the right of the "people" of a distinct territorial unit or even of individuals (human right) in the light of Art. 1, sec. 1, of the UN Convenant on Civil and Political Rights and of the UN Covenant on Economic, Social, and Cultural Rights of December 19, 1966. This right is considered as jus cogens (cf. J. A. Frowein, "Jus Cogens," in EPIL, Instalment 7 [1984], p. 328). If a "unity," e.g., Berlin, is considered to be a sufficiently objective element to create a right of self-determination of the population of Berlin or even West Berlin (cf. Doehring [note 4], p. 44 ff.), that right cannot be refused to the population of colonies like Hong Kong. This is all the more true if the right of self-determination as a human right gives individuals the right to "constitute" a "people" (the right to be "apart") and to exercise thereby the most elementary form of self-determination (cf. W. Wengler, "Das Selbstbestimmungsrecht der Völker als Menschenrecht," in Vorträge, Reden, und Berichte aus dem Europa-Institut, no. 76 [Saarbrücken, 1986], p. 10 ff.).

25. This is the view of the government of the PRC (pt. 1 of the Joint Declaration) according to which the recovering of the Hong Kong area is the common aspiration "of the entire Chinese people." Cf. in this respect also a letter dated March 10, 1972, addressed by the PRC's UN ambassador to the chairman of the Special Committee on Colonialism of the United Nations (quoted in J. A. Cohen and Hungdah Chiu, eds., People's China and International Law: A Documentary Study, vol. 1 [Princeton, N.J.: Princeton University Press, 1974], p. 384).

26. "Any colonial situation which partially or completely destroys the national unity and territorial integrity of a country is incompatible with the purposes and principles of the Charter of the U.N. and specifically with paragraph 6 of GA Res. 1514 (XV)." This argument has also played some role in the discussion of the Falkland's question; cf. J. Houbert, The Falklands: A Hiccup of Decolonization; Current Research on Peace and Violence (n.p.: n.p., 1982), p. 8: "It is ironic that a Colonial Power is able to use the very principle of self-determination, the weapon of the nationalists, to perpetuate a colonial situation." Cf. also Dolzer (note 21), p. 137 f.

27. Howard S. Levie, The Status of Gibraltar (Boulder, Colo.: Westview Press, 1983), p. 113. It is interesting to compare the suggested solution of Levie for the Gibraltar question (p. 117 ff.) with the solution in the Joint Declaration. On the forms of "participation" of the population of Hong Kong in treating their own affairs after 1997, cf. Kaul (note 1), p. 2, and L. Rayner, "ASEAN and Hong Kong," Round Table, no. 292 (1984), p. 383 ff., 388.

28. Cf. Dicks (note 1), p. 427 f.

29. The Treaty of Nanking, signed on August 29, 1842 (ratified on June 26, 1843). The full text is in Treaties, Conventions, etc., Between China and Foreign States: China, the Maritime Customs III, Miscellaneous Series no. 30, vol. 1, 2d ed. (Shanghai: Inspectorate General of Customs, 1917), pp. 351–356. According to the third annex of the Treaty of Nanking, the "Emperor of China cedes to . . . the Queen of Great Britain . . . the island of Hongkong, to be possessed in perpetuity by the Britannic Majesty, Her Heirs and Successors, and to be governed by such

laws and regulations as Her Majesty the Queen of Great Britain shall see fit to direct." In the first Convention of Peking of October 24, 1860, the Emperor of China "agrees to cede . . . that portion of the township of Cowloon, in the Province of Kwang-tung of which a lease was granted in perpetuity" (text in ibid., vol. 1, pp. 429–434). The acquisition of the New Territories (lease for ninety-nine years) took place in the second Convention of Peking of June 9, 1898 (cf. Dicks [note 1], p. 446).

30. Quoted in Dicks (note 1), p. 428. Cf. also Karamanian (note 1), p. 185 f. It seems to be an interesting legal question whether the government of the PRC regards "unequal" treaties as null and void (ab initio and automatically) or whether it considers them only as "not binding," with the effect that the issue can be reopened at its initiative.

31. For a discussion, see W. Morvay, "Unequal Treaties," in *EPIL*, Instalment 7 (1984), p. 514, with further references; P. Wesley-Smith, *Unequal Treaty 1898–1997: China, Great Britain, and Hong Kong's New Territories* (London: Oxford University Press (1980); H. G. Tanneberger, *Das Verhältnis der Volksrepublik China zum Völkerrecht—unter besonderer Berücksichtigung der historischen Erfahrungen des Landes mit den sog: "Ungleichen Verträgen" seti dem Frieden von Nanking (1842) und der eigenen Vertragspraxis gegenüber den sechs asiatischen Staaten (Afghanistan, Birma, Ceylon, Indonesien, Nepal, Pakistan* (Doctoral thesis, University of Bochum, 1974); and A. Verdross and B. Simma, *Universelles Völkerrecht*, 3d ed. (Berlin: Duncker and Humblot, 1984), p. 479. Cf. also K. A. Greenberg, "Hong Kong's Future: Can the People's Republic of China Invalidate the Treaty of Nanking as an Unequal Treaty?" *Fordham International Law Journal* 7 (1984), p. 534, and Newsham (note 1), p. 253 ff.

32. Cf. the references in H. Chiu, "Comparison of the Nationalist and Communist Chinese Views of Unequal Treaties," in J. A. Cohen, ed., *China's Practice of International Law* (Cambridge, Mass.: Harvard University Press, 1972), pp. 239–267, and A. N. Talalaev and V. G. Boyrshinov, "Unequal Treaties as a Mode of Prolonging the Colonial Dependence of the New States of Asia and Africa," in *Soviet Yearbook of International Law* (Moscow: Soviet Association of International Law, 1961), pp. 156–170 (in Russian with English summary). Further references in Dicks (note 1), p. 434; Landry (note 1), p. 253; and Tso, "The Legal Implications of the Sino-British Treaties Regarding Hong Kong," *Loyola of Los Angeles International and Comparative Law Annual* 4 (1981), pp. 111–136.

33. If Art. 52 of the VCLT had been in force in 1842 or in 1860, two of the three treaties from which the British claim to sovereignty over Hong Kong is derived would have been—according to Dicks (note 1), p. 435—null and void.

34. Landry (note 1), p. 253. On the question of the nonretroactive effect of the VCLT, cf. Art. 4 of the convention and Greenberg (note 31), p. 549; cf. also L. A. Castle, "The Reversion of Hong Kong to China: Legal and Practical Questions," *Willamette Law Review* 21 (1985), p. 330.

35. Landry (note 1), p. 253 note 22.

36. The Four Power Munich agreement (Hitler, Mussolini, Chamberlain, Daladier) of September 30, 1938, on the cession from Czechoslovakia to Germany of the "Sudeten" territory, initiated by a German ultimatum, was communicated to the Czechoslovak government, which replied that it would comply with the terms agreed upon "without us and against our will." Cf. T. Schieder, "Munich Agreement," in, *EPIL*, Instalment 3 (1982), p. 285.

37. Treaty of Prague of December 11, 1973, ILM 13 (1974), p. 19 ff.; cf. D. Blumenwitz, *Der Prager Vertrag* (Bonn: Kulturstiftung der deutchen Vertriebenen, 1985), with further references.

38. According to Art. 2, para. 2, the "present Treaty shall not affect the nationality of living or deceased persons ensuing from the legal system of either of the Contracting parties." On the consequences of this "agreed and limited" nullity of the Munich agreement, see Blumenwitz (note 37), p. 63 ff.

39. Cfs. Hungdah Chiu, "The 1984 Sino-British Agreement on Hong Kong and Its Implications on China's Unification," *Issues and Studies* 21 (April 1985), p. 13 ff., 19 ff.

40. FBIS (China), October 5, 1984, p. 5 (quoted by Chiu [note 39], p. 14 note 14).

41. A well-known example of such a recognition of "sovereignty" without full legal substance was the British-Egypt Treaty of August 28, 1936. Cf. W. Kewenig, "Grenzen der Souveränität," in *Aussenpolitische Perspektiven des westdeutschen Staates, Das Ende des Provisoriums*, vol. 1 (Munich and Vienna: R. Oldenbourg Verlag, 1971), p. 144.

42. Art. 1, para. 1, of the Hong Kong Act 1985.

43. Cf. "Art. 2 of the Convention on Relations Between the Three Powers and the Federal Republic of Germany, May 26, 1952 (October 23, 1954)," *AJIL* 49 (1955), suppl. 57.

44. Of December 21, 1972 (ILM 12 [1973], p. 16 ff.); cf. B. Simma, "Der Grundvertrag und das Recht der völkerrechtlichen Verträge," *Archiv des öffentlichen Rechts* 100 (1975), p. 4 ff. The situation can be compared with the recognition of a state by treaty. If the state violates provisions of the treaty, the suspension or termination does not revoke the recognition.

45. Suspension and termination are legally possible; if a material breach of the treaty occurs (cf. E. Klein, *Statusverträge im Völkerrecht, Rechtsfragen territorialer Sonderregime*, Beiträge zum ausländischen öffentlichen Recht und Völkerrecht, vol. 76 [Berlin: Springer Verlag, 1980], p. 254 ff.), but state practice demonstrates that often such a breach has been tolerated because of the factual situation (ibid., p. 257).

46. Cf. ibid., p. 239 note 220. Even under those circumstances it is doubtful, in the light of the principle of self-determination, whether the United Kingdom could ever regain a title for the recovery of sovereignty over the crown colony (except the New Territories).

47. According to Art. 70, sec. 1(b), of the VCLT, the termination of a treaty "does not affect any right, obligation or legal situation of the parties created through the execution of the treaty prior to its termination." D. Evrigenis pointed out that the words, "legal situation of the parties created through the execution of the treaty," applied to any legal situation all the conditions of which had been fulfilled by the execution of the treaty prior to the termination and that "subsequent nonexecution of the treaty . . . did not have the automatic effect of reversing that situation" (A/CONF. 39/11, p. 447; quoted in Klein [note 45], p. 302).

48. Whether also for treaties "establishing territorial status" the application of the rule of *rebus sic stantibus* is excluded is a matter of dispute. The inclusion in Art. 62, sec. 2, was rejected because of the vagueness of the notion of "territorial status" (cf. Klein [note 45], p. 289 ff.).

49. Cf. C.H.M. Waldock, YILC (1966), vol. 1, pt. 1, p. 86: "treaties of that type were intended to create a stable position. It would be inconsistent with the very nature of those treaties to make them subject to the rebus sic stantibus rule" (further references in Klein [note 45], p. 292 ff.).

50. As to the notion of guarantee, cf. G. Ress, "Guarantee Treaties," in *EPIL*, Instalment 7 (1984), p. 109 ff.

51. H. Steinberger, "Einflüsse der Ostverträge auf Deutschland als Ganzes," in *Finis Germaniae?* ed. I. von Münch, T. Oppermann, and R. Stödter (Frankfurt am Bain: Metzner Verlag, 1977), p. 265; cf. also A. M. de Zayas, "Peace Treaty of Westphalia 1968," in *EPIL*, Instalment 7 (1984), p. 536.

52. Cf. para. 4 of the Final Protocol of June 3, 1973, to the agreement. The three Western powers and the Soviet Union undertook "to ensure the observance of the commitments undertaken on behalf of the Federal Republic of Germany and the German Democratic Republic, respectively." Cf. H. Schiedermair, *Der völkerrechtliche Status Berlins nach dem Viermächte-Abkommen vom 3. September 1971*, Beiträge zum ausländischen öffentlichen Recht und Völkerrecht, vol. 64 (Berlin: Springer Verlag, 1975), p. 185 ff.

53. Cf. Chiu (note 39), p. 14, who cites in this respect Art. 4 of the Harvard *Research in International Law*. Cf. also Kaul (note 1), p. 3, and Karamanian (note 1), p. 181.

54. On this special technique, cf. Schiedermair (note 52), p. 64 ff.

55. Also, according to Landry (note 1), p. 253, the words "upon resuming the exercise of sovereignty" appear to be a diplomatic solution to the problem of avoiding either the British or the Chinese position regarding the history and legal status of Hong Kong. On the historical background, cf. Karamanian (note 1), p. 168 ff., and Greenberg (note 31), p. 535 f. On the economic situation and effects, cf. L. Dunn, "Hong Kong After the Sino-British Declaration," *International Affairs* 61 (1985), p. 197 ff.

56. Dicks (note 1), p. 427 ff., 441 f.

57. The word "cession," which was used in the Treaty of Nanking and the first Peking Convention, is carefully avoided, even if the whole legal procedure can only be interpreted as being a cession of the island of Hong Kong and of Kowloon to the PRC. The idea that the United Kingdom waives unilaterally the exercise of sovereignty (cf. Art. 1, sec. 1, of the Hong Kong Act 1985: "As from 1st July 1997 Her Majesty shall no longer have sovereignty or jurisdiction over any part of Hong Kong"), thus leaving for a logical second a *terra nullius* before the PRC establishes its own sovereignty, does not meet the substance of the procedure because the United Kingdom "restores" the Hong Kong area to the PRC.

58. Nevertheless, the PRC has, for all practical purposes, not objected to the exercise of British sovereignty over Hong Kong. The Chinese attitude may therefore be described "as one of acquiescence" (Dicks [note 1], p. 439). The relationship between Hong Kong and the United Kingdom is of a domestic nature. The United Kingdom has concluded not only treaties and other international agreements that apply to Hong Kong but others in which Hong Kong has specifically been mentioned as a separate territory (e.g., GATT). The Hong Kong government, acting with the "consent" of the U.K. government, has directly concluded agreements not only with foreign states but also with the provincial government of Guangdong (e.g., for water supply, etc.). The legislation of the PRC for certain fiscal and administrative purposes has treated the boundary between Hong Kong and China "as an international boundary" (ibid.). Air traffic rights and regulations, rules on the flying of ships' flags, legal and judicial acts under the law of Hong Kong "are recognized in the normal way in China" (ibid.). On the other hand, Chinese legislation has to avoid referring to Hong Kong as a foreign country. Dicks (note 1), p. 440, gives an example from the field of monetary law that is of particular importance to the relationship between China and Hong Kong. The status of the currency issued by or on behalf of the British administration in Hong Kong has been recognized in Chinese legislation ever since 1949. At the same time, in China's foreign exchange control legislation,

Hong Kong as a territory, although "external" to China, is separately mentioned, together with Macao, in such a way as to make it clear that it is not a "foreign country." In other matters, the PRC has enacted legislation "which appears to be applicable to Hong Kong or is at least equivocal in this respect. The most important example is the Law on Nationality of the People's Republic of China, which contains provisions relating to persons born in foreign countries while making no mention of Hong Kong, leaving it to be inferred, in the light of the more usual legislative practice, that Hong Kong is to be included into China. If this is correct, the provision of Art. 3, whereby China makes it clear that dual nationality is not recognized in relation to any Chinese national, appears to create a direct conflict with the British law of nationality as it has been applied in Hong Kong (including the New Territories)" (ibid., p. 440 f.).

59. The British position in the past has been quite clear. In September 1982, in connection with the meeting in Peking, the prime minister told the public that the United Kingdom "had not yet conceded sovereignty to China." She continued: "There are treaties in existence. We stick by our treaties unless we decide on something else. At the moment we stick by our treaties" (quoted in ibid., p. 472). On September 27, 1982, the prime minister, in Hong Kong, concluded: "But one point about the treaties, I believe they are valid at international law, and if countries try to abrogate treaties like that, then it is very serious indeed, because if a country will not stand by one treaty it will not stand by another treaty, and that's why you enter into talks" (ibid., p. 428).

60. PRC Constitution (adopted by the Fifth National People's Congress on December 4, 1982); cf. T. Hsia, K. Haun, and C. Johnson, "People's Republic of China," in A. Blaustein and G. Flanz, Constitutions of the World (Dobbs Ferry, N.Y.: Oceana Publications, 1983). According to Art. 31 of the constitution, the state can, if necessary, establish special administrative regions. The systems in the SARs shall be prescribed by the National People's Congress in the light of the specific conditions (cf. also Art. 62, para. 13, of the constitution).

61. White Paper (note 18), pp. 33, 31. The two memoranda relate only to physical, not juridical, persons.

62. On the question of diplomatic and consular protection in cases of dual nationality, cf. G. Ress, "Diplomatischer Schutz," in I. Seidl-Hohenveldern, Lexikon des Rechts, Völkerrecht (Neuwied and Darmstadt: Luchterhand Verlag, 1985), p. 54 ff. The principle of effective nationality has been generally recognized (cf. "Mergé Claim," ILR 22 [1955], p. 443).

63. A quite similar question is discussed in relation to those German nationals residing in the German Democratic Republic and seeking diplomatic protection by the Federal Republic of Germany in third countries; cf. Ress (note 19), p. 212 ff.

64. The notion of "internationalization" is not very clear; cf. R. Wolfrum, Die Internationalisierung staatsfreier Räume, Beiträge zum ausländischen öffentlichen Recht und Völkerrecht, vol. 85 (Berlin: Springer Verlag, 1984), p. 10 f. Forms of coimperium and condominium have been qualified as "internationalization" (cf. U. Nussbaum, Rohstoffgewinnung in der Antarktis [Vienna and New York: Springer-Verlag, 1985], p. 58 f.). The Hong Kong agreement establishes neither the one nor the other. The United Kingdom does not continue to exercise territorial jurisdiction, but only a limited form of personal jurisdiction (BDTCs—now BNOs).

65. Cf. para. 3, secs. 9 and 10. According to sec. 9, the Hong Kong SAR "may establish mutually beneficial economic relations with the United Kingdom and other countries, whose economic interests in Hong Kong will be given due regard." It is obvious that the PRC can control the "mutual benefit" of any "relation" through

the chief executive, who will be appointed—and also recalled—by the Central People's government. Sec. 10 provides the capacity not only to conclude agreements but also, the Hong Kong SAR government "may on its own issue travel documents for entry into and exit from Hong Kong" (immigration control; "present practice" of entrance regulations will apply in relation to persons from other parts of China— cf. Annex I, Art. 14). Landry (note 1), p. 254 note 26, evaluates these powers as being "substantially comparable to those currently enjoyed by Hong Kong." Cf. also Miners (note 20), p. 283.

66. Cf. the respective provisions of the constitution of the Federal Republic of Germany (Art. 32, Basic Law).

67. Cf. Joint Declaration, para. 3, sec. 10, and Annex I, Art. 11. The capacity to maintain treaty relations shall include "participation in the GATT through which Hong Kong enjoys most-favored-nation status in its major markets" (Landry [note 1], p. 254 note 27). Cf. also Annex I, Art. 6.

68. Annex I, Art. 11. Hong Kong already has a form of membership in both the Asian Development Bank and the Economic and Social Commission for Asia and the Pacific.

69. This procedure will be necessary at least for all those treaties implemented in Hong Kong to which the PRC is not a party. These treaties "may remain implemented in the Hong Kong Special Administrative Region" (Annex I, Art. 11), but this provision depends not only on the PRC but also on the decision of the parties to the treaty. On the renewal or amendment of air service agreements actually in force in Hong Kong, see Annex I, Art. 9 (renewal only "in principle" and bound to "specific authorisations from the Central People's Government"). Cf. Karamanian (note 1), p. 177 f.

70. Cf. the declaration of the United Kingdom in GATT press release, April 4, 1986 (GATT/1384), and the communication from the PRC in GATT L/5987 of April 24, 1986; cf. also F. K. Liebig, *Das GATT als Zentrum der internationalen Handelspolitik* (Baden-Baden: Nomos Verlag, 1971), p. 51 note 44.

71. Cf. Karamanian (note 1), p. 176. Landry (note 1), p. 253, is of the opinion that the capitalist structure of the Hong Kong SAR will operate "at least" until June 30, 2047. The continuation is possible, but so far the PRC is not legally obligated to do so. A continuation of the capitalist status of the Hong Kong SAR after 2047 on the initiative of the PRC, without any international agreement or commitment, would hardly attract foreign investors in the same way as before. The situation would perhaps be different if after 2047 the PRC entered into an international commitment by a unilateral act addressed to the United Kingdom or to the GA of the United Nation.

72. Chiu (note 39), p. 15.

73. Cf. the references in ibid.

74. The United Kingdom perhaps might not be interested in such an arrangement because it would be brought in in a kind of guarantor position.

75. Cf. the examples in G. Ress, "The Demarcation of Frontiers in International Treaties and Maps," in *National and International Boundaries, Thesaurum Acroasium,* vol. 14, ed. D. S. Constantopoulos (Thessaloníki: Institute of Public International Law and International Relations, 1985), p. 433 ff.

76. Within the period up to 1997, para. 3 of the schedule of the Hong Kong Act 1985 allows Hong Kong to adopt local laws to replace those U.K. enactments that currently form part of the law of Hong Kong, e.g., civil aviation and shipping. Hong Kong may make laws "having extraterritorial operation," for instance, in connection with air piracy and regulations for shipping. In 1997, Hong Kong laws must be "self-contained" (Howe [note 13], p. 740).

77. Joint Declaration, para. 3, sec. 2.
78. Chiu (note 39), p. 17.
79. Joint Declaration, para. 3, sec. 12.
80. Chiu (note 39), p. 17.
81. Annex I, Art. 2, para. 1. In Hong Kong, various sources of law are in force, e.g., common law, ordinances, subordinate legislation, etc. Cf. V. A. Penlington, *Law in Hong Kong* (Hong Kong: SCMP, 1978), p. 14.
82. Cf. Chiu (note 39), p. 18. The Standing Committee can also annul new laws of the Hong Kong SAR. According to Annex I, Art. 2, para. 2, the Hong Kong legislature "may on its own authority enact laws in accordance with the provisions of the Basic Law and legal procedures, and report them to the Standing Committee of the National People's Congress for the record. Laws enacted by the legislature which are in accordance with the Basic Law and legal procedures shall be regarded as valid." On the question of the superiority of final judicial decisions in Hong Kong, cf. Castle (note 34), p. 340.
83. Cf. Art. 13 of Annex I. Even "the provisions of the International Covenant on Civil and Political Rights and the International Covenant on Economic, Social and Cultural Rights as applied to Hong Kong shall remain in force" (ibid., para. 4). Cf. the White Paper (note 18), p. 42, on the reservations made by the United Kingdom in order to take account of Hong Kong's particular conditions. The conclusion that the Basic Law has to be interpreted in the light of the Joint Declaration—and therefore in the light of these guaranties of human rights—cannot be outweighed by the fact that Art. 2 of Annex I itself refers to the Basic Law as the governing maxim. This reference does not put the Basic Law on an independent level; it remains submitted to an interpretation in the light of all principles agreed upon between the parties in the Joint Declaration. Cf. on this question Finer (note 3), p. 262 ff.; Kaul (note 1), p. 6; and Castle (note 34), p. 336.
84. Chiu (note 39), p. 18.
85. Ibid.; cf. Finer (note 3), p. 265 f., and Castle (note 34), p. 338 note 77.
86. Chiu ([note 39], p. 19) concludes from an article in the *People's Daily* that the special administrative region and the high degree of autonomy are all "special favors" granted by the PRC's central authorities and there is no credible guarantee that they will not be changed in "appropriate time." The text in the *People's Daily* (*Renmin ribao*) on special administrative regions (FBIS [China], October 2, 1984, p. K19; cited by Chiu [note 39], p. 18 f.) may indicate this conclusion, because it states: "First of all, to safeguard China's sovereignty, unity, and territorial integrity is a basic principle we should adhere to in establishing special administrative regions. Our country should be a unified country. There is only one China in the world, and that is the People's Republic of China. It exercises sovereignty over its special administrative regions. Ours is a socialist country with the unitary system. It is not a federal country. The NPC is the supreme power organ of the state and its permanent body is the NPC Standing Committee. Both exercise the legislative power of the state. The State Council, that is central people's government, is the executive body of the supreme power organ of the state and the highest organ of the state administration. The special administrative regions are local administrative regions under the unified central leadership. They are not member states. The relationship between the special administrative regions and the central authorities is one between localities and central authorities. They must exercise their powers within the limits of their authority as prescribed by the laws enacted by the NPC." Nevertheless, from a legal point of view, China is bound to observe the specific regulations in the Joint Declaration, and it would be a breach of treaty obligations if the NPC

were to enact laws contrary to paragraph 3 of the Joint Declaration. It is true that no credible "guarantee" (or any guarantee at all) in the legal sense of that notion exists. There is no third power guaranteeing the fulfillment of the Joint Declaration.

87. Chiu (note 39), p. 19 f. The costs of the Chinese forces will be borne by the PRC. There is no indication in the Joint Declaration whether Hong Kong's inhabitants may be required to serve as conscripts in the People's Liberation Army.

88. Cf. *Der Spiegel* 38:39 (September 1984), p. 136, and *Frankfurter Allgemeine Zeitung*, September 27, 1984, p. 7.

89. The judges will be appointed by the chief executive who will act "in accordance with the recommendation of an independent commission composed of local judges, persons from the legal profession and other eminent persons" (Annex I, Art. 3). The removal of judges is made rather difficult (cf. Landry [note 1], p. 257).

90. E. Klein, "Treaties, Effects of Territorial Changes," in *EPIL*, Instalment 7 (1984), p. 473.

91. H. Waldock, "Third Report on the Law of Treaties," *YILC* (1969), pt. 2, p. 52.

92. Liebig (note 70), p. 51 note 44.

93. On the question of membership of China, cf. *GATT Newsletter (Focus)*, no. 40 (July/August/September 1986), p. 6.

94. Cf. T. Kunugi, "States Succession in the Framework of GATT," *AJIL* 59 (1965), p. 285 note 65.

95. Annex I, Art. 14. On the question of nationality of the Hong Kong population, cf. Tun-Ri Chen, "The Nationality Law of the People's Republic of China and the Overseas Chinese in Hong Kong, Macao, and Southeast Asia," *New York Law School Journal of International and Comparative Law* 5 (1984), p. 281 ff.

96. These persons will obtain permanent identity cards from the SAR. "Passports" of the Hong Kong SAR are restricted to Chinese nationals who hold permanent identity cards. Other persons lawfully residing in Hong Kong may receive travel documents from the Hong Kong SAR. On the treatment of the non-Chinese Hong Kong residents, cf. Karamanian (note 1), p. 181, and note 100 below.

97. A. N. Makarov, "Staatsangehörigkeit," in K. Strupp and H. J. Schlochauer, *Wörterbuch des Völkerrechts*, vol. 3, 2d ed. (Berlin: de Gruyter, 1962), p. 328.

98. Ibid.

99. White Paper (note 18), p. 31, item (b). The use of the word "may" rather than "shall" in para. 2(1) (b) of the Schedule of the Hong Kong Act 1985 (see note 2) raised considerable concern in Hong Kong (cf. H.C., January 21, 1985, p. 736), but the problem was solved in the Hong Kong (British Nationality) Order 1986, Art. 4, sec. 2 (cf. White Paper on the Draft Hong Kong [British Nationality Order] 1986 [published October 17, 1985]). Cf. the Hong Kong (British Nationality) Order 1986, SI 1986/948 (note 6).

100. The connection with Hong Kong is defined in relation to birth or registration of the person or parents (father or mother) in Hong Kong, and in the case of registration outside of Hong Kong, descent from a person born in Hong Kong having residence there, Crown service under the government of Hong Kong, etc., are relevant. The date of January 1, 1983, is decisive as for registration in Hong Kong. A person born in Hong Kong on or after that date shall not be taken to have a connection with Hong Kong unless one of his or her parents was settled in Hong Kong or a BDTC by virtue of having a connection with Hong Kong as specified.

The order regulates, inter alia, the removal of Hong Kong from the list of dependent territories. The British Nationality Act of 1981 and the British Nationality (Falkland Islands) Act of 1983 are amended, and "British National (Overseas)" is inserted as new category besides the BDTCs.

101. The British announcements are somewhat euphemistic. "The title 'British National (Overseas)' makes clear that we are dealing with a form of British nationality. Nothing less than that would be acceptable in Hong Kong. On the other hand, it is essential that the title . . . must clearly carry no implication of a continuing constitutional relationship between Britain and Hong Kong after 1997" (Howe [note 13], p. 735). Who is eligible to acquire the new form of nationality is now regulated in the Hong Kong (British Nationality) Order of 1986. "For technical reasons" it was deemed not possible to rely on the words "by virtue of a connection with Hong Kong" in the title of the "new form of British nationality" (cf. Art. 4, para. 1, of the order).

102. The British government told Parliament that the order will include any measures necessary to ensure "that no British national or any child born after 1st July 1997 to a British national is made stateless as a result of the agreements (H.C., January 21, 1985, p. 736)." Such people may acquire British Overseas citizenship.

Art. 6 of the order sets out the provisions for avoiding or reducing statelessness. The underlying principle is that no one who loses his or her BDTC status as a result of the order nor any child born on or after July 1, 1997, to such a person, should be stateless as a result of the Joint Declaration. The principle was extended to the grandchildren of former BDTCs if they are born stateless (cf. White Paper of October 17, 1985 [note 99], p. 6 f.).

103. Cf. this definition in the Chinese Memorandum, White Paper (note 18).

104. Ibid., p. 45. Cf. also the questions in the British Parliament (H.C., 1985, p. 736). The same statement is to be found in the White Paper of October 17, 1985 (note 99), p. 2: "Her Majesty's Government . . . state that all those who on 30 June 1997 are BDTCs by virtue of a connection with Hong Kong will cease to have that status with effect from 1 July 1997, and it will not be possible to acquire BDT citizenship by virtue of a connection with Hong Kong on or after 1 July 1997. But those who will lose BDT citizenship will be eligible to retain an appropriate status (not to be acquired by anyone born on or after 1 July 1997) which will enable them to continue to use British passports before 1 July 1997 (or up to 31 December 1997 if born in the first six months of that year). Arrangements will be made for the renewal and replacement of those passports by United Kingdom Consular Officers, and for the holders of such passports to receive British consular protection when in third countries."

105. The only real relationship being the fact of having been formerly a British Dependent Territories citizen.

106. *ICJ Reports*, 1955, p. 4.

107. Note 18, p. 45.

108. Nevertheless, a nationality without the basic rights of a national is a contradiction in itself. Where is "his" country to which a BNO has the human right to return (cf. Art. 13, para. 2, of the General Declaration of Human Rights)? Where is "his" country in which he has the right of access to public functions according to Art. 25(c) of the UN Covenant on Civil and Political Rights? The British government is responsible at least for granting to its "nationals," whatever form of nationality they may have, access to one of its territories. This problem may be of importance not only in relation to the BNOs but also to third countries that want to extradite a BNO.

109. Those inhabitants of Hong Kong who are British Dependent Territories citizens but not "Chinese compatriots" will or can become BNOs, but their dependents will become stateless unless they fall under the categories of Art. 6 of the order (cf. note 102).

110. Cf. *Frankfurter Allgemeine Zeitung*, November 7, 1985, p. 7. The right of residence is restricted to holders of permanent identity cards of the SAR (Annex I, Art. 14), and this fact may be stated in the travel documents of the SAR.

111. Even if there does not exist any international obligation of third states to recognize BNO passports or to grant access to their holders, some Western governments have declared their willingness to recognize them, e.g., U.S. Vice-President Bush has declared that the United States will recognize these passports (cf. *Frankfurter Allgemeine Zeitung*, November 7, 1985, p. 7), and Switzerland has reached an agreement with Britain to accept the new Hong Kong passports and to grant access to their holders (cf. *Frankfurter Allgemeine Zeitung*, December 26, 1986, p. 5). The key to a solution seems to have been found in an endorsement to appear in the new passports that will link the document to the bearer's certificate of identity (cf. Chiu [note 39], p. 18) which will state that he or she has a right of abode in Hong Kong.

112. H.C., January 12, 1985, p. 739. Home Secretary D. Hurd has rejected a plea for 11,500 nonethnic Chinese citizens of Hong Kong to be granted full British citizenship (cf. *Times*, April 4, 1986). However, he has given "an amber light" for 270 Hong Kong veterans of the Second World War to acquire British citizenship or to settle in Britain. The new British National (Overseas) passport (for 3.5 million Hong Kong Chinese) will carry an endorsement that the holder does not need a visa or entry certificate to visit Britain.

113. Cf. Art. 48, EEC treaty. On these provisions, cf. G. Ress, "Free Movement of Persons, Services, and Capital," in *Thirty Years of Community Law*, ed. the Commission of the European Communities, the European Perspectives Series (Luxembourg, 1983), p. 285 ff. However, the right to free movement under Art. 48 of the EEC treaty is granted only to British citizens, not to BDTCs (with some exceptions). Hong Kong is not mentioned in Annex 4 to the EEC treaty (cf. Art. 227, para. 3, subpara. 2, EEC treaty). Hong Kong is not part of the EEC territory; therefore, holders of a "British Passport Hong Kong" are not entitled to the right of free movement of workers (cf. BayVGH NJW [1985], p. 1304, and A. Randelzhofer in E. Grabitz, *Kommentar zum EWG-Vertrag*, Art, 48 marginal note 9 [Munich: Beck-Verlag, 1986]). Cf. also K. R. Simmonds, "The British Nationality Act 1981 and the Definition of the Term 'National' for Community Purposes," *CMLR* 21 (1984), p. 675.

114. H. Hecker, "Staatsangehörigkeit," in Seidl-Hohenveldern (note 62), p. 262; Makarov (note 97), p. 328; and Verdross and Simma (note 31), p. 788 (§ 1193).

115. Cf. Art. 1, para. 1, of the International Covenant on Civil and Political Rights of December 19, 1966.

116. R. Bernhardt, "Option," in K. Strupp and H. J. Schlochauer, *Wörterbuch des Völkerrechts*, vol. 2 (Berlin: Duncker and Humblot, 1966), p. 663; cf. also K. M. Meessen, *Die Option der Staatsangehörigkeit* (Berlin: Duncker and Humblot, 1966).

117. Cf. Klein (note 45), p. 191 ff.

118. Cf. Scheuner (note 4), p. 61.

119. Landry (note 1), p. 263.

120. *Frankfurter Allgemeine Zeitung*, November 7, 1985, p. 7: "If the PRC already one year after the conclusion of the Joint Declaration attempts to interpret it in

her own way, the prospects for Hong Kong look rather dark. The result is that the more wealthy Hong Kong Chinese people continue to establish a second position in western countries." Cf. also *Die Welt*, October 10, 1985, p. 5.

121. This formula of "full implementation" is well known from the dispute between the USSR and the three Western powers concerning the Berlin agreement of 1971. The USSR urges the strict application; the three Western powers, the full application and implementation.

122. Howe (note 13), p. 734.

123. Ibid., p. 741.

124. *Der Spiegel* 39, no. 49 (December 2, 1985), p. 146, referring to a commentary in the *South China Morning Post*.

125. Until that date there was "virtually no public demand for representation" in Hong Kong, and no political parties existed. Hong Kong was and is run "by professional bureaucrats, in a spirit of benevolent paternalism" (cf. Finer [note 3], p. 266).

126. According to a Chinese representative on the question of Hong Kong, Mr. Xu, it would be "ideal if both systems would be in concordance. It would be a misfortune for China and the U.K. if one or both would try to implement its own political system in Hong Kong" (quoted in *Der Spiegel*, p. 147).

127. It has been noted that "on its face," the Joint Declaration appears to establish an executive branch predominantly under NPC influence, a legislative branch responsive to the demands of the Hong Kong population and a judiciary with special ties to the United Kingdom (Landry [note 1], p. 261). The Joint Declaration does not give any indication of the manner in which elections will be conducted, and Landry rightly concludes that the method employed "could have crucial implications, since the legislature of the Hong Kong SAR will be able to enact laws on its own authority, without the assent of the chief executive" (ibid., p. 262).

128. Cf. Chiu (note 39), p. 19 ff.

129. Cf. the discussion of different proposals in *Frankfurter Allgemeine Zeitung*, March 3, 1986, p. 12.

130. Cf. D. Murswiek, "Systematische Überlegungen zum Selbstbestimmungsrecht des deutschen Volkes," in G. Zeiger, ed., *Deutschland als Ganzes, Festschrift für Herbert Czaja* (Cologne: Verlag Wissenschaft und Politik, 1985), p. 233 ff., 257; G. Ress, *Die Rechtslage Deutschlands nach dem Grundlagenvertrag vom 21. Dezember 1972* (Berlin: Springer Verlag, 1978), p. 108; and E. Klein, "Das Selbstbestimmungsrecht der Ostdeutschen unter Berücksichtigung der Selbstbestimmungsdiskussion in den Vereinten Nationen," in *Reden zu Deutschland 1980* (Bonn: Kulturstiftung der deutschen Vertriebenen, 1981), p. 82.

131. On the prerequisites of public international law as to the free exercise of the right of self-determination, cf. H. von Mangoldt, *Die West-Iran-Frage und das Selbstbestimmungsrecht der Völker*, Zeitschrift für ausländisches öffentliches Recht und Völkerrecht, vol. 31 (Stuttgart: Kohlhammer, 1971), p. 197 ff., 235.

9

The Hong Kong Agreement and
Its Impact on the World Economy

Jan S. Prybyla

Jane said passionately: "What's needed is a new heaven and a new earth! And you sit there eating kidneys?"

Agatha Christie
An Overdose of Death

Hong Kong

To Lord Palmerston, Hong Kong was "a barren island with hardly a house upon it," and perhaps also the added inconvenience that there was nowhere to play cricket.[1] Some one hundred years later, after the Japanese imperial armies were done with it, Hong Kong was "a run-down, war-damaged, pre-industrial society with no very evident future."[2] Sixteen years after that, in 1961, with a half million refugees from Communist China and many more on the way, it was "dirty, overcrowded, often very thirsty, and obviously fighting hard for 'a place in the sun.'"[3] But an interesting dimension now appears in the assessment: Hong Kong "was sometimes chaotic and always opportunist. . . . [It] is at all levels . . . permeated with the idea of working and making money. . . . There is not much sympathy or public support for those who do not or cannot work."[4] In the words of one of its native sons, Hong Kong is "a money-making machine."[5] It is that, but it is also more than that.

For the student of politics, it is a singular colonial city-state, which, when compared with most postcolonial states, splendidly illustrates Joan Robinson's (rather atypical) proposition that "the misery of being exploited by capitalists is nothing compared to the misery of not being exploited at all."[6] It is a Chinese city with British law and, more important, the British instinct for the rule of law. For the humanist, it is not just a place where, if we had a hedonimeter, it would register—on a scale of 0 to 10—Hong Kong residents at 9.9. It is also a city of refugees, the largest of its kind in the world; of family loyalties and sacrifices; not just of competition, but

167

of that other indispensable (but theoretically neglected) ingredient of the free competitive society, voluntary cooperation.

For the economist, Hong Kong is the nearest living thing to Adam Smith's "obvious and simple system of natural liberty," or laissez-faire, a credit to the idea of the competitive market and the presumption against government involvement in what Alfred Marshall has called "the ordinary business of life."[7] Although the Hong Kong phenomenon is not as simple and obvious as it is sometimes made out to be, it is still the most obvious and simplest of the lot.[8]

Under the Hong Kong government's policy of active nonintervention, the greater part by far of the ordinary business of life is left to individuals and families to do with as they please. The government has limited its actions to the three duties of the sovereign listed in the *Wealth of Nations* and a fourth duty added, curiously enough, by Milton Friedman. The first three are protection of society from the violence and invasion of other independent societies; protection of every member of the society from the injustice or oppression of every other member of it, or the duty of establishing an exact administration of justice; and the provision of "public works," which might not "be for the interest of any individual or small number of individuals to erect or maintain . . . though it may frequently do much more than repay it to a great society."[9] The fourth duty, the Friedman duty, is the protection of members of the community who cannot be regarded as "responsible" individuals.[10] Even the harsher critics of the Hong Kong government would, I think, agree that these four duties, quite narrowly interpreted, have been discharged in a very exemplary manner over the years, under the most trying of conditions. Although the private sector has had its share of disorder and crime and the public sector its scandals, by and large, the society has been an orderly one with an administration that is both apolitical and uncorrupt.[11] It will be difficult to replicate this combination.

Under this benevolent nonrule, where "every man . . . [was] left perfectly free to pursue his own interest his own way, and to bring his industry and capital into competition with those of any other man,"[12] Hong Kong has grown and prospered. With refugees from China arriving in staggering numbers, the colony—in the 1960s and 1970s—increased its per capita gross national product (GNP) at an average annual rate of 7 percent, surpassed in the whole (non-oil-exporting) world only by Singapore (7.4 percent). By 1982, its per capita GNP reached $5,340, putting it in the upper reaches of what the World Bank calls "middle-income economies" (MIEs) or, alternatively, in the lower reaches of the "industrial market economies" (IMEs), roughly on a par with Ireland, Spain, and Israel. In those terms, Hong Kong is the third most materially comfortable place in Asia, well behind Japan ($10,080 in 1982) but right behind Singapore. By comparison, Communist China's per capita GNP in 1982 was $310, comparable to Somalia or the Central African Republic.[13] Today, after much improvement, the PRC is probably at the level of Sierra Leone.

Data on the distribution of income and wealth in Hong Kong are largely, but not altogether, impressionistic. The impression conveyed by one longtime observer is that

the contrast between the lives of the wealthy and the lives of the poor is very great, and this contrast is unusually evident in Hong Kong where there are many people and little room, so that no one can hide himself away or separate himself from his fellow citizens for very long. But although the contrast is obvious, it is not so extreme or disagreeable as in many countries. On the one hand the rich are rarely idle; and on the other poverty is seldom abject or degrading. . . . Between the new and the old and the rich and the poor there is an enormous volume of plain but evidently quite tolerable living, geared to modern patterns of work and consumption.[14]

Less impressionistic investigations carried out by Steven Chow and Gustav Papanek suggest that income distribution in Hong Kong has been relatively equitable: relative even to the more redistributively inclined industrial market economies like Britain and France.[15] The findings of decile and quintile income distribution analysis for Hong Kong are indirectly confirmed by the leading social indicators, such as life expectancy, infant mortality, calorie intake, education, adult literacy, and the physical quality of life index, all of which have shown dramatic improvement since the early 1960s.[16]

Hong Kong's movement toward middle-class prosperity among the nations of the world has not only been rapid and comparatively equitable but also "modern" in the sense that export-oriented industrialization has progressively emphasized higher value-added through increasing intensity of skills and rising technological level ("going up the market," as this tendency is sometimes called). In this way, Hong Kong has managed to keep a step or two ahead of the competition on the world market coming from the low-income economies (LIEs), which are now in the cheap garment and plastic flower businesses, whereas Hong Kong increasingly works for the fashion houses of Europe and America and is into fairly complex electronics. It has also been modernized in the sense that an expanding share of business is accounted for by the tertiary sector, including the provision of sophisticated banking, financial, and professional services. In 1984, manufacturing contributed 22 percent of Hong Kong's gross domestic product; transport, financial, real estate, and business services, 27 percent; the distributive and catering trades, 21 percent; and ownership of premises, 16 percent.[17] In short, "services" accounted for 64 percent of the GDP.

Looked at from a different, causal angle, this modern economic performance has been, in very large measure, the result of the unfettered exercise of choice by private economic agents. This freedom, and the pressures that go with it, have given Hong Kong a flexibility and a quickness of response to changing conditions in the world market that are without equal.[18] They have also contributed greatly to the nervousness, speculativeness, and volatility of the economy and its very erratic upward course.[19]

The tense condition of the Hong Kong psyche must be insisted upon since it has an important bearing on the city's future. Of course, fascination with risk, speculative activity, the cycles of exuberance and anxiety, impatience, and frayed nerves are among the facts of life of any free market. In Hong Kong, these qualities are merely carried to something like near extreme. The people there, it has been said, have "difficulty finding middle ground between smugness and panic."[20] If Hong Kong is, as some people have suggested, money, and if money is confidence, then the slightest change in the complex and delicate pattern of factual information, rumor, and interpretation on which confidence rests will have instant, large multiplier effects on decisions to consume, save, invest, stay put, or leave for more congenial climes.[21] Like its owners, big money is extremely mobile. It is the perception of events by financial and mercantile decision makers, both domestic and foreign, that is a key determinant of Hong Kong's economic viability in the future. Although domestic and foreign moneys work in tandem, the domestic component of the combination is the more influential if simply by reason of numbers. Only 10 percent of investment in Hong Kong is foreign;[22] the rest is local Chinese money, much of it big. Practically all local Chinese money belongs to people who are either themselves refugees from China or are descended from refugees. This fact cannot but influence the perception of events and, hence, Hong Kong's economic future.[23]

Hong Kong and the World Economy

Thus far, I have concentrated on the meaning and significance of Hong Kong to itself: as a place to live, work, and make money in. But what does Hong Kong mean to the outside world? How important is it in this wider context?

Hong Kong's merchandise trade with the outside world in 1982 was 182 percent of Hong Kong's GDP,[24] and Hong Kong exported about 98 percent of what it manufactured.[25] It is one of the top twenty trading countries in the world. Its exports equal those of China, which has 200 times more people and 9,600 times more territory. Hong Kong is the world's largest exporter of garments, plastic toys (some of them manufactured under license), and watches (with quartz watches now on the rise), and it is one of the world's larger exporters of electronic products (transistor radios, cassette recorders, computer memory systems, calculators, transistors, circuits, semiconductors, electronic modules, television games, and assembled television sets);[26] photographic equipment; textile yarns; fabrics; made-up articles; electric household goods; materials made of polyvinyl-chloride for use in upholstery, clothing, floor tiles, and indoor paneling; metal manufactures; and travel goods.

Hong Kong has a lively reexport trade (60 percent by value of domestic exports in 1984) in textiles, clothing, precious stones (especially diamonds), watches, clocks, and electric machinery. Its entrepôt trade with China is significant and growing. It is a communications center serving Southeast

Asia, a major foreign exchange market, and an important regional center for fund management. It is home to a large number of financial and other companies, local and foreign (including 800 American corporations with offices, factories, or joint ventures there).[27] It is Asia's leading center for the setting of precious stones and one of the world's largest gold markets. And it is, of course, a great tourist city (3.2 million visitors in 1984; 20 percent of them American, another 20 percent Japanese).[28] Not included in this impressive, if somewhat promotional, list is Hong Kong's reputation for pirating intellectual property in a perfectly nonchalant and evenhanded way. Although the press is free and lively, Hong Kong is not otherwise noted for extraordinary literary or artistic accomplishments.

This wide-brush, broad-stroke portrait of tiny Hong Kong as a world-class economic heavyweight is, on closer examination, somewhat deceiving. Hong Kong's permanent case of nerves is not altogether paranoid in origin. It is, on the contrary, rationally justified on at least three grounds, two of which predate the agreement. The third consists of some troubling questions and uncertainties raised by the agreement itself.

The Preagreement Vulnerability of Hong Kong

In an article commenting on the unenviable situation in which the Mexican middle class finds itself, Mary Walsh (a reporter for the *Wall Street Journal*) said something that without much stretching applies also to Hong Kong: "The rich . . . have the savvy and political clout to stay rich; the poor stay poor no matter what. But the middle class bounces up and down with each new jolt of the economy. Its morale is shot."[29] The fact that Hong Kong has reached an upper-middle-income status among the nations of the world, while laudable and fairly unusual, puts the colony in an ambivalent position. It is not poor enough to engender the kind of benevolent feelings in IME governments and the World Bank inspired by the likes of Ethiopia and other unfortunate and/or mismanaged economies, and it is not rich enough to have any kind of credible political or economic clout in world affairs. Its reputation for being a money-making machine does not help; nobody loves a slot machine. It arouses emotions of anger and resentment when things go wrong, as when the bottom falls out of the local real estate market or when U.S. and West European textile and garment workers are put out of work by what they and their unions perceive to be "unfair" Hong Kong competition.

The fact of the matter is that nobody anywhere outside Hong Kong really cares what happens to the place so long as the money is safe and can be profitably turned over or pulled out fast enough. Much investment in Hong Kong, foreign as well as domestic, is of the relatively short-term type: It can be recouped in five years or less, with handsome profits into the bargain. "Almost everybody agrees that there is that much time, perhaps more, before the shadows of 1997 cast a pall."[30] The old Chinese saying, "Drink your wine today and get drunk," applies exceptionally well to Hong

TABLE 9.1. Composition of Hong Kong's domestic exports, 1979–1984 (percent)

All commodity exports	100
Apparel and clothing accessories	33–36 } 39–43
Textiles	6–7
Plastic toys and dolls	6
Watches and clocks	6–8
Household electrical and nonelectrical equipment	2–4
Electronic components and parts for computers	1–5
Telecommunications equipment and parts	1–4

Source: Hong Kong, Census and Statistics Department, *Hong Kong in Figures 1985* (Hong Kong, 1985).

Kong before and after the agreement. Naturally, bankers lead the cheering section. A 1985 survey of 194 top bank executives in East and Southeast Asia (excluding Japan) revealed that 41 percent of them thought Hong Kong would show the "most dramatic banking growth" in the next ten years, preceded only by Tokyo (57 percent) and well ahead of Singapore (27 percent) and Sydney, Australia (24 percent).[31] (It will be recalled that leading bank executives also thought that Brazil, Mexico, and Poland were good credit risks.) In the meantime, the smart long-term money is finding a niche in the real estate market of Vancouver, British Columbia, which is fast becoming a barometer of the fluctuating state of confidence in Hong Kong.

The second preagreement vulnerability of Hong Kong has been the colony's lack of diversification, or conversely, its reliance for its commodity exports on a relatively few light industrial products, concentration on a few export markets where buyer tastes are fickle, dependence on China for essentials such as water and food, and the large role played by U.S. capital in the colony's foreign investment picture. Although there has been a diversification of economic activities as a part of Hong Kong's modern growth (both a "deepening," in the sense of rising technical sophistication and skill improvement, and a "spreading-out," in the sense of the growing importance of services in the GDP), manufacturing exports continue to be dominated by apparel and textiles, which account for more than two-fifths of total export value and employ two-fifths of the manufacturing labor force (see Table 9.1). Garment and textile exports are highly recession sensitive, and they are the favorite targets of protectionists in the importing countries. It has been estimated that the Jenkins Bill, vetoed by President Reagan, would have caused a 12 percent overall reduction in Hong Kong textile exports to the United States (70 percent for nonmultifiber agreement exports), which would have resulted in foreign exchange losses to Hong Kong of $1 billion.[32]

Almost half of Hong Kong's commodity exports go to one market, the United States (see Table 9.2). Another 20 to 30 percent go to the European Economic Community (EEC), mainly to West Germany and the United

TABLE 9.2. Main markets for Hong Kong domestic exports and main sources of imports, 1979–1984 (percent)

Markets for Domestic Exports		
All markets	100	
United States	34–45	} 54–75
European Economic Community (EEC)	20–30	
Federal Republic of Germany	7–11	
United Kingdom	8–11	
Japan	4–5	
Canada	3–4	
People's Republic of China	1–8	

Sources of Imports	
All sources	100
United States	11–12
European Economic Community	11–14
United Kingdom	4–5
Japan	23–24
People's Republic of China	18–25
Republic of China on Taiwan	7–8
Singapore	6

Source: Hong Kong, Census and Statistics Department, *Hong Kong in Figures 1985* (Hong Kong, 1985).

Kingdom (about 10 percent to each).[33] This situation is not altogether satisfactory, particularly in view of the U.S. trade deficit with Hong Kong, which in 1984 exceeded $6 billion (almost 5 percent of the total U.S. trade deficit that year). In 1984, Hong Kong domestic exports to the United States went up 40 percent from the year before, and Hong Kong's reexports to the United States jumped by 51 percent. Hong Kong's imports from the United States, on the other hand, increased by only 27 percent.[34] This imbalance is the kind of thing that raises protectionist ire, despite free trade arguments that stress the benefits gained by U.S. consumers because goods can be imported from Hong Kong cheaply.[35] Hong Kong's import sources are more diversified, but they are still dominated by China and Japan, each of which contributes roughly one-quarter of Hong Kong's imports, with China's share rising in recent years (see Table 9.2).

Almost half of all foreign investment in Hong Kong is American. Japan is second, with about one-quarter, and Britain a distant third, with 6 percent.[36] China's relative share is growing fast. Despite recurrent jitters, foreign capitalist investors, especially Americans, keep coming in. This "strikes some Chinese [in Hong Kong] as the entrepreneurial equivalent of

TABLE 9.3. Hong Kong in world trade, 1984

Hong Kong Exports	
(Percentage share of each country's total imports)	
United States	2.6
European Economic Community	7.1
Federal Republic of Germany	9.1
United Kingdom	1.6
Japan	0.6
People's Republic of China	11.4

Hong Kong Imports	
(Percentage share of each country's total exports)	
United States	1.4
European Economic Community	5.2
Federal Republic of Germany	3.5
United Kingdom	1.3
Japan	3.9
People's Republic of China	26.5

Source: International Monetary Fund, *Direction of Trade Statistics Yearbook 1985* (Washington, D.C., 1985).

rats swimming toward a sinking ship."[37] However, as noted already, a good deal of that investment is liquid and short term. Besides, some of the bigger money has already either migrated or diversified. Jardine Matheson has moved its corporate headquarters to Bermuda, and the Hong Kong and Shanghai Bank, which derives 60 percent of its earnings from business in Hong Kong, now has 70 percent of its assets outside the colony, mainly in North America (over 40 percent).[38] So, the real direction of the swim is not so clear-cut as it might at first appear.

What all these factors mean is that the United States, Western Europe, Japan, and, increasingly, China are very important to the Hong Kong economy but the reverse is much less true, except for China. Big trader that it certainly is, Hong Kong is only eighteenth among U.S. trading partners. Imports of Wisconsin ginseng, Florida oranges, and cufflinks notwithstanding, Hong Kong is not a significant buyer of U.S. products (see Table 9.3). It is handy as a stepping-stone for U.S. business dealings with China, assuming that Chinese development continues along the lines traced by the Teng Hsiao-p'ing regime.[39] To the IMEs (essentially the United States, EEC countries, and Japan), Hong Kong is useful and convenient as a place to do business and make fast profits, but it is not indispensable. Garments, plastic dolls, watches, and home computers can be made and imported from elsewhere without much disturbance of comparative advantage. There are many Third World countries and a few NICs (newly industrialized countries) waiting to take over chunks of the Hong Kong trade in goods and services (including offshore banking) should Hong Kong turn from a NIC into what Chalmers Johnson calls a CRIC ("collapsing recently industrialized country").[40] The real loser would be China. But China has survived the domestication of Shanghai, although to this day the PRC has not properly understood what has been lost in proletarianizing that international city.[41] If to the IMEs Hong Kong is useful but replaceable, to Hong Kong the IMEs are the world in which Hong Kong has prospered. The alternative world of Communist China is unattractive; a darkness, perhaps under some future less-benevolent Chinese Communist leader, a *Kristallnacht*-style pogrom.

Vulnerability Under the Agreement

After the British "surrendered" to the Chinese in October 1983, things became much more amiable around the negotiating table. With insouciant bonhomie, the Chinese now promised almost everything short of a three-week, all-expenses-paid vacation in Bermuda for each and every Hong Kong compatriot.[42] The terms of the agreement are generally known.[43] On the question of what to make of the assurances contained in the document, there are three schools of thought represented by the people who take the promises seriously, the people who think that to believe them is like believing that Calcutta has a brilliant future, and the people in-between. I am inclined to take the third position. "It is a mistake," says Yuan-li Wu,

> to look for the economic consequences of the Agreement per se. In a sense, the terms of the September Agreement are really quite irrelevant because no one, not even the PRC leaders, can say for certain today whether the terms will be honored. All they can tell us, and have been telling us, is their present intention to honor these terms if nothing untoward happens. In addition, all parties agree that as of now it is in the PRC's economic self-interest to leave Hong Kong as it is. Beyond this one cannot really be sure of anything.[44]

Prediction is a dicey affair. "Heaven," said Mencius, "does not speak."

The problem can be broken down into two parts. There is, first of all, the question of present intent by the people presently in power in the PRC. And here, I think, one can give them the benefit of the doubt. They are, as Communist leaders go, levelheaded and down-to-earth people who perhaps mean it when they say they want to leave Hong Kong pretty much as it is; for a while anyway. It is undoubtedly in the present economic self-interest of the PRC to do so. The economic benefits derived by China from Hong Kong are many, and they are not limited to the earning of a substantial portion of China's hard currencies. As Frank Ching points out, the PRC "can expect to learn modern management methods, import Western technology, and attract funds for investment. . . . Many foreign companies with offices in China prefer to bring in staff from Hong Kong rather than hire unskilled and unreliable personnel in China or bring in expensive expatriates from their own countries. Tour guides in the major tourist centers in China have had to learn Cantonese because of the big influx of free-spending Hong Kong visitors."[45]

On the other hand, if Hong Kong falters, its 5 million people and its cathedrals of profit, emptied of their priests (the skilled professionals) and deprived of their capitalist soul (freedom), will be a drain on China's meager purse. Since 1979, Hong Kong's trade exchanges with the PRC have risen dramatically and today make up roughly one-fourth of Hong Kong's foreign trade turnover. Exports to China have risen eighteen times (albeit from miserly levels) and imports, four times. The Bank of China has become an increasingly influential presence in the city, slowly displacing the Hong Kong and Shanghai Banking Corporation, once known as "the bank." Peking money has propped up the failing, locally founded Ka Wah Bank and bailed out Conic Investments Ltd., a major manufacturer of television sets, radios, and electronic components. Peking's China Resource Holding Company has invested heavily in Hong Kong businesses and now controls more than 300 firms in the territory, encroaching on the preserves of traditional British companies such as Jardine Matheson and Swire Pacific Ltd. China has a substantial interest in the newly founded Dragon Airlines (chairman, Sir Yue-kong Pao), which competes with Swire's Cathay Pacific Airways and intends to cash in on Peking's takeover of Hong Kong's Kai Tak airport. China has also invested heavily in the territory's real estate market. It owns some choice properties in downtown Victoria, including the site for the seventy-story new Bank of China building designed by I. M. Pei. Hong Kong investors have been active in China's special economic zones, especially Shenzhen.[46] Hong Kong's economy is already being restructured away from the traditional export industries, and redirected from its cosmopolitan orientation toward rustic China. Hong Kong is reverting to its traditional role as an entrepôt and a conduit for China, but on a larger scale.

Even if one grants the sincerity of the PRC's present intent with respect to the economic configuration of Hong Kong, troubling questions remain. Economic self-interest is, for Peking, a necessary but not a sufficient condition for what it does. The insufficiency stems from Chinese nationalism and from Leninism. During the early stage of the negotiations, the British (and some Hong Kongers) let it be bruited about that the most rational way for the Chinese side to demonstrate its grasp of what China's economic self-interest meant would be to throw a big party at which Chinese sovereignty over Hong Kong would be vociferously acknowledged, and then quietly let the British run the place as they used to. This idea was not lost on Peking, which interpreted it as implying that the Chinese were not capable of running Hong Kong. The raw nerve of Chinese cultural nationalism was touched to the quick, and, as Chalmers Johnson has shown, the PRC immediately "mousetrapped" Hong Kong.[47] Whatever it was that the British were or were not suggesting, the real point surely is that a Communist system is incapable of running a market economy. However, once offended, nationalism insinuated itself into the argument, and the idea of Chinese sovereignty cum British administration was dead.

Peking not only thinks it can run Hong Kong but has always argued that without China's help in supplying food, water, labor (albeit of the refugee variety), and the China market, Hong Kong would not have survived. This Sino-centric understanding of international commercial interdependencies is not new. Lin Tse-hsü, imperial commissioner at Canton in 1839, composed a letter to Queen Victoria pointing out Britain's dependence on Chinese rhubarb, without which the English would die of constipation.[48] Prime Minister Thatcher has been censured for unnecessarily raising the question of sovereignty and so provoking a rebuff. However that may be, politics in command of economics, though not very Marxist, is very Leninist indeed, and Leninism is what counts. Thatcher's gaffe or not, the political issue could not be avoided. It was decisive. In this respect, the Chinese Communist leadership acted in a perfectly orthodox, predictable, and correct Party way. But what this situation does is raise serious questions about the validity of the economic self-interest *über Alles* argument. So, there is a problem even on the side of China's present intent.

The second and real part of the problem, however, is on the side of the execution of the intent. And here profound skepticism is in order. First, the actuarial tables are against Teng Hsiao-p'ing's presiding for very long over pragmatism in China. His appointees lack the prestige and power bases that Teng possesses, and there is a rather large and strong political constituency that does not like what's going on in China today. Within that constituency, the neo-Stalinist conservatives, à la Ch'en Yün and Teng Li-ch'ün have demonstrated uncommon staying power. Then there are many frustrated Maoists, who are now lying low.[49] Second, China's track record of policy stability has been, to put it mildly, disquieting. So the present intent could be simply thrown away somewhere down the road in accordance with the ancient law that things that happen once may happen twice.[50] But these are subsidiary matters. There is something else, permanent and important, that argues persuasively against the present intent being carried out in the future. And that is the nature of the socialist system.

The socialist system is constitutionally incapable of leaving people alone. Capitalism (which the agreement promises to keep in Hong Kong for fifty years—why not seventy-five?) is what people do when you leave them alone. Socialism—Stalinist, Maoist, Tengist—is in different degrees the antithesis of the noble quality of laissez-faire. The triumph of an idea over common sense, a socialist system will not let things be. The socialist administrative command economy, which despite some modifications is still what China has, rests on philosophical premises and demands intellectual qualities and temperamental predispositions of its operators that are fundamentally and irreconcilably at variance with the premises, qualities, and temperament of a free market economy. The command economy and the market economy do not mix. "Market socialism," now being touted in China under the appellation of "socialism with Chinese characteristics," is a contradiction in terms.[51] Instead of socialism with Chinese characteristics, what the Chinese are getting on the mainland is mercantilism with corrupt characteristics. So, it is not a deliberate repudiation of the agreement's promises that is the main threat to Hong Kong. Rather, it is the ineluctable damage done to markets when Leninists (no matter how "rightist" or "revisionist") lay their hand on the delicate mechanism that freedom of economic choice represents: "A speck of rat's dirt will spoil a bowl of rice," as the Chinese say.

It is easy to "muck up" Hong Kong. There is a strong case to be made that such a mucking up will occur naturally and effortlessly, certainly after 1997 and probably before, by reason of the structure and inner dynamics of the socialist system, despite contrary present intent.[52] The history of Marxism everywhere has been that of a dream destructively applied.

Conclusion

So what happens if Hong Kong is mucked up? From the standpoint of the world economy (which in this instance means the United States and three or four other IMEs), nothing much. Such a change will be an inconvenience. Other great business and financial city-states have disappeared in the past without pulling the mercantile world down with them. A couple of NICs may benefit, if they are quick enough to pick up the pieces by liberalizing their still rather restrictive financial and banking arrangements. The big loser will be mainland China, but the damage there will not be lethal: more of a shame than a loss. The biggest loser will be Hong Kong.

Notes

1. Cited by Hugh D.R. Baker, "'Greatness Thrust Upon Them': Hong Kong Before and After the British," *Asian Affairs* 16, pt. 1 (1985), p. 47.
2. A. J. Youngson, *Hong Kong Economic Growth and Policy* (Hong Kong: Oxford University Press, 1982), p. 2.
3. Ibid., p. 7.
4. Ibid., p. 19.
5. Frank Ching, *Hong Kong and China: For Better or for Worse* (New York: China Council of the Asia Society and the Foreign Policy Association, 1985), p. 60.
6. Joan Robinson, *Economic Philosophy* (Chicago: Aldine, 1963), p. 45.
7. Alfred Marshall, *Principles of Economics*, 8th ed. (London: Macmillan, 1949), p. 1.
8. On the less than obvious and simple role of government in Hong Kong in the areas of education, health care, transport, housing, land, money, rents, and rice, see Youngson, *Hong Kong Economic Growth*, pp. 119–136, and Hugh D.R. Baker, "Life in the Cities: The Emergence of Hong Kong Man," *China Quarterly*, no. 95 (September 1983), pp. 469–479.
9. Adam Smith, *The Wealth of Nations*, 5th ed., ed. Edwin Cannan (New York: Modern Library, Random House, 1937), p. 651.

10. Milton Friedman and Rose Friedman, *Free to Choose: A Personal Statement* (New York: Harcourt Brace Jovanovich, 1980), pp. 32–33.

11. "The Hong Kong China Needs," *Economist*, October 1, 1983, pp. 8–9.

12. Smith, *Wealth of Nations*, p. 651.

13. World Bank, *World Development Report 1984* (New York: Oxford University Press, 1984), table 1, p. 219.

14. Youngson, *Hong Kong Economic Growth*, pp. 52–53.

15. Steven C. Chow and Gustav F. Papanek, *"Laissez-faire*, Growth and Equity—Hong Kong," *Economic Journal* 91:362 (June 1981), pp. 466–468. See also, World Bank, *World Development Report 1984*, table 28, p. 273 (data for 1980).

16. World Bank, *World Development Report 1984*, tables 23, 24, and 25, pp. 263, 265, 267, and John A. Mathieson, *The Advanced Developing Countries: Emerging Actors in the World Economy*, Development Paper no. 28 (Washington, D.C.: Overseas Development Council, November 1979), table 4, p. 21. The physical quality of life index is a composite indicator giving equal weight to life expectancy, infant mortality, and literacy. It is measured on a scale of 0 to 100 with 0 representing worst possible performance and 100 representing best possible performance. In the mid-1970s the index was 87 for Hong Kong (95 for the IMEs and the United States).

17. Hong Kong, Census and Statistics Department, *Hong Kong in Figures 1985* (Hong Kong: 1985).

18. Willard Sharpe, Hong Kong area economist for Chase Manhattan Bank, lists ten ingredients for Hong Kong's success: free enterprise, market determined pricing, free movement of goods and people, market access for Hong Kong goods, the British legal system, freedom of information, free movement of funds, an independent currency, a range of financial institutions, and a simple, low tax structure. Kevin Rafferty, "Hong Kong," *Asia and Pacific* (1984), p. 140.

19. For a more exhaustive analysis of the internal and external causes of Hong Kong's success, see Jan S. Prybyla, "The 'Gang of Four's' Economic Miracle: Hong Kong, Singapore, South Korea, Taiwan," in *America's New Pacific Era: Five Lectures on U.S.-Asian Relations*, Heritage Lecures no. 43 (Washington, D.C.: Heritage Foundation, 1985), Lecture 3, pp. 53–90. On the erratic path of Hong Kong's growth, see Youngson, *Hong Kong Economic Growth*, table 1.1, p. 8.

20. Robert Keatley, "Jittery Hong Kong Frets About Its Future," *Wall Street Journal*, August 30, 1982, p. 13.

21. Y. C. Yao, "The 1997 Issue and Hong Kong's Financial Crisis," *Journal of Chinese Studies* 2:1 (April 1985), pp. 124, 131–132, 140, and Ching, *Hong Kong and China*, pp. 12–13.

22. James P. Sterba, "Hong Kong's Chinese Fearing '97 Takeover, Seek Capitalist Havens," *Wall Street Journal*, June 22, 1984, p. 13.

23. The influence, however, is not as straightforward as it might seem. Some of Hong Kong's leading capitalists (for example, Sir Yue-kong Pao, the shipping and real estate magnate) have been assiduously courting Peking, building luxury hotels in China and endowing universities in their places of birth. In their view, the best insurance policy for *nous après le déluge* ("after the catastrophe") survival is a network of highly placed personal connections (*guanxi*) with the men in charge in Peking. They also seem to believe, despite the Shanghai precedent, that they can "educate" China's Communist leaders in the capitalist mechanics and ethics of Hong Kong. Feelings of Chinese patriotism also enter into this delusion (see "The Rich Folk Go Courting Peking," *New York Times*, December 29, 1985).

24. World Bank, *World Development Report 1984*, tables 3 and 9, pp. 223, 235.

25. Len Dunning, executive director Hong Kong Trade Development Council, in the *Wall Street Journal*, June 21, 1982, p. 13.

26. Reacting to quotas and other trade restrictions imposed by the IMEs, Hong Kong's textile and garment industries have moved upmarket, and many of them are now working for Pierre Cardin, Calvin Klein, Fiorucci, and Yves St. Laurent. Hong Kong boosters hope that the electric and electronics industries will follow the same path. One obstacle is that most of the 1,300 Hong Kong electronics workshops are very small: 80 percent of them employ fewer than 100 workers each. They compete on their own against government-aided or otherwise subsidized Singapore firms and Taiwan's government-supported push toward high technology (Rafferty, "Hong Kong," p. 139).

27. James P. Sterba, "Although Hong Kong Reverts to China Soon, U.S. Influence Prevails," *Wall Street Journal*, October 10, 1985, p. 26.

28. Hong Kong, Census and Statistics Department, *Hong Kong in Figures 1985.*

29. Mary Williams Walsh, "Mexico's Middle Class Blames Government for Economic Crunch," *Wall Street Journal*, December 30, 1985.

30. John Burns, "Hong Kong Savors Its Interlude," *New York Times*, December 29, 1985. "For the last two decades, Hong Kong has been a place where investors could pour capital into hotels, office blocks, and cross-harbor tunnels and retrieve it with a profit in as little as three to five years" (ibid.).

31. *Wall Street Journal*, December 10, 1985, p. 34.

32. *Asian Pacific Monitor* (Washington, D.C.), December 1985, p. 1.

33. Hong Kong, Census and Statistics Department, *Hong Kong in Figures 1985.*

34. International Monetary Fund, *Direction of Trade Statistics Yearbook 1985* (Washington, D.C., 1985), pp. 28–29, 58–59, 112, 186, 399, and *New York Times*, November 18, 1985.

35. The Hong Kong Trade Development Council took out an advertisement in the *New York Times* (November 18, 1985) to educate Americans about the benefits they derive from their Hong Kong connection. Although the textile problem was skirted and the pirating was not mentioned, two themes were stressed. The first was the importance to the United States of exports to Hong Kong: $3.1 billion in 1984 (nearly one-third reexported to China), with Hong Kong being the leading global importer of U.S. razors and razor blades, ginseng from Wisconsin, dressed poultry, cigarettes, buttons, studs and cufflinks, oranges, lemons, and $70 million worth of diamonds and other precious and semiprecious stones (making Hong Kong the third-largest customer in the world for New York dealers and cutters in this trade). The theme is appealing and stimulating, especially the ginseng part of it, but it is not convincing. For one thing, U.S. exports to Hong Kong represented just 1.4 percent of all U.S. exports in 1984. The second theme was the importance of Hong Kong's role as an intermediary with China for U.S. goods and other exports.

36. *Wall Street Journal*, June 22, 1984, p. 13, and October 10, 1985, p. 26; T. B. Lin, "Foreign Investment in the Economy of Hong Kong," *Economic Bulletin for Asia and the Pacific* (UN) 35:2 (December 1984), pp. 96–106.

37. *Wall Street Journal*, June 24, 1984, p. 13.

38. Ibid.

39. See "Big Business Sees Profit in a Chinese Flag Over Hong Kong," *Business Week*, October 8, 1984, p. 55.

40. Chalmers Johnson, "The Mousetrapping of Hong Kong: A Game in Which Nobody Wins," *Asian Survey* 24:9 (September 1984), p. 887.

41. Throughout the Sino-British negotiations, Peking kept repeating that "if we can rule Shanghai, we can surely rule Hong Kong," without realizing what this statement was doing to Hong Kong's Hang Seng index, the exchange rate of the Hong Kong dollar, and the curbside passport market (see "Hearts Ill at Ease," *Far Eastern Economic Review*, March 17, 1983, pp. 43–45).

42. A Hong Kong businessman interviewed by Frank Ching put it this way: "If I were looking for a job, and I know I'm worth $30,000, but they offer me $60,000, I'd think there was something fishy" (Ching, *Hong Kong and China*, p. 43).

43. See, for example, Hungdah Chiu, ed., *Symposium on Hong Kong 1997*, with articles by Hungdah Chiu, Y. C. Yao, and Chu-yuan Cheng, in *Journal of Asian Studies* 2:1 (April 1985), pp. 95–163, available also in *Occasional Papers/Reprints Series in Contemporary Asian Studies*, no. 3, 1985 (68) (Baltimore: University of Maryland School of Law, 1985).

44. Yuan-li Wu, "The Future of Hong Kong Before and After 1997," *American Asian Review* 2:4 (Winter 1984), p. 13. At one point in what, with poetic license, might be called the negotiations on the future of Hong Kong, Teng Hsiao-p'ing tried to reassure nervous investors in the colony. He told them that with him in charge, they could put their hearts at ease. That caused immediate panic for, among other things, it was not their hearts the investors were worried about.

45. Ching, *Hong Kong and China*, p. 60. A good source for the economic relationship between China and Hong Kong is A. J. Youngson, ed., *China and Hong Kong: The Economic Nexus* (Hong Kong: Oxford University Press, 1983).

46. Louise de Rosario, "Into the Red Zone," *Far Eastern Economic Review*, September 19, 1985, p. 61.

47. Johnson, "The Mousetrapping of Hong Kong."

48. Baker, "'Greatness Thrust Upon Them,'" p. 46, citing Arthur Waley, *The Opium War Through Chinese Eyes* (London: Allen and Unwin, 1958), p. 33.

49. From an interview of Hu Yao-pang by Hong Kong journalist Lu Keng, on May 10, 1985, *Pai-hsing* [The common people] (Hong Kong), no. 97 (June 1985), pp. 3–16, in *Foreign Broadcast Information Service—China*, June 3, 1985, pp. W19, W22, W23:

Lu: I would like to tell you some reactions in overseas areas, and please do not take offense. Outside people are worried that once Mr. Deng [Teng Hsiao-p'ing] goes to see Marx, some Army generals may try to emerge, big and strong, and our General Secretary Hu [Yaobang] may not have peremptory command of the Army!

Hu: This is not quite right!

Lu: Another point is linked to policies. Everyone holds that in the economic reform, the old gentleman Chen Yun [Ch'en Yün] opposes the reform policy of the revered Deng.

Hu: That is not true.

Lu: I do not believe it much either. However, this is what people say: "Chen Yun, Peng Zhen [P'eng Chen], and Wang Zhen [Wang Chen] oppose the revered Deng." . . .

Hu: Our Comrade Chen Yun . . . has been in poor health for the past two years and his energy has flagged a bit.

50. John F. Burns, "China On the Move: Will the Changes Last?" *New York Times Magazine*, December 8, 1985, pp. 38–42, 86–94, and Burns, "China Grain Crop Dips; Setback Seen for Policy," *New York Times*, December 23, 1985.

51. On the theoretical deficiency and impracticality of market socialism, see Jan S. Prybyla, *Market and Plan Under Socialism: The Bird in the Cage* (Stanford, Calif.: Hoover Institution Press, 1986). Cf. Don Lavoie, *Rivalry and Central Planning: The*

Socialist Calculation Debate Reconsidered (New York: Cambridge University Press, 1985).

52. The mucking up has already begun. Timid British attempts to translate *Kang-jen chih Kang* ("Hong Kong people ruling Hong Kong") into something more than a cardboard socialist united front slogan have met with hardly disguised Communist fury (see Emily Lau, "No More Velvet Glove," *Far Eastern Economic Review,* September 19, 1985, p. 27, and Lau, "Long, Slow March . . ." ibid., October 31, 1985, p. 18). John Burns, "Hong Kong Has Seen the Future and Has Doubts," *New York Times,* January 7, 1986. The precedent of preemptive surrender set by the British in the negotiations leading to the agreement is being followed by influential sections of Hong Kong society as they kowtow to what they perceive to be the wishes and modus operandi of the new masters in Peking. Hong Kong's independent journalism has "begun to steer clear of politics and concentrate on less controversial subjects, such as juvenile delinquency or bus-fare increases." This voluntary abdication of freedom of speech is one of many incremental accommodations to socialist rule, the pace and scope of which may be expected to accelerate and expand as the countdown to 1997 proceeds (see Julia Leung, "Hong Kong Press Cooling Criticism of Peking Rulers," *Wall Street Journal,* February 7, 1986, p. 18).

10

The Hong Kong Agreement and U.S. Foreign Policy

Hungdah Chiu

During the nineteenth century, Great Britain concluded three treaties with the Chinese (Ch'ing) government relating to Hong Kong: the Treaty of Nanking, signed in 1842 and ratified in 1843, under which Hong Kong Island was ceded in perpetuity;[1] the Convention of Peking in 1860, under which the southern part of the Kowloon Peninsula and Stonecutters Island were ceded in perpetuity;[2] and the Convention of Peking in 1898, under which the New Territories (also referred to as Kowloon Leased Territories in the Chinese documents, comprising 92 percent of the total land area of present-day Hong Kong) were leased to Great Britain for ninety-nine years beginning July 1, 1898.[3] The United States has never challenged the legality of the British acquisition of these areas from China. In fact, the United States also followed a similar practice in seizing territories; for instance, after the United States defeated Spain in 1898, it forced Spain to cede the Philippine Islands to the United States.[4] Later, the United States also obtained a permanent lease of Guantánamo from Cuba.[5]

After the United States and the United Kingdom entered into war against Japan on December 8, 1941, the Republic of China, under the leadership of Chiang Kai-shek, became an ally of those two countries. In late 1942, both countries entered into negotiation with the Republic of China on the abolition of their extraterritorial and other special rights in China. The U.S. negotiations with China went very smoothly, but the negotiations between the Republic of China and the United Kingdom remained deadlocked over the Chinese demand for the return of the leased territories of Kowloon (the so-called New Territories). In order not to delay the abrogation of British extraterritorial and other special rights in China, the Chinese side finally agreed to drop the Kowloon leased territories issue, but it made clear that it reserved the right to reopen negotiations in the future.[6] On January 11, 1943, both countries signed treaties with the Republic of China abrogating their extraterritorial and other special rights in China.[7]

At that time, U.S. policy was to make China a strong and stabilizing force in East Asia after the defeat of Japan. Therefore, the United States was sympathetic to the Chinese aspiration to restore their country's territorial integrity by regaining its lost territories. In March 1943, President Roosevelt proposed to Mr. T. V. Soong, the Chinese representative in the United States, that he, if it was agreeable to the Republic of China, would propose to the United Kingdom a voluntary return of Hong Kong to China. At the same time, Roosevelt suggested that China should designate Hong Kong and part or all of Kowloon as a free port to preserve part of the British nationals' interest there. Mr. Soong reported the proposal to Chiang Kaishek, who referred the proposal to the Supreme National Defense Council for deliberation. The Council resolved that if the United Kingdom returned Hong Kong to China, the Chinese government would voluntarily declare Hong Kong and the old Kowloon area (i.e., not including the New Territories) as a customs free port. However, the return of Hong Kong to China could not be preconditioned on this basis. The designation of Hong Kong and the Kowloon area as a customs free port had to be done voluntarily by China. Mr. Soong transmitted this message to President Roosevelt who, the Chinese side believed, conveyed the message to the United Kingdom. Because the United Kingdom did not sincerely intend to return Hong Kong to China, no response was made to this message.[8]

After the Chinese Communists took over the Chinese mainland in 1949, the United States, until recently, appeared to take a hands-off policy toward Hong Kong. It has not committed itself to defending Hong Kong in the case of a Chinese invasion, and in 1972, when the PRC requested the Special Committee on Colonialism of the UN General Assembly to remove Hong Kong and Macao from its list of colonial territories entitled to self-determination,[9] the United States did not oppose the Chinese request. It was not until the PRC and the United Kingdom began their negotiations on the future of Hong Kong that the United States publicly renewed its concern over Hong Kong's future. Although the United States has, since 1949, taken a low posture on the Hong Kong question, the United States does have an important political and economic stake in Hong Kong.

The U.S. Political and Economic Stake in Hong Kong

Immediately after the Chinese Communist takeover of the Chinese mainland, U.S. interest in Hong Kong was primarily for intelligence gathering. The number of staff members of the U.S. consulate-general in Hong Kong was increased from fewer than twelve to several hundred, and most of them were engaged in gathering, analyzing, and translating Chinese Communist materials. One major publication has been the *Survey of China Mainland Press*, which for many years has been an important source of information on China for U.S. officials, news people, and scholars.

In the early 1950s, the U.S. economic stake was minimal or of adverse impact. When the United States instituted an embargo against the PRC after the Chinese intervention in Korea, many strategic materials were smuggled to China through Hong Kong. Moreover, after the Korean armistice agreement was signed in 1953, Britain's concern over its interests in Hong Kong prompted the British government to withdraw from the U.S. effort to enforce a collective embargo against the PRC.

On the political side, despite support for principles of decolonialization and self-determination at the United Nations, the United States has never attempted to apply these principles to Hong Kong. Since the PRC has made it clear that the Hong Kong question is not the business of the United Nations or any country (except the United Kingdom),[10] the hands-off attitude of the United States is understandable.

Over the years, the nature of the U.S. stake in Hong Kong has undergone a significant change. With the gradual opening of China and improved U.S.-PRC relations, Hong Kong's role as an intelligence gathering post has gradually diminished. On the other hand, the spectacular economic development of Hong Kong under British laissez-faire policy has transformed it into a significant economic power in East Asia and a major trading partner of the United States. Moreover, the United States has a significant amount of private investments and connections in Hong Kong. The following is a summary of U.S. economic and business interests there.

In 1984, Hong Kong imported US$3.1 billion worth of goods from the United States. Because the British ran Hong Kong as a customs free port, all U.S. exports were free of import duty. In per capita terms, imports from the United States were about US$577 per Hong Kong resident, a figure higher than those for the European Economic Community (US$172), Japan (US$198), the Republic of Korea (US$150), the Republic of China on Taiwan (US$268), and Australia (US$312). Major items of imports from the United States in 1984 included integrated circuits (US$326 million), electronic components (US$305 million), tobacco (US$173 million), and vegetables and fruit (US$161 million). The Hong Kong–based airline Cathay Pacific has a fleet of nineteen aircraft, comprising ten U.S.-made Boeing 747s and nine Lockheed Super Tri-Stars.[11] On the export side, the United States is Hong Kong's largest market; in 1984, Hong Kong exported $7.9 billion of goods to the United States which constituted 45 percent of Hong Kong's total exports. Textiles made up 31 percent of Hong Kong's exports to the United States in 1984.[12]

Hong Kong is also an important location for U.S. business interests. There are approximately 14,000 U.S. residents in Hong Kong, and approximately half a million U.S. nationals visit Hong Kong annually. Many large U.S. firms, such as Wang Laboratories, Westinghouse, Hercules Inc., Bank America Trading Corp., Mast Industries, and Allen-Bradley, have set up the Asia-Pacific regional headquarters in Hong Kong. There are over 800 U.S. firms in Hong Kong, including 3M, Dow Chemical, IBM, Mobil Oil, Exxon, Eastman Kodak, Texas Instruments, Sea-Land, and Xerox. Moreover, there are twenty U.S. banks, including Citibank, Bank of America, and Chase Manhattan Bank; thirty-six U.S. deposit-taking companies; thirty-one wholly U.S.-owned insurance companies;[13] and branches of many U.S. law firms in Hong Kong. Total U.S. investment is difficult to estimate because there is no foreign exchange control in Hong Kong. However, the U.S. consulate-general estimates that U.S. firms have invested between US$4 billion and $5 billion in Hong Kong, thus putting it second in Asia, after Japan, as a locale for U.S. investment.[14] With regard to the manufacturing industry, U.S. investment in 1983 constituted 46.2 percent of all foreign investment, the highest among foreign countries.[15] Furthermore, the United States also has a strong interest in using Hong Kong as a base for promoting investment and business interests in China.

Because of the existence of important U.S. trade, investment, and business interests in Hong Kong, the U.S. consulate-general remains the largest of the sixty-one consular offices there.[16] Hong Kong maintains an office at the British Embassy in Washington, D.C.; an office of the Commission for Hong Kong Commercial Affairs at the British consulate-general in New York; an industrial promotion office in San Francisco; five Hong Kong development councils, in New York, Chicago, Dallas, Los Angeles, and Miami; and three Hong Kong tourist associations, in San Francisco, New York, and Chicago.[17]

Internationally, the British government concluded only two postal agreements with the United States on behalf of Hong Kong (one relates to parcel and the other to express mail),[18] but Hong Kong has participated, through the United Kingdom, in more than eighty-five multilateral treaties or agreements to which the United States is also a contracting party. These treaties and agreements include matters relating to arbitration, aviation, copyright, customs, trade, health, protection of industrial property, settlement of investment disputes, judicial assistance, maritime matters, the control of narcotic drugs, patents, publications, satellite communications, telecommunications, and other matters.[19] Hong Kong is also a full member of the Asian Development Bank[20] and an associate member of the International Maritime Organization.[21]

The United States and the Negotiations on the Restoration of Hong Kong to China

On September 24, 1982, following a meeting between Prime Minister Margaret Thatcher and Chairman Teng Hsiao-p'ing, the following statement was issued:

> Today the leaders of both countries held far-reaching talks in a friendly atmosphere on the future of Hong Kong. Both leaders made clear their respective positions on this subject.
> They agreed to enter talks through diplomatic channels following the visit with the common aim of maintaining the stability and prosperity of Hong Kong.[22]

The negotiations lasted two years, and the Draft Agreement was initialed on September 26, 1984,[23] and formally signed on December 19, 1984. Instruments of ratification were exchanged on May 27, 1985.[24]

The important economic and business interests of the United States in Hong Kong made it necessary for the United States to pay special attention to the negotiations. Moreover, U.S. interest in the PRC's future policy toward Taiwan also prompted the United States to follow closely the PRC's approach to Hong Kong's future, since that would provide an indication of how the PRC intends to deal with Taiwan. Finally, the United States has an interest in the future well-being and security of the Chinese in Hong Kong, especially those who left China in 1948 and 1949 to make their home in Hong Kong.[25]

In view of the strong U.S. interest in Hong Kong's future, should the United States have tried to play an active role in the Sino-British negotiations? One view is that the United States should have tried to intercede with the PRC privately in order to encourage a restrained PRC policy toward Hong Kong to preserve the economic and social status quo there. Along this line, some people suggest that U.S. officials could have attempted to influence the course of events indirectly, especially through U.S. business leaders who have a strong interest in Hong Kong and enjoy good ties with the PRC leaders; or that U.S. officials might have encouraged Hong Kong leaders to be more assertive in their discussions with PRC leaders in emphasizing the need for Chinese restraint.[26]

Despite the possibility of the United States playing an active role in the Sino-British negotiations, the U.S. official position appeared to restrict involvement to the role of an interested bystander during the period of the Sino-British negotiations. In an interview on January 20, 1984, Eugene Lawson, a senior official at the East Asian Bureau of the U.S. Department of State, stated:

> While we have a considerable interest in how these talks progress, we have no intention of inserting ourselves and our views when they are going on.
>
> We accept that a peaceful and satisfactory solution is possible to preserve the investment climate and the political and economic freedom that makes Hong Kong what it is.
>
> Hong Kong is unique in the world. We appreciate that it will not take too much to change that climate and bring about economic disaster.
>
> We have an interest in how the talks progress, but we have no intention of interposing our views at the present time. We look at it as strictly an issue between the UK and the People's Republic of China.[27]

While maintaining the position of an interested bystander toward the Sino-British negotiations, Mr. Lawson still took the opportunity to discuss U.S. policy toward Hong Kong to remind the PRC of the implications of Hong Kong's future on the Taiwan question, where the United States has a strong political, moral, and legal interest because of the U.S. Taiwan Relations Act of 1979.[28] Thus, in the same interview, he also said: "A smooth transition for Hong Kong would serve as a model for the future of Taiwan and encourage the Taiwanese to accept the sovereignty of China. The PRC could never hope to enter into negotiations with the Taiwanese on any basis unless there has been a smooth transition in Hong Kong that is satisfactory to the people of Hong Kong."[29]

A more elaborate discussion on the future of Hong Kong and U.S. policy was made on June 7, 1984, by Burton Levin, U.S. consul-general in Hong Kong, in a speech delivered at a meeting sponsored by the Asia Society in New York City. In addition to the economic aspect of U.S. interest in Hong Kong, he also pointed out the cultural and human relations aspects of U.S. concern about the future of Hong Kong.

> As a prosperous and creative society, we have attracted thousands of students from Hong Kong to our universities and hundreds of thousands of Hong Kong tourists and businessmen to our cities and towns. Many of the three quarters of a million Chinese living in the States have family ties in Hong Kong. Millions of Americans have visited Hong Kong. Over the past few decades the people of the United States and Hong Kong have gotten to know each other much better. Americans come away from this relationship with respect and admiration for a group of people who have worked hard, endured many hardships over the decades and have contributed in many ways to the world community. We believe they deserve a secure future.[30]

Despite the existence of important U.S. stakes in Hong Kong's future, he did not, however, see any U.S. role in the Sino-British negotiations: "The United States does not see a role for itself in the present negotiations. We have made clear our interest in a settlement that preserves Hong Kong's prosperity and stability and our pleasure that both the U.K. and the PRC share and are working toward this objective. We will be supportive in any appropriate way we can."[31]

Similar to Lawson's reference to the Taiwan issue to indirectly influence the Sino-British negotiations, Levin also took the opportunity to remind the PRC of the implications of the Hong Kong question on Taiwan's future.

> China . . . has a major political interest in Hong Kong. One of its most important national objectives is Taiwan's reunification with the mainland. China has stated that it seeks to accomplish this by peaceful means. In recognition of the different systems and styles of life, China is proposing to Taiwan a high degree of autonomy under a confederational arrangement featuring one state, two systems. Its promises to Taiwan closely resemble those made to Hong Kong. China has publicly proclaimed that Hong Kong is to serve as a model for Taiwan's reunification. It has to be presumed that China would want to make that model as attractive as possible to the people of Taiwan.[32]

In one aspect Levin's speech went beyond Lawson's interview when, for the first time, he indicated that the United States "would continue its support of Hong Kong's participation in such arrangements as international postal and telecommunications organizations, the GATT, and the multi-fiber arrangements following restoration of Chinese sovereignty."[33] He was silent, however, on the crucial immigration quota problem with respect to Hong Kong people. At present, Hong Kong, with its status as a British colony, is entitled to have a 600 U.S. immigrant quota annually.[34] After losing its colonial status, the quota would presumably be automatically canceled unless the U.S. Congress is willing to amend the law and the PRC is agreeable to the amendment.[35]

Judging from the fact that the United Kingdom and the PRC did not ask the United States to play a role in their negotiations, China's sensitivity to its sovereignty, the lack of any solid legal basis for the United States to intervene in the negotiations, and the absence of U.S. domestic pressure to get the United States involved in the Hong Kong question, it appears that the U.S. government's decision to refrain from an active role in the Sino-British negotiations was only natural.[36]

The U.S. Response to the Joint Declaration

On September 26, 1984, an agreement in the form of a Joint Declaration on the Question of Hong Kong was initialed by the United Kingdom and the PRC.[37] The Joint Declaration contains more than 8,000 words and is, perhaps, the second-longest international agreement ever concluded by the PRC.[38] It spells out in detail the PRC's policy toward Hong Kong, the post-1997 Hong Kong regime, and its international relations. The highlights of the Declaration are as follows:

1. After 1997, Hong Kong will become a special administrative region of the PRC under Art. 31 of the PRC constitution.[39] It will enjoy a "high degree of autonomy" except in foreign and defense affairs.
2. Hong Kong will be vested with executive, legislative, and independent judicial powers, including that of final adjudication.
3. Hong Kong's chief executive will be appointed by the PRC after elections or consultation in Hong Kong. The government of Hong Kong will be composed of local people.
4. Hong Kong shall maintain the capitalist economic and trade systems for fifty years after 1997.
5. The existing social and economic systems will remain unchanged. Freedoms of speech, movement, the press, assembly, strike, religion, and others will be protected by law. Similarly, private property rights will be protected.
6. In addition to displaying the national flag and the national emblem of the PRC, Hong Kong may use a regional flag and an emblem of its own.
7. Hong Kong may participate in relevant international organizations and international trade agreements. It may establish official and semiofficial economic and trade missions in foreign countries. Using the name

"Hong Kong China," it can maintain and develop relations and conclude and implement agreements with states, regions, and relevant international organizations in appropriate fields.

8. The PRC defense force stationed in Hong Kong shall not interfere in the internal affairs of Hong Kong, and the expenditures for these military forces shall be borne by the PRC's Central People's government.

The official U.S. response to this Declaration has been extremely positive. Acting U.S. Department of State spokesman Alan Romberg stated, at a September 26, 1984, press conference:

The U.S. Government welcomes the successful conclusion of 2 years of negotiations between the United Kingdom and the People's Republic of China over the future of Hong Kong.

The United States has a strong interest in the continued stability and prosperity of Hong Kong and believes the agreement will provide a solid foundation for Hong Kong's enduring future progress.

In this regard, we have noted statements by both sides indicating that Hong Kong's way of life will be guaranteed for 50 years from 1997 and that systems existing in Hong Kong will continue in the special administrative region.

We expect the American business communities, both in the United States and Hong Kong, will see in this agreement good reason for sustained confidence in the future of Hong Kong as an attractive and thriving commercial center.

The United States will provide any assistance it can, in close cooperation with the United Kingdom and the People's Republic of China, to maintain Hong Kong's appropriate participation in international bodies.[40]

Despite the official optimistic response to the Sino-British agreement on Hong Kong, there is serious doubt that the future of Hong Kong will meet U.S. expectations because the Declaration does not insulate Hong Kong from future Chinese political development. As analyzed by a leading U.S. newspaper:

China's constitution promises its own citizens many of the same rights and freedoms now promised for Hong Kong, but they are honored only in the breach. . . .

China will now go about fashioning a so-called Basic Law for Hong Kong after 1997; this will offer its cadres a chance to "reform" the current system, if they so wish, and not necessarily for the better. The declaration also allows China to appoint its own chief executive for Hong Kong after 1997, heeding either local "elections or consultations," though *whom* China will consult with isn't stated. What has been a growing movement for democratic rule by Hong Kongers themselves seems to have been overruled.

Can the Chinese then be trusted to appoint someone who understands the rule of law and a free economy? And more important, will the successors to China's 80-year-old leader, Deng Xiaoping, also honor the pact? In short, Hong Kong will now live or die by Peking's political whim.[41]

Aside from making a positive statement regarding U.S. confidence on the future of Hong Kong and encouraging the PRC to honor its promise to Hong Kong, there appear to be only limited options available to U.S. policymakers to deal with the situation. This question is described by a U.S. specialist on East Asian affairs as follows:

One U.S. option would be to intercede strongly with Chinese leaders, using U.S. influence to advocate policies toward Hong Kong that would take U.S. interests into account. Nevertheless, such a maneuver could backfire, because the PRC has always been sensitive to matters involving its sovereignty. Any appearance that the United States was attempting to interfere might offend Chinese leaders and adversely affect U.S.-China relations. In particular, Beijing might resent such American action coming at a time when PRC leaders still see the United States repeatedly affronting Chinese sovereignty with arms sales to Taiwan. Moreover, U.S. willingness to discuss Hong Kong's status with the PRC could put the United States into the compromising position of appearing also to be willing to bargain with Beijing over Taiwan's future.

A second option available to U.S. policy makers is to play a greater role in Hong Kong's political affairs prior to 1997, encouraging Hong Kong's officials and residents to demand a greater voice in their own government on the theory that more active participation now could mean greater autonomy in the future. Advocates of this view pointed to the increased political activity in heretofore apathetic Hong Kong over the past two years as evidence that Hong Kong's citizens are interested in self-government and may respond to U.S. encouragement in this area. However, this option could seriously complicate Sino-American relations by setting the United States directly against PRC plans for the territory, and it could set a precedent for a similarly activist U.S. approach for political organization and self-determination in Taiwan—a position strongly opposed by both the Nationalist government in Taipei and the Communist government in Beijing.

Those advocating a stronger stand on Hong Kong's future have expressed support for use of U.S. trade sanctions involving Hong Kong should China's rule contribute to a serious decline in Hong Kong's status quo. According to these observers, the U.S. trade relationship is so important to Hong Kong's economic survival that trade sanctions would be an effective means in influencing events there. In particular, the United States could threaten to reduce the benefit Beijing derives from the territory and thereby prompt the Chinese to follow a policy in Hong Kong more compatible with U.S. interests. Others, however, have pointed out that trade sanctions against other countries in the past have rarely proven successful in influencing policy. Moreover, for the United States to protect its significant economic interests in Hong Kong by imposing economic sanctions would seem to be counterproductive.[42]

Although the United States was not actively involved in the negotiations, it has adopted the policy of supporting the Sino-British Joint Declaration in order to stabilize Hong Kong's situation during the transitional period. It has also taken concrete steps to achieve this goal. For instance, when the British government proposed issuing a new British National (Overseas) passport to Hong Kong residents, many people in Hong Kong wondered whether this passport would be recognized by other countries, and the

United States was the first country to announce that it would recognize the validity of that passport.[43]

Conclusion

Despite the extensive U.S. economic and business stake in Hong Kong, it does not appear feasible for the United States to play a more active role in the Sino-British negotiations on the future of Hong Kong. Under international law, there is no basis for the United States to intervene in either the return of Hong Kong to the PRC or the Sino-British negotiations. Strategically, Hong Kong is indefensible since the PRC can force Hong Kong's surrender simply by cutting off its water supply. Moreover, any confrontation between the United States or the United Kingdom and the PRC over Hong Kong can only trigger a large exodus of refugees and severely undermine U.S. economic and business interests there.

In view of this situation, the policy options of the United States are very limited, and its present policy appears to be the only sensible one. Whether this policy will succeed is beyond U.S. control because Hong Kong's fate is now tied to political developments in China. Any political turmoil in China from now on would have a serious impact on Hong Kong. One may argue that during the Cultural Revolution period, except for a brief period during 1967, the high degree of political turmoil in China did not affect Hong Kong. However, the situation now is different. At that time, the British presence in Hong Kong served as a buffer to minimize the effects of political turmoil in China on Hong Kong. With the removal of that buffer in 1997, without providing a creditable substitute, one can hardly see how Hong Kong can be insulated from any future drastic political changes in China.

In commenting on the Hong Kong question, U.S. officials have, on several occasions, reminded the PRC of the implication of the Hong Kong settlement on the PRC's goal of "peaceful unification" with Taiwan.[44] Such comments appear to be the only effective restraining factor, in addition to the PRC's self-interest in maintaining Hong Kong as a foreign exchange earning commercial center, on the PRC's policy toward Hong Kong. The effectiveness of this factor is, however, dependent on Taiwan's ability to maintain a sufficient deterrence capability to discourage the PRC from changing its "peaceful unification" policy to one of "military unification." In view of this delicate situation, any U.S. effort to strengthen the self-defense capability of the Republic of China on Taiwan, as long as the latter maintains its one-China policy principle to keep the peaceful unification option open, would indirectly enhance the chance of success of U.S. policy toward Hong Kong.

Notes

1. Article 3 of the 1842 treaty (*Consolidated Treaty Series*, vol. 93 [Dobbs Ferry, N.Y.: Oceana Publications, 1963], p. 467).

2. Article 6 of the 1860 convention (*Consolidated Treaty Series*, vol. 123 [Dobbs Ferry, N.Y.: Oceana Publications, 1963], pp. 73–74).

3. *Consolidated Treaty Series*, vol. 186 (Dobbs Ferry, N.Y.: Oceana Publications, 1979), pp. 310–311.

4. Treaty of Paris between the United States and Spain, signed on December 10, 1898. United States, *Statutes at Large* (hereafter cited as *Stat.*), vol. 30, p. 1754; *Treaty Series* (hereafter cited as *TS*) 343; and Charles I. Bevans, *Treaties and Other International Agreements of the United States of America, 1776–1949* (hereafter cited as Bevans), vol. 11 (Washington, D.C.: Government Printing Office, 1974), p. 615.

5. U.S.-Cuba agreement for the lease to the United States of lands in Cuba for coaling and naval stations, signed in Havana, February 16, 1903, and in Washington, D.C., February 23, 1903 (*TS* 866, and Bevans, vol. 6 [Washington, D.C.: Government Printing Office, 1971], p. 1113).

6. Wang Shih-chieh and Hu Ching-yu, *Chung-kuo pu-p'ing-teng t'iao-yueh chih fei-ch'u* [Abolition of China's unequal treaties] (Taipei: Central Cultural Supply Press, 1967), p. 296.

7. Text of the treaties can be found in, Republic of China, Ministry of Foreign Affairs, ed., *Treaties Between the Republic of China and Foreign States (1927–1957)* (Taipei: Taiwan Commercial Press, 1958), pp. 589–602, Great Britain; pp. 659–668, United States.

8. Chang Chun and Huang Shao-ku, *Chiang tsung-t'ung wei tzu-yu cheng-yi yu ho-p'ing fen-tou shu-lueh* [President Chiang's struggle for the cause of freedom, justice, and peace] (Taipei: Central Cultural Supply Press, 1968), p. 277.

9. Jerome Alan Cohen and Hungdah Chiu, *People's China and International Law: A Documentary Study*, vol. 1 (Princeton, N.J.: Princeton University Press, 1974), p. 384.

10. At the World Youth Forum held on September 23, 1964, the Chinese delegate denounced the Soviet attempt to put Hong Kong and Macao on the list of colonies and demanded their "independence" in a draft resolution. He pointed out that Hong Kong and Macao are Chinese territories occupied by British and Portugese imperialists on the strength of unequal treaties. The Chinese people, he said, would recover them without fail at an appropriate time. The demand for "independence" for the two places, as proposed in the Soviet supported resoltuion, meant in fact to demand their detachment from China (see Cohen and Chiu [note 9], pp. 381–382).

11. British Hong Kong Government, Trade Department, *United States and Hong Kong: Some Important Facts* (Hong Kong, August 1985), p. 1.

12. Ibid., p. 2.

13. Ibid., p. 1.

14. See U.S. Consul-General to Hong Kong Burton Levin's speech delivered to the Asia Society (New York, June 7, 1984, mimeograph), p. 3.

15. U.S. nationals or corporations have seventy-eight wholly owned and fifty-four joint venture manufacturing factories, with a total employment of 40,379 persons. Information supplied by British Embassy, Hong Kong Office, Washington, D.C.

16. In addition to sixty-one consulates, eight British Commonwealth countries maintain a commissioner's office in Hong Kong. For a list of these countries, see *Hong Kong 1985* (Hong Kong: Government Information Services, n.d.), p. 305.

17. Ibid., pp. 306–307.

18. U.S.–Hong Kong Parcel Post Agreement and Regulations of Execution, signed in Hong Kong January 18, 1961, and in Washington, D.C., February 2, 1961; entered into force July 1, 1961 (*United States Treaties and Other International Agreements*

[hereafter cited as UST]) [Washington, D.C.: Government Printing Office, 1984], vol. 12, p. 328 ff., and *Treaties and Other International Acts Series* [hereafter cited as TIAS], no. 4721). U.S.–Hong Kong International Express Mail Agreement, with Detailed Regulations, signed in Hong Kong and Washington, D.C., January 2 and February 6, 1979; effective February 1, 1979 (UST, vol. 30, p. 3427 ff., and TIAS, no. 9398).

19. For a list of these treaties and agreements, see *Treaties in Force: A List of Treaties and Other International Agreements of the United States in Force on January 1, 1985* (hereafter cited as *Treaties in Force 1985*) (Washington, D.C.: U.S. Government Printing Office, 1986).

20. Articles of Agreement Establishing the Asian Development Bank, with Annexes, Manila, December 4, 1965; entered into force August 22, 1966 (UST, vol. 17, p. 1418 ff.; TIAS, no. 6103; and *United Nations Treaty Series* [hereafter cited as UNTS], vol. 571, p. 123 ff). See also *Treaties in Force 1985*, p. 239, for a list of all members.

21. Convention on the Intergovernmental Maritime Consultative Organization, signed in Geneva March 6, 1948; entered into force March 17, 1958 (UST, vol. 9, p. 621; TIAS, no. 4044; and UNTS, vol. 289, p. 48). The title of the convention was changed to the Convention of International Maritime Organization by amendment adopted by the organization on November 14, 1975; effective May 22, 1982 (TIAS, no. 10374). See also *Treaties in Force 1985*, p. 257, for a list of all members.

22. *Hong Kong 1985*, p. 17.

23. For text of the agreement and related documents, see ibid., pp. 1–16, and *International Legal Materials* 23:6 (November 1984), pp. 1366–1387.

24. *Facts on File, 1985* 45:2323 (May 31, 1985), p. 412 A3.

25. See a high U.S. State Department Official's view reported in Winsome Lane, "U.S. Confident About 1997," *South China Morning Post*, January 1, 1984, p. 6.

26. See Robert Sutter, "The United States and Hong Kong's Future: Important Interests, Limited Options" (Report prepared for Congressional Research Service, n.d.), pp. 15–16.

27. Lane, "U.S. Confident About 1997," p. 6.

28. U.S. Public Law 96-8, *Stat.*, vol. 93, p. 14 ff.

29. Lane, "U.S. Confident About 1997," p. 1.

30. Levin's speech, pp. 10–11.

31. Ibid., p. 11.

32. Ibid., pp. 8–9.

33. Ibid., p. 11.

34. S 202(3) of the U.S. Immigration and Naturalization Act as amended through 1984 (*United States Code Annotated*, vol. 8, S 1101 et seq.; reprinted in Thomas Alexander Aleinikoff and David A. Martin, *Immigration: Process and Policy* [St. Paul, Minn.: West Publishing Company, 1985], p. 954).

35. The PRC strongly opposed the U.S. grant of a separate 20,000 immigrant quota to Taiwan in 1981 under sec. 714 of the International Security Act of 1981, Public Law, 97-113 (*Stat.*, vol. 95, p. 1548 [December 29, 1981]).

36. Timothy Elder, "U.S. Shuns Active Interest in Hong Kong Negotiations," *Washington Times*, April 6, 1984, p. 7A.

37. For text, see note 23.

38. The longest PRC treaty is the 1962 boundary treaty with Mongolia (see *Chung-ha jen-min kung-ho kuo t'iao-yueh chi* [Collection of treaties of the People's Republic of China], vol. 11 [1962], pp. 19–36).

39. Article 31 provides: "The state may establish special administrative regions when necessary. The systems to be institutionalized in special administrative regions shall be prescribed by law enacted by the National People's Congress in the light of the specific conditions."

40. "U.K. and China Reach Agreement on Hong Kong," *Department of State Bulletin* 84:292 (November 1984), p. 56.

41. "Promises, Promises," *Wall Street Journal*, October 10, 1984, pp. 32(W), 32(E). For an analysis of the durability and credibility of the PRC's promised "high degree of autonomy" to Hong Kong, see Hungdah Chiu, "The 1984 Sino-British Settlement on Hong Kong: Problems and Analysis," *Journal of Chinese Studies* 2:1 (April 1985), pp. 105–107; reprinted in Hungdah Chiu, ed., *Symposium on Hong Kong 1997, Occasional Papers/Reprints Series in Contemporary Asian Studies*, no. 3, 1985 (68) (Baltimore: University of Maryland School of Law, 1985), pp. 11–13.

42. Kerry B. Dumbaugh, "Hong Kong: Issues for U.S. Policy," *Major Issues System, Issue Brief*, December 28, 1984 (Washington, D.C.: Congressional Research Service, Library of Congress), pp. 6–7.

43. On October 19, 1985, U.S. Vice President Bush said at a press conference that the U.S. government will recognize the proposed British National (Overseas) passport (information provided by British Embassy, Hong Kong Office, Washington, D.C., January 8, 1986).

44. See notes 29 and 32 and quotations in the text.

11

The Hong Kong Agreement and Its Impact on the International Position of Japan

Mineo Nakajima

If Hong Kong were a colony or protectorate having little influence in international society, just like Goa in India or Brunei on Borneo, a move toward its restoration or independence would not attract so much international attention as a major problem. Because of its economic growth, however, Hong Kong attained a GNP of US$5,390 per capita in real terms in 1983, its wealth ranking second after Japan's in Asia and surpassing that of Singapore. This success strongly implies that economically prosperous Hong Kong is positioned at the intersection of East and West, as a crossroads of Asia or as a contact point between the socialist and capitalist worlds. The colony is also often referred to as an international financial center next to New York and London.

Although Hong Kong is physically as small as a pinhead, consisting of islands and areas scattered along the coast of the Chinese mainland, its per capita GNP is about twenty times as high as that in the PRC. Even Hong Kong's trade with the external world amounts to US$44,229 million (as of 1983), a level almost equal to the total of imports and exports of the PRC. The economic status of Hong Kong today is far beyond that of mainland China in all senses.

It is not easy to fully appreciate the prospect of such a fluid and multidimensional international society, or "city-state," as Hong Kong, in which the developing climate of China, still controversial with many unknowns, would reflect accurately. Forecasting Hong Kong's future is made more difficult by the fact that the PRC, expected to guide Hong Kong's future, has just started a full-scale "takeoff" toward modernization after the long-standing turmoil created by the "angry lion" (Mao Tse-tung).

Since the PRC has already pledged internationally, in the historical Sino-British agreement, that the status quo of Hong Kong will be maintained for fifty years after the Chinese resumption of sovereignty on July 1, 1997, by designating Hong Kong as a special administrative region, to be called "Hong Kong China," the future of Hong Kong may be guaranteed as far as its legal status is concerned. However, that statement does not imply that the social realities in Hong Kong today will remain unchanged; in fact, Hong Kong society has already begun to change, step by step.

If the question about Hong Kong's future is viewed from the basis of the above premises, in the light of historical probability a certain gradually developing course seems likely. This course will bring Hong Kong into the scope of political influence of Peking, and thus it indicates the extinction of the freedom and vitality hitherto evidenced in every sector of Hong Kong society. It can also be said that whether the socioeconomic prosperity is retained in Hong Kong under such situation depends heavily on the direction mainland China is heading in. China will probably make substantial efforts to facilitate the maintenance and good use of freedom and vitality because the socioeconomic prosperity of Hong Kong is indispensable. However, it is as yet uncertain whether the retention of prosperity can be assured when the government and "red merchants" and "red capitalists" of the PRC assume the leadership instead of the Royal Crown government and British capital of Hong Kong. It should be said that Hong Kong will be put to the test of the century. The idea of "one country, two systems" (or "one country, three systems" if special economic zones such as Shenzhen collectively count as another separate system) or that of *Kang-jen chin Kang* (the administration of Hong Kong by Hong Kong residents) may denote a sort of solution that will alleviate the political instability, but neither has yet matured as a complete means for endorsing the future.

Needless to say, the Communist Chinese society would be greatly influenced by the outstanding energy that Hong Kong's socioeconomic prosperity holds if the PRC government continues to exercise the open-door policy. This issue further implies the possibility that Hong Kong's economic future will be linked and gradually integrated with that of Shenzhen and other special economic zones, and with the coastal "open" cities of the mainland as well. The Chinese leaders designated those special economic zones and open cities, and set up large barriers (represented by the secondary control line in Shenzhen) against other Chinese societies, because they wanted to limit the possible influence of nonsocialistic property on the interior.

Speaking in the extreme, Hong Kong will be changing from a British colony to a socialist Chinese colony. All directions running counter to the intentions of the Chinese authorities—for example, the conventional antisocialistic and anticommunistic features of Hong Kong, including a wide range of freedom (of speech, thought, etc.)—will therefore be restricted gradually. The position of the head (administrative secretary) of the future Hong Kong SAR should naturally be assigned to a person favorable to the central government in Peking. It is impossible for Hong Kong to avoid moving in this direction after it comes under the PRC's sovereignty, despite its status as a SAR. But, under these conditions, China will undoubtedly implement a variety of economic undertakings, ranging from those monetary and speculative activities that can never happen in the internal arena to those of free market categories, under the leadership of "red merchants" and "red capitalists." This is one tentative projection for the future of Hong Kong, and the years until 1997, during which Hong Kong will remain a British colony, can be defined as a transition period toward a "Chinese Hong Kong."

Because the intrinsic feature of Hong Kong society—that it is basically characterized by a house of cards—will not change soon, all individuals in Hong Kong have to share, for the time being, the fear that the distinguishable property of today could quickly turn out to be only the "aftertaste of a dream." Thus, everything about Hong Kong is solely dependent on the future of China, and the situation allows for no easy approach to an optimistic conclusion.

As is well known, China has established the goal of achieving a per capita GNP performance of US$1,000 by the end of this century under a new national goal called "the four modernizations." It should be remembered, however, that the Chinese leaders themselves have admitted that attaining this goal will be somewhat difficult. Since the current GNP falls between US$250 and $350 per capita, improving it three- to fourfold by the year 2000 is not a simple target to achieve in the light of the PRC's economic statistics in the past, even if there were brisk movement in part of the market. In addition, the attainment of this goal hinges on the premise that not a single increase occurs in the current 1 billion-odd population—a precondition impossible in Chinese society without a miracle, no matter how strictly the population control policy is carried out throughout the country. The more the Chinese society becomes civilized, the more criticism about the forcible population control measures will spread.

The PRC will need to pay continuously for the large debts resulting from Mao Tse-tung's policies based on the "theory of human capitalism" until the twenty-first century, and even if this is the only problem lying ahead, one cannot help but reach a considerably pessimistic view about the future of China. Even if the four modernizations program is accomplished satisfactorily, with the expected outcome of US$1,000 per capita GNP, the gap between mainland China and its neighbors—such as Japan, Taiwan, and South Korea—will be widened because the economies of those countries should also expand, probably by an increment greater than can be achieved in the PRC.

In this context, the experiment called an "open economic system" will not prove to be easy. The road that China is likely to follow until the twenty-first century will be steep and winding, and those windings will also influence the future of Hong Kong. The Chinese society will gain the maturity and stability of the sort that the countries within the "Confucian culture area" of Asia (i.e., the so-called Asian NICs) enjoy today sometime during the twenty-first century when its per capita GNP exceeds the US$2,000 level. Although this GNP level is used as a guideline for the modernization of a state, there is an anxiety at the same time that the socialist system under the one-party rule of the Chinese Communist party might be thoroughly questioned in a modernized Chinese society. And perhaps the true stabilization of Hong Kong will not be realized until that time.

The Japanese influence is currently felt to a great degree in the society of Hong Kong. Anyone can see how closely Hong Kong is linked with Japan, even by glancing at the advertisements and neon signs of typical Japanese enterprises displayed in the busy streets while on a Star Ferry boat crossing the harbor between Hong Kong Island and Kowloon. Japanese goods flood the marketplace, and representatives of Japanese firms, banks, and manufacturers actively promote business to the best of their abilities.

Especially today, when the Chinese economy is shifting toward the open-door system, Hong Kong means a direct gateway to a more "liberal" China for Japanese enterprises. The approximately 10,000 Japanese in Hong Kong and the number of Japanese tourists, which averages nearly 1,500 per day, also indicate the important role of Japan in Hong Kong. The visibility of the Japanese is intensified by the small size of the territory.

So, there is some possibility that "Chinese Hong Kong," once released from the British rule, might suddenly turn out to be the base for a fierce anti-Japanese movement if relations between Peking and Tokyo deteriorated or if any change occurred in Peking's policies toward Japan.

It is true that the process of fostering friendship between China and Japan, which started in the early 1970s, has had a great influence on Hong Kong. The Japanese influence in Hong Kong also increased dramatically during the years when Britain was devaluing the pound sterling and withdrawing from the Suez and the eastward arena and when the United States was tending to withdraw from Asia in the aftermath of the Vietnam War failure.

British capital investors and corporations have been gradually withdrawing their funds and assets from Hong Kong ever since the conclusion of the Sino-British agreement, but Japanese investment in Hong Kong is becoming brisk again, and so is U.S. investment. The recent economic climate between Japan and Hong Kong can well be indicated by some trade figures for 1984. Out of the total value of trade of HK$62,404 million (US$8,000.51 million), Hong Kong merchandise exports to Japanese markets amounted to HK$5,151 million (US$660.38 million) and reexports, HK$4,633 million (US$593.97 million). At the same time, Hong Kong's imports from Japan accounted for HK$52,620 million (US$6,746.15 million), a lopsided surplus of HK$42,836 million (US$5,491.79 million) in favor of Japan. These figures collectively point to the existence of very strong demand in Hong Kong for Japanese products.

Japan furnishes 23.6 percent of Hong Kong's total volume of imports, ranking second after China (25.0 percent), compared to a fifth-largest share in terms of export (figures also as of 1984). Japan's stock of direct investment in manufacturing industries in Hong Kong is HK$2,306 million (US$295.64 million), proportionally the second in rank (29.4 percent) after that of the United States (46.2 percent). Looking at these comparisons from the Japanese

side, Hong Kong denotes the fifth-largest export market with a share of
3.6 percent of Japan's total foreign exports. Hong Kong also constitutes the
seventh significant market economy (or country) for Japanese direct investment
abroad (figures here are for 1983).

Because of the importance of Hong Kong, Hiroaki Fujii, the Japanese
consul-general to the territory, stated the following three basic points in
explaining the necessity for the maintenance of Hong Kong's prosperity:

> In the first place, Hong Kong's role is essential in attaining modernization in
> China; secondly, Hong Kong is capable of providing substantial contribution
> to the economic development of ASEAN and other Asian countries; thirdly,
> Hong Kong is the most internationalized city in the entire region of Asia and
> will probably act as a catalytic agent for attracting the attention of non-Asian
> countries to the region.[1]

Since Hong Kong's importance to Japan is so high, there is also a natural
fear that Japan might suffer a strong impact from any political changes in
China in future because of its deep commitment to the Hong Kong society.
Referring to this question, Chinese Secretary-General Hu Yao-pang reassured
Japanese businessmen after the Hong Kong dollar had dropped suddenly
due to anxiety about the consequences of the Sino-British negotiations.
On September 30, 1983, when he met a Japanese Socialist party delegation
headed by Chairman Tansan Ishibashi, he said, "There are many Japanese
enterprises in Taiwan and Hong Kong, and we will avoid harming those
enterprises. We guarantee to let them grow further."[2]

Furthermore, when Japanese Foreign Minister Shintaroh Abe had a
meeting with Chinese Foreign Minister Wu Hsüeh-ch'ien in Tokyo on
August 18, 1984, the former received a favorable response from Wu regarding
protection. In the response Wu stated that the rights and interests of
foreign enterprises would be protected to maintain their economic activities
in Hong Kong even after the restoration of sovereignty to China.[3]

After the initial shock of the Sino-British agreement, inroads by Japanese
enterprises into Hong Kong have been revitalized, especially in the distribution
industry. Apart from Daimaru Hong Kong, established in the early 1960s,
three Japanese department stores—Isetan, Matsuzakaya, and Mitsukoshi—
had begun business in Hong Kong in the 1970s. Recently, Yaohan, one of
biggest supermarket corporations in Japan, opened a branch in the New
Territories, and it was followed by a Sogo department store launched in
Causeway Bay close to Daimaru Hong Kong. The scales of their business
and the severe competition among them are becoming topics of conversation
among the Hong Kong people.

There is also an influx of Japanese undertakings in sectors other than
distribution and commerce. For example, a large building has been constructed
in Tuen Mun, a new town in the New Territories, to become the second
plant in Hong Kong of Yoshida Kogyo Company. In addition, more than
50 percent of the contracts for the subway extension project has been given

to major civil engineering corporations from Japan. Economic interdependence between Hong Kong and Japan is thus increasing, helped by an improvement in their political relations, but a few problems yet remain to be solved.

In November 1978—that is, around the time Hong Kong bought a number of semifinished goods and other production materials from Japan and constituted a market excessively favorable to Japan—a group of representatives including Hong Kong Governor Sir Murray Maclehorse and chairman of the Bank of East Asia, Y. K. Kan, visited Japan on an economic mission to improve relations between the two countries and achieved the establishment of a Japan–Hong Kong Economic Joint Committee. After the Sino-British agreement in September 1984, another economic mission paid a visit to Japan, headed by Governor Sir Edward Youde together with a member of the executive council, S. Y. Chung; chairman of the Hong Kong and Shanghai Bank, M.G.R. Sandberg; and a representative of the Worldwide Shipping Group, Y. K. Pao. This group made a strong demand for Japan's policy measures concerning correcting trade unequilibrium and removing items excluded from preferential tariff treatment.

There are growing private exchanges between the two countries today. For example, approximately 1,000 Japanese enterprises are open for business in Hong Kong, and 500,000 Japanese tourists go to Hong Kong annually while 200,000 Hong Kongers visit Japan. In addition, there is a remarkable preference for learning the Japanese language in the Hong Kong society. It is because of these close ties that a steady and calm observation is needed on the future course of Hong Kong, which can be regarded as a historic experiment.

Needless to say, there would be no impact of vital importance on Japan's economy if Hong Kong's prosperity were lost, for Taiwan or Singapore could then be expected to be the crossroads of the Asia-Pacific region instead of Hong Kong. More important than the economic relations between Hong Kong and Japan is the question of any possible influence that future changes in Hong Kong may have on Japan's diplomatic and security operations.

Such an influence is likely to be small because China's forthcoming resumption of sovereignty over Hong Kong has already been taken into account by Japan and friendly relations are maintained between China and Japan. But the influence would increase substantially if disorder in Hong Kong in the future, because of political and economic insecurity, social disturbance, or another unexpected event, were to have repercussions in the international environment around Hong Kong, particularly with regard to safety in the Taiwan Strait, for Japan is highly dependent on external conditions. It is therefore natural for Japan to be greatly concerned about the future stability and prosperity of the Taiwan society along with the security of the Taiwan Strait area. For myself, I am rather optimistic about Taiwan's future because I have doubts about the future of Hong Kong.[4]

Notes

1. Hiroaki Fujii, "The Future of Hong Kong and Japan," speech at the Japan Universities Alumni Society, Hong Kong, October 9, 1984.

2. Jiji Press wire report from Peking, printed in *Sankei*, September 30, 1983.

3. *Asahi*, August 18, 1984.

4. For further details on my view regarding the history, status quo, and future of Hong Kong, see Mineo Nakajima, *Hon-kon Utsuriyuku Toshi-kokka* [Hong Kong: A changing city-state] (Tokyo: Jiji Press, 1985).

PART FOUR

Hong Kong: The Future

12

Hong Kong's Future as a Free Market Economy

Y. C. Jao

Under the terms of the Sino-British Joint Declaration signed on December 19, 1984, Hong Kong, widely regarded as the last bastion of laissez-faire capitalism, will fall under the rule of a Communist state on July 1, 1997.[1] The purpose of this chapter is to appraise Hong Kong's prospects as a free market economy in the light of the agreement and current developments.

Factors for Hong Kong's Economic Miracle

Hong Kong's *Wirtschaftswunder* ("economic miracle") during the past four decades has been well documented elsewhere, and only the briefest summary is necessary here.[2] From being a relatively poor and obscure entrepôt before the Second World War, Hong Kong had by the mid-1960s, transformed itself into an export-oriented, industrial city-state, and since the late sixties, it has been further emerging as a leading financial center in the Asia-Pacific region. Hong Kong's per capita GDP, measured at current prices and exchange rates, increased by twenty-four times from US$243 in 1947 to US$5,951 in 1984, the third highest in Asia, after Japan and Singapore. This increase was achieved during a period when the population had more than tripled, largely through immigration, to 5.5 million. The average annual growth rate of the economy in real terms from 1947 to 1984 was 8.3 percent; in the more recent period, 1976–1981, it was an incredible 11.9 percent, arguably one of the highest in the world. Despite its minuscule size, Hong Kong ranked fifteenth among exporting nations of the world in 1984. It is also reputedly the largest exporter, in terms of value, of garments and toys; the third-largest container port; and the third-largest gold and diamond trading center in the world.

For a tiny territory of only 1,067 square kilometers, with virtually no natural resources, this record of economic growth is remarkable by any standard. What are the reasons, the driving forces, for this brilliant achievement? Undoubtedly, there are alternative scholarly interpretations of Hong

Kong's success story, but three key factors can be briefly identified to explain Hong Kong's economic miracle.

The first is internal political and social stability. Like all other countries, Hong Kong is not immune to the repercussions of wars, revolutions, and the other great upheavals of the twentieth century. But as a British crown colony, Hong Kong has, since 1945, enjoyed a high degree of internal political and social stability, except perhaps for 1967 when the Cultural Revolution spilled over in the form of a violent anti-British campaign launched by a small group of extreme Maoists without any support whatsoever from the population. Hong Kong has been ruled by a paternalistic and enlightened colonial civil service, led by British nationals, who, while not directly responsible to the local population, have been responsive to their wishes and demands. The bureaucracy has shown considerable skill in coopting the elite through an elaborate system of consultation, recognition, and awards. This system of implicit "rule by consent" has secured a high degree of political stability, despite the fact that colonialism has gone out of fashion since 1945. Furthermore, a huge influx of immigrants has created a "refugee mentality" that is highly conducive to social cohesion and stability. Refugees from repression and tyranny value Hong Kong as a haven and regard with distaste political turmoil and social strife. Indeed, in a dynamic and growing economy, the scope for political and social agitation is limited. One important manifestation of social stability is, for example, the lack of militant trade unionism.

The second key factor is economic freedom. Hong Kong has often been cited as almost a textbook version of the classic laissez-faire economy. The label "laissez-faire" is now misleading for Hong Kong if it is interpreted in the Smithsian sense that the government confines its functions to defense and law and order. The Hong Kong government, for instance, is responsible for the construction and management of a huge subsidized housing program, which now houses 2.2 million people of the lower-income groups and is expected to accommodate some 3.2 million people (57 percent of the estimated population) by 1990. It owns and operates a number of enterprises such as the airport, the Kowloon-Canton Railway (British section), and the Mass Transit Railway Corporation; it regulates the prices and fees of privately owned electric, telephone, bus, and ferry companies; it is heavily involved in financing and subsidizing education at all levels; it has imposed rent control on residential premises for extended periods of time; and it has become increasingly active in social welfare and labor legislation, recent examples being the increase in public assistance allowance to the poor and paid holidays for workers. Last but not least, because of a series of crises and scandals, the government is tightening supervision of depository financial institutions.

Nevertheless, despite the increasing role of the public sector, Hong Kong probably enjoys more economic freedom than any other country in the contemporary world. The Hong Kong government prides itself upon its policy of "positive noninterventionism," which, in the words of its leading exponent, "involves taking the view that in the great majority of circumstances it is futile and damaging to the growth rate of the economy for attempts to be made to plan the allocation of resources available to the private sector and to frustrate the operation of market forces which, in an open economy, are difficult enough to predict, let alone to control."[3] In other words, the government normally refrains from interfering with the market mechanism unless there is a clear-cut case of market failure. Subject to the usual legal prohibitions and government regulations, the domain of which is small, it may be said that private citizens in Hong Kong may engage in any form of economic activity. Hong Kong is one of the few remaining free ports in the world. The scope of freedom is particularly striking in the realm of money and finance, where there is not only no foreign exchange control of any kind, either on current or capital account, but also no restriction on the circulation of foreign currencies, following the recent repeal of the Foreign Notes Ordinance of 1913. This lack of restriction is unusual even for major international financial centers, where foreign currencies are routinely borrowed and lent, or held as financial assets, but hardly permitted to circulate as a medium of exchange. Another manifestation of minimal government intervention is the low level of taxation and the simplicity of the tax system. Despite increases over the years, the standard rate of 17 percent (with a corporation profit tax of 18.5 percent) is still, leaving aside tax havens, one of the lowest in the world.

The third major factor is the rule of law. Hong Kong is fortunate in having a well-established legal system, which, administered by an independent judiciary, effectively protects personal liberty and other human rights as well as private property and contracts. The economic significance of a sound legal framework can hardly be exaggerated. Recent theoretical and empirical research in economics has emphasized the importance of property rights for the efficient allocation of resources and the effective preservation of incentives to all economic agents, especially entrepreneurs.[4] Moreover, being largely based on English common law and equity, the Hong Kong legal system is widely understood and appreciated by civilized nations, particularly English-speaking countries sharing the same tradition, with whom Hong Kong maintains close economic and commercial ties. There can be little doubt that the legal system has played a vital role in Hong Kong's evolution into a major international financial, commercial, and manufacturing center.[5]

In short, it may be stated without exaggeration that, excepting the lack of political democracy, Hong Kong approximates in most respects an "open society" in the Popperian or Hayekian sense.[6] As a concrete example, consider the aspect of freedom of speech. In Hong Kong today, there are some 66 newspapers and 473 periodicals whose political views range from the far Left to the far Right, from rigidly pro-Peking to fervently pro-Taipei. But apart from the usual legal restrictions against libel, obscenity, etc., common to all free societies, there is no censorship or prohibition on dissident political views. Moreover, government policies and government officials are routinely criticized and attacked by the media and the more articulate citizens without any fear of official repression or retaliation.

In stating these facts I should hasten to add that I am not attempting to idealize Hong Kong. Indeed, I would be the first to admit that many unsavory features of capitalism are highly visible in Hong Kong, such as erratic cyclical fluctuations, a wide discrepancy in income and wealth, recurrent banking crises, and insiders' manipulation of the stock market, not to mention other social and environmental problems. Consciousness of these defects is the main reason why I cannot agree with the fulsome praise of Hong Kong by some foreign admirers.[7] However, in mitigation, it may be reasonably argued that Hong Kong's boom-and-bust phenomena are at least partly a consequence of its extreme openness and heavy dependence on foreign trade. Although the discrepancy in income and wealth is still wide, it has not engendered any social strife, because the benefits of rapid economic growth have filtered down to the lower-income groups.[8] Moreover, in an open society like Hong Kong, there is no insurmountable barrier to social mobility, the clearest evidence of which is the fact that many of Hong Kong's wealthiest and most successful entrepreneurs come from very humble origins. A high amount of social mobility implies a lack of social rigidities, which can also partly account for Hong Kong's renowned flexibility and resilience in coping with adversity and external shocks during the past four decades.

The three key factors responsible for Hong Kong's past success can now be used to also explain the confidence crisis of 1982–1984 and the euphoria (however transient it may be) that immediately followed the initialing of the Sino-British agreement on September 26, 1984. China's demand for the return of sovereignty over the whole Hong Kong area, made public in the summer of 1982 and confirmed during Prime Minister Margaret Thatcher's visit to Peking in September of the same year, immediately touched off a profound crisis of confidence for the very simple reason that the People's Republic, to put it mildly, has a most undistinguished record, especially during the Maoist era, with respect to the three key factors that have made Hong Kong what it is today. Since over half of Hong Kong's population is composed of first- or second-generation refugees from the mainland, and nearly all Chinese families in Hong Kong have relatives and friends inside China who they support financially and in other ways,[9] it is hardly surprising that people became extremely concerned about the viability of the social, legal, and economic systems; the protection of private property; and the respect for personal liberty and human rights consequent on a change in regimes.

The shattering blow to confidence manifested itself in a dramatic financial crisis in 1982–1984. As I have analyzed in detail elsewhere, the financial crisis comprised three conceptually distinct, but mutually interdependent, components: a currency crisis, a banking crisis, and a fiscal crisis.[10] The origins of the crisis can be traced to the heady days of 1977–1981, when excessive monetary growth and credit creation fueled rampant speculation on the stock and property markets, but the proximate cause was the profound negative impact of China's claim to sovereignty over Hong Kong.

Uncertainty and apprehension about the future triggered off a massive capital flight and portfolio shift that directly led to an almost continuous depreciation of the Hong Kong dollar and the collapse of the stock and property markets. These factors, in turn, resulted in heavy loan losses to the less prudently managed banks and deposit-taking companies, which gave rise to a series of runs on the depository institutions and their failures. Furthermore, the collapse of the property market resulted in a sharp fall in land sales revenue to the government, which, compounded by the government's enforced rescue of financial institutions in distress, in turn led to an unprecedented three-year fiscal deficit. Thus, a "domino effect" was initiated by a political shock. At the height of the financial crisis on September 24, 1983, marked by a massive run on the Hong Kong currency and some banks, the whole financial system was tottering on the brink of a total breakdown. This collapse was only narrowly averted by the government's takeover of one bank and assistance to another bank in late September and the implementation of a currency stabilization program in October.

By contrast, the Sino-British agreement appeared to produce at least a temporary respite or even euphoria. Thus, the Hang Seng index of stock prices, a sensitive though volatile barometer of public confidence, rose steadily from 746 on July 13, 1984, when there was still great tension concerning the outcome of the Sino-British negotiations, to 1752 on December 31, 1985.[11] Equally impressive was the recovery of the real estate market. Land and property prices in 1985 were reported to have risen by 30 to 50 percent, depending on location, size, and other attributes, compared to a trough in 1982.[12] As a result, government land sales also recovered sharply in 1985, giving rise to hopes that a balanced budget could be reached once again in fiscal year 1986-1987. Inflation, as measured by consumer price index, plummeted from 11 percent in 1982 to 3.5 percent in 1985, and unemployment fell from 4.5 percent in early 1983 to 3.4 percent in September 1985. Meanwhile, the Hong Kong dollar, pegged to the U.S. dollar at the fixed rate of US$1 = HK$7.8 under the currency reform mentioned earlier, has remained remarkably steady, the market variations from the official parity being no more than 2 percent either way. The trade-weighted exchange rate index of the Hong Kong dollar (December 18, 1971 = 100) rose steadily from 57.2 on the "black Saturday" of September 24, 1983, to 78.1 on February 28, 1985, before drifting lower, along with a weakening U.S. dollar, to 70.6 on December 31, 1985.

Finally, the real economy recovered much earlier, aided by the U.S. recovery. The real growth rate of the GDP, which had dropped to only 1.1 percent in 1982 from 9.4 percent a year earlier, rose to 5.9 percent in 1983 and further to 9.4 percent in 1984. Although the export-led expansion due to U.S. boom was the main factor for this remarkable performance, there can be little doubt that the psychological boost from the political settlement also played a role. In 1985, mainly because of the U.S. slowdown, the growth rate has been estimated at less than 4 percent. This figure is of course unsatisfactory according to Hong Kong's past record, but it is still much better than, for example, Singapore's negative growth of about −2 percent.

Indeed, there were incipient signs that export orders were again picking up, and provided there is no radically adverse development on the political front, or an uncontrollable surge in protectionism in the advanced industrialized countries, the flexible and resilient Hong Kong economy should be able to benefit from an improved world economic outlook based on lower energy prices, inflation, and interest rates. Over the near term, say 1986–1988, an average annual growth rate of 4–5 percent is definitely within Hong Kong's capability. In short, at the end of 1985, far from being a CRIC ("collapsing recently industrializing country"),[13] Hong Kong has recovered from an excruciating ordeal and is likely to maintain a positive, though slower, rate of growth in real terms at least over the near term.

Many skeptics would undoubtedly describe the postsettlement euphoria in Hong Kong as shortsighted and illusory. But, even as a transient phenomenon, it needs to be explained, as Hong Kong's imminent economic breakdown was widely predicted as recently as the summer of 1984. To understand the present situation, one must first recall the state of mind in Hong Kong between July 1982 and September 1984, which was extremely nervous and jittery. Especially in the summer of 1983, when China launched a strident anti-British propaganda campaign, there was a real possibility that the negotiations on the future of Hong Kong might end in failure. In that event, many people feared China would unilaterally take over Hong Kong before 1997, as it had threatened to do. Prohibition on the movement of money and capital, restrictions on personal freedom, nationalization of private enterprises, etc., might follow immediately. With the conclusion of an agreement, which is an international treaty in all but name, most people reasoned that the period up to June 30, 1997, at least would be fairly safe.

Second, the provisions of the Joint Declaration itself are more detailed and reassuring than expected. Except for defense and foreign affairs, Hong Kong will be given a high degree of autonomy, and the existing social, economic, and legal systems will be preserved for another fifty years after 1997. Hong Kong is to continue as an international financial center and free port and can conduct negotiations with foreign countries on commercial and economic matters as an independent economic entity. In addition to these freedoms, one surprising feature is that "the provisions of the International Covenant on Civil and Political Rights and the International Covenant on Economic, Social and Cultural Rights as applied to Hong Kong shall remain in force."[14] Thus, there is a widespread perception that, at least on paper, the three key factors of Hong Kong's success have been enshrined in the Joint Declaration. Although it is realized that the post-1997 special administrative region government will be ultimately controlled by Peking, the SAR arrangement is still thought to be much more preferable to direct rule by Communist cadres sent from the mainland should there have been no agreement.

Third, the quick endorsement of the Sino-British agreement by the United States, Japan, the European Economic Community, and other countries in the Asia-Pacific area (except Taiwan) has given a veneer of international respectability to the agreement, which undoubtedly has considerable soothing effect on public confidence. Fourth, the more rational and outward-looking policies pursued by the post-Mao leadership, especially after the downfall of Hua Kuo-feng in 1981, have given rise to hopes that after years of turmoil, China has at long last taken a sensible road to economic development. Many people reason that as long as China keeps moving on the right track, the standards of living and life-styles of the mainland and Hong Kong will hopefully converge over the long run, in which case 1997, instead of being the end of the world, might well represent a new chapter in Hong Kong's history.

Again I must hasten to add that in describing this sense of relief after the Sino-British accord, I am not suggesting for a moment that the people of Hong Kong actually welcomed the agreement with open arms. Polls taken before the settlement all indicated that the majority of the population preferred the status quo to Chinese sovereignty.[15] But given China's determination and intransigence over the sovereignty issue, and the reluctance or inability of Britain and other Western democracies to confront China, what can the unarmed and politically unorganized people of Hong Kong do, short of physical emigration, to escape Communist rule? The stark fact is that Hong Kong is left with no choice but to accept the fait accompli.

The China Factor

Given that there is no viable alternative to the Sino-British agreement, Hong Kong's future now depends on the faithful observance and implementation of the agreement itself. More specifically, the questions to be asked are, Will China conscientiously honor the agreement? and Will the "one country, two systems" formula work over the long run? These questions have already generated heated controversy, and undoubtedly both optimists and pessimists can marshal valid reasons for their arguments. Only time will tell which is right. My own view is that there are two aspects to China's attitude toward the Joint Declaration. One is China's willingness, and other is its ability, to honor the agreement.

On the willingness to observe the agreement, I personally think China should be given the benefit of the doubt. Hong Kong is indefensible either militarily or politically, and China could have taken over the territory any time during the past thirty-six years, either by force, much like what India did to Goa, or simply by cutting off the water supply from the East River. But even during the most xenophobic years of the Maoist era, China by and large observed the existing treaties on which British rule is based, though they have never been formally recognized. It seems far-fetched to suggest that China took the trouble of negotiating with Britain for two years and signed an international agreement, only to repudiate it deliberately.

TABLE 12.1. Net financial transactions between Hong Kong and China (million HK$)

End of Quarter		Licensed Banks	Deposit-taking Companies	Total
1979	Q1	+4,725	+96	+4,821
	Q2	+5,231	+102	+5,333
	Q3	+5,266	+116	+5,382
	Q4	+5,701	+32	+5,733
1980	Q1	+5,386	+190	+5,576
	Q2	+4,676	+445	+5,121
	Q3	+4,617	+390	+5,007
	Q4	+5,352	+445	+5,797
1981	Q1	+5,984	+588	+6,572
	Q2	+4,291	+487	+4,778
	Q3	+3,343	+64	+3,407
	Q4	+2,567	−597	+1,970
1982	Q1	−100	−613	−713
	Q2	−2,010	−641	−2,651
	Q3	−2,677	−404	−3,081
	Q4	−4,933	−525	−5,458
1983	Q1	−5,468	−1,446	−6,914
	Q2	−5,366	−1,803	−7,169
	Q3	−7,001	−1,868	−8,869
	Q4	−7,333	−1,822	−9,155
1984	Q1	−9,710	−694	−10,404
	Q2	−12,473	−1,235	−13,708
	Q3	−12,670	−1,114	−13,784
	Q4	−10,020	−659	−10,679
1985	Q1	−5,022	−1,222	−6,244
	Q2	−2,204	−306	−2,510
	Q3	+6,416	−112	+6,304

Note: A negative sign denotes net liabilities to China, and a positive sign denotes net claims on China.

Source: Banking Commissioner's Office, Hong Kong.

References have often been made to the previous duplicity with respect to Shanghai, Tibet, etc., but although the historical facts are indisputable, the historical analogy is valid only if China remains the same Maoist China it was before 1977. The Sino-British agreement represents a considerable diplomatic victory for China, and a stable and prosperous Hong Kong, for economic and financial reasons alone, is of vital importance to China's modernization program.[16] On these grounds it is in China's own interest to observe the agreement correctly.

Evidence can be cited that China, extremely concerned about Hong Kong's deteriorating confidence after 1982, has been trying hard to stabilize the local economy through various channels. One manifestation, which can be quantified, is the net transactions with Hong Kong's financial institutions. As shown in Table 12.1, between the first quarter of 1979 and the end of 1981, Hong Kong's financial institutions as a whole had net claims on their

Chinese counterparts, a state of affairs fully consistent with Hong Kong's status as a major financial center in the Pacific. However, from the first quarter of 1982 through the second quarter of 1985, Hong Kong's financial institutions became net debtors to their Chinese counterparts. The net indebtedness to China reached a peak of HK$13,784 million (US$1,758 million) in the third quarter of 1984, not an inconsiderable sum considering China's own financial capability. As I have argued elsewhere, there can be various plausible interpretations of why China became a net lender to Hong Kong, but the fact that this change occurred at a time when Hong Kong was experiencing great financial strains and stresses is suggestive.[17] However, from the end of 1984 onward, after the accord was signed and confidence in Hong Kong gradually recovered, China's net claims on Hong Kong fell sharply to HK$2,510 million (US$322 million) in the second quarter of 1985, and in the third quarter, China once again became a net debtor to Hong Kong. Although it is still too early to say whether a new trend has been established, there are signs that Hong Kong, having survived the financial crisis of 1982–1984, is reasserting its role as a financial center with respect to China.

It is also known that China has invested heavily in all sectors of the Hong Kong economy in recent years. Although economic motivations probably predominate, a desire to boost confidence during the delicate Sino-British negotiations also played a significant role. According to Wang Kuang-ying, chairman of the Peking-owned Everbright Industrial Corporation, China had, by early 1984, invested some US$4 million in more than 300 Hong Kong projects through fifty representative and trade offices.[18] An estimate by the Industry Department of the Hong Kong government reveals that at the end of March 1985, Peking owned or controlled 124 firms in trade and industrial promotion, 44 in banking and finance, 5 in insurance, 19 in manufacturing, 4 in publishing and printing, 53 in transportation and tourism, and 26 in real estate and construction.[19] These figures do not, however, include hundreds of department stores and retail outlets selling Chinese products. During Hong Kong's currency crisis of 1982–1983, China lost, according to my estimate, about US$1.1 billion as a result of the sharp depreciation of the Hong Kong dollar, and yet it has refrained so far from passing on the loss to Hong Kong consumers by raising sharply the supply prices of Chinese goods.

Two other examples of China's concern for Hong Kong's stability are the takeover in 1984 of two large Hong Kong industrial firms that nearly went bankrupt[20] and the support by the Bank of China of a small local bank, Ka Wah Bank, which suffered a rumor-inspired run in June 1985. In December, China Hwa Jian Company, a state-run enterprise under the State Council's Overseas Chinese Affairs Office, took a substantial equity in Ka Wah Bank through a joint venture with Singapore interests. Earlier, in June 1985, the China Merchant Steam Navigation Company, another China-owned shipping company, acquired a 25 percent equity in another small local bank, the Far East Bank, for about HK$90 million.

TABLE 12.2 Merchandise trade between Hong Kong and China (million HK$)

	Domestic Exports to China		Total Exports to China		Imports from China	Trade Balance for Hong Kong
1977	31		206		8,115	−7,909
1978	11	(−64.5)	225	(+9.2)	10,597 (+30.6)	−10,302
1979	603	(+5,381.8)	1,918	(+752.4)	15,201 (+43.5)	−13,283
1980	1,605	(+166.2)	6,247	(+225.7)	21,948 (+44.4)	−15,701
1981	2,924	(+82.2)	10,968	(+75.6)	29,510 (+34.5)	−18,542
1982	3,806	(+30.2)	11,798	(+7.6)	32,935 (+11.6)	−21,137
1983	6,223	(+63.5)	18,406	(+56.0)	42,821 (+30.0)	−24,415
1984	11,283	(+81.3)	39,347	(+113.8)	55,753 (+30.2)	−16.406
1985 (first 10 months)	12,686	(+47.4)	51,539	(+77.0)	46,334 (+0.6)	+17,891

Note: Total exports = domestic exports + reexports; figures in parentheses are year-on-year percentage growth.

Source: Hong Kong government, Census and Statistics Department.

TABLE 12.3. Entrepôt trade between Hong Kong and China (million HK$)

	Reexports to China		Reexports from China Through Hong Kong	
1977	175		2,492	
1978	214	(+22.3)	3,659	(+46.8)
1979	1,315	(+514.5)	5,663	(+54.8)
1980	4,642	(+253.0)	8,394	(+48.2)
1981	8,044	(+73.3)	12,834	(+52.9)
1982	7,992	(−0.005)	14,694	(+14.5)
1983	12,183	(+52.4)	19,680	(+33.9)
1984	28,064	(+130.4)	28,107	(+42.8)
1985 (first 10 months)	28,853	(+89.4)	27,976	(+21.1)

Note: Figures in parentheses are year-on-year percentage growth.

Source: Hong Kong government, Census and Statistics Department.

Leaving aside these aspects of "crisis management," one salient feature of the post-Mao era is the rapidly growing trade and investment flows between China and Hong Kong. China replaced Japan as Hong Kong's largest supplier in 1982; it also became Hong Kong's fourth-largest export market in the same year, then the second largest in 1984. In entrepôt trade, China became Hong Kong's largest country of destination in 1980, and the largest country of origin as early as 1969. Tables 12.2 and 12.3 summarize merchandise and entrepôt trade between China and Hong Kong for the period 1977 through the first ten months of 1985, and several important features may be noted. One is the impressive year-on-year growth rates in all trade categories. Although these are expressed in value terms in the tables, the growth rates in real terms are also very high: The volume growth rate of domestic exports to China in 1984, for example, was as high as 60 percent. Second, the phenomenal growth of domestic exports to China is perhaps the most surprising development in the post-Mao era. Over the period of less than eight years, such exports had increased by nearly forty times, from almost nothing to over HK$11.3 billion (US$1.45 billion). China's purchase of Hong Kong goods partly reflects modernization requirements, partly pent-up consumer demand, and partly a much improved foreign exchange position—the country's total foreign exchange reserves having increased from US$2.345 billion in 1977 to US$17.302 billion in September 1984. Third, the equally phenomenal growth of reexports to and from China in the post-Mao years has unequivocally confirmed Hong Kong's reemergence as the leading entrepôt for China and the whole Pacific area. However, unlike the pre-1950 entrepôt, Hong Kong today is a highly sophisticated financial and trading center with a respectable manufacturing base, in which entrepôt trade is a nice complement, but not a key pillar, of the economy.

In May 1985, as a result of heavy loss of reserves, China reimposed drastic curbs on imports, which were bound to eventually affect Hong Kong's domestic exports to China. Thus, the upsurge in exports to China, which helped to compensate for the slump in exports to the United States and Europe in 1985, cannot be sustained for long unless China's reserve position shows substantial recovery. Nevertheless, the trade data do clearly demonstrate that China's modernization program and outward-looking development strategy have produced a significant and positive impact on Hong Kong.

Mention has been made of China's injection of funds into Hong Kong and other investments by state corporations. The investment flow is by no means unidirectional however. Since China opened its door to foreign investment in 1979, Hong Kong interests have topped all other foreign investors in either joint ventures or wholly owned enterprises.[21] In the special economic zone of Shenzhen, Hong Kong's position is particularly predominant, accounting for about 80 percent of total foreign investment. Indeed, it is not an exaggeration to say that Shenzhen has become virtually a satellite of Hong Kong.[22] Elsewhere, I have shown how Hong Kong, apart from regularly providing about one-third of China's hard currency earnings, also serves as an unexcelled financial center, entrepôt, and information center for China.[23] If Peking plays its cards wisely, it will be able to acquire from Britain in 1997, virtually without cost, all these first-rate facilities, which it knows quite well can never be replicated elsewhere in China.

The other aspect of the question, namely, China's ability to observe and implement the Sino-British agreement, depends on China's internal political stability and policy continuity. China's own record during the past four decades is not one that inspires either domestic or international confidence. The death of Mao, however, ushered in a new era of relative stability and progress. Economically, the adoption by the post-Mao leadership of a more pragmatic and outward-looking economic policy that recognizes the importance of incentives, price mechanisms, and property rights has resulted in substantial gains in output, particularly in agriculture, and some improvement in the standard of living of the population, as has been shown by careful studies by economists in the West.[24]

In external relations, since 1978 China has actively tried to attract foreign investment and technology by setting up four special economic zones on the southern coast, opening fourteen coastal cities and the whole coastal area to foreign investment, and by enacting various forms of "economic legislation." In October 1984, the Chinese Communist party's Central Committee decided that the reform program, based on the so-called responsibility system so successfully applied to the rural sector, would be extended to the urban areas with an emphasis on freeing prices and wages from rigid state control and granting greater autonomy to enterprises. In social, cultural, and intellectual life, there has also been a noticeable depoliticization or loosening of the total regimentation that was so characteristic of the Maoist era. There has also been a belated awareness of the importance of knowledge, technology, education, and the role of intellectuals in China's modernization program. The pre-1949 tradition of sending promising students to study at institutions of higher learning abroad, particularly in the United States, has been revived. In short, there is abundant evidence that Teng's China is settling down to become what might be called a "post-revolutionary society," whose primary goals are economic reconstruction and modernization rather than class struggle and world revolution.[25]

Despite this more hopeful development in China, some nagging questions remain: How long will the current period of relative stability, progress, and reform last? Will the modernization program succeed in lifting China out of abject poverty by the year 2000, as promised by the leadership? Will Teng's policies survive after him? Peking is not unaware of the doubts that persist in Hong Kong and abroad, and recent developments suggest that Teng and his followers have achieved a considerable victory in enlarging and consolidating their power base. In June 1985, Teng announced the demobilization of 1 million soldiers and a long list of reshuffles of key military personnel. Then in September, at a meeting of the Communist party's Central Committee and a specially convened national conference, some 131 old guards were retired, and younger and better-educated cadres known to be Teng's protégés were promoted to the Politburo and the Central Committee. A new Five-Year Plan for 1986–1990 was also released, and it stressed the continuation of Teng's modernization program and the open-door policy.

However, the fact that Teng's China has firmly turned its back on the Maoist past does not imply that there are no serious domestic conflicts and difficulties or that it has ceased to be a totalitarian society. There are many signs that the urban reform program, initiated with such fanfare in October 1984, has not been going well. Indeed, it has given rise to inflation, corruption, nepotism, tax evasion, smuggling, profiteering, prostitution, pornography, and other "unhealthy" trends. Moreover, the rejection of the simple-minded Maoist egalitarianism has engendered widening discrepancies in income and wealth, not only among various social strata, but also among the various regions in the country—an issue that can become potentially explosive in a poor country like China. Already there are reports that widespread anger at inflation, corruption, and income discrepancies has caused student and labor unrest. And despite some liberalization in the economic, social, and cultural spheres, China's human rights record, particularly with regard to political dissidents, is still most unsatisfactory.[26]

The gap in income and wealth is particularly pertinent to Hong Kong. In 1984, Hong Kong's GDP per capita, measured at current prices and exchange rate, was US$5,951. China's gross social product (GSP), the nearest equivalent to the GDP, in the same year was about US$443.[27] The difference means that China's nominal income per head is only one-thirteenth of Hong Kong's. To be sure, these figures do not necessarily measure the gap in real income, since purchasing power discrepancies have to be allowed for as well, but it is reasonable to infer that even after purchasing power adjustments on assumptions most favorable to China, an extremely wide gap will still remain.

Ideally, China's economy should grow at a higher rate than Hong Kong's so that, over time, the gap would eventually diminish, but so far the empirical record has shown the reverse. According to the World Bank, the average annual growth rate of China's GNP per capita at constant prices was 3.5 percent in the period 1957–1979.[28] By contrast, the average annual growth rate of Hong Kong's GDP at constant prices in 1961–1979, according to Hong Kong government estimates, was about 6.9 percent, nearly twice that of China's for roughly the same period.[29] Another World Bank study gives the GNP per capita growth rates of China and Hong Kong in real terms at 4.5 percent and 6.8 percent, respectively, for the period 1973–1982.[30] In 1984, China's nominal GSP per capita is reported to have grown by 12 percent. There is no information about the deflator, but the retail price index is said to have risen by 2.8 percent.[31] However, China's price index is widely regarded as an unreliable indicator of inflation.[32] The true inflation rate for 1984 was, according to my best guess, at least 7 percent. Real income per head therefore grew at most by 5 percent, and Hong Kong's growth rate of real GDP per capita in the same year was 8.2 percent. It may well be that as the Hong Kong economy becomes more mature, its growth rate will slow down, even in the absence of any catastrophe, while China's growth rate will accelerate with the progress in modernization and reform. But even assuming that China will grow at a higher rate than Hong Kong from 1985 onward, it may still take at least two generations before China can catch up with Hong Kong.

The huge gap in income, not to mention the personal freedom and other benefits of an open society, is the major reason why Hong Kong is such an irresistible magnet for the people of China, particularly those living in the southern province of Guangdong. Ignoring the previous influx, and confining ourselves to the period from 1977 to 1980 alone, at least 211,900 illegal immigrants entered Hong Kong from China and were allowed to remain after having "reached base." This large influx was in addition to some 55,000 legal immigrants from the mainland.[33] Faced with this avalanche, the Hong Kong government was forced to abandon the so-called reached-base policy in October 1980 and repatriate all illegal immigrants on capture or detection.[34] Whether immigration can be effectively controlled after 1997 will be a severe test for the future Hong Kong Special Administrative Region government.

The dilemma for China is that in 1997, Hong Kong will become China's responsibility and China's authority and prestige would be severely damaged if Hong Kong should stagnate and decline under Chinese rule after the British era of economic progress and prosperity. Purely from the political and psychological point of view, China will be compelled to do everything possible to prop up the Hong Kong economy. To do so, however, would mean diverting scarce investable resources to Hong Kong and, paradoxically, would perpetuate the wide gap in income and wealth that is the source of so many difficulties. Resentment against the "special policy" toward Hong Kong will no doubt grow among the populace, and the political and social consequences of this resentment cannot be lightly dismissed.

Even assuming that China is both willing and able to observe and implement the Joint Declaration, interpretations of the agreement may differ. Currently, a highly sensitive topic in Hong Kong is political reform. In anticipation of British withdrawal, the Hong Kong government published two official papers in 1984—one green and one white—on the development of representative government.[35] Pursuant to this objective, elections to the district boards and the Legislative Council were held in March and September 1985. China is extremely suspicious of this move toward parliamentary democracy, regarding it as an attempt to nurture popularly elected but pro-British leaders who can take over power in 1997.

Hsü Chia-t'un, director of the Hong Kong Xinhua news agency (New China News Agency, China's de facto diplomatic mission in Hong Kong), publicly warned in August 1985 against any hasty change in Hong Kong's governmental structure before 1997, and the Communist press in Hong Kong quickly followed by reminding the British, in none too subtle terms, that sovereignty is to be transferred to the People's Republic, not Hong Kong. Then on November 21, 1985, Hsü dropped a bombshell by bluntly charging that "some people are not observing the Joint Declaration."[36] Although Hsü refused to identify what he meant by "some people," there is no doubt that the British and Hong Kong governments were his targets. The next day the Hang Seng index of stock prices dropped nearly fifty points, reflecting Hong Kong's extreme nervousness to any sign of a Sino-British rift. Although subsequently the rift appeared to have been papered over during the visit of Chi P'eng-fei, director of China's Hong Kong and Macao Affairs Office, to Hong Kong in December 1985, it has been reliably learned that the tension eased only because Britain, yielding to Chinese pressure, agreed to discuss Hong Kong's poliltical reforms at the regular meetings of the Joint Liaison Group, which was established under the terms of the agreement to monitor developments in Hong Kong up to January 1, 2000.

It may well be that certain vested interests in Hong Kong, especially the wealthy industrialists, bankers, and merchants, etc., also do not wish to see any over-hasty democratization lest populist demands for more government spending and taxation might result. But China's heavy-handed approach to this matter, especially its implacable opposition to any form of parlilamentary democracy, however cautious and timid it may be, does not augur well for Hong Kong.

The most charitable interpretation of China's stance is that Peking does not want to see Hong Kong's stability and prosperity threatened by political agitation and social strife because of democratization. According to this view, China is still prepared to grant Hong Kong considerable freedom and autonomy in economic, social, and cultural affairs, but it will certainly not tolerate any move toward an independent polity or any form of political dissidence. What China favors is a kind of "authoritarian capitalism" on the model of Taiwan or Singapore: The only political change that is permitted is the replacement of London by Peking as the ultimate master of Hong Kong.[37]

Longer-term Economic Issues

The previous analysis makes it clear that China's intention and behavior with respect to its treaty obligations are the key determinants of Hong Kong's future as a free market economy. On this major premise, let us examine some concrete economic issues in the years up to 1997 and beyond.

The first is the stability of the financial sector. I have mentioned how the currency crisis of September 1983 nearly caused the total collapse of the financial system. The "linked rate system" introduced in October 1983, under which the Hong Kong dollar was linked to the U.S. dollar at the rate of US$1 = HK$7.8, has proved to be surprisingly successful. In normal times, the present system relies on the automatic mechanism of "arbitrage and competition" for its efficacy; in an emergency, however, the decisive factor is the resources of the Exchange Fund.[38] Although a recurrence of Maoist turmoils in China is highly unlikely, some pressure on the Hong Kong dollar can be expected on Teng's death or as the result of other events that might be perceived as signs of instability. There has been much speculation about the outflow of capital from Hong Kong since 1982, but there is hardly any precise quantification, since, for various reasons, Hong Kong does not yet have a comprehensive balance of payments accounting system.[39] Only a trade account, including invisibles, is now available.

As may be seen from Table 12.4, Hong Kong's trade account has improved considerably in recent years, with a surplus of HK$11.644 billion (US$1.49 billion) in 1984 and a trade surplus (excluding invisibles) of HK$4,106 billion

TABLE 12.4. Visible and invisible trade accounts (million HK$)

	1979	1980	1981	1982	1983	1984
Visible Trade						
Domestic exports	55,912	68,171	80,423	83,032	104,405	137,936
Reexports	20,022	30,072	41,739	44,353	56,294	83,504
Total exports of goods	75,934	98,242	122,163	127,385	160,699	221,441
Imports of goods	85,908	111,651	138,375	142,893	175,442	223,370
Visible trade balance	−9,974	−13,408	−16,212	−15,508	−14,743	−1,929
Visible trade gap (%)[a]	11.6	12.0	11.7	10.9	8.4	0.9
Imports of goods adjusted[b]	86,339	111,794	139,246	143,769	176,574	224,812
Visible trade balance adjusted[b]	−10,405	−13,552	−17,083	−16,384	−15,875	−3,371
Visible trade gap adjusted (%)[b]	12.1	12.1	12.3	11.4	9.0	1.5
Invisible Trade						
Exports of services	19,258	22,203	27,218	30,671	36,922	44,455
Imports of services	11,968	14,912	19,234	20,889	25,081	29,440
Invisible trade balance	7,290	7,291	7,984	9,782	11,841	15,015
Visible and Invisible Trade						
Exports of goods and services	95,192	120,445	149,381	158,056	197,621	265,896
Imports of goods and services[b]	98,307	126,706	158,480	164,658	201,655	254,252
Visible and invisible trade balance	−3,115	−6,261	−9,099	−6,602	−4,034	11,644
Visible and invisible trade gap (%)[c]	3.2	4.9	5.7	4.0	2.0	(4.6)

[a]Visible trade gap, that is, the proportion of the value of imports of goods not covered by the value of total exports of goods.
[b]Adjusted to take account of imports of gold for industrial and commercial use.
[c]VIsible and and invisible trade gap, that is, the proportion of the value of imports of goods and services not covered by the value of exports of goods and services. The figures in brackets denote a visible and invisible trade surplus expressed as a percentage of the value of imports of goods and services.
Source: Hong Kong government.

(US$526 million) in the first eleven months of 1985. But the trade account, unlike the capital account, is more a function of economic performance than intangibles like political uncertainty and confidence. Before October 1983, a net outflow of capital showed up in the rapid depreciation of the domestic currency. After the implementation of the linked rate system, the stability of the Hong Kong dollar would seem to suggest that net outflow has become less of a problem. However, capital flow is highly reversible and unpredictable: A massive outflow could resume anytime due to an adverse development on the political front, or as 1997 draws nearer.

Another element of the financial crisis, illiquidity or insolvency of depository institutions, can arise, not only from political uncertainty, but also from mismanagement and criminal fraud. The bankruptcy of the Overseas

Trust Bank and the Hong Kong Industrial and Commercial Bank in June 1985 are cases in point. Another indication that the repercussions of the 1982–1984 crisis are by no means over is the fact that in December 1985, Wing On Bank, which used to be a respected medium-sized bank, had to cede majority equity control, because of heavy loan losses, to Hang Seng Bank, which in turn is 61 percent controlled by the powerful Hong Kong and Shanghai Banking Corporation. Currently, the Hong Kong regulatory authorities are trying to tighten up prudential regulation by requiring, among other things, a higher capital/risk assets ratio and tougher examination and reporting procedures. The reform proposals have met with strong opposition from certain foreign banks, particularly Japanese and Korean institutions. It appears that the latter have made use of Hong Kong's lax regulation in the past for circumventive purposes and now threaten to scale down their operations in Hong Kong if the reforms are implemented. This example underlines a dilemma: Hong Kong's liberal environment is one of the important factors for its rise as a financial center, but at the same time, the lack of adequate control on mismanagement and fraud has also caused heavy losses to depositors and investors. How to tighten and improve prudential supervision without adversely affecting Hong Kong's status as a major international financial center is an important, but by no means easy, task.

The second major concern is the rate of capital formation. In 1982–1984, largely because of the confidence crisis, the growth rate of capital formation in real terms was −2.4 percent, against an average rate of 8.7 percent in 1966–1981. For 1985, the real capital formation was initially forecast in February 1985 to recover modestly to 3 percent, on a GDP growth of 7.2 percent, but subsequently, owing to the sharp slump in exports, the GDP growth rate was scaled down to about 3.5 percent (the corresponding figure for capital formation was not available at the time of writing). Over the longer horizon, it is almost impossible to predict how this component of GDP, which is vitally important for the economy's long-term growth, will behave.

Public sector capital formation is presumably more stable, being under the direct control of the government, but public sector investment is a function of government revenue, and large-scale and persistent deficit financing is out of the question. Private sector capital formation is governed, not only by the prospective yield on real investment, but also by long-term expectations about political stability, personal freedom, and property rights. By its very nature, therefore, it is much more volatile. Within the private sector, there is also a notable difference in attitude and outlook between foreign and local firms. By and large, foreign firms appear to take a more sanguine view of Hong Kong's future than their local counterparts. For example, according to a recent survey, foreign investment in Hong Kong's manufacturing industries increased by 19.3 percent from US$1,230 million in August 1981 to US$1,468 million in September 1984 while investment per worker increased by 30.9 percent from US$15,614 to US$20,436. The three largest source countries are the United States (53.7 percent), Japan (21.1 percent), and the United Kingdom (6.9 percent), and the three largest industries are electronics (35.5 percent), textiles and garments (9.9 percent), and electrical products (8 percent).[40] Similarly, in the financial sector, the 1982–1984 crisis did not seem to have stopped foreign financial institutions from pouring into Hong Kong.

The apparent paradox is, however, not difficult to explain. Typically, a multinational firm's investment in Hong Kong is a calculated risk that is quantitatively trivial in relation to the firm's global assets but nevertheless forms an integral part of the firm's global strategy. Given Hong Kong's congenial environment and proximity to the potentially vast China market, it is entirely rational for a multinational firm to establish and maintain a presence in Hong Kong. The firm also has reasons to believe that it will command more respect from China after 1997, backed as it is by its home government. If the firm is prestigious enough, it may even use its name to tap the local capital market without tying up too much of its own funds. Thus, the Security Pacific Bank of California made a HK$500 million commercial paper issue in November 1984 to finance its takeover of minority interests in a Hong Kong bank, the Bank of Canton.

By contrast, an indigenous entity typically has most of its assets concentrated in Hong Kong, and given the uncertainty about the future, it is entirely rational for the firm to diversify its assets away from Hong Kong as much as possible. Unlike a foreign firm, after 1997 an indigenous firm can expect protection only from the Hong Kong SAR government, which will be ultimately responsible to the Central People's government in China. One can therefore expect that local firms will increasingly follow the strategy of "precautionary diversification" or "precautionary internationalization" as best as they can. This strategy may take many forms, but the principal elements are (1) transfer of liquid assets abroad, leaving only money balances enough for transaction purposes in Hong Kong; (2) establishment of branches or offices in foreign countries or acquisition of foreign firms in whole or in part; (3) sale of the firm's equity to a foreign firm or formation of a joint venture with a foreign firm in Hong Kong; and (4) removal of a firm's registered head office from Hong Kong to a foreign country, especially a tax haven.

It should be emphasized that this strategy does not necessarily imply outright withdrawal. Unless conditions become utterly intolerable, very few firms will actually abandon Hong Kong even after 1997, because the attractions of doing business in Hong Kong and the lure of the China market will still be very considerable. As an illustration, the decision of Jardine Matheson— the oldest British conglomerate in Hong Kong—to move its legal domicile to Bermuda in 1984 has not resulted in the winding down of its operations. Instead, the company is expanding its business with China, having reportedly explained its corporate policy to Peking's satisfaction. It is also well known that virtually all of Hong Kong's shipping companies are already incorporated in countries like Liberia and Panama for tax purposes. The fact that many

Hong Kong firms invest in China is also by no means inconsistent with the "precautionary diversification" hypothesis. The hypothesis requires only that a firm diversity its assets away from Hong Kong; it does not require a total abandonment of Hong Kong or China.

The third issue is whether Hong Kong's status as a separate economic entity, enshrined in the Sino-British agreement, will be accepted by the international community. Although most of Hong Kong's trade partners have welcomed the settlement, the goodwill is couched in vague terms and can be taken as no more than a diplomatic gesture. One critical concern, for example, is Hong Kong's quota under the multifiber arrangement. The textile and garment industries now still account for about 41 percent of Hong Kong's industrial work force and 40 percent of its total domestic exports. Any attempt by an importing country to abolish Hong Kong's independent quota and merge it with that of China would deal a severe blow to Hong Kong, and it could well be disastrous if such a tactic were widely copied by others.[41] Similar considerations apply to other international organizations and institutions such as the General Agreement on Tariffs and Trade, the Coordinating Committee on Export Controls, most-favored-nation treatment, and the Asian Development Bank. A related problem concerns those countries that have no diplomatic relations with China. Because Hong Kong is apolitical, it has been able to maintain normal and even thriving economic and financial ties with them and also to serve as an intermediary between them and China, to the benefit of all concerned. Both aspects may be jeopardized when Hong Kong comes under Chinese sovereignty.

But although the international attitude toward post-1997 Hong Kong may create problems, there is a positive side to the issue. If China really wants to maintain Hong Kong's stability and prosperity, it must respect Hong Kong's status as a separate economic entity, otherwise international recognition will be withheld. Thus, China does face some external constraints, even if they are implicit, on its behavior toward Hong Kong.

The fourth issue is long-term development strategy. Even before 1997 surfaced as a diplomatic issue, many analysts had already pointed out that Hong Kong could no longer rely on its labor-intensive industries to sustain growth in an age of rapid technological innovations and structural changes. Critics are especially concerned about the heavy government involvement in guiding and establishing "strategic industries" and about various forms of direct and indirect subsidies to industrial development in Singapore, South Korea, and Taiwan—Hong Kong's main rivals in international trade. However, recent careful studies have shown that state-sponsored projects in heavy industries, refineries, and petrochemicals, etc., in those countries have turned out to be financial losers. In the case of Singapore, an overly interventionist policy resulted in negative growth in 1985 and possibly also in 1986.[42] By contrast, Hong Kong's policy of avoiding government intervention and grandiose schemes, relying instead on the flexibility of private entrepreneurs and the law of comparative advantage, has generally served Hong Kong well.[43]

But Hong Kong cannot afford to be smug. There are already a number of government-subvented organizations, such as the Trade Development Council, Productivity Center, Vocational Center, and Management Association, doing useful work in promoting Hong Kong products abroad, disseminating information on technological innovations and management skills, and training personnel, etc. These bodies, which generate positive externalities for the whole economy, should be strengthened and subsidized by public revenue, and indeed this course has been recommended by the government's advisory committee on diversification.[44] But direct subsidy and guidance to individual firms or industries has wisely been avoided by the government. The fiscal crisis of 1982–1984 in any case rendered any proposal about large-scale government assistance to industrial development irrelevant. However, there is no lack of pressure groups of various kinds constantly clamoring for more government aid to industries and other forms of government spending. Whether the pre-1997 colonial government or the post-1997 SAR government can resist such demands, which many economists fear could undermine the famed efficiency, flexibility, and resilience on which Hong Kong's free market economy rests, remains to be seen.

Over the very long run, Hong Kong's manufacturing industries will have to compete, not only with those of the other three "little dragons" of Asia, but also with those of China. Despite its backwardness, China has a much broader and deeper industrial base than Hong Kong. It has established sizable industries like iron and steel, heavy engineering, coal, petroleum, petrochemicals, automobile, and armaments that are totally absent in Hong Kong. Moreover, since 1978 China's consumer goods industries, which were given low priority during the Maoist era, have grown rapidly and made their impact felt in international markets. As the Soviet experience shows, a totalitarian society can always mobilize resources to achieve what it regards as priority targets regardless of human cost.

Over the long run, it will be increasingly difficult for Hong Kong, where wages are determined by market forces, to compete in manufactured products with China, where wages are determined by administrative decrees. On the other hand, Hong Kong's port facilities and other aspects of its infrastructure are at least a generation ahead of those in China's seaports. The freedom Hong Kong allows with respect to the movement and trading of money, goods and services, and securities; the flow of information; and the employment of foreign nationals is unrivaled even by the other three "little dragons," let alone China. Hong Kong's comparative advantage and long-term future therefore lie in its being the financial center, information center, and entrepôt, not only for China, but also for the whole Asia-Pacific region.

Some clues to the structural change in the Hong Kong economy are presented in Table 12.5. Based on the "production" method of GDP estimation, the table shows the relative contribution of various sectors in the period 1980–1983. As may be seen, the primary sector (Divisions 1 and 2) is now negligible. The share of manufacturing declined during the period from 23.9 percent to 21.9 percent, and if the secondary sector is defined

TABLE 12.5. Contribution of economic sectors to the gross domestic product at current prices, 1980–1983 (million HK$)

	1980		1981		1982		1983a	
	$	%	$	%	$	%	$	%
1. Agriculture and fishing	1,109	0.9	1,122	0.7	1,229	0.7	1,242	0.6
2. Mining and quarrying	213	0.2	253	0.2	308	0.2	328	0.2
3. Manufacturing	30,549	23.9	36,049	22.8	36,390	20.6	44,231	21.9
4. Electricity, gas, and water	1,703	1.3	2,229	1.4	3,243	1.8	4,142	2.1
5. Construction	8,570	6.7	11,922	7.5	12,904	7.3	12,002	5.9
6. Wholesale and retail, import/export trades, restaurants and hotels	26,169	20.4	30,749	19.4	33,647	19.1	42,535	21.1
7. Transport, storage, and communication	9,645	7.5	11,853	7.5	13,632	7.7	16,049	7.9
8. Financing, insurance, real estate, and business services	29,292	22.9	37,688	23.8	39,746	22.5	37,944	18.8
9. Community, social, and personal services	15,696	12.3	20,995	13.3	27,428	15.6	31,696	15.7
10. Ownership of premises	12,297	9.6	15,638	9.9	19,317	11.0	23,395	11.6
11. Nominal sector (adjustment for financial services)	−7,200	−5.7	−10,325	−6.5	−11,405	−6.5	−11,738	−5.8
GDP at factor cost (production-based estimate)	128,043	100.0	158,173	100.0	176,439	100.0	201,826	100.0
Indirect taxes less subsidies	5,196		6,117		6,230		7,932	
GDP at market prices (production-based estimate)	133,239		164,290		182,669		209,758	

aProvisional estimates.

Source: Hong Kong government, Census and Statistics Department, *Estimates of Gross Domestic Product 1966 to 1984* (Hong Kong, 1985).

to include manufacturing, public utilities, and construction, then that sector's share declined from 31.9 percent to 29.9 percent. One puzzle concerns the behavior of Division 8, comprising financing, insurance, real estate, and business services. This division used to be a high flier, but after advancing to 23.8 percent in 1981, its share dropped over the next two years to 18.8 percent. The most plausible cause for this reversal was the financial crisis and real estate slump in 1982–1983, and although the trend is probably a temporary aberration, the figures for 1984-1985 were not available at the time of writing.

Comparison over a longer period is difficult because the time series on GDP by industrial origin for 1970–1980 was computed by another method, and the data before 1970 are even more sketchy. Roughly, it appears that the share of manufacturing in GDP rose from 24.7 percent in 1960 to 30.9 percent in 1970 and then declined to 21.9 percent in 1983. The financial services industry rose sharply from 9.7 percent in 1960 to 23.8 percent and then declined to 18.8 percent in 1983. Even so, its share nearly doubled in a generation. The primary sector, however, exhibited a long-term decline from 3.6 percent to less than 1 percent during the same period. Although there are year-to-year fluctuations, the general pattern is that the tertiary sector (Divisions 6 through 10) has gained at the expense of the primary and secondary sectors, a trend that is more or less consistent with the experiences of most industrialized countries, which suggests that the Hong Kong economy is maturing. However, despite their declining share in the GDP, the manufacturing industries remain the largest employing sector, with some 904,709 workers in 1984, or 37 percent of the total labor force. The retraining and relocation of displaced workers from the manufacturing to the tertiary industries will present a gigantic challenge to the economy in the coming decades.

Conclusion

In this chapter I have explained in some detail the key factors responsible for Hong Kong's economic miracle after the Second World War, namely, political and social stability, economic freedom, and the rule of law. Fears that these factors would no longer operate after the return of sovereignty to China underlay the profound confidence crisis that shook the Hong Kong economy to its very foundations in 1982–1984. By explicitly recognizing the importance of the three factors, the Sino-British Joint Declaration of September 1984 brought a short-term relief or even euphoria to Hong Kong. But the settlement per se does not constitute a permanent guarantee for Hong Kong's stability and prosperity, and prospects for the longer run remain uncertain. Much will depend on the stability of the political system, the continuity of pragmatic policies, and the progress of the modernization and reform program in China. In the last analysis, Hong Kong's future as a free market economy is a function of China's conduct and performance. At the same time, however, China cannot act with impunity with respect to Hong Kong, for apart from its rational self-interest, it also faces some implicit external constraints, such as the existence of a strong and stable Taiwan, the impact of international public opinion, and the possibility of international economic sanctions. To that extent, it can be hoped that the Sino-British Joint Declaration will not be just a piece of paper.

Notes

1. For the full text of the Joint Declaration, as well as a collection of essays on the future of Hong Kong, see Y. C. Jao, C. K. Leung, Peter Wesley-Smith, and S. L. Wong, eds., *Hong Kong and 1997: Strategies for the Future* (Hong Kong: Center of Asian Studies, University of Hong Kong, 1985).

2. See the essays by E.K.Y. Chen, Y. C. Jao, and C. L. Hung on the economy, financial structure, and foreign investment, respectively, in D. G. Lethbridge, ed., *The Business Environment in Hong Kong*, 2d ed. (Hong Kong: Oxford University Press, 1984), and the extensive bibliography cited therein.

3. Sir Philip Haddon-Cave, "The Making of Some Aspects of Public Policy in Hong Kong," in ibid., p. xiv.

4. See, inter alia, R. H. Coase, "The Problem of Social Cost," *Journal of Law and Economics* (October 1960), pp. 1–44, and H. Demsetz, "The Exchange and Enforcement of Property Rights," *Journal of Law and Economics* (October 1964), pp. 11–26.

5. For Hong Kong's evolution into a major financial center, see Y. C. Jao, "Hong Kong's Rise as a Financial Center," *Asian Survey* 19:7 (July 1979), pp. 674–694; Y. C. Jao, "Hong Kong as a Regional Financial Center: Evolution and Prospects," in C. K. Leung, J. W. Cushman, and Wang Gungwu, eds., *Hong Kong: Dilemmas of Growth* (Canberra: Australian National University Press, 1980), pp. 161–194; and Y. C. Jao, "Hong Kong's Future as a Financial Center," *Three Banks Review* (March 1985), pp. 35–53.

6. K. R. Popper, *The Open Society and Its Enemies*, 2 vols. (London: Routledge and Kegan Paul, 1945); F. A. Hayek, *The Constitution of Liberty* (London: Routledge and Kegan Paul, 1960); and F. A. Hayek, *Law, Legislation, and Liberty*, 3 vols. (London: Routledge and Kegan Paul, 1973–1979).

7. See the references to Hong Kong in Milton Friedman and Rose Friedman, *Free to Choose* (Harmondsworth, Eng.: Penguin Books, 1980), and A. Rabushka, *Hong Kong: A Study in Economic Freedom* (Chicago: University of Chicago Press, 1979).

8. The Gini coefficient dropped from 0.48 in 1957 to 0.4 in 1980, indicating a considerable improvement in income distribution, but the coefficient worsened again in 1981 to 0.48, mainly due to massive immigration from mainland China, which depressed wages of industrial and clerical workers (see L. C. Chau, "Economic Growth and Income Distribution of Hong Kong Since Early 1950s," Discussion Paper no. 38, Department of Economics, University of Hong Kong, October 1984, and R. Hsia and L. C. Chau, *Industrialization, Employment, and Income Distribution: A Case Study of Hong Kong* [London: Croom Helm, 1978]).

9. For an analysis of Hong Kong residents' financial contributions to China in the form of remittances, gifts, donations, etc., since 1949, see Y. C. Jao, "Hong Kong's Role in Financing China's Modernization," in A. J. Youngson, *China and Hong Kong: The Economic Nexus* (Hong Kong: Oxford University Press, 1983), chapter 1.

10. See Y. C. Jao, "The 1997 Issue & Hong Kong's Financial Crisis," *Journal of Chinese Studies* 2:1 (April 1985), pp. 113-153; reprinted in *Occasional Papers/ Reprints Series in Contemporary Asian Studies*, no. 3, 1985 (68), (Baltimore: University of Maryland School of Law, 1985).

11. At its worst, the Hang Seng index fell to 676 in December 1982.

12. Rating and Valuation Department, *Property Review* (Hong Kong, 1984); "Strong Recovery in the Property Market," *Hong Kong Bank Economic Report* (Hong Kong, June 1985); and "Business News," *South China Morning Post*, December 28, 1986.

13. Chalmers Johnson, "The Mouse-trapping of Hong Kong: A Game in Which Nobody Wins," *Asian Survey* 24:9 (September 1984), pp. 887-909.

14. Joint Declaration, Annex 1, sec. 13.

15. For a documentation of the public opinion polls, see J.Y.S. Cheng, ed., *Hong Kong In Search of a Future* (Hong Kong: Oxford University Press, 1984).

16. For a fuller analysis, see Jao, "Hong Kong's Role in Financing China's Modernization."

17. Y. C. Jao, "The Enigma of Hong Kong's Financial Transactions with China," *Asian Monetary Monitor* (May-June 1984), pp. 26-31.

18. *South China Morning Post*, April 26, 1984. Wang is the brother-in-law of Liu Shao-ch'i, the late president of the People's Republic of China. Sent to Hong Kong in 1983, Wang's mission was to calm the jittery colony. The same figure of US$4 billion was also mentioned by P. E. Johnson, an assistant director of the Industry Department of the Hong Kong government, in a speech to the Arizona World Trade Association on March 19, 1985. However, according to the general manager of the Bank of China in Hong Kong, the figure was close to US$5 billion (see Zhang Xueyao, "China-Hong Kong Economic Relationships," speech to the symposium, The New Economic Challenges and Opportunities: Hong Kong Moving into the 90s and Beyond, Hong Kong Affairs Society, Hong Kong, March 31, 1985).

19. Private correspondence with the Industry Department.

20. These two companies are Conic Investments Ltd., an electronics firm, and China Cement (H.K.) Ltd., a cement company.

21. *Beijing Review*, September 16, 1985.

22. See various studies in Y. C. Jao and C. K. Leung, eds., *China's Special Economic Zones: Policies, Problems, and Prospects* (Hong Kong: Oxford University Press, 1986).

23. See Jao, "Hong Kong's Role in Financing China's Modernization."

24. See various articles in "Readjustment in the Chinese Economy," *China Quarterly*, no. 100 (December 1984); Chu-yuan Cheng, "China's Economy: Advances and Dilemmas," *Current History* (September 1984), pp. 257-274; Nai-ruenn Chen and Jeffrey Lee, *China's Economy and Foreign Trade* (Washington, D.C.: U.S. Department of Commerce, September 1984); and Gregory Chow, *The Chinese Economy* (New York: Harper and Row, 1985).

25. For perceptive studies of China's political and social changes, see Harry Harding, "The Transformation of China," *Brookings Review* (Spring 1984), pp. 3-7; and Kenneth Lieberthal, "China's Political Reforms: A Net Assessment," *Annuals of the American Academy* (Washington, D.C., 1984), pp. 19-33.

26. For a documented study, see J. F. Copper, F. Michael, and Yuan-li Wu, *Human Rights in Post-Mao China* (Boulder, Colo.: Westview Press, 1985).

27. Computed from data contained in "Bulletin of the State Statistical Bureau on the National Economy and Social Development," *Renmin ribao* [People's daily], March 10, 1985.

28. World Bank, *China: Socialist Economic Development* (Washington, D.C., 1983), vol. 1, p. 17.

29. Hong Kong government, Census and Statistics Department, *Estimates of the Gross Domestic Product* (Hong Kong: Government Printer, various years).

30. World Bank, *The World Bank Atlas 1985* (Washington, D.C., 1985).

31. "Bulletin of the State Statistical Bureau."

32. For an interesting analysis of the true inflation rate in China, see G. Peebles, "Inflation in the People's Republic of China, 1950–1982," *Three Banks Review* (June 1984), pp. 37–57.

33. *Hong Kong Annual Report 1981* (Hong Kong: Government Printer, 1981), chap. 11. According to Tao Siju, China's deputy minister of public security, in August 1985 there was a backlog of 600,000 applications by Chinese citizens to emigrate to or to visit Hong Kong (see *Liaowang* [Outlook], October 7, 1985, p. 16).

34. The "reached-base" policy means that once an illegal immigrant escaped capture at the border and reached the urban area, he or she would be allowed to stay.

35. *Green Paper: The Further Development of Representative Government in Hong Kong* (July 1984) and *White Paper: The Further Development of Representative Government in Hong Kong* (November 1984), both published in Hong Kong by the Government Printer.

36. "Xu's Speech Jolts Hong Kong Optimism," *Asian Wall Street Journal*, November 25, 1985.

37. For a broadly similar view but with more detailed hypothetical scenarios, see B. B. de Mesquita, D. Newman, and A. Rabushka, *Forecasting Political Events: The Future of Hong Kong* (New Haven and London: Yale University Press, 1985).

38. For an exposition of the new monetary arrangement, see J. G. Greenwood, "The Monetary Framework Underlying the Hong Kong Dollar Stabilization Scheme," *China Quarterly*, no. 99 (September 1984), pp. 631–636, and Y. C. Jao, "The Monetary System and the Future of Hong Kong," in Jao, et al., eds., *Hong Kong and 1997*, pp. 361–395.

39. According to Hong Kong's then-deputy secretary of monetary affairs, "there is sufficient evidence to support the view that there has been an increased outflow of certain types of capital" in 1982–1984, though he did not quantify it (see A. R. Latter, "Changing Patterns of External Flows" [Paper presented to the Hong Kong Management Association, August 22, 1984]). According to Robert F. Emery of the Division of International Finance, Board of Governors of the Federal Reserve System, official data in *Treasury Bulletin* and *Survey of Current Business* show that "there has generally been an outflow of capital from the U.S. to Hong Kong, rather than an inflow" (letter to the author dated February 21, 1985).

40. Hong Kong government, Industry Department, "Report on the Survey of Overseas Investment in Hong Kong's Manufacturing Industry" (Hong Kong, November 1984, Mimeograph).

41. See K. Sung, "Trading On from 1997, With Special Reference to Hong Kong's Textile Agreements," in Jao, et al., eds., *Hong Kong and 1997*, pp. 305–324.

42. This was disclosed by Prime Minister Lee Kuan Yew in his New Year message for 1986. For a concise analysis of what went wrong in Singapore, see Augustine H.H. Tan, "Putting the Spark Back in Singapore," *Asian Wall Street Journal*, November 11, 1985.

43. See Y. W. Sung, "The Role of the Government in the Future Industrial Development of Hong Kong," in Jao, et al., eds., *Hong Kong and 1997*, pp. 405–440.

44. Hong Kong government, *Report of the Advisory Committee on Diversification* (Hong Kong, 1979).

13

Hong Kong After the Sino-British Agreement: The Illusion of Stability

George L. Hicks

The Sino-British agreement on Hong Kong has given both the optimists and the pessimists a maximum incentive to invest in the short run. Most investors had adopted a wait-and-see attitude during the uncertainty of the negotiations, but the two years of trauma ended with the announcement of the details of the agreement on September 26, 1984. This agreement was met with relief rather than optimism. The people who trusted the Chinese promises took it as a green light to resume investing, and even those who had no trust whatsoever in China realized that the agreement had given Hong Kong a breathing space. During the course of the negotiations it had sometimes looked as if China might take over at any time or that the Hong Kong economy might collapse under the pressure of uncertainty. As Y. C. Jao says in Chapter 12, by September 24, 1983, Hong Kong's "whole financial system was tottering on the brink of a total breakdown." The agreement gave everyone a respite; even the most pessimistic knew that China would not have spent two years negotiating with the British if Peking had intended an early takeover. As a result of the agreement, many business people thought that Hong Kong would be all right at least until 1990, time enough to make good profits and recover capital outlay on most Hong Kong investments.

Thus, even the people who were extremely pessimistic about the outlook for Hong Kong after about 1990 had every incentive to invest in 1985. In some ways, the pessimists had more incentive to invest than the optimists. For the former, it was imperative to maximize profits and savings in the short run in order to accumulate enough funds to migrate or, at the very least, to see them through the expected hard times.

In the absence of any investment surveys, it is impossible to prove the proposition that most investors had confidence in Hong Kong for a few years, little confidence after 1990, and none after 1997. The brutal fact is that hardly anyone trusts China, which, given events since 1949, is not surprising. This mistrust is heightened by Hong Kong's refugee mentality;

by and large Hong Kong people are either refugees from communism or the children of such refugees. Surveys taken in 1982 showed that most people were overwhelmingly in favor of maintaining the status quo and that a high percentage would do everything possible to leave Hong Kong if China took over.[1]

The Sino-British agreement gave Hong Kong a short-term stability that put it in the ideal position to benefit from its neighbors' woes. Singapore experienced negative growth in 1985, and most of the other countries of the region were beset by severe problems. For the Hong Kong investor, given the options, Hong Kong appeared the best place to invest. Many of the Southeast Asian investors felt the same way, and there were many reports during 1985 of substantial investments in Hong Kong from Singaporean, Malaysian, and Indonesian interests. Political turmoil in the Philippines also ensured a substantial capital inflow from that source, and uncertainty in Indonesia encouraged capital flight to Hong Kong.

Hong Kong optimists and official spokespeople are fond of pointing out that plenty of long-term investment was taking place in 1985, indicating long-term confidence in the future of Hong Kong. The major long-term investments, in fact, were either government projects or financed by bank loans or shareholders' funds. Very few private investors were putting their own money into long-term investments.

In short, the stability of 1985 was illusory. The local investors of 1985 were almost certain to become disinvestors by 1988, if not earlier. The blunt truth is that most people will not be able to leave Hong Kong, but would leave if they could. Such is the mistrust of China that given the offer of a passport and financial assistance, few people would refuse the opportunity to leave Hong Kong before 1997. The professional classes are especially fearful of Communist rule, and most of the wealthy business classes already have their U.S. green card or equivalent and will leave some time before 1997. Under the most optimistic scenario, a slow decline of the economy before 1997 appears inevitable; at worst, civil disorder and a financial collapse cannot be ruled out.

The near financial collapse in September 1983 showed how vulnerable the Hong Kong economy was to a loss of confidence. The famed resilience of the Hong Kong economy is a resilience to normal commercial buffetings, associated, for example, with a rapidly changing pattern of world demand for Hong Kong products. This kind of reversal is of a different order than a loss of confidence that brings about a bank run. Adverse developments in China that caused a loss of confidence leading to a massive outflow of Hong Kong dollars would be quite unstoppable. Hong Kong almost reached the point of no return in September 1983, and the chances of getting anywhere near to 1997 without a similar or greater blow to confidence must be slight.

The optimists who maintain that Hong Kong will remain stable and prosperous up to 1997 and beyond rest their case mainly on the arguments that it is in China's interest to keep Hong Kong prosperous, that China would never renege on the terms of the agreement, and that China wants to set a good example to Taiwan in order to speed up the process of peaceful reunification. Some writers draw a distinction between China's willingness to carry out the terms of the agreement and its ability to do so. This approach assumes a literal interpretation of the agreement, which leads to immediate difficulties.

Once the agreement is viewed as a legally binding international agreement or an international treaty in all but name, then its absurdities are all too apparent. The attempt to provide a detailed blueprint for fifty years after 1997 is only the most obvious absurdity. China's guarantees to Hong Kong of freedom of the press, of assembly, of association, etc., are almost identical to those in Art. 35 of the Chinese constitution and should be taken with a similar grain of salt. The agreement cannot be viewed in a legal or literal sense but has to be seen in a political and psychological context. The agreement, a masterstroke, brought immense relief to Hong Kong and bought time for China. The slogans "one country, two systems," "Hong Kong people rule Hong Kong," and "stability and prosperity"—just what Hong Kong wanted to hear—were grasped by a people desperate for straws. These were just the right notes for a traumatized Hong Kong. The agreement served its purpose brilliantly, but in no sense can it be construed as a legally binding document that pins China down until 2047. It was simply a tract of the times, which like all such tracts will quickly outlive its usefulness. This situation was sensed by many people who said the agreement was "too good to be true."

I do not mean to suggest that China feels free to renege openly on the agreement. Such an action is neither necessary nor desirable as China can easily achieve all its objectives by simple reinterpretation. In the nine months that followed the ratification of the agreement, China's reinterpretation dramatically changed the agreement's meaning. For example, China conspicuously distanced itself from the concept of Hong Kong people ruling Hong Kong, and even the definition of "Hong Kong people" was held by high official Lu P'ing to be "unscientific." More ominously, Lu redefined the meaning of "accountability" out of existence. Annex I of the agreement says, "The executive authorities shall abide by the law and shall be accountable to the legislature." According to Lu, "accountability" only means that the legislature has the right to be consulted by the executive and that the executive would explain its actions to the legislature. "Accountability" in Lu's book certainly does not imply limits on executive authority. Hsü Chia-t'un, China's chief representative in Hong Kong, said that "consultations were a form of election."

Perhaps most startling of all was Lu's discourse on press freedom. He said, "Press freedom would be allowed after 1997 so long as it did not damage China's sovereignty." In other words, the press would be free so long as it did not criticize China. The Hong Kong press was not slow to realize that such an interpretation would mean the end of press freedom as it is known in Hong Kong. The *Financial Daily*, for instance, pointed out, "To bar the press from saying anything about China's sovereign rights over Hong Kong means that Hong Kong would not enjoy press freedom because anything could be interpreted as a breach of the principle of sovereignty."[2]

Once such crucial terms as "freedom of the press," "Hong Kong people ruling Hong Kong," "elections," and "accountability" can be defined out of existence, then the whole agreement means exactly what China wants it to mean—neither more nor less.

Although the agreement does not tie China's hands in the least, it is extremely effective in tying Britain's. So long as China does not openly renege on the agreement, Britain is obliged to remain in Hong Kong until 1997. This arrangement was China's real masterstroke. While giving away nothing itself, it forced Britain to abandon the one real card it had: the right to pull out at a time of its own choosing. With Britain effectively locked in and deprived of any significant bargaining power, it is inevitable that it will give in to China every time a potential conflict arises. Britain has to give highest priority to international geopolitical considerations, its own bilateral relations with Peking, and British trade prospects with China. It is hardly surprising that under Chinese pressure, Britain is willing to sacrifice Hong Kong interests. In effect, Britain is China's proxy in Hong Kong until 1997, or to put it crudely, Peking's hatchet man. As Timothy Renton, the British official in charge of Hong Kong affairs, has made clear, Britain's job in Hong Kong is to ensure a smooth transfer of power in 1997, and to do so, it is necessary to bring about a convergence of the Hong Kong and Chinese systems. Needless to say, the Hong Kong system must converge with the Chinese, not vice versa.

It is, of course, very much easier for Britain to bring about a convergence than it would be for China to do so through a direct takeover of Hong Kong. China could only bring about convergence at the cost of Hong Kong's prosperity, but it is hoped that Britain can do it smoothly. Britain took the first major steps in bringing about "convergence" in late 1985, when under Chinese pressure Britain backed away from the concept of Hong Kong people ruling Hong Kong, which had been proposed in the 1984 Green and White Papers entitled *The Further Development of Representative Government in Hong Kong*. The aims of these proposals were "to develop progressively a system of government the authority for which is firmly rooted in Hong Kong, which is able to represent authoritatively the views of the people of Hong Kong, and which is more directly accountable to the people of Hong Kong."

During the second half of 1985, China made clear its opposition to this British objective. In August, the director of the Xinhua news agency in Hong Kong, Hsü Chia-t'un, said that Hong Kong people probably did not realize that Britain would be transferring sovereignty and administration to China, not to the Hong Kong people. So there was no question of self-rule. Whatever right of self-government the Hong Kong people might get would come from Peking. This stand effectively ruled out the approach adopted by the British, so it was then up to them whether to stand firm or backtrack and fall in line with China's views. The outcome was never really in doubt.

The director of the Hong Kong and Macao Affairs Office, Chi P'eng-fei, made his opposition to the British proposals clear to various visiting groups. Although the message was a coded one, it was obvious that China opposed the British reform proposals as well as the formation of political parties and direct elections. China made it clear that Hong Kong would have to follow the Basic Law—Peking's constitution for Hong Kong—which would not be promulgated until 1990 although a draft would be available by 1988. In the meantime, any changes introduced by the British must be purely cosmetic; once the Basic Law was known, then Hong Kong must fall into line. The British capitulated under this pressure and agreed to "consult" with China before introducing any new political reforms.

Instead of direct elections or representative government, Communist terminology and methods obviously would be the order of the day. The Hong Kong Basic Law Consultative Committee, which was established to advise the Peking Basic Law Drafting Committee, quickly showed that it intended to run its affairs the Communist way through "democratic consultation" with "elections" à la China. "Elections" became appointments in all but name.

The clearest message of all was delivered by Hsü Chia-t'un on November 21, when he warned that incompatibility between the Basic Law and the representative government system may present a very significant problem. He warned of a possible "misfortune" if China and Britain work toward different systems for Hong Kong and said that current moves indicated a deviation from the spirit and principles of the Declaration. Although he did not name Britain, Hsü was obviously accusing it of "deviation" and demanding that it get back into line.

This open attack created turmoil in Hong Kong. The Hang Seng index responded by plunging fifty points. If the British were unable to reply effectively, then Hsü's statement came close to a de facto takeover, or at the very least left Hong Kong with a powerless, discredited, lame duck government. The Hong Kong government's response was to deny that it had deviated from the Joint Declaration, but London capitulated on the issue by agreeing to discuss the proposed political reforms in the Joint Liaison Group. Prior to Hsü's bombshell, Britain had resisted discussing the issue in that group, arguing correctly that under the terms of the agreement, such matters did not have to be discussed until 1990. Britain's humiliating capitulation on this issue showed how powerless it was to resist Chinese pressure.[3] As if to make the point clear beyond all doubt, Chi P'eng-fei followed up Hsü Chia-t'un's November 21 attack with the demand that Hong Kong's political reforms must toe the line of the Basic Law starting from 1990. Changes prior to the promulgation of the Basic Law must be minimal.

The British appeared to think that they had little choice but to give in to Chinese demands. To stand firm in the face of Chinese firepower would have thrown Hong Kong into turmoil and damaged London-Peking bilateral relations. The message from London to the Hong Kong government was widely held to be the avoidance of confrontation at all costs.

Political reform was not the only area in which the British capitulated to Chinese demands. The Sino-British aviation talks of November 1985, far from correcting the imbalance on the Hong Kong–Peking route, actually increased it. Peking viewed the route as a domestic one, seeing no imbalance in the fact that between China and Hong Kong, the former's airline had fifty-eight flights compared to the latter's three. Another example of British capitulation came in the area of sport. On March 1, 1986, it was reported:

> China is putting pressure on Hong Kong sports federations to impose a localization policy on team selections for international events, Amateur Sports Federation and Olympic Committee of Hong Kong president Mr. A. de O. Sales admitted yesterday. As a result of this pressure the government would no longer fund sporting associations who choose competitors with less than a seven-year local residency.[4]

Yet another capitulation came in the negotiations for the Daya Bay nuclear power plant. Under relentless Chinese pressure, the British supplier, General Electric, halved the price of its equipment, from £500 million to £250 million, which aroused strong suspicions of a disguised U.K. government subsidy. The most costly surrender to Chinese demands may well prove to be the Chinese International Trust and Investment Corporation (CITIC) takeover of the Ka Wah Bank. CITIC was able to obtain this bank on bargain terms with all its bad and doubtful debts underwritten by the Hong Kong government's exchange fund.

Although it was thought that 1986 would be a relatively quiet year in Sino-British relations over Hong Kong, it was expected that 1987 would be something else. The British scheduled a major political review for 1987 before the Chinese warning that no significant changes should precede the Basic Law. No doubt the British can fudge the review and arrive at cosmetic proposals that will not anger China, but to do so might cause a major confidence crisis in Hong Kong, especially if the results of the review were clearly at variance with public opinion. China may try to preempt the British political review by making known the outlines of the Basic Law early in 1987; that would put irresistible pressure on Britain to follow the Basic Law, which would emasculate the projected political review.

China has made clear that it does not recognize any of the colonial political institutions, such as the Legislative and Executive Councils. If the Basic Law indicates that the traditional institutions will be scrapped in 1997 and that a Hong Kong ruled by Hong Kong people with a high degree of autonomy really has gone by the board, then Hong Kong could face a major confidence crisis, even as early as 1987, that could take it past the point of no return. Britain may be willing to guide Hong Kong in the direction proposed by China, but it is far from certain that to do so would be consistent with the maintenance of stability. It will certainly require more finesse and understanding of the Hong Kong situation than China has shown in the past. Britain may try to bring about the convergence of Hong Kong and China, but a willingness to be China's proxy is one thing, success is another.

The events of 1985 clarified China's future intentions for Hong Kong. Clearly, China would not tolerate press freedom, free elections, genuine representative government, or any political dissidence. The concept of Hong Kong people ruling Hong Kong with a high degree of autonomy was also effectively ruled out. Not that any of these actions were surprising. China has always been a highly centralized state, so the concept of local autonomy has never gained legitimacy. China's position is just further evidence that the Joint Declaration should be seen as a political and psychological document, not a policy guide, because it is unrelated and even in conflict with the political, economic, and above all, historical realities of China.

I do not mean to imply, however, that China intends to absorb Hong Kong into the Communist system. Far from it. Y. C. Jao is on the mark when he says, "What China favors is a kind of 'authoritarian capitalism' on the model of Taiwan or Singapore." The central question is, Will China, assisted by Britain and the Hong Kong business elite, be able to establish a viable right-wing, authoritarian regime in Hong Kong?

The triple alliance of China, the British Hong Kong government, and the Hong Kong business elite has immense, overwhelming power and should have little difficulty in suppressing the political activists, liberal democrats, and "human rightists" who call for a literal interpretation of the Joint Declaration and frequent direct elections with one person, one vote. The Hong Kong business elite is fiercely opposed to serious elections in any form, fearing that any move toward more representative government will be destabilizing and lead to demands for government welfare expenditures and higher taxes. Both the business elite and China share the same antilabor, elitist philosophy. Peking has appointed many members of the Hong Kong business elite to the Basic Law Consultative Committee where some of them play leading roles. T. K. Ann, a leading industrialist; Sir Y. K. Pao, the shipping magnate; and David Li of the Bank of East Asia are the leading pro-Peking business figures. The firm alliance between Peking and a large part of the business elite creates a strong antidemocratic lobby. How far and for how long they can trust each other remains to be seen.

Lord Kadoorie, a leading Hong Kong businessman, can hardly be put in the camp of T. K. Ann, et al., who have gone all the way with Peking, but he well expresses their antidemocratic, elitist, and oligarchic philosophy. According to Lord Kadoorie, "The people who govern Hong Kong should be chosen from those members of the community who created the prosperity." Kadoorie maintains that Hong Kong can best survive under a "benevolent oligarchy. . . . All Hong Kong is one big business, and it must have good management and a well-chosen board of directors." Kadoorie agrees that his view of "the right of the few" to govern means that he is not in favor of the general push toward a more representative government. As he put it, Hong Kong should not "fall into the trap of advocating Western democracy which was foreign to the freedoms and business concepts of Hong Kong." Most significantly, Kadoorie has brushed aside criticisms that Hsü Chia-t'un was meddling in local affairs when he warned against reforming the territory's political structure.[5]

Kadoorie's call for Hong Kong to be governed by an oligarchy of elite business people was attacked by the political activists but strongly endorsed by Sir Y. K. Pao. Few, if any, of the elite business class attacked him, and it can only be assumed that his views are widely supported among top business groups. In a comment on the Peking–Hong Kong elite business alliance and Lord Kadoorie's philosophy, Professor Joseph Silverstein of Rutgers said: "It just shows that elitists never die, they don't even fade away, but go on in their myth world. Since they share the same elitist values as the communists, they will have no difficulty working out a way to share the future with them. The people get screwed from the Left and the Right, and doubly when the two find ways to combine."[6]

Another factor working in favor of the successful imposition of right-wing, authoritarian capitalism on Hong Kong concerns the changes taking place in China. A number of observers have argued that China is converting from a left-wing totalitarian dictatorship to a right-wing authoritarian government and that the Communist party in China will soon be Communist in name only. This line of thought holds that the expansion of the market economy is eroding the economic justification of the Communist system. If the modernization policy succeeds, then by 1997 China will be practicing authoritarian capitalism and should have no trouble imposing it on Hong Kong.

Be that as it may, it seems safer to assume here that China is Communist and will remain so up to 1997 and beyond. On the other hand, it is also assumed, perhaps optimistically, that Teng's reforms will outlive him and that the open-Door policy will be continued up to 1997 and beyond. It is most useful to draw up a scenario for Hong Kong based on generally optimistic assumptions about China with the knowledge that if things go badly in China, then the outcome for Hong Kong can only be worse than projected.

Based on these simple assumptions, what is the outlook for Hong Kong in the years leading up to 1997? What is very clear from the events of 1985 is that the sort of "liberal democracy" implied by the Joint Declaration is a nonstarter. Freedom of the press and the other Western, liberal freedoms will die, probably well before 1997. The concept of Hong Kong ruled by Hong Kong people with a high degree of autonomy also has to be dismissed as a pipe dream. Legislative Councillor Allen Lee recognized this reality when he announced on December 29, 1985, that his plan to form a political party had died on the vine. Lee said:

> Despite the provisions in the Joint Declaration on the future political set-up of the Special Administrative Region Government, China would not allow Hong Kong to be ruled by the people of Hong Kong.

The chief executive in all likelihood would be appointed by the central Chinese government. . . . A political party as a means to fill a vacuum would be meaningless as there would be no vacuum to fill.[7]

Lee also said that once China had made clear its opposition to direct elections, it became pointless to pursue the issue. Whereas members of Lee's political group had been in favor of direct elections, China's opposition caused most of them to have second thoughts. Only Martin Lee remained openly and publicly in favor of direct elections while others, Stephen Cheong, a local businessman, for example, now found direct elections "untimely."

Lee's statement brought to the forefront the central issue of intimidation. China had only to hint that it opposed direct elections to almost entirely suppress discussion of the issue. China's veiled opposition to political parties is more than enough to discourage their emergence. Fear of future reprisals are so widespread that hardly anyone dares advocate a course of action that they even think China might oppose.

Covert intimidation makes it so easy for China to use Britain as its proxy during the transition to 1997. If, for example, China wants Britain (the Hong Kong government) to restrict the freedom of the press in Hong Kong, it is not necessary for Britain to take *active* steps against press freedom. All that has to happen is for China to circulate coded messages that it disapproves of any criticism of China in the Hong Kong press. Unless Britain springs to the *active* defense of press freedom, the Hong Kong press, feeling abandoned by its government, and will naturally exercise self-censorship to avoid any criticism of China.

This is the pattern that developed in the second half of 1985. Britain began to adopt a hands-off policy and refused to stand up to China for Hong Kong's rights. This inaction exposed Hong Kong to the full blast of China's intimidation, which was made even more effective by Britain's constant reiteration of its tough immigration stance. By stressing that almost no one was going to be given the right of abode in the United Kingdom who did not already have it, Hong Kong people felt even more trapped and intimidated.

There is little doubt that Britain will also implement active policies to fall in line with China's wishes. The whole new theme of both London's spokesman, Timothy Renton, and Hong Kong Chief Secretary Sir David Akers-Jones is convergence. On December 30, 1985, Akers-Jones held a long briefing with the press, the entire thrust of which was that the "systems must converge." Earlier Renton, in a press statement from Peking, had used the word "convergence" some eight times. There was an implicit admission that Hong Kong and China had been in danger of divergence, but this situation was being corrected to bring about steady convergence. China, with 1 billion people, a Communist system, and sovereignty over Hong Kong, is hardly going to change direction and converge with Hong Kong. Clearly, Hong Kong must do all the converging, so that, as Akers-Jones and Renton stress, the transition will be smooth. This admission does not mean that the Hong Kong government has to turn Hong Kong into the mirror image of China by 1997. China has in mind, not a Communist Hong Kong, but authoritarian capitalism with none of the West's democratic and liberal trappings. After all, the lack of a complete free press and political dissent has not held back the economic growth of Taiwan or Singapore.

In the task of converting Hong Kong into a right-wing, authoritarian capitalist state before 1997, China can count on enthusiastic support from the business elite. Y. K. Pao has already earned his spurs and is an expert in "democratic consultation" through his handling of the "elections" in the Basic Law Consultative Committee. Lord Kadoorie and some of the other business people will not go all the way to Peking's bedroom, but by and large, the extremely conservative Hong Kong business elite will go along with Peking's antiwelfare, antidemocratic, authoritarian, capitalist philosophy.

Britain may have some qualms, but given the alternative of a new nuclear power plant sale to China and a little less press freedom in Hong Kong—which could be lost by default anyway—the issue should not be in doubt. Assuming that this unlikely triple alliance of China, London (Hong Kong government), and the Hong Kong business elite does hold together, it will do so under the umbrella of an all-pervasive atmosphere of intimidation that frightens any opposition and provides a protective screen for the inroads that have to be made on traditional freedoms. Those freedoms can now be largely lost by default.

The successful evolution of a right-wing, authoritarian capitalist state by 1997 brilliantly serves the interests of each of the members of the triple alliance. All three groups want to keep Hong Kong stable and prosperous, and this method seems to be the best, and perhaps only, way to do so. China wants to inherit the British colonial structure, which will give it total control without any nonsense about democracy or Hong Kong rights. Britain wants to trade with China, a quiet life in Hong Kong, and to exit in glory. The business elite wants profits plus a sense of importance on the Chinese political scene. As well as being a billionaire, it is even better to be a "patriot" and to be feted in Peking. Full participation in Peking organizations, such as the Basic Law Consultative Committee, is especially sweet for those Chinese business people who missed out under the British honors system.

Unfortunately, the plan will not work, and not primarily because of opposition on the part of political activists. The lawyers, Martin Lee and his friends, can be humored and ignored, and the triple alliance can encircle, stifle, and ultimately demoralize and defeat this tiny, brave, articulate, and ultimately irrelevant minority. The plan to impose authoritarian capitalism on Hong Kong will founder mainly because it will be resisted, or rather undermined, by two large and influential classes: the small businessman, who is excluded from a cosy alliance with Peking, and the professional classes and the civil servants, who value their present freedoms, detest communism, and can see in the future only danger with no positive potential. Unlike the business elite, members of these classes cannot dream of deals with China but can only see that one day they or their children will lose their freedom. The civil servants may not be able to emigrate in large numbers, but the elite groups will, the rest will become demoralized, and public services will suffer.

Peking fondly imagines that the Hong Kong business elite controls the Hong Kong economy. In this, as in other matters, they see the Hong Kong economy through the prism of their own experience. In China, it may be true that only a few dozen or a few hundred people really count, but the Hong Kong economy is dominated by the small businessmen, each of whom makes his or her own decision. China thinks that the small businessmen—and Hong Kong in general—will be happy if they are free to make money and go to the races, but the Hong Kong people value the freedoms they have enjoyed under enlightened British colonial rule so authoritarian capitalism under the shadow of communism has nothing to offer them.

Even if authoritarian capitalism were to work, the great majority of the people will have sacrificed freedom for no economic gain. Above all, they will continue to fear that full-scale communism will one day be imposed on them. Given no positive potential, but unlimited negative possibilities, most of those who can get out, will. The very people Hong Kong needs most will be lost. The resultant brain drain and capital drain will erode Hong Kong's stability and prosperity, leading to a crumbling of the triple alliance. The cement that holds the alliance together is stability, prosperity, and intimidation. Although the last can easily be maintained, the loss of stability and prosperity will destroy the alliance. Members of the Hong Kong business elite will be allies of China only as long as it pays them, and in the context of declining prosperity it is inevitable that China will blame Britain and mutual recrimination will bring the deep-seated differences and mutual mistrust between Britain and China into the open.

With China insisting that Hong Kong follow the Basic Law and prosperity declining, the British will resent their role as transparent caretakers for Peking. Why should they stay until 1997 just to engineer convergence for Peking? At the moment Britain appears bound by the Joint Declaration to stay until then, but that fact does not prevent an early withdrawal negotiated with Peking. Once the Basic Law is in place, there seems little point in the British staying. If the promulgation of the Basic Law takes place in the context of a mounting capital outflow, a massive brain drain, and general acrimony, then both Britain and China are likely to favor an early transfer of authority. Hong Kong will have become a millstone around Britain's neck, and China will want to step in both to stop the hemorrhaging and to assert its national destiny.

Britain will also run into resistance in Hong Kong as it attempts to impose a more authoritarian cast on its management of Hong Kong affairs. The Hong Kong people are extremely mistrustful—with good reason—of both the British and Chinese governments. As Lau Siu-Kai and Kuan Hsin-Chi have pointed out, this mistrust "is especially true when the effect of some of the policies is to strengthen the power of the government and by derivation threaten the social and economic freedom of the people. While the desire of the populace to participate in politics is far from impressive, their determination to resist the encroachment of the government on social and economic liberty is quite persistent."[8]

During the course of 1985, the Hong Kong people dealt the Hong Kong government several nasty shocks, which serve as a warning of what the government can expect if it takes steps perceived as a potential threat to traditional liberties. In the past, the Hong Kong government has had no difficulty in introducing new laws, which were hardly scrutinized let alone opposed by the appointed legislature. All that has changed. The Legislative Council, now partly elected, is no longer a rubber stamp. Even more effective as public watchdogs are various pressure groups of concerned citizens. When the government attempted to pass the Legislative Council Powers and Privileges Bill in 1985, it was not the Legislative Council but outside groups who first blew the whistle. The public outcry that followed resulted in the almost complete rewriting of the bill. The Commercial Crimes Bill, which would have led to the elimination of juries in complex commercial crimes, had to be withdrawn because of intense opposition. The attempt to introduce electronic road tolls was also defeated by a public that saw it as a potential threat to freedom and privacy.

Although the extreme Western liberals, such as lawyer Martin Lee, cannot arouse much popular support for political parties and direct elections, the people will fight if they feel their freedoms are threatened. Consequently, Britain will find it difficult to bring about "convergence" and impose authoritarian capitalism. Its clumsy attempts to move in this direction in 1985 were all defeated, and the government is now moving with a new caution.

To satisfy China, Britain must bury the promises of the Green and White Papers on representative government and render meaningless the political review. This effort will not be easy and could well destroy what little remaining trust Hong Kong has in Britain. Hong Kong people, who are more prosperous than their compatriots in Taiwan and Singapore, also enjoy far more freedom, and they want to keep it that way as long as possible. Britain's attempt to impose China's vision of convergence and authoritarian capitalism was resisted in 1985 and will be resisted in the future.

Thus, the tidy Peking vision of the Hong Kong economic structure will not work. Authoritarian capitalism imposed by the triple alliance is a seductive blueprint, especially with the successful Singapore and Taiwan examples in the background. Perhaps if Peking could really learn to act like a right-wing authoritarian capitalist, the scheme might have some faint hope of success. Right-wing governments, while not allowing political dissent or press freedom, leave people alone in the other areas of their lives. By contrast, Communist governments have an irresistible urge to interfere in almost every aspect of existence. As Lee Yee, the editor of the *Nineties*, pointed out, the Chinese government is used to having absolute control and doesn't feel comfortable otherwise. The Hong Kong people know that China could never run the free, liberal capitalist Hong Kong outlined in the Joint Declaration, and they doubt it could run an authoritarian capitalist version either. Robert Elegant, the novelist, summed up the situation: "I'm certain the Chinese have nothing but the best intentions regarding Hongkong, but that doesn't make me very confident. It's the unwritten thing about this place—its ethos for want of a better word—that will be the most difficult for the Chinese to understand and deal with."[9]

Conclusion

No one knows what China is planning for Hong Kong. Probably China doesn't know itself, and any plans it has now may well be changed several times before 1997. Nevertheless, China has come out strongly against any significant changes, especially those that would devolve any power on the people of Hong Kong. It wants to inherit unchanged the British colonial structure. This structure, which is highly centralized with the governor and the top bureaucrats monopolizing all power, is ideal for China. On paper, the Hong Kong governor has virtually absolute authority; his position is the same as that of the sovereign he represents. In practice, his power is as limited as that of the sovereign.

Power is not used by British governors in arbitrary, authoritarian ways because of the rules of British political life. The Hong Kong government, which is accountable to the British Parliament, is effectively an extension of British democracy except for the fact that the Hong Kong people do not have the vote and cannot choose their own government. In Chinese hands, this structure would work very differently and would be ideal for right-wing, centralized, authoritarian capitalism. The idea surely appeals to China, especially in view of its desire to keep Hong Kong prosperous and the successful Chinese examples of Taiwan and Singapore. Such a system could be imposed without renouncing the Joint Declaration and, in fact, by claiming to follow it.

From China's point of view, Britain can play an important role in the transition period by leading Hong Kong in this direction, thus making China's ultimate task much easier. Britain has now thrown its weight behind the convergence process because it lacks both the power and the will to reject the role of China's handmaiden. The members of the Hong Kong business elite, many of whom are dependent on China for business and who enjoy China's flattery and general ego boosting, have largely thrown in their lot with Peking.

The move to authoritarian capitalism has won the support of this powerful triple alliance, which uses intimidation—the fear of future reprisals—to stifle overt opposition. Nevertheless, as I have argued in this chapter, authoritarian capitalism will not work, and the triple alliance will break up. Hong Kong people will fight to preserve their freedoms, and fatally large numbers will leave.

In the end, of course, the people of Hong Kong will lose their freedom and probably their prosperity as well. Hundreds of thousands of the more prosperous and qualified, however, will escape to rebuild their lives in other parts of the world, taking with them the energy and dynamism that has made Hong Kong one of the great economic miracles in history. Other nations will benefit from the Hong Kong tragedy, although East Asia as a region will be the poorer for the loss of its most dynamic member. Britain and China will have to share the responsibility for what is a predictable, but avoidable, disaster. Fortunately, neither is likely to escape unscathed.

Notes

1. A survey conducted by Survey Research HongKong Ltd. showed that the political confidence index declined substantially between May 1985 and January 1986. The percentage of people who were very confident about the future dropped from 23 percent to 13 percent over this period (*South China Morning Post*, February 18, 1986). For details of earlier surveys, see Joseph Y.S. Cheng, "The Future of Hong Kong: A Study of the Hong Kong People's Attitudes," *Australian Journal of Chinese Affairs*, no. 12 (July 1984):113–142, and Joseph Y.S. Cheng, *Hong Kong: In Search of a Future* (Hong Kong: Oxford University Press, 1984).

2. *Financial Daily*, January 1, 1986; author's translation.

3. China's insistence on discussing political reforms in the Joint Liaison Group is not the only example of its breaking the Sino-British agreement. The agreement effectively defines Hong Kong people as Chinese and all other persons who have resided in Hong Kong for seven years or more (Annex I, sec. 14). This definition makes it clear that Chinese from the mainland cannot come and automatically be regarded as Hong Kong people. The Basic Law Consultative Committee constitution, for which Peking must take responsibility, undermines this safeguard by stating in Art. 8 that only foreigners require a seven-year residence period in order to qualify for membership. The implication is that any Chinese is automatically recognized as a "Hong Kong person," which makes nonsense of the concept of Hong Kong people ruling Hong Kong (see Frank Ching, *Ta Kung Pao*, October 10, 1985).

Yet another example of China's redefining the meaning of a word and effectively undermining the spirit of the agreement is the interpretation by the Basic Law Consultative Committee of the word "nonsubordination." Annex I, sec. 13 of the Sino-British agreement states, "The relationship between religious organisations in the Hong Kong Special Administrative Region and those in other parts of the People's Republic of China shall be based on the principles of non-subordination, non-interference and mutual respect." The key word is "nonsubordination," that is, the religious organizations in Hong Kong will not be subordinate to bodies under the Party or government such as the Religious Affairs and Bureau of the State Council. However, the constitution of the Basic Law Consultative Committee shows that China means something entirely different by "nonsubordination." Paragraph 1 of the consultative committee's constitution says, "The Consultative Committee shall be independent of and not subordinate to each other." In fact, however, all the members of the consultative committee were appointed by the drafting committee and the officers of the consultative committee were appointed by the vice-chairman of the drafting committee although the word "elected" was used. The key people in control of the drafting committee are from the consultative committee so that it cannot possibly be held that the consultative committee is not subordinate to the drafting committee. This reinterpretation of the word "subordination" bodes ill for the future freedom of religion in Hong Kong and is a clear example of China's twisting the meaning of a crucial clause in the Sino-British agreement (Frank Ching, *South China Morning Post*, March 18, 1986).

4. *South China Morning Post*, March 1, 1986.

5. Ibid., January 6, 1986. Later, Lord Kadoorie had more to say on this subject. In a submission to the Basic Law Consultative Committee, he spoke out strongly against the formation of political parties. "It is unwise at this delicate stage in Hong Kong's history to introduce and encourage political partices thus detracting from confidence and making it more difficult for the Government both in this interim period and after 1997" (ibid., March 1, 1986).

6. Private communication, February 9, 1986.

7. *Hongkong Standard*, December 29, 1985.

8. Lau Siu-Kai and Kuan Hsin-Chi, "Hong Kong After the Sino-British Agreement," *Pacific Affairs* (forthcoming).

9. *South China Morning Post*, January 23, 1986.

About the Editors and Contributors

Hungdah Chiu is professor of law at the University of Maryland. He is the author of *The Capacity of International Organizations to Conclude Treaties* and *The People's Republic of China and the Law of Treaties* and coauthor of *People's China and International Law: A Documentary Study* and *Criminal Justice in Post-Mao China: Analysis and Documents*. He has edited *China and the Question of Taiwan, China and the Taiwan Issue,* and *Agreements of the People's Republic of China, 1966–80: A Calendar of Events* and coedited *Agreements of the People's Republic of China, 1949–1967: A Calendar, Law in Chinese Foreign Policy,* and *China: Seventy Years After the 1911 Hsin-hai Revolution.* He has also contributed many articles to various learned journals.

Jürgen Domes is professor of political science, chairman of the Political Science Section, and director of the Research Unit on Chinese and East Asian Politics at the Faculty of Law and Economics, the Saar University, Saarbrücken, West Germany. His publications in English include *The Internal Politics of China, 1949–1972, China After the Cultural Revolution, Socialism in the Chinese Countryside, The Government and Politics of the PRC: A Time of Transition* (Westview, 1985), and *Peng Te-huai: The Man and the Image* as well as numerous contributions in the field of Chinese politics to symposium volumes and academic journals.

Dennis Duncanson, OBE, is a former soldier, colonial administrator, diplomat, and professor of political science at the University of Kent at Canterbury. Now retired, he held appointments in Macao and Hong Kong for five years. He is the author of *Government and Revolution in Vietnam, Changing Qualities of Chinese Life,* and other works.

Henry N. Geraedts is a banker and business consultant of Dutch nationality living in Canada. He earned his doctorate at the University of Lund, Sweden. He has published *The PRC: Foreign Economic Relations and Technology Acquisition, 1972–1981* and numerous articles in symposium volumes and academic journals.

George L. Hicks is an Australian businessman who has been living in the Far East for the last twenty-five years. He has now retired from business and has concentrated his research on Hong Kong. He is the author of "Hong Kong on the Eve of Communist Takeover" (in *The Future of Hong*

Kong: Toward 1997 and Beyond, ed. Hungdah Chiu, Y. C. Jao, and Yuan-li Wu).

Y. C. Jao is reader in economics at the University of Hong Kong, where he also served as the dean of the Faculty of Social Sciences in 1978–1981. He is the author of *Banking and Currency in Hong Kong: A Study of Postwar Financial Development* and *Hong Kong: Economic Prospects to 1987;* coauthor of *Financial Structures and Monetary Policies in Southeast Asia;* coeditor of *Hong Kong and 1997: Strategies for the Future* and *China's Special Economic Zones: Policies, Problems, and Prospects;* and contributor to *China and Hong Kong: The Economic Nexus.*

Ambrose Y.C. King is professor and chairman of the Department of Sociology and the head of the New Asia College, the Chinese University of Hong Kong. He is the author of *The Ecology of Public Administration, From Tradition to Modernity: An Analysis of Chinese Society and Its Change,* and *The Historical Development of Chinese Democratic Thought.*

Mineo Nakajima is professor of international relations and contemporary China studies at the Tokyo University of Foreign Studies. He is the author of *Era of the New Cold War, Beijing in Flux, China: History, Society, and International Relations, Shock at the Sino-Soviet Alliance, Politics and Civilization of Contemporary China, Hong Kong: A Changing City State, China: Ten Years from Now,* and other works.

Jan S. Prybyla is professor of economics at Pennsylvania State University. He is the author of *The Political Economy of Communist China, The Chinese Economy: Problems and Policies, Issues in Socialist Economic Modernization, Market and Plan Under Socialism: The Bird in the Cage,* and numerous articles on Asian economic affairs and comparative economic systems.

Georg Ress holds doctorates in law and economics and is professor of public, international, and European law, director of the Institute for European Community Studies, and currently first vice-president of the Saar University. He is also a judge of the Saarland Constitutional Court and honorary secretary, the German branch of the International Law Association. He is the author of *Die Entscheidungsbefugnis in der Verwaltungsgerichtsbarkeit, Die Rechtslage Deutschlands nach dem Grundlagenvertrag vom 21. Dez. 1972,* and numerous contributions to symposium volumes and academic journals and the coauthor of *Verfassungstreue im öffentlichen Dienst europäischer Staaten* and *Rechtsfragen grenzüberschreitender Umweltbelastungen.*

Yu-ming Shaw is director-general of the Government Information Office, Republic of China, professor of history of international relations at the Graduate School of International Law and Diplomacy, National Chengchi University, Taipei, Taiwan, and former director of the Institute of International Relations in that city. His publications include *China and Christianity, Twentieth Century Sino-American Relations,* and *From the Open Door Policy to the U.S. Diplomatic Rupture with the Republic of China.* He is the editor of *Chinese Modernization; Power and Policy in the PRC* (Westview, 1985);

Mainland China: Politics, Economics, and Reform (Westview, 1985); and *Reform and Revolution in Twentieth-Century China* (Westview, 1988).

Teh-pei Yu is professor in the Economics Department, Soochow University, and research associate of the First Institute (Economic Research on Mainland China) of the Chung Hua Institution for Economic Research in Taipei, Taiwan. She is—together with Kang Chao, C. T. Lu, and others—the author of *The Economic Development in Mainland China and Its Influences on Taiwan, 1997 and Economic Prospects in Hong Kong, An Analysis of Competition Between Mainland China and Taiwan in Their Major Markets, The Economic Effects of ASEAN Tariffs on Taiwan's Exports to Southeast Asia,* and numerous contributions on economic and trade problems of Taiwan and other newly industrialized countries.

Appendix

JOINT DECLARATION

Of the Government of the People's Republic of China And The Government of the United Kingdom of Great Britain and Northern Ireland On the Question of Hong Kong

The Government of the People's Republic of China and the Government of the United Kingdom of Great Britain and Northern Ireland have reviewed with satisfaction the friendly relations existing between the two Governments and peoples in recent years and agreed that a proper negotiated settlement of the question of Hong Kong, which is left over from the past, is conducive to the maintenance of the prosperity and stability of Hong Kong and to the further strengthening and development of the relations between the two countries on a new basis. To this end, they have, after talks between the delegations of the two Governments, agreed to declare as follows:

1. The Government of the People's Republic of China declares that to recover the Hong Kong area (including Hong Kong Island, Kowloon and the New Territories, hereinafter referred to as Hong Kong) is the common aspiration of the entire Chinese people, and that it has decided to resume the exercise of sovereignty over Hong Kong with effect from 1 July 1997.

2. The Government of the United Kingdom declares that it will restore Hong Kong to the People's Republic of China with effect from 1 July 1997.

3. The Government of the People's Republic of China declares that the basic policies of the People's Republic of China regarding Hong Kong are as follows:

(1) Upholding national unity and territorial integrity and taking account of the history of Hong Kong and its realities, the People's Republic of China has decided to establish, in accordance with the provisions of Article 31 of the Constitution of the People's Republic of China, a Hong Kong Special Administrative Region upon resuming the exercise of sovereignty over Hong Kong.

(2) The Hong Kong Special Administrative Region will be directly under the authority of the Central People's Government of the People's Republic of China. The Hong Kong Special Administrative Region will enjoy a high degree of autonomy, except in foreign and defence affairs which are the responsibilities of the Central People's Government.

(3) The Hong Kong Special Administrative Region will be vested with executive, legislative and independent judicial power, including that of final adjudication. The laws currently in force in Hong Kong will remain basically unchanged.

(4) The Government of the Hong Kong Special Administrative Region will be composed of local inhabitants. The chief executive will be appointed by the Central People's Government on the basis of the results of elections or consultations to be held locally. Principal officials will be nominated by the chief executive of the Hong Kong Special Administrative Region for appointment by the Central People's Government. Chinese and foreign nationals previously working in the public and police services in the government departments of Hong Kong may remain in employment. British and other foreign nationals may also be employed to serve as advisers or hold certain public posts in government departments of the Hong Kong Special Administrative Region.

(5) The current social and economic systems in Hong Kong will remain unchanged, and so will the life-style. Rights and freedoms, including those of the person, of speech, of the press, of assembly, of association, of travel, of movement, of correspondence, of strike, of choice of occupation, of academic research and of religious belief will be ensured by law in the Hong Kong Special Administrative Region. Private property, ownership of enterprises, legitimate right of inheritance and foreign investment will be protected by law.

(6) The Hong Kong Special Administrative Region will retain the status of a free port and a separate customs territory.

(7) The Hong Kong Special Administrative Region will retain the status of an international financial centre, and its markets for foreign exchange, gold, securities and futures will continue. There will be free flow of capital. The Hong Kong dollar will continue to circulate and remain freely convertible.

(8) The Hong Kong Special Administrative Region will have independent finances. The Central People's Government will not levy taxes on the Hong Kong Special Administrative Region.

(9) The Hong Kong Special Administrative Region may establish mutually beneficial economic relations with the United Kingdom and other countries, whose economic interests in Hong Kong will be given due regard.

(10) Using the name of "Hong Kong, China", the Hong Kong Special Administrative Region may on its own maintain and develop economic and cultural relations and conclude relevant agreements with states, regions and relevant international organisations.

The Government of the Hong Kong Special Administrative Region may on its own issue travel documents for entry into and exit from Hong Kong.

(11) The maintenance of public order in the Hong Kong Special Administrative Region will be the responsibility of the Government of the Hong Kong Special Administrative Region.

(12) The above-stated basic policies of the People's Republic of China regarding Hong Kong and the elaboration of them in Annex I to this Joint Declaration will be stipulated, in a Basic Law of the Hong Kong Special Administrative Region of

the People's Republic of China, by the National People's Congress of the People's Republic of China, and they will remain unchanged for 50 years.

4. The Government of the People's Republic of China and the Government of the United Kingdom declare that, during the transitional period between the date of the entry into force of this Joint Declaration and 30 June 1997, the Government of the United Kingdom will be responsible for the administration of Hong Kong with the object of maintaining and preserving its economic prosperity and social stability; and that the Government of the People's Republic of China will give its cooperation in this connection.

5. The Government of the People's Republic of China and the Government of the United Kingdom declare that, in order to ensure a smooth transfer of government in 1997, and with a view to the effective implementation of this Joint Declaration, a Sino-British Joint Liaison Group will be set up when this Joint Declaration enters into force; and that it will be established and will function in accordance with the provisions of Annex II to this Joint Declaration.

6. The Government of the People's Republic of China and the Government of the United Kingdom declare that land leases in Hong Kong and other related matters will be dealt with in accordance with the provisions of Annex III to this Joint Declaration.

7. The Government of the People's Republic of China and the Government of the United Kingdom agree to implement the preceding declarations and the Annexes to this Joint Declaration.

8. This Joint Declaration is subject to ratification and shall enter into force on the date of the exchange of instruments of ratification, which shall take place in Beijing before 30 June 1985. This Joint Declaration and its Annexes shall be equally binding.

Done in duplicate at Beijing on 1984 in the Chinese and English languages, both texts being equally authentic.

(Signed)   (Signed)

For the   For the
Government of the   Government of the United
People's Republic of China   Kingdom of Great Britain
                                                and Northern Ireland

ANNEX I

Elaboration by the Government of The People's Republic of China Of Its Basic Policies Regarding Hong Kong

The Government of the People's Republic of China elaborates the basic policies of the People's Republic of China regarding Hong Kong as set out in paragraph 3 of the Joint Declaration of the Government of the People's Republic of China and the Government of the United Kingdom of Great Britain and Northern Ireland on the Question of Hong Kong as follows:

I

The Constitution of the People's Republic of China stipulates in Article 31 that "the state may establish special administrative regions when necessary. The systems to be instituted in special administrative regions shall be prescribed by laws enacted by the National People's Congress in the light of the specific conditions." In accordance with this Article, the People's Republic of China shall, upon the resumption of the exercise of sovereignty over Hong Kong on 1 July 1997, establish the Hong Kong Special Administrative Region of the People's Republic of China. The National People's Congress of the People's Republic of China shall enact and promulgate a Basic Law of the Hong Kong Special Administrative Region of the People's Republic of China (hereinafter referred to as the Basic Law) in accordance with the Constitution of the People's Republic of China, stipulating that after the establishment of the Hong Kong Special Administrative Region the socialist system and socialist policies shall not be practised in the Hong Kong Special Administrative Region and that Hong Kong's previous capitalist system and life-style shall remain unchanged for 50 years.

The Hong Kong Special Administrative Region shall be directly under the authority of the Central People's Government of the People's Republic of China and shall enjoy a high degree of autonomy. Except for foreign and defence affairs which are the responsibilities of the Central People's Government, the Hong Kong Special Administrative Region shall be vested with executive, legislative and independent judicial power, including that of final adjudication. The Central People's Government shall authorise the Hong Kong Special Administrative Region to conduct on its own those external affairs specified in Section XI of this Annex.

The government and legislature of the Hong Kong Special Administrative Region shall be composed of local inhabitants. The chief executive of the Hong Kong Special Administrative Region shall be selected by election or through consultations held locally and be appointed by the Central People's Government. Principal officials (equivalent to Secretaries) shall be nominated by the chief executive of the Hong Kong Special Administrative Region and appointed by the Central People's Government. The legislature of the Hong Kong Special Administrative Region shall be constituted by elections. The executive authorities shall abide by the law and shall be accountable to the legislature.

In addition to Chinese, English may also be used in organs of government and in the courts in the Hong Kong Special Administrative Region.

Apart from displaying the national flag and national emblem of the People's Republic of China, the Hong Kong Special Administrative Region may use a regional flag and emblem of its own.

II

After the establishment of the Hong Kong Special Administrative Region, the laws previously in force in Hong Kong (i.e. the common law, rules of equity, ordinances, subordinate legislation and customary law) shall be maintained, save for any that contravene the Basic Law and subject to any amendment by the Hong Kong Special Administrative Region legislature.

The legislative power of the Hong Kong Special Administrative Region shall be vested in the legislature of the Hong Kong Special Administrative Region. The legislature may on its own authority enact laws in accordance with the provisions of the Basic Law and legal procedures, and report them to the Standing Committee of the National People's Congress for the record. Laws enacted by the legislature which are in accordance with the Basic Law and legal procedures shall be regarded as valid.

The laws of the Hong Kong Special Administrative Region shall be the Basic Law, and the laws previously in force in Hong Kong and laws enacted by the Hong Kong Special Administrative Region legislature as above.

III

After the establishment of the Hong Kong Special Administrative Region, the judicial system previously practised in Hong Kong shall be maintained except for those changes consequent upon the vesting in the courts of the Hong Kong Special Administrative Region of the power of final adjudication.

Judicial power in the Hong Kong Special Administrative Region shall be vested in the courts of the Hong Kong Special Administrative Region. The courts shall exercise judicial power independently and free from any interference. Members of the judiciary shall be immune from legal action in respect of their judicial functions. The courts shall decide cases in accordance with the laws of the Hong Kong Special Administrative Region and may refer to precedents in other common law jurisdictions.

Judges of the Hong Kong Special Administrative Region courts shall be appointed by the chief executive of the Hong Kong Special Administrative Region acting in accordance with the recommendation of an independent commission composed of local judges, persons from the legal profession and other eminent persons. Judges shall be chosen by reference to their judicial qualities and may be recruited from other common law jurisdictions. A judge may only be removed for inability to discharge the functions of his office, or for misbehaviour, by the chief executive of the Hong Kong Special Administrative Region acting in accordance with the recommendation of a tribunal appointed by the chief judge of the court of final appeal, consisting of not fewer than three local judges. Additionally, the appointment or removal of principal judges (i.e. those of the highest rank) shall be made by the chief executive with the endorsement of the Hong Kong Special Administrative Region legislature and reported to the Standing Committee of the National People's Congress for the record. The system of appointment and removal of judicial officers other than judges shall be maintained.

The power of final judgment of the Hong Kong Special Administrative Region shall be vested in the court of final appeal in the Hong Kong Special Administrative Region, which may as required invite judges from other common law jurisdictions to sit on the court of final appeal.

A prosecuting authority of the Hong Kong Special Administrative Region shall control criminal prosecutions free from any interference.

On the basis of the system previously operating in Hong Kong, the Hong Kong Special Administrative Region Government shall on its own make provision for local lawyers and lawyers from outside the Hong Kong Special Administrative Region to work and practise in the Hong Kong Special Administrative Region.

The Central People's Government shall assist or authorise the Hong Kong Special Administrative Region Government to make appropriate arrangements for reciprocal juridical assistance with foreign states.

IV

After the establishment of the Hong Kong Special Administrative Region, public servants previously serving in Hong Kong in all government departments, including the police department, and members of the judiciary may all remain in employment and continue their service with pay, allowances, benefits and conditions of service no less favourable than before. The Hong Kong Special Administrative Region Government shall pay to such persons who retire or complete their contracts, as well as to those who have retired before 1 July 1997, or to their dependants, all pensions, gratuities, allowances and benefits due to them on terms no less favourable than before, and irrespective of their nationality or place of residence.

The Hong Kong Special Administrative Region Government may employ British and other foreign nationals previously serving in the public service in Hong Kong, and may recruit British and other foreign nationals holding permanent identity cards of the Hong Kong Special Administrative Region to serve as public servants at all levels, except as heads of major government departments (corresponding to branches or departments at Secretary level) including the police department, and as deputy heads of some of those departments. The Hong Kong Special Administrative Region Government may also employ British and other foreign nationals as advisers to government departments and, when there is a need, may recruit qualified candidates from outside the Hong Kong Special Administrative Region to professional and technical posts in government departments. The above shall be employed only in their individual capacities and, like other public servants, shall be responsible to the Hong Kong Special Administrative Region Government.

The appointment and promotion of public servants shall be on the basis of qualifications, experience and ability. Hong Kong's previous system of recruitment, employment, assessment, discipline, training and management for the public service (including special bodies for appointment, pay and conditions of service) shall, save for any provisions providing privileged treatment for foreign nationals, be maintained.

V

The Hong Kong Special Administrative Region shall deal on its own with financial matters, including disposing of its financial resources and drawing up its budgets and its final accounts. The Hong Kong Special Administrative Region shall report its budgets and final accounts to the Central People's Government for the record.

The Central People's Government shall not levy taxes on the Hong Kong Special Administrative Region. The Hong Kong Special Administrative Region shall use its financial revenues exclusively for its own purposes and they shall not be handed over to the Central People's Government. The systems by which taxation and public expenditure must be approved by the legislature, and by which there is accountability to the legislature for all public expenditure, and the system for auditing public accounts shall be maintained.

VI

The Hong Kong Special Administrative Region shall maintain the capitalist economic and trade systems previously practised in Hong Kong. The Hong Kong Special Administrative Region Government shall decide its economic and trade policies on its own. Rights concerning the ownership of property, including those relating to acquisition, use, disposal, inheritance and compensation for lawful deprivation (corresponding to the real value of the property concerned, freely convertible and paid without undue delay) shall continue to be protected by law.

The Hong Kong Special Administrative Region shall retain the status of a free port and continue a free trade policy, including the free movement of goods and capital. The Hong Kong Special Administrative Region may on its own maintain and develop economic and trade relations with all states and regions.

The Hong Kong Special Administrative Region shall be a separate customs territory. It may participate in relevant international organisations and international trade agreements (including preferential trade arrangements), such as the General Agreement on Tariffs and Trade and arrangements regarding international trade in textiles. Export quotas, tariff preferences and other similar arrangements obtained by the Hong Kong Special Administrative Region shall be enjoyed exclusively by the Hong Kong Special Administrative Region. The Hong Kong Special Administrative Region shall have authority to issue its own certificates of origin for products manufactured locally, in accordance with prevailing rules of origin.

The Hong Kong Special Administrative Region may, as necessary, establish official and semi-official economic and trade missions in foreign countries, reporting the establishment of such missions to the Central People's Government for the record.

VII

The Hong Kong Special Administrative Region shall retain the status of an international financial centre. The monetary and financial systems previously practised in Hong Kong, including the systems of regulation and supervision of deposit taking institutions and financial markets, shall be maintained.

The Hong Kong Special Administrative Region Government may decide its monetary and financial policies on its own. It shall safeguard the free operation of financial business and the free flow of capital within, into and out of the Hong Kong Special Administrative

Region. No exchange control policy shall be applied in the Hong Kong Special Administrative Region. Markets for foreign exchange, gold, securities and futures shall continue.

The Hong Kong dollar, as the local legal tender, shall continue to circulate and remain freely convertible. The authority to issue Hong Kong currency shall be vested in the Hong Kong Special Administrative Region Government. The Hong Kong Special Administrative Region Government may authorise designated banks to issue or continue to issue Hong Kong currency under statutory authority, after satisfying itself that any issue of currency will be soundly based and that the arrangements for such issue are consistent with the object of maintaining the stability of the currency. Hong Kong currency bearing references inappropriate to the status of Hong Kong as a Special Administrative Region of the People's Republic of China shall be progressively replaced and withdrawn from circulation.

The Exchange Fund shall be managed and controlled by the Hong Kong Special Administrative Region Government, primarily for regulating the exchange value of the Hong Kong dollar.

VIII

The Hong Kong Special Administrative Region shall maintain Hong Kong's previous systems of shipping management and shipping regulation, including the system for regulating conditions of seamen. The specific functions and responsibilities of the Hong Kong Special Administrative Region Government in the field of shipping shall be defined by the Hong Kong Special Administrative Region Government on its own. Private shipping businesses and shipping-related businesses and private container terminals in Hong Kong may continue to operate freely.

The Hong Kong Special Administrative Region shall be authorised by the Central People's Government to continue to maintain a shipping register and issue related certificates under its own legislation in the name of "Hong Kong, China".

With the exception of foreign warships, access for which requires the permission of the Central People's Government, ships shall enjoy access to the ports of the Hong Kong Special Administrative Region in accordance with the laws of the Hong Kong Special Administrative Region.

IX

The Hong Kong Special Administrative Region shall maintain the status of Hong Kong as a centre of international and regional aviation. Airlines incorporated and having their principal place of business in Hong Kong and civil aviation related businesses may continue to operate. The Hong Kong Special Administrative Region shall continue the previous system of civil aviation management in Hong Kong, and keep its own aircraft register in accordance with provisions laid down by the Central People's Government concerning nationality marks and registration marks of aircraft. The Hong Kong Special Administrative Region shall be responsible on its own for matters of routine business and technical management of civil aviation, including the management of airports, the provision of air traffic services within the flight information region of the Hong Kong Special Administrative Region, and the discharge of other responsibilities allocated under the regional air navigation procedures of the International Civil Aviation Organisation.

The Central People's Government shall, in consultation with the Hong Kong Special Administrative Region Government, make arrangements providing for air services between the Hong Kong Special Administrative Region and other parts of the People's Republic of China for airlines incorporated and having their principal place of business in the Hong Kong Special Administrative Region and other airlines of the People's Republic of China. All Air Service Agreements providing for air services between other parts of the People's Republic of China and other states and regions with stops at the Hong Kong Special Administrative Region and air services between the Hong Kong Special Administrative Region and other states and regions with stops at other parts of the People's Republic of China shall be concluded by the Central People's Government. For this purpose, the Central People's Government shall take account of the special conditions and economic interests of the Hong Kong Special Administrative Region and consult the Hong Kong Special Administrative Region Government. Representatives of the Hong Kong Special Administrative Region Government may participate as members of delegations of the Government of the People's Republic of China in air service consultations with foreign governments concerning arrangements for such services.

Acting under specific authorisations from the Central People's Government, the Hong Kong Special Administrative Region Government may:

— renew or amend Air Service Agreements and arrangements previously in force; in principle, all such Agreements and arrangements may be renewed or amended with the rights contained in such previous Agreements and arrangements being as far as possible maintained;

— negotiate and conclude new Air Service Agreements providing routes for airlines incorporated and having their principal place of business in the Hong Kong Special Administrative Region and rights for overflights and technical stops; and

— negotiate and conclude provisional arrangements where no Air Service Agreement with a foreign state or other region is in force.

All scheduled air services to, from or through the Hong Kong Special Administrative Region which do not operate to, from or through the mainland of China shall be regulated by Air Service Agreements or provisional arrangements referred to in this paragraph.

The Central People's Government shall give the Hong Kong Special Administrative Region Government the authority to:

— negotiate and conclude with other authorities all arrangements concerning the implementation of the above Air Service Agreements and provisional arrangements;

— issue licences to airlines incorporated and having their principal place of business in the Hong Kong Special Administrative Region;

— designate such airlines under the above Air Service Agreements and provisional arrangements; and

— issue permits to foreign airlines for services other than those to, from or through the mainland of China.

X

The Hong Kong Special Administrative Region shall maintain the educational system previously practised in Hong Kong. The Hong Kong Special Administrative Region Government shall on its own decide policies in the fields of culture, education, science and technology, including policies regarding the educational system and its administration, the language of instruction, the allocation of funds, the examination system, the system of academic awards and the recognition of educational and technological qualifications. Institutions of all kinds, including those run by religious and community organisations, may retain their autonomy. They may continue to recruit staff and use teaching materials from outside the Hong Kong Special Administrative Region. Students shall enjoy freedom of choice of education and freedom to pursue their education outside the Hong Kong Special Administrative Region.

XI

Subject to the principle that foreign affairs are the responsibility of the Central People's Government, representatives of the Hong Kong Special Administrative Region Government may participate, as members of delegations of the Government of the People's Republic of China, in negotiations at the diplomatic level directly affecting the Hong Kong Special Administrative Region conducted by the Central People's Government. The Hong Kong Special Administrative Region may on its own, using the name "Hong Kong, China", maintain and develop relations and conclude and implement agreements with states, regions and relevant international organisations in the appropriate fields, including the economic, trade, financial and monetary, shipping, communications, touristic, cultural and sporting fields. Representatives of the Hong Kong Special Administrative Region Government may participate, as members of delegations of the Government of the People's Republic of China, in international organisations or conferences in appropriate fields limited to states and affecting the Hong Kong Special Administrative Region, or may attend in such other capacity as may be permitted by the Central People's Government and the organisation or conference concerned, and may express their views in the name of "Hong Kong, China". The Hong Kong Special Administrative Region may, using the name "Hong Kong, China", participate in international organisations and conferences not limited to states.

The application to the Hong Kong Special Administrative Region of international agreements to which the People's Republic of China is or becomes a party shall be decided by the Central People's Government, in accordance with the circumstances and needs of the Hong Kong Special Administrative Region, and after seeking the views of the Hong Kong Special Administrative Region Government. International agreements to which the People's Republic of China is not a party but which are implemented in Hong Kong may remain implemented in the Hong Kong Special Administrative Region. The Central People's Government shall, as necessary, authorise or assist the Hong Kong Special Administrative Region Government to make appropriate arrangements for the application to the Hong Kong Special Administrative Region of other relevant international agreements. The Central People's Government shall take the necessary steps to ensure that the Hong Kong Special Administrative Region shall continue to retain its status in an appropriate capacity in those international organisations of which the People's Republic of China is a member and in which Hong Kong participates in one capacity or another. The Central People's Government shall, where necessary, facilitate the continued participation of the Hong Kong Special Administrative Region in an appropriate capacity in those international organisations in which Hong Kong is a participant in one capacity or another, but of which the People's Republic of China is not a member.

Foreign consular and other official or semi-official missions may be established in the Hong Kong Special Administrative Region with the approval of the Central People's Government. Consular and other official missions established in Hong Kong by states which have established formal diplomatic relations with the People's Republic of China may be maintained. According to the circumstances of each case, consular and other official missions of states having no formal diplomatic relations with the People's Republic of China may either be maintained or changed to semi-official missions. States not recognised by the People's Republic of China can only establish non-governmental institutions.

The United Kingdom may establish a Consulate-General in the Hong Kong Special Administrative Region.

XII

The maintenance of public order in the Hong Kong Special Administrative Region shall be the responsibility of the Hong Kong Special Administrative Region Government. Military forces sent by the Central People's Government to be stationed in the Hong Kong Special Administrative Region for the purpose of defence shall not interfere in the internal affairs of the Hong Kong Special Administrative Region. Expenditure for these military forces shall be borne by the Central People's Government.

XIII

The Hong Kong Special Administrative Region Government shall protect the rights and freedoms of inhabitants and other persons in the Hong Kong Special Administrative Region according to law. The Hong Kong Special Administrative Region Government shall maintain the rights and freedoms as provided for by the laws previously in force in Hong Kong, including freedom of the person, of speech, of the press, of assembly, of association, to form and join trade unions, of correspondence, of travel, of movement, of strike, of demonstration, of choice of occupation, of academic research, of belief, inviolability of the home, the freedom to marry and the right to raise a family freely.

Every person shall have the right to confidential legal advice, access to the courts, representation in the courts by lawyers of his choice, and to obtain judicial remedies. Every person shall have the right to challenge the actions of the executive in the courts.

Religious organisations and believers may maintain their relations with religious organisations and believers elsewhere, and schools, hospitals and welfare institutions run by religious organisations may be continued. The relationship between religious organisations in the Hong Kong Special Administrative Region and those in other parts of the People's Republic of China shall be based on the principles of non-subordination, non-interference and mutual respect.

The provisions of the International Covenant on Civil and Political Rights and the International Covenant on Economic, Social and Cultural Rights as applied to Hong Kong shall remain in force.

XIV

The following categories of persons shall have the right of abode in the Hong Kong Special Administrative Region, and, in accordance with the law of the Hong Kong Special Administrative Region, be qualified to obtain permanent identity cards issued by the Hong Kong Special Administrative Region Government, which state their right of abode:

— all Chinese nationals who were born or who have ordinarily resided in Hong Kong before or after the establishment of the Hong Kong Special Administrative Region for a continuous period of 7 years or more, and persons of Chinese nationality born outside Hong Kong of such Chinese nationals;

— all other persons who have ordinarily resided in Hong Kong before or after the establishment of the Hong Kong Special Administrative Region for a continuous period of 7 years or more and who have taken Hong Kong as their place of permanent residence before or after the establishment of the Hong Kong Special Administrative Region, and persons under 21 years of age who were born of such persons in Hong Kong before or after the establishment of the Hong Kong Special Administrative Region;

— any other persons who had the right of abode only in Hong Kong before the establishment of the Hong Kong Special Administrative Region.

The Central People's Government shall authorise the Hong Kong Special Administrative Region Government to issue, in accordance with the law, passports of the Hong Kong Special Administrative Region of the People's Republic of China to all Chinese nationals who hold permanent identity cards of the Hong Kong Special Administrative Region, and travel documents of the Hong Kong Special Administrative Region of the People's Republic of China to all other persons lawfully residing in the Hong Kong Special Administrative Region. The above passports and documents shall be valid for all states and regions and shall record the holder's right to return to the Hong Kong Special Administrative Region.

For the purpose of travelling to and from the Hong Kong Special Administrative Region, residents of the Hong Kong Special Administrative Region may use travel documents issued by the Hong Kong Special Administrative Region Government, or by other competent authorities of the People's Republic of China, or of other states. Holders of permanent identity cards of the Hong Kong Special Administrative Region may have this fact stated in their travel documents as evidence that the holders have the right of abode in the Hong Kong Special Administrative Region.

Entry into the Hong Kong Special Administrative Region of persons from other parts of China shall continue to be regulated in accordance with the present practice.

The Hong Kong Special Administrative Region Government may apply immigration controls on entry, stay in and departure from the Hong Kong Special Administrative Region by persons from foreign states and regions.

Unless restrained by law, holders of valid travel documents shall be free to leave the Hong Kong Special Administrative Region without special authorisation.

The Central People's Government shall assist or authorise the Hong Kong Special Administrative Region Government to conclude visa abolition agreements with states or regions.

ANNEX II

Sino-British Joint Liaison Group

1. In furtherance of their common aim and in order to ensure a smooth transfer of government in 1997, the Government of the People's Republic of China and the Government of the United Kingdom have agreed to continue their discussions in a friendly spirit and to develop the cooperative relationship which already exists between the two Governments over Hong Kong with a view to the effective implementation of the Joint Declaration.

2. In order to meet the requirements for liaison, consultation and the exchange of information, the two Governments have agreed to set up a Joint Liaison Group.

3. The functions of the Joint Liaison Group shall be:

(a) to conduct consultations on the implementation of the Joint Declaration;

(b) to discuss matters relating to the smooth transfer of government in 1997;

(c) to exchange information and conduct consultations on such subjects as may be agreed by the two sides.

Matters on which there is disagreement in the Joint Liaison Group shall be referred to the two Governments for solution through consultations.

4. Matters for consideration during the first half of the period between the establishment of the Joint Liaison Group and 1 July 1997 shall include:

(a) action to be taken by the two Governments to enable the Hong Kong Special Administrative Region to maintain its economic relations as a separate customs territory, and in particular to ensure the maintenance of Hong Kong's participation in the General Agreement on Tariffs and Trade, the Multifibre Arrangement and other international arrangements; and

(b) action to be taken by the two Governments to ensure the continued application of international rights and obligations affecting Hong Kong.

5. The two Governments have agreed that in the second half of the period between the establishment of the Joint Liaison Group and 1 July 1997 there will be need for closer cooperation, which will therefore be intensified during that period. Matters for consideration during this second period shall include:

(a) procedures to be adopted for the smooth transition in 1997;

(b) action to assist the Hong Kong Special Administrative Region to maintain and develop economic and cultural relations and conclude agreements on these matters with states, regions and relevant international organisations.

6. The Joint Liaison Group shall be an organ for liaison and not an organ of power. It shall play no part in the administration of Hong Kong or the Hong Kong Special Administrative Region. Nor shall it have any supervisory role over that administration. The members and supporting staff of the Joint Liaison Group shall only conduct activities within the scope of the functions of the Joint Liaison Group.

7. Each side shall designate a senior representative, who shall be of Ambassadorial rank, and four other members of the group. Each side may send up to 20 supporting staff.

8. The Joint Liaison Group shall be established on the entry into force of the Joint Declaration. From 1 July 1988 the Joint Liaison Group shall have its principal base in Hong Kong. The Joint Liaison Group shall continue its work until 1 January 2000.

9. The Joint Liaison Group shall meet in Beijing, London and Hong Kong. It shall meet at least once in each of the three locations in each year. The venue for each meeting shall be agreed between the two sides.

10. Members of the Joint Liaison Group shall enjoy diplomatic privileges and immunities as appropriate when in the three locations. Proceedings of the Joint Liaison Group shall remain confidential unless otherwise agreed between the two sides.

11. The Joint Liaison Group may by agreement between the two sides decide to set up specialist sub-groups to deal with particular subjects requiring expert assistance.

12. Meetings of the Joint Liaison Group and sub-groups may be attended by experts other than the members of the Joint Liaison Group. Each side shall determine the composition of its delegation to particular meetings of the Joint Liaison Group or sub-group in accordance with the subjects to be discussed and the venue chosen.

13. The working procedures of the Joint Liaison Group shall be discussed and decided upon by the two sides within the guidelines laid down in this Annex.

ANNEX III

Land Leases

The Government of the People's Republic of China and the Government of the United Kingdom have agreed that, with effect from the entry into force of the Joint Declaration, land leases in Hong Kong and other related matters shall be dealt with in accordance with the following provisions:

1. All leases of land granted or decided upon before the entry into force of the Joint Declaration and those granted thereafter in accordance with paragraph 2 or 3 of this Annex, and which extend beyond 30 June 1997, and all rights in relation to such leases shall continue to be recognised and protected under the law of the Hong Kong Special Administrative Region.

2. All leases of land granted by the British Hong Kong Government not containing a right of renewal that expire before 30 June 1997, except short term tenancies and leases for special purposes, may be extended if the lessee so wishes for a period expiring not later than 30 June 2047 without payment of an additional premium. An annual rent shall be charged from the date of extension equivalent to 3 per cent of the rateable value of the property at that date, adjusted in step with any changes in the rateable value thereafter. In the case of old schedule lots, village lots, small houses and similar rural holdings, where the property was on 30 June 1984 held by, or, in the case of small houses granted after that date, the property is granted to, a person descended through the male line from a person who was in 1898 a resident of an established village in Hong Kong, the rent shall remain unchanged so long as the property is held by that person or by one of his lawful successors in the male line. Where leases of land not having a right of renewal expire after 30 June 1997, they shall be dealt with in accordance with the relevant land laws and policies of the Hong Kong Special Administrative Region.

3. From the entry into force of the Joint Declaration until 30 June 1997, new leases of land may be granted by the British Hong Kong Government for terms expiring not later than 30 June 2047. Such leases shall be granted at a premium and nominal rental until 30 June 1997, after which date they shall not require payment of an additional premium but an annual rent equivalent to 3 per cent of the rateable value of the property at that date, adjusted in step with changes in the rateable value thereafter, shall be charged.

4. The total amount of new land to be granted under paragraph 3 of this Annex shall be limited to 50 hectares a year (excluding land to be granted to the Hong Kong Housing Authority for public rental housing) from the entry into force of the Joint Declaration until 30 June 1997.

5. Modifications of the conditions specified in leases granted by the British Hong Kong Government may continue to be granted before 1 July 1997 at a premium equivalent to the difference between the value of the land under the previous conditions and its value under the modified conditions.

6. From the entry into force of the Joint Declaration until 30 June 1997, premium income obtained by the British Hong Kong Government from land transactions shall, after deduction of the average cost of land production, be shared equally between the British Hong Kong Government and the future Hong Kong Special Administrative Region Government. All the income obtained by the British Hong Kong Government, including the amount of the above-mentioned deduction, shall be put into the Capital Works Reserve Fund for the financing of land development and public works in Hong Kong. The Hong Kong Special Administrative Region Government's share of the premium income shall be deposited in banks incorporated in Hong Kong and shall not be drawn on except for the financing of land development and public works in Hong Kong in accordance with the provisions of paragraph 7 (d) of this Annex.

7. A Land Commission shall be established in Hong Kong immediately upon the entry into force of the Joint Declaration. The Land Commission shall be composed of an equal number of officials designated respectively by the Government of the People's Republic of China and the Government of the United Kingdom together with necessary supporting staff. The officials of the two sides shall be responsible to their respective governments. The Land Commission shall be dissolved on 30 June 1997.

The terms of reference of the Land Commission shall be:

(a) to conduct consultations on the implementation of this Annex;

(b) to monitor observance of the limit specified in paragraph 4 of this Annex, the amount of land granted to the Hong Kong Housing Authority for public rental housing, and the division and use of premium income referred to in paragraph 6 of this Annex;

(c) to consider and decide on proposals from the British Hong Kong Government for increasing the limit referred to in paragraph 4 of this Annex;

(d) to examine proposals for drawing on the Hong Kong Special Administrative Region Government's share of premium income referred to in paragraph 6 of this Annex and to make recommendations to the Chinese side for decision.

Matters on which there is disagreement in the Land Commission shall be referred to the Government of the People's Republic of China and the Government of the United Kingdom for decision.

8. Specific details regarding the establishment of the Land Commission shall be finalised separately by the two sides through consultations.

MEMORANDA

(To Be Exchanged Between the Two Sides)

Memorandum

In connection with the Joint Declaration of the Government of the United Kingdom of Great Britain and Northern Ireland and the Government of the People's Republic of China on the Question of Hong Kong to be signed this day, the Government of the United Kingdom declares that, subject to the completion of the necessary amendments to the relevant United Kingdom legislation:

(a) All persons who on 30 June 1997 are, by virtue of a connection with Hong Kong, British Dependent Territories citizens (BDTCs) under the law in force in the United Kingdom will cease to be BDTCs with effect from 1 July 1997, but will be eligible to retain an appropriate status which, without conferring the right of abode in the United Kingdom, will entitle them to continue to use passports issued by the Government of the United Kingdom. This status will be acquired by such persons only if they hold or are included in such a British passport issued before 1 July 1997, except that eligible persons born on or after 1 January 1997 but before 1 July 1997 may obtain or be included in such a passport up to 31 December 1997.

(b) No person will acquire BDTC status on or after 1 July 1997 by virtue of a connection with Hong Kong. No person born on or after 1 July 1997 will acquire the status referred to as being appropriate in sub-paragraph (a).

(c) United Kingdom consular officials in the Hong Kong Special Administrative Region and elsewhere may renew and replace passports of persons mentioned in sub-paragraph (a) and may also issue them to persons, born before 1 July 1997 of such persons, who had previously been included in the passport of their parent.

(d) Those who have obtained or been included in passports issued by the Government of the United Kingdom under sub-paragraphs (a) and (c) will be entitled to receive, upon request, British consular services and protection when in third countries.

Memorandum

The Government of the People's Republic of China has received the memorandum from the Government of the United Kingdom of Great Britain and Northern Ireland dated   1984.

Under the Nationality Law of the People's Republic of China, all Hong Kong Chinese compatriots, whether they are holders of the "British Dependent Territories citizens Passport" or not, are Chinese nationals.

Taking account of the historical background of Hong Kong and its realities, the competent authorities of the Government of the People's Republic of China will, with effect from 1 July 1997, permit Chinese nationals in Hong Kong who were previously called "British Dependent Territories citizens" to use travel documents issued by the Government of the United Kingdom for the purpose of travelling to other states and regions.

The above Chinese nationals will not be entitled to British consular protection in the Hong Kong Special Administrative Region and other parts of the People's Republic of China on account of their holding the above-mentioned British travel documents.

Bibliography

Abbreviations: FEER *Far Eastern Economic Review*
SCMP *South China Morning Post*

Adley, Robert. 1984. *All Change Hong Kong.* Poole, Eng.: Blandford Press.
Amnesty International. 1984. *China: Violations of Human Rights.* London: Amnesty International Publications.
Baker, Hugh D.R. 1983. "Life in the Cities: The Emergence of Hong Kong Man." *China Quarterly,* no. 95 (September):469–479.
Bernstein, Thomas P. 1985. "China in 1984: The Year of Hong Kong." *Asian Survey* 25:1 (January):33–50.
Biddulph, Jim. 1985. "Putting the Squeeze on the Hong Kong Press." *Asian Wall Street Journal,* June 12.
Blaustein, Albert P. 1984. "Drafting a New Constitution for the Hong Kong SAR." Paper presented at conference on Hong Kong and 1997: Strategies for the Future, December 6–8, Centre of Asian Studies, University of Hong Kong.
Bonavia, David. 1985. *Hong Kong and 1997: The Final Settlement.* 2d ed. Hong Kong: South China Morning Post.
Bond, Michael H. 1984. "Coping with the Threat of Westernization in Hong Kong." Paper presented at a symposium, Alternative Models of Development, May 2–5, third Asian regional meeting of the Association of Cross-Cultural Psychology, Kuala Lumpur.
———. 1985. "Inter-Group Relations in Hong Kong." Paper presented at conference on Interethnic Conflict and Aggression, March 5–12, East West Center, Honolulu.
Bueno de Mesquita, Bruce; David Newman; and Alvin Rabushka. 1985. *Forecasting Political Events: The Future of Hong Kong.* New Haven: Yale University Press.
Burns, John P. 1985. "Immigration from China and the Future of Hong Kong." Paper prepared for spring 1985 regional seminar in Chinese Studies, April 12–13, University of California, Berkeley.
Burns, John P., and H. J. Bacon-Shone. 1984. "The Localization of the Hong Kong Civil Service." Paper presented at conference on Hong Kong and 1997: Strategies for the Future, December 6–8, Centre of Asian Studies, University of Hong Kong.
Buruma, Ian. 1985. "Changing Cultural Climate: Bending to the North Wind." *FEER,* May 30.
Butler, Stuart M. 1983. "How Guam Can Become America's Hong Kong." Heritage Foundation Asian Studies Center, *Backgrounder,* no. 1 (April 19).
Cha, Louis. 1984. *On Hong Kong's Future: A Collection of Ming Pao's Editorials.* Hong Kong: Ming Pao Daily News.

Chang, Kuo-sin. 1984a. "China and Hong Kong See Same Thing in Different Light."
    Hongkong Standard, November 7.
_____. 1984b. "One Country, Two Systems—How It Did the Trick." Hongkong
    Standard, November 21.
_____. 1985a. "It Is Time Now to Say Goodbye." Hongkong Standard, June 25.
_____. 1985b. "There's No Viable Substitute for British Admin." Hongkong Standard,
    June 11.
_____. 1985c. "'Two Systems' Isn't Working Well in Shenzhen Zone." Hongkong
    Standard, June 18.
Chang, Shin. 1984. "The 1982-83 Overinvestment Crisis in China." Asian Survey
    24:12 (December):1275–1301.
"Changing of the Guard." 1985. Asiaweek (August 2):7–13.
Chen, Albert. 1984a. "Further Aspects of the Autonomy of Hong Kong Under the
    PRC Constitution." Hong Kong Law Journal 14, pt. 3 (September):341–347.
_____. 1984b. "Hong Kong's Legal System: Adaptation for 1997 and Beyond."
    Paper presented at conference on Hong Kong and 1997: Strategies for the Future,
    December 6–8, Centre of Asian Studies, University of Hong Kong.
Cheng, Chu-yuan. 1985. "Hong Kong's Prosperity: Foundation and Prospects."
    Journal of Chinese Studies 2:1 (April):155–163.
Cheng, Joseph Y.S. 1984a. "The Future of Hong Kong: A Study of the Hong Kong
    People's Attitudes." Australian Journal of Chinese Affairs, no. 12 (July):113–142.
_____. 1984b. Hong Kong in Search of a Future. Hong Kong: Oxford University
    Press.
Cheng, Terry. 1985. "Consultative Committee Could Be Controversial." SCMP, July
    4.
Cheng, Tong-yung. 1982. The Economy of Hong Kong. 2d ed. Hong Kong: Far East
    Publications.
China Daily Commentator. 1985. "The Rule of Law." China Daily, June 30.
"China Trader: A Survey." 1985. Economist (May 15):1–26.
Ching, Frank. 1985. Hong Kong and China: For Better or for Worse. New York:
    China Council of the Asia Society.
Chiu, Hungdah. 1985. "The 1984 Sino-British Settlement on Hong Kong: Problems
    and Analysis." Journal of Chinese Studies 2:1 (April):95–112.
Chung, Chalina. 1985. "Double Say for HK in Law Draft." Hongkong Standard,
    July 3.
Chung, S. Y. 1984. Interview by Anthony Paul. Asiaweek. June 1.
Clarke, W. S. 1984a. "The Constitution of Hong Kong and 1997." Paper presented
    at conference on Hong Kong and 1997: Strategies for the Future, December 6–
    8, Centre of Asian Studies, University of Hong Kong.
_____. 1984b. "Hong Kong Under the Chinese Constitution." Hong Kong Law
    Journal 14, pt. 1 (January):71–81.
The Constitution of the People's Republic of China. 1983. Beijing: Foreign Languages
    Press.
Cooper, Gene. 1981. "Hong Kong: Liberation Without Liberation." Bulletin of
    Concerned Asian Scholars 13:2 (April):61–63.
Copper, John F. 1983. "The Lessons of Playing Tough with China." Heritage
    Foundation Asian Studies Center, Backgrounder, no. 4 (August 23).
Davies, Derek. 1984a. Asia 1985 Yearbook. Hong Kong: FEER.
_____. 1984b. "Dark Voices Prophesying Doom." FEER, October 11.
_____. 1984c. "Initialled, Sealed, and Delivered: An Unprecedented Agreement
    Guarantees the Future." FEER, October 4.

————. 1985. "Wanted: A Government Confidence in Hong Kong." *FEER*, July 25.

Davies, S.N.G. 1983. Review of *Society and Politics in Hong Kong* by Lau Siu-kai. *Hong Kong Law Journal* 13, p. 2 (May):246–254.

Dicks, Anthony. 1983. "Treaty, Grant, Usage, or Sufferance? Some Legal Aspects of the Status of Hong Kong." *China Quarterly*, no. 95 (September):427–455.

Editorial. 1984. "The Legal System, the Constitution, and the Future of Hong Kong." *Hong Kong Law Journal* 14, pt. 2 (May):137–141.

————. 1985a. "The Aim: To Seek No Changes." *Ming Pao Daily News*, June 19.

————. 1985b. "Censored in Hong Kong." *Asian Wall Street Journal*, June 6.

————. 1985c. "Correctly Assessing SEZ Experiment." *SCMP*, July 4.

————. 1985d. "Criticizing and Inheriting Confucianism." *Ming Pao Daily News*, June 16.

————. 1985e. "Damage Done to Confidence Makes People Worried." *Ming Pao Daily News*, June 18.

————. 1985f. "Garner's Blow for Death Penalty." *SCMP*, July 2.

————. 1985g. "Is Hong Kong Watching?" *Asian Wall Street Journal*, June 26.

————. 1985h. "Lessons to Be Learned from Powers Bill Controversy." *Ming Pao Daily News*, June 27.

————. 1985i. "A Preliminary Concept on Basic Law." *Ming Pao Daily News*, June 20.

————. 1985j. "Self-Disciplined Organization and Disciplinary Organization." *Ming Pao Daily News*, June 29.

————. 1985k. "Wage Reform in Mainland." *Ming Pao Daily News*, July 2.

————. 1985l. "The Way the Basic Law Drafting Committee Works." *Ming Pao Daily News*, July 7.

————. 1985m. "We Are Learning Democracy." *Ming Pao Daily News*, March 7.

Emmons, Charles F. 1984. "Public Opinion and Political Participation in Pre-1997 Hong Kong." Paper presented at conference on Hong Kong and 1997: Strategies for the Future, December 6–8, Centre of Asian Studies, University of Hong Kong.

Finer, Samuel. 1985. "Hong Kong 1997: When the Kissing Has to Stop." *Political Quarterly* 56 (1985).

Fung, Vigor. 1985a. "Economic Reforms Trim China's Exports." *Asian Wall Street Journal*, July 2.

————. 1985b. "Partners in China Hat-Making Venture Bump Heads." *Asian Wall Street Journal*, July 17.

Goodstadt, Leo. 1984a. "The Flight from Hong Kong." *Euromoney* (July).

————. 1984b. "The Hong Kong Special Administrative Region." *Asiabanking* (October).

Greenwood, John. 1983. "Stabilization of the Hong Kong Dollar." *Asian Monetary Monitor* 7:6 (November):9–37.

————. 1984a. "The Monetary Framework Underlying the Hong Kong Dollar Stabilization Scheme." *China Quarterly*, no. 99 (September):631–636.

————. 1984b. "Operation of the New Exchange Rate." *Asian Monetary Monitor* 8:1 (January):2–12.

————. 1984c. "Why the HK$/US$ Linked Rate System Should Not Be Changed." *Asian Monetary Monitor* 8:6 (November):2–17.

Guterres, Halima. 1984. "Casting Lifeline for Belongers." *SCMP*, December 12.

————. 1985a. "Lawyers United to Defer the 'Botched' Legco Bill." *SCMP*, June 11.

———. 1985b. "Loophole in EEC Status: Link with Macau Under Scrutiny." *SCMP*, August 5.

———. 1985c. "Powers Bill Loses Punch in Passing." *SCMP*, June 27.

Hamrin, Carol Lee. 1984. "Competing 'Policy Packages' in Post-Mao China." *Asian Survey* 24:5 (May):487–518.

Han, Seung Soo. 1984. "Of Economic Success and Confucianism." *FEER*, December 20.

Hicks, George L. 1985. "Hong Kong on the Eve of Communist Rule." Paper presented at the annual meeting of the Western Social Science Association, April 24–27, Fort Worth, Texas.

Hong Kong—China Risk. 1984–. Published fortnightly by Asiabanking.

Hong Kong Government. 1984a. *Green Paper: The Further Development of Representative Government in Hong Kong.*

———. 1984b. *White Paper: The Further Development of Representative Government in Hong Kong.*

———. 1985a. *1984 Economic Background.*

———. 1985b. *1985 Economic Prospects.*

———. 1985c. *Powers and Privileges Bill: The Amended Text.*

Hong Kong Observers. 1982. *The Hong Kong Observers Poll.* Hong Kong: Survey Research Hongkong.

———. 1983. *Pressure Points.* Hong Kong: Summerson Educational Research Centre.

———. 1984. "A Question of Freedom." *SCMP*, December 11.

———. 1985a. "Accountability Must Be Put into Practice." *SCMP*, August 5.

———. 1985b. "Bill Is Better Dead than Read." *SCMP*, June 10.

———. 1985c. "The Committees Must Be Receptive to Public Views." *SCMP*, September 6.

———. 1985d. "Government Must Win Back Our Confidence." *SCMP*, June 21.

Hook, Brian. 1983. "The Government of Hong Kong: Change Within Tradition." *China Quarterly*, no. 95 (September):491–511.

Howe, Christopher. 1983. "Growth, Public Policy, and Hong Kong's Economic Relationship with China." *China Quarterly*, no. 95 (September):512–533.

Hughes, Richard. 1976. *Borrowed Time, Borrowed Place: Hong Kong.* 2d ed. London: Andre Deutsch.

Jao, Y. C. 1983a. *Hong Kong: Economic Prospects to 1987. Economist Intelligence Unit*, Special Report no. 156.

———. 1983b. "Hong Kong's Role in Financing China's Modernization." In *China and Hong Kong: The Economic Nexus*, edited by A. J. Youngson, chap. 1. Hong Kong: Oxford University Press.

———. 1984a. "The Enigma of Hong Kong's Financial Transactions with China." *Asian Monetary Monitor* 8:3 (May):26–31.

———. 1984b. "Hong Kong Dollar Looking for Political Parity." *Asiabanking* (September):47–55.

———. 1984c. "The Monetary System of and the Future of Hong Kong." Paper presented at conference on Hong Kong and 1997: Strategies for the Future, December 6–8, Centre of Asian Studies, University of Hong Kong.

———. 1985. "Hong Kong's Economic Prospects After the Sino-British Agreement: A Preliminary Assessment." Paper presented at the annual meeting of the Western Social Science Association, April 24–27, Fort Worth, Texas.

Johnson, Chalmers. 1984. "The Mousetrapping of Hong Kong: A Game in Which Nobody Wins." *Asian Survey* 24:9 (September):887–909.

Jones, Dorothy E., and Marc Frons. 1985. "Why Y. K. Pao Is So High on Hong Kong." *Business Week* (May 20):53–54.

King, Ambrose Y.C. 1975. "Administrative Absorption of Politics in Hong Kong: Emphasis on the Grass Roots Level." *Asian Survey* 15:5 (May):422–439.

———. 1982. "The Confucian Paradigm of Men: A Sociological View." Paper presented at conference on Chinese Culture and Mental Health, March 1–7, East West Center, Honolulu.

King, Ambrose Y.C., and Rance P.L. Lee, eds. 1981. *Social Life and Development in Hong Kong.* Hong Kong: Chinese University Press.

Knight, Bill. 1985. *Hong Kong 1985.* Hong Kong: Government Printer.

Lao, Sze-kwang. 1985. "Will 'One Country, Two Systems' Work?" *Asiaweek,* January 11.

Lasater, Martin L. 1985. "Hong Kong's Future—and Taiwan's." Heritage Foundation, *Executive Memorandum,* no. 65 (October 3).

Lau, Emily. 1984a. "Another British Sunset." FEER, November 15.

———. 1984b. "Assessment Assessed." FEER, December 13.

———. 1984c. "A Shade of Difference." FEER. November 29.

———. 1984d. "Time to Face the Challenge of 1997." FEER, November 22.

———. 1985a. "Basic Differences." FEER, July 18.

———. 1985b. "The Big Backdown." FEER, June 27.

———. 1985c. "More Problems Ahead." FEER, January 10.

———. 1985d. "One Small Step for Voters: For the First Time, 24 Councillors Are to Be Elected." FEER, September 5.

———. 1985e. "The Rising Red Tide: Under Surface China Is Establishing Its Own Structure." FEER, August 1.

———. 1985f. "When Is a Passport Not a Passport?" FEER, February 7.

Lau, Siu-kai. 1981. "Government Intermediate Organizations and Grass-Roots Politics in Hong Kong." *Asian Survey* 21:8 (August):865–884.

———. 1982a. "Local Administrative Reform in Hong Kong: Promises and Limitations." *Asian Survey* 22:9 (September):858–873.

———. 1982b. *Society and Politics in Hong Kong.* Hong Kong: Chinese University Press.

———. 1983. "Bureaucratic Rule and Emergent Political Issues in Hong Kong." *World Politics* 35 (July):544–562.

———. 1984. "Political Reform and Political Development in Hong Kong: Dilemmas and Choices." Paper presented at conference on Hong Kong and 1997: Strategies for the Future, December 6–8, Centre of Asian Studies, University of Hong Kong.

Lau, Siu-kai, and Hsin-chi Kuan. 1983. *The District Board Elections in Hong Kong.* Hong Kong: Chinese University of Hong Kong.

———. 1985. "The 1985 District Board Election in Hong Kong: The Limits of Political Mobilization in a Dependent Policy." Department of Sociology, Chinese University of Hong Kong. Photocopy.

Lau, Siu-kai; Hsin-chi Kuan; and Kam-fai Ho. 1983. *Leaders, Officials, and Citizens in Urban Service Delivery: Comparative Studies in Four Localities of Hong Kong.* Hong Kong: Chinese University.

Lee, Jane. 1984. "Pressure Groups and Political Participation in Hong Kong." Seminar paper, Research School of Pacific Studies, Australian National University, Canberra.

Lee, Mary. 1985. "The Curtain Goes Up: Peking Permits Foreign Investment All Along Its Coastline." FEER, January 31.

Lee, Ta-ling. 1985. "Hong Kong: The Human Rights Dimension." Department of History, Southern Connecticut State University. Photocopy.

Lethbridge, H. J. 1985. *Hard Graft in Hong Kong*. Hong Kong: Oxford University Press.

Levin, Barnard. 1984. "Hong Kong." *Times*, September 5.

Lewis, D. K. 1982. *The Prospects for Hong Kong*. London: Institute for the Study of Conflict.

Liu, Louis. 1985. "HK Will Have Power to Interpret Basic Law." *SCMP*, June 17.

Loh, Christine. 1985. "Watching over Hong Kong's Watchdog." *Asian Wall Street Journal*, June 21.

Luard, Evan. 1962. *Britain and China*. London: Chatto and Windus.

Macpherson, I.F.C. 1984a. *Report of the Assessment Office*. Hong Kong: Assessment Office.

———. 1984b. *Report of the Assessment Office: Submissions Made by Organizations to the Assessment Office*. 2 vols. Hong Kong: Assessment Office.

Menezes, Victor. 1984. "Hong Kong: Financial Centre for the Future." Paper presented at conference on Hong Kong and 1997: Strategies for the Future, December 6–8, Centre of Asian Studies, University of Hong Kong.

Miners, N. J. 1981. *The Government and Politics of Hong Kong*. 3d ed. Hong Kong: Oxford University Press.

———. 1984. "Alternative Governmental Structure for a Future Self-Governing Hong Kong." Paper presented at conference on Hong Kong and 1997: Strategies for the Future, December 6–8, Centre of Asian Studies, University of Hong Kong.

Mushkat, Miron. 1982. *The Making of the Hong Kong Administrative Class*. Hong Kong: Centre of Asian Studies, University of Hong Kong.

Ng, Margaret. 1985a. "Ministers Will Have Wider Powers." *SCMP*, June 18.

———. 1985b. "Towards a New Democracy." *SCMP*, June 17.

"No Cheering over Hong Kong." 1985. *Economist*, September 22.

Overholt, William H. 1984. "Hong Kong and the Crisis of Sovereignty." *Asian Survey* 24:4 (April):471–484.

———. 1985. "Hong Kong After the Chinese-British Agreement." *Asian Perspective* 9:2 (Fall-Winter).

Pang, Eng Fong. 1985. "Distinctive Features of Two City-States' Development." Paper presented at symposium, In Search of an East Asian Development Model, June 28–30, Council on Religion and International Affairs, New York.

Parsons, Melinda J., ed. 1984. *Hong Kong 1984*. Hong Kong: Government Printer.

Patel, D. K. 1984. "One Country, Two Systems: Prospects for Hong Kong's Economy Under Chinese Sovereignty." Paper presented at conference on Hong Kong and 1997: Strategies for the Future, December 6–8, Centre of Asian Studies, University of Hong Kong.

Pye, Lucian W. 1982. *Chinese Commercial Negotiating Style*. Cambridge, Mass.: Oelgeschlager, Gunn and Hain.

———. 1983. "The International Position of Hong Kong." *China Quarterly*, no. 95 (September):456–468.

———. 1984. "The New Asian Capitalism: A Political Portrait." Paper presented at symposium, In Search of an East Asian Development Model, June 28–30, Council on Religion and International Affairs, New York.

Quon, Ann. 1985. "Maria Tam: Power but No Privilege." *SCMP*, June 23.

Rabushka, Alvin. 1985. "China, Taiwan, and Hong Kong: Economic Development in Three Chinas." Hoover Institution, Stanford University. Mimeograph.

Scott, Ian. 1985. "The Sino-British Agreement and Political Power in Hong Kong." Paper presented at workshop, The Future of Hong Kong, April 19, University Joint Centre on Modern Eastern Asia, University of Toronto–York, Toronto.

Southerland, Damiel. 1985. "Do the People in China Really Hate Foreigners?" *Hongkong Standard*, June 25.

Stockwin, Harvey. 1984a. "Dissecting Mrs. Thatcher." *SCMP*, December 23.

———. 1984b. "Hongkong in Wonderland." *SCMP*, November 25.

———. 1985a. "Checks Needed as the Plot Thickens." *SCMP*, June 16.

———. 1985b. "Clause 14 Still Rankles." *SCMP*, June 30.

———. 1985c. "The Great Legco Identity Parade." *SCMP*, June 20.

"Stormy Passage." 1985. *Asiaweek*, July 5.

Survey Research (Hong Kong). 1984. *Researching the 1997 Agreement*. 6 vols. Hong Kong: Survey Research.

Taylor, Edward. 1984. "Why Britain Gave Back Hong Kong." *Asian Wall Street Journal*, December 5.

Thatcher, Margaret. 1984. "Press Conference in Hong Kong Following the Signing of the Sino-British Agreement." *SCMP*, December 21.

Tier, Mark. 1984. *How to Get a Second Passport*. Hong Kong: WMA Publishing Company.

Tisdall, Brian. 1984. "Less Than a Frank Affair." *SCMP*, December 28.

United Kingdom. 1984a. *A Draft Agreement Between the Government of the United Kingdom of Great Britain and Northern Ireland and the Government of the People's Republic of China on the Future of Hong Kong*. London: Her Majesty's Stationery Office.

———. 1984b. *Parliamentary Debates* (Commons). Vol. 19, no. 22; vol. 60, no. 162; vol. 65, no. 209; vol. 69, no. 22; vol. 69, no. 23.

———. 1984c. *Parliamentary Debates* (Lords). Vol. 452, no. 127; vol. 456, no. 177; vol. 458, no. 17.

———. 1985a. *Parliamentary Debates* (Commons). Vol. 70, no. 36; vol. 71, no. 43; vol. 72, no. 55; vol. 72, no. 56.

———. 1985b. *Parliamentary Debates* (Lords). Vol. 459, no. 40; vol. 460, no. 46.

United Kingdom. Parliament. 1985. *Hong Kong Bill*. February.

Unofficial Members of the Legislative Council (UMELCO). 1984. *The Future of Hong Kong*. Hong Kong: Government Printer.

Walden, John. 1983. *Excellency, Your Gap Is Showing*. Hong Kong: Corporate Communications.

———. 1984a. "The Plight of Hong Kong's Silent Majority." *Asian Wall Street Journal*, November 17.

———. 1984b. "Safeguarding Self-Rule for Hong Kong." *Asian Wall Street Journal*, March 7.

Wang, Jersic. 1985. "Shenzhen Mirrors Frustration of China: Economic Zone Finds There Is No Shortcut to Modern Economy." *Asian Wall Street Journal*, July 8.

Wang, Kwan-yin, ed. 1982. *Shenzhen Special Economic Zone*. Hong Kong: Hong Kong Geographical Association.

Wesley-Smith, Peter. 1983. *Unequal Treaty 1898–1997: China, Great Britain, and Hong Kong's New Territories*. 2d ed. Hong Kong: Oxford University Press.

Wu, Yuan-Li. 1984. "The Future of Hong Kong Before and After 1997." *American Asian Review* 11:4 (Winter):13–23.

Yao, Y. C. 1985. "The 1997 Issue and Hong Kong's Financial Crisis." *Journal of Chinese Studies* 2:1 (April):113–154.

Youngson, A. J., ed. 1983. *China and Hong Kong: The Economic Nexus*. Hong Kong: Oxford University Press.

Index